TIGER & BUNNY 3

ART BY **MIZUKI SAKAKIBARA**
PLANNING / STORY **SUNRISE** | ORIGINAL SCRIPT **Masafumi Nishida**
ORIGINAL CHARACTER AND HERO DESIGN **Masakazu Katsura**

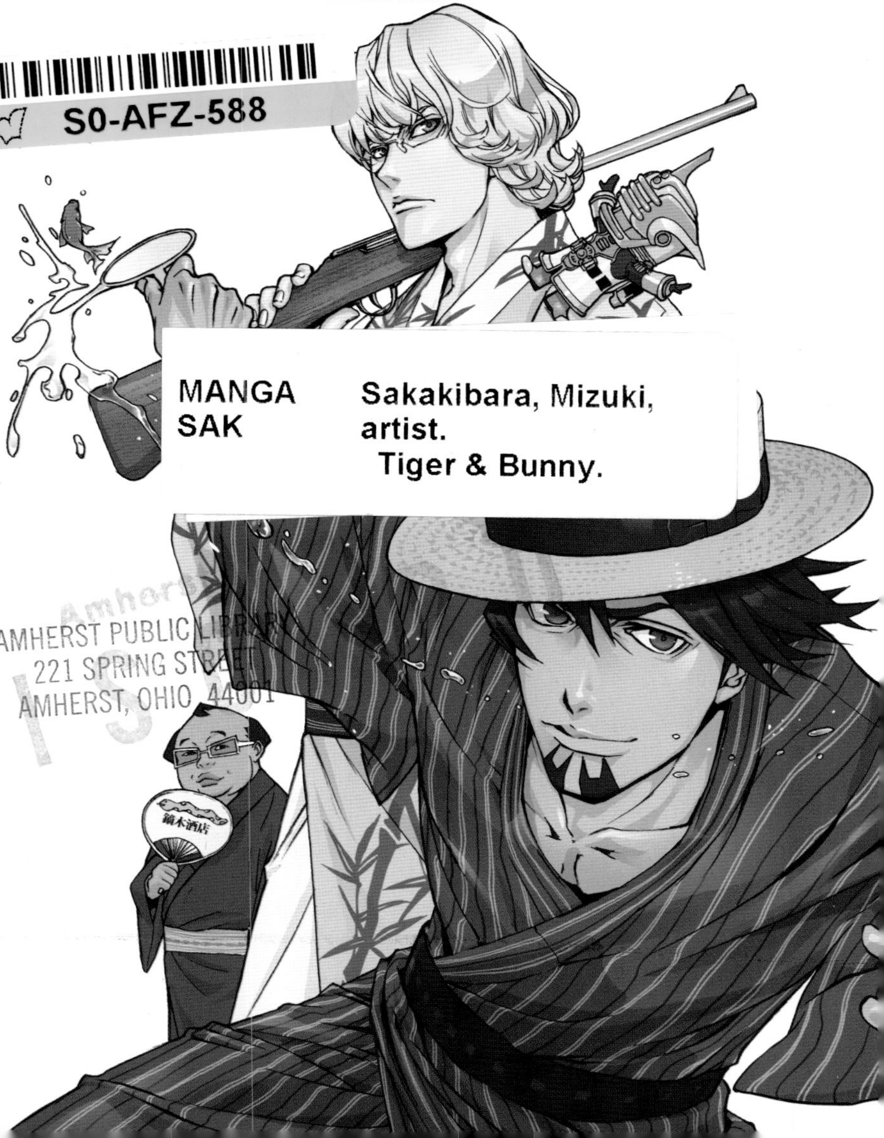
鏑木酒店

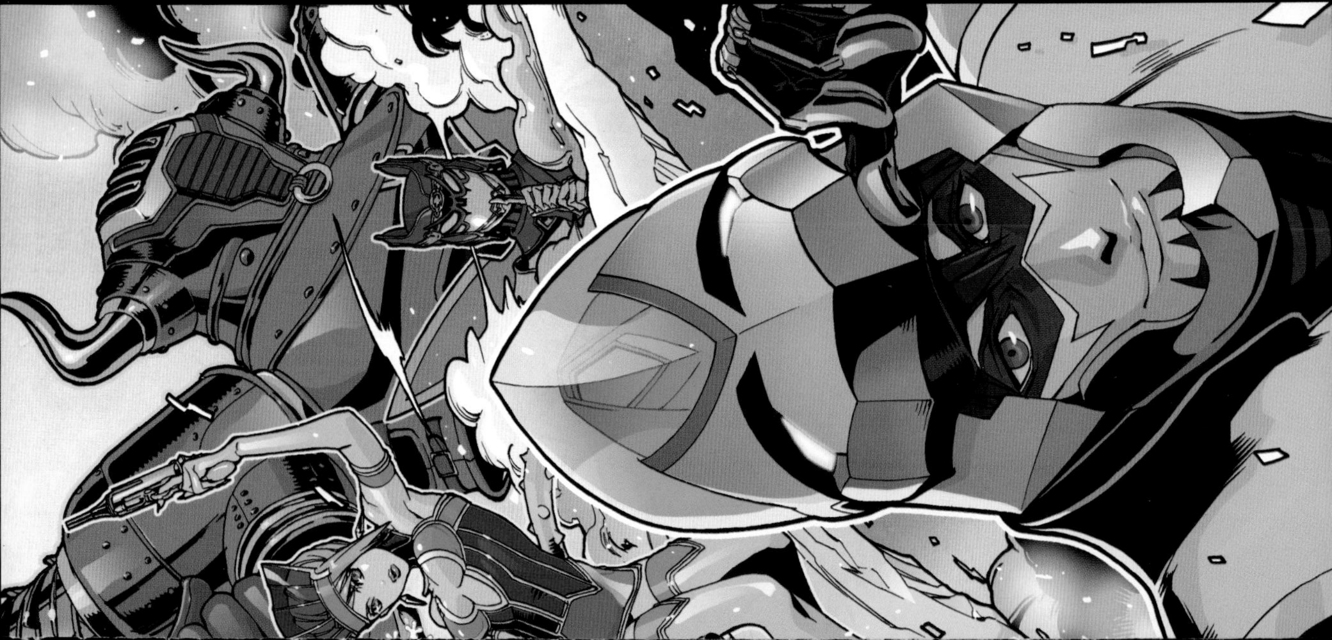

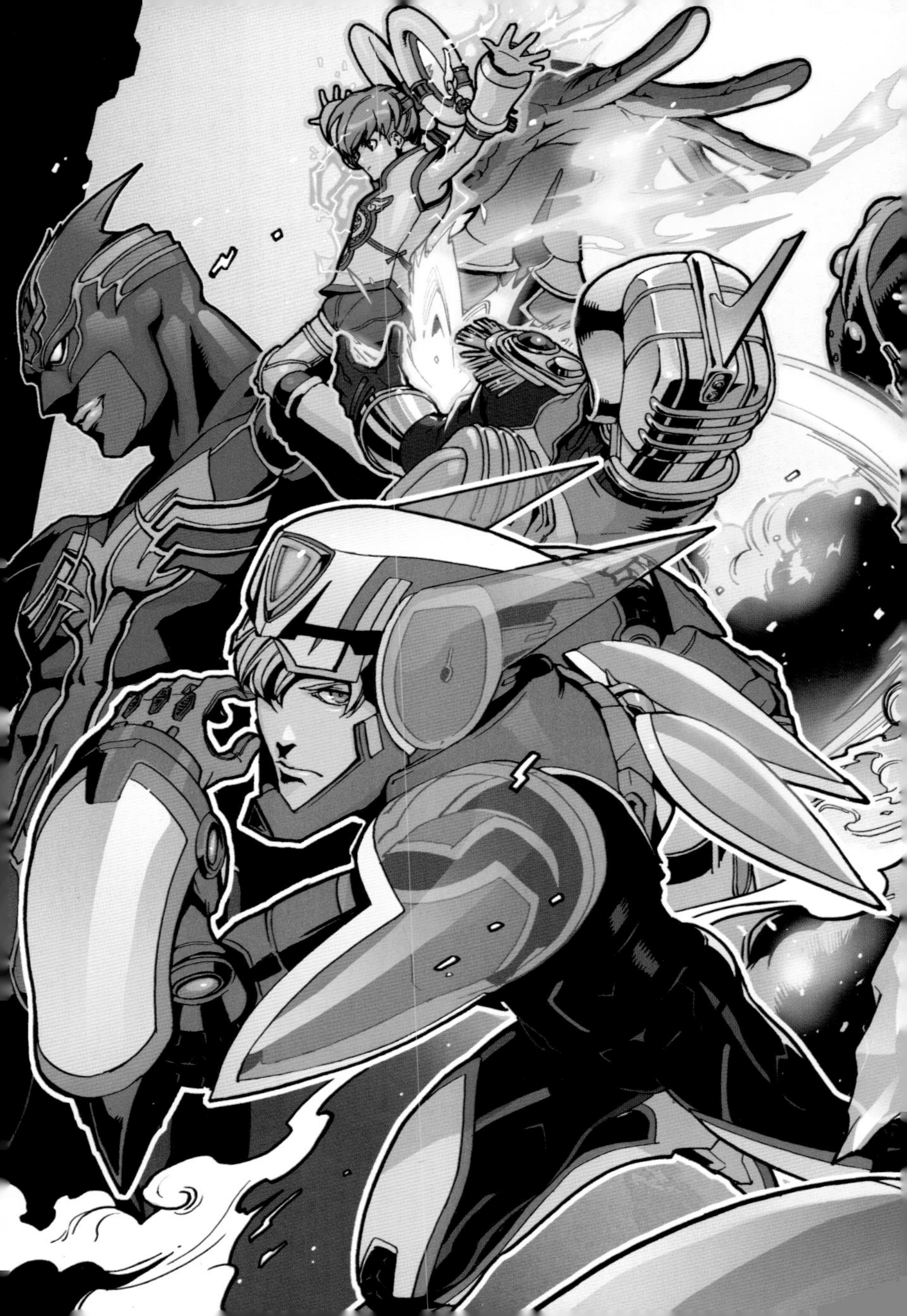

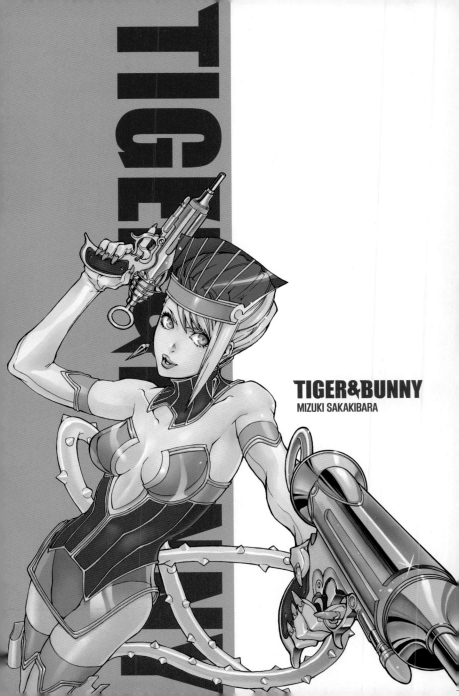

TIGER&BUNNY
MIZUKI SAKAKIBARA

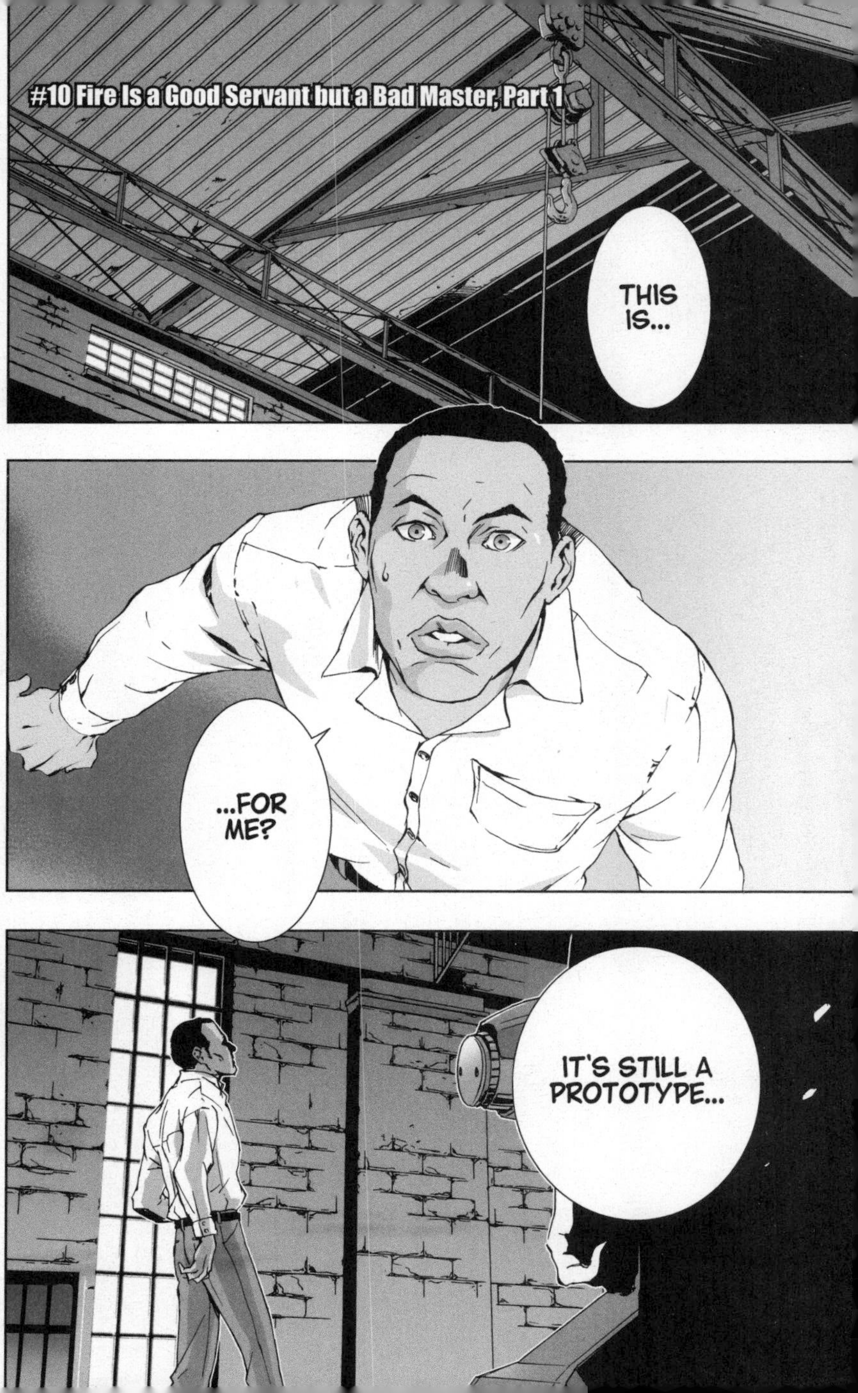
#10 Fire Is a Good Servant but a Bad Master, Part 1
THIS IS...
...FOR ME?
IT'S STILL A PROTOTYPE...

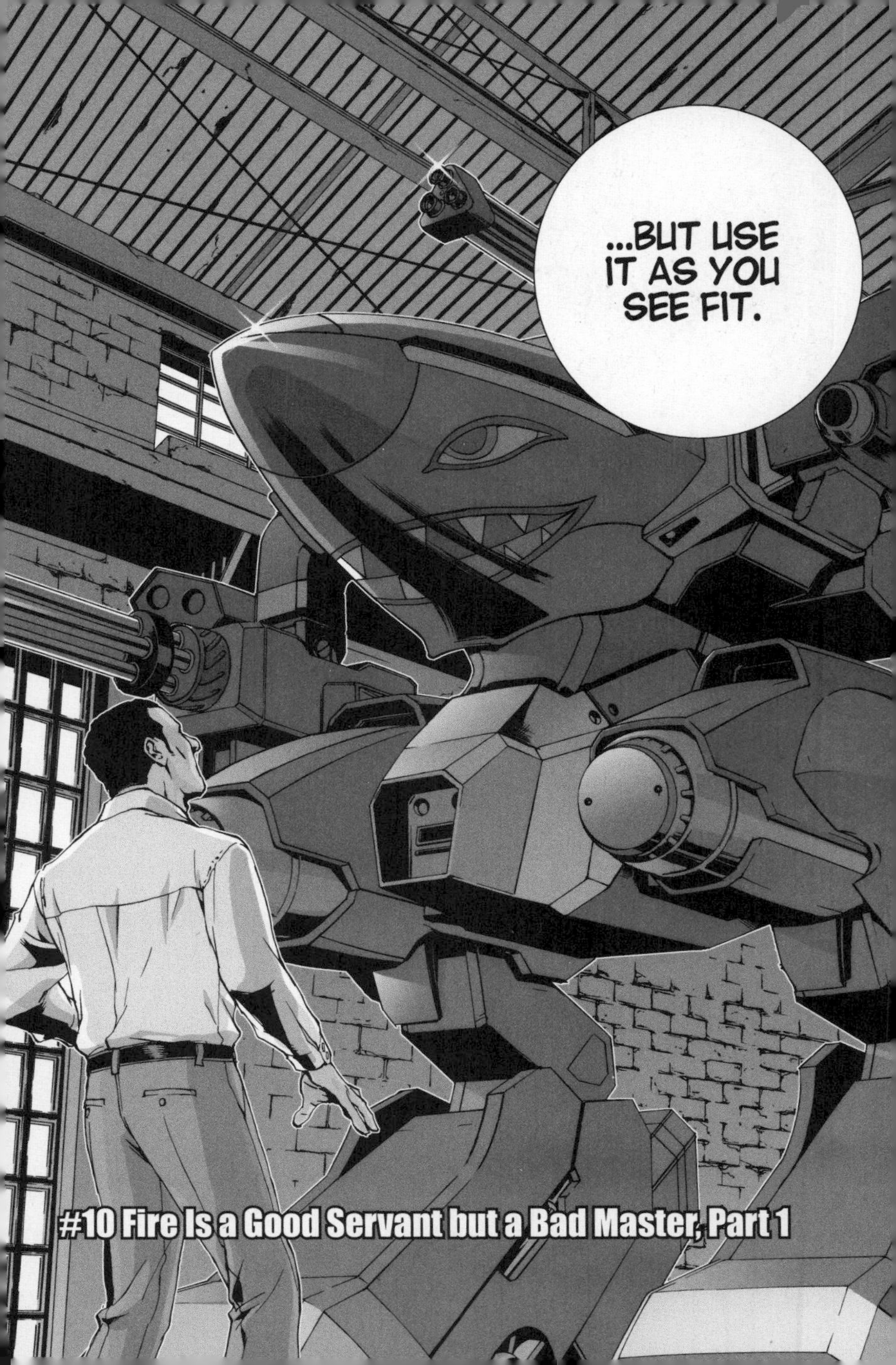
...BUT USE IT AS YOU SEE FIT.
#10 Fire Is a Good Servant but a Bad Master, Part 1

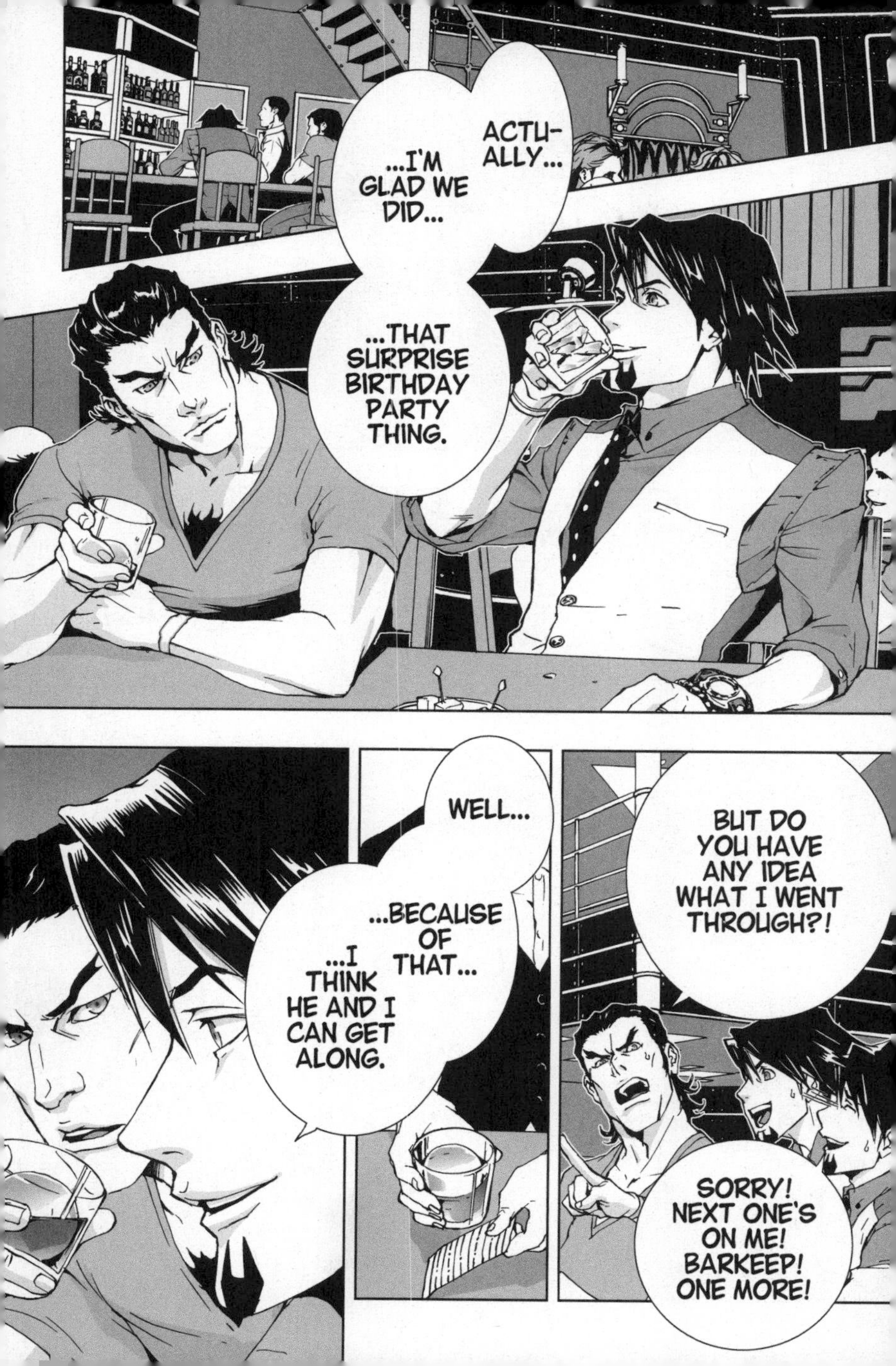
ACTU-ALLY...
...I'M GLAD WE DID...
...THAT SURPRISE BIRTHDAY PARTY THING.
BUT DO YOU HAVE ANY IDEA WHAT I WENT THROUGH?!
SORRY! NEXT ONE'S ON ME! BARKEEP! ONE MORE!
WELL...
...BECAUSE OF THAT...
...I THINK HE AND I CAN GET ALONG.

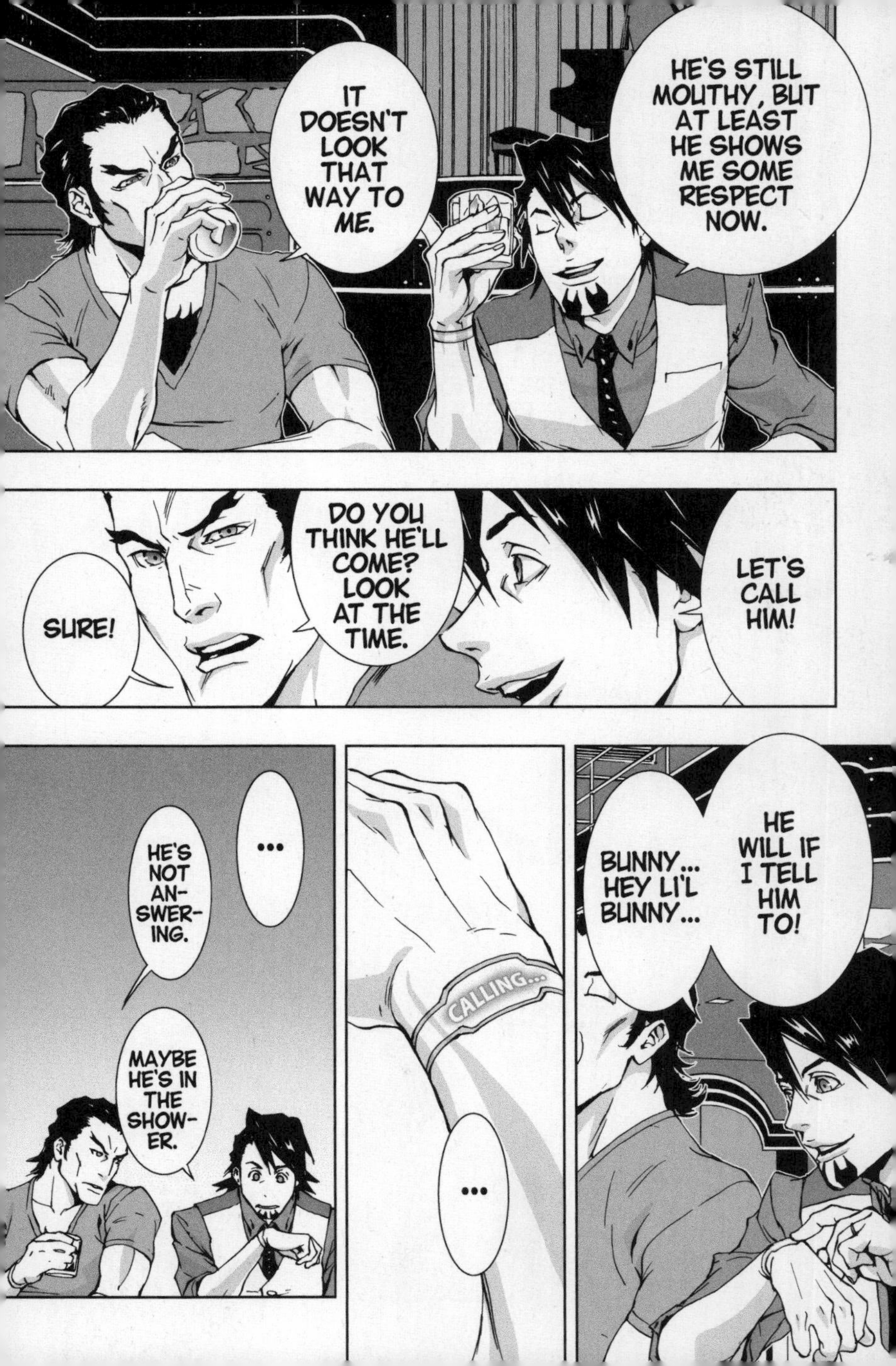
HE'S STILL MOUTHY, BUT AT LEAST HE SHOWS ME SOME RESPECT NOW.
IT DOESN'T LOOK THAT WAY TO ME.
LET'S CALL HIM!
DO YOU THINK HE'LL COME? LOOK AT THE TIME.
SURE!
HE WILL IF I TELL HIM TO!
BUNNY... HEY LI'L BUNNY...
CALLING...
...
...
HE'S NOT AN-SWER-ING.
MAYBE HE'S IN THE SHOW-ER.

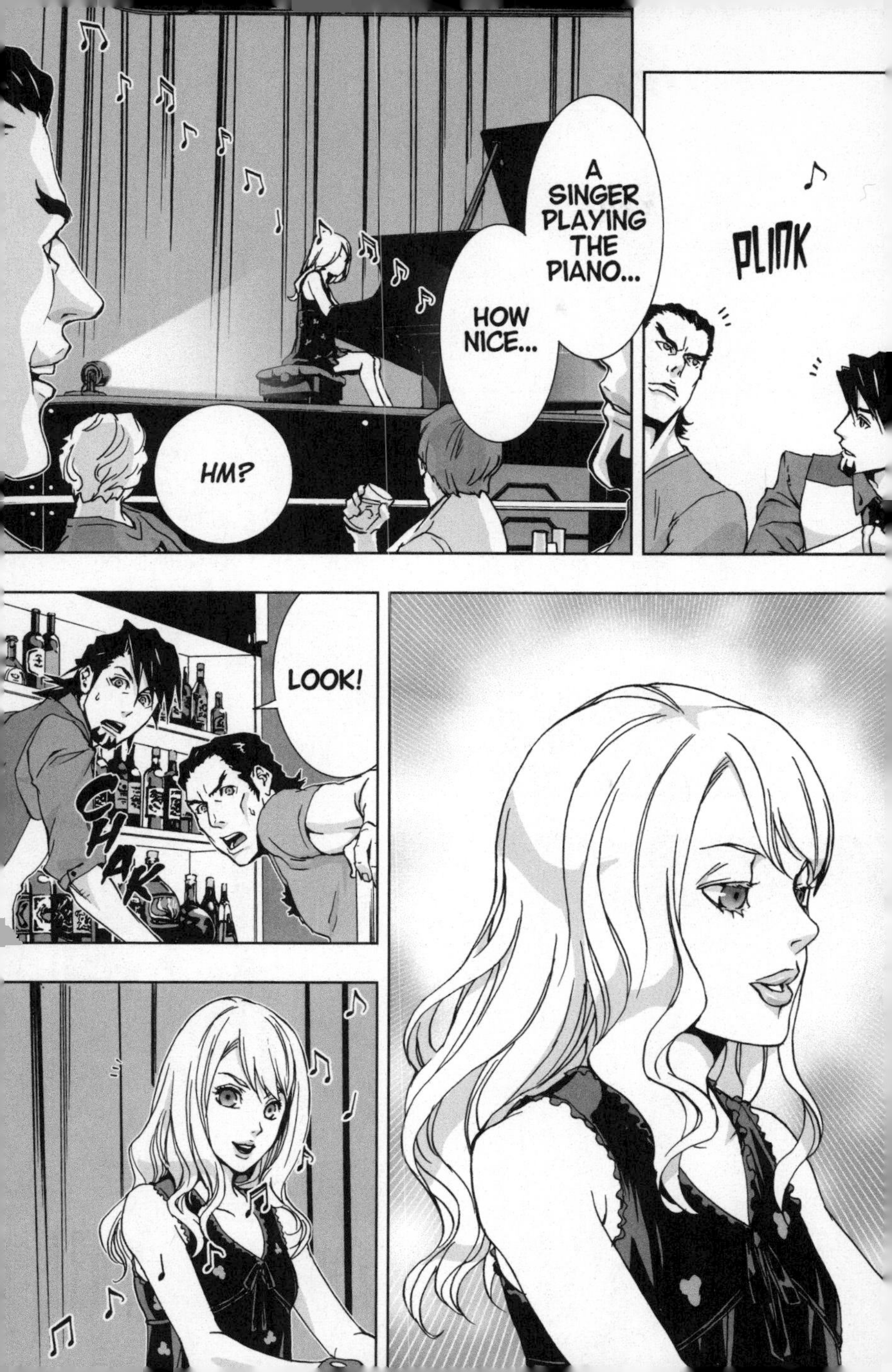
PLINK
A SINGER PLAYING THE PIANO...
HOW NICE...
HM?
LOOK!
CHAK

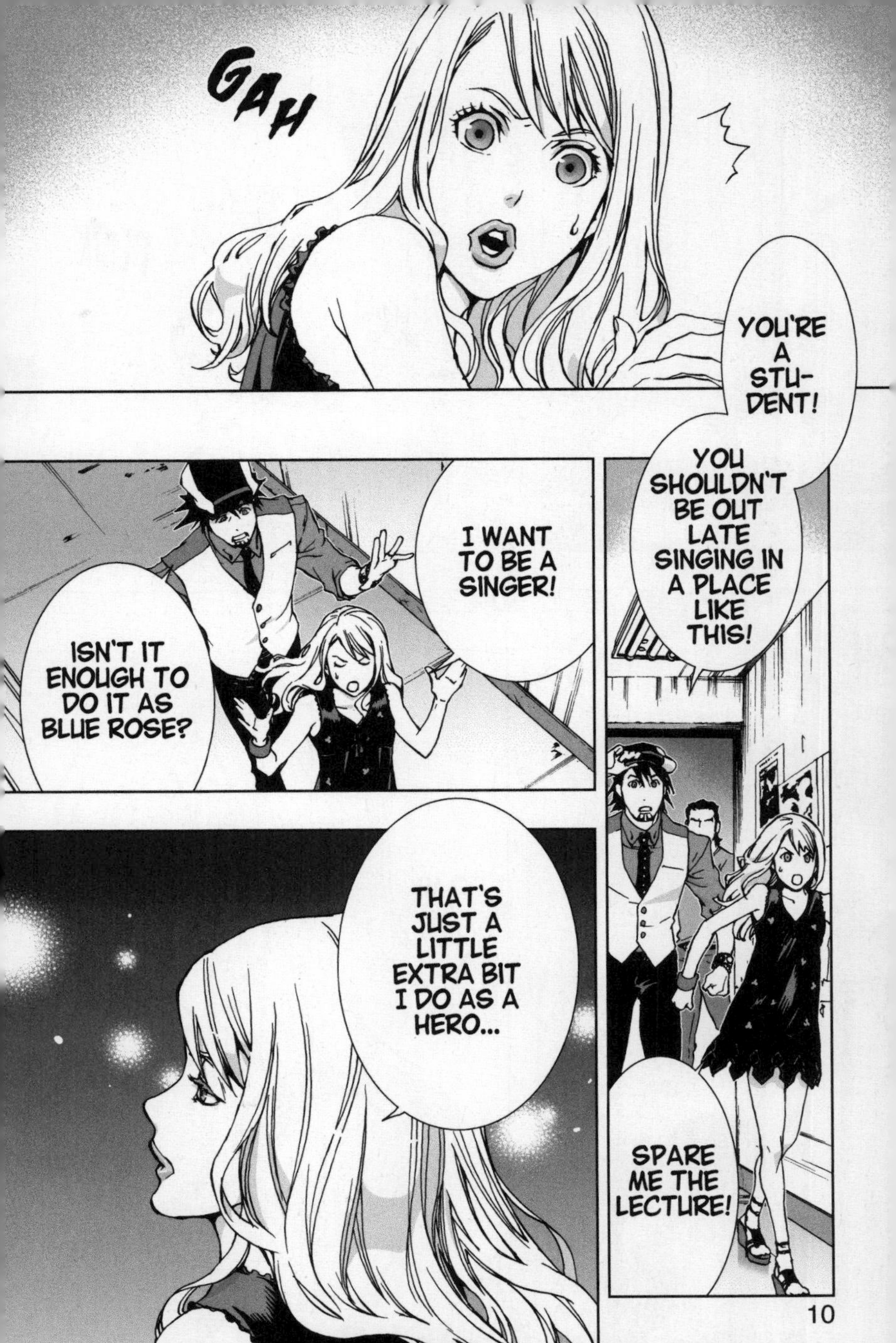
GAH
YOU'RE A STU-DENT!
YOU SHOULDN'T BE OUT LATE SINGING IN A PLACE LIKE THIS!
SPARE ME THE LECTURE!
I WANT TO BE A SINGER!
ISN'T IT ENOUGH TO DO IT AS BLUE ROSE?
THAT'S JUST A LITTLE EXTRA BIT I DO AS A HERO...

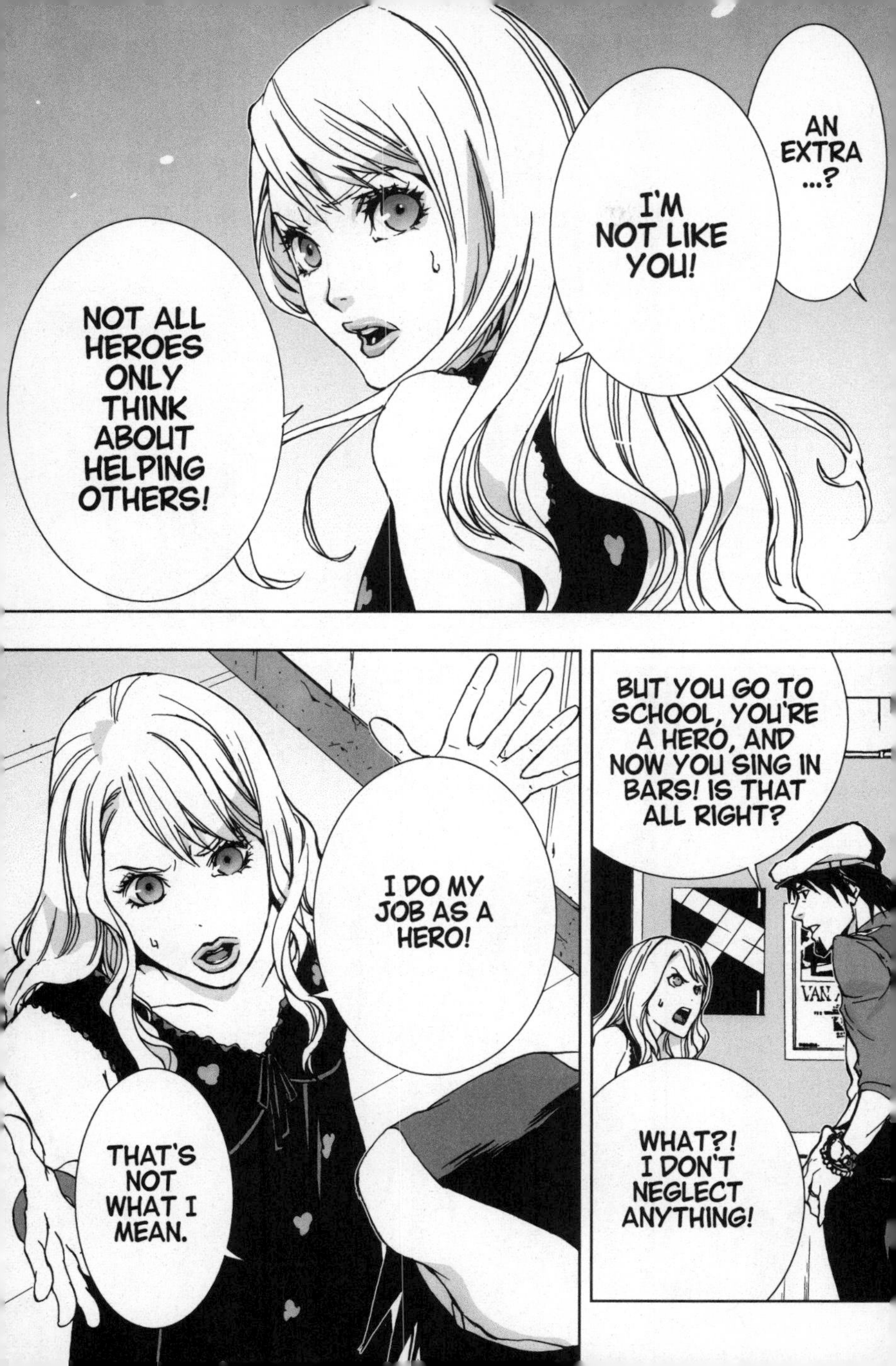
AN EXTRA ...?
I'M NOT LIKE YOU!
NOT ALL HEROES ONLY THINK ABOUT HELPING OTHERS!
BUT YOU GO TO SCHOOL, YOU'RE A HERO, AND NOW YOU SING IN BARS! IS THAT ALL RIGHT?
WHAT?! I DON'T NEGLECT ANYTHING!
I DO MY JOB AS A HERO!
THAT'S NOT WHAT I MEAN.

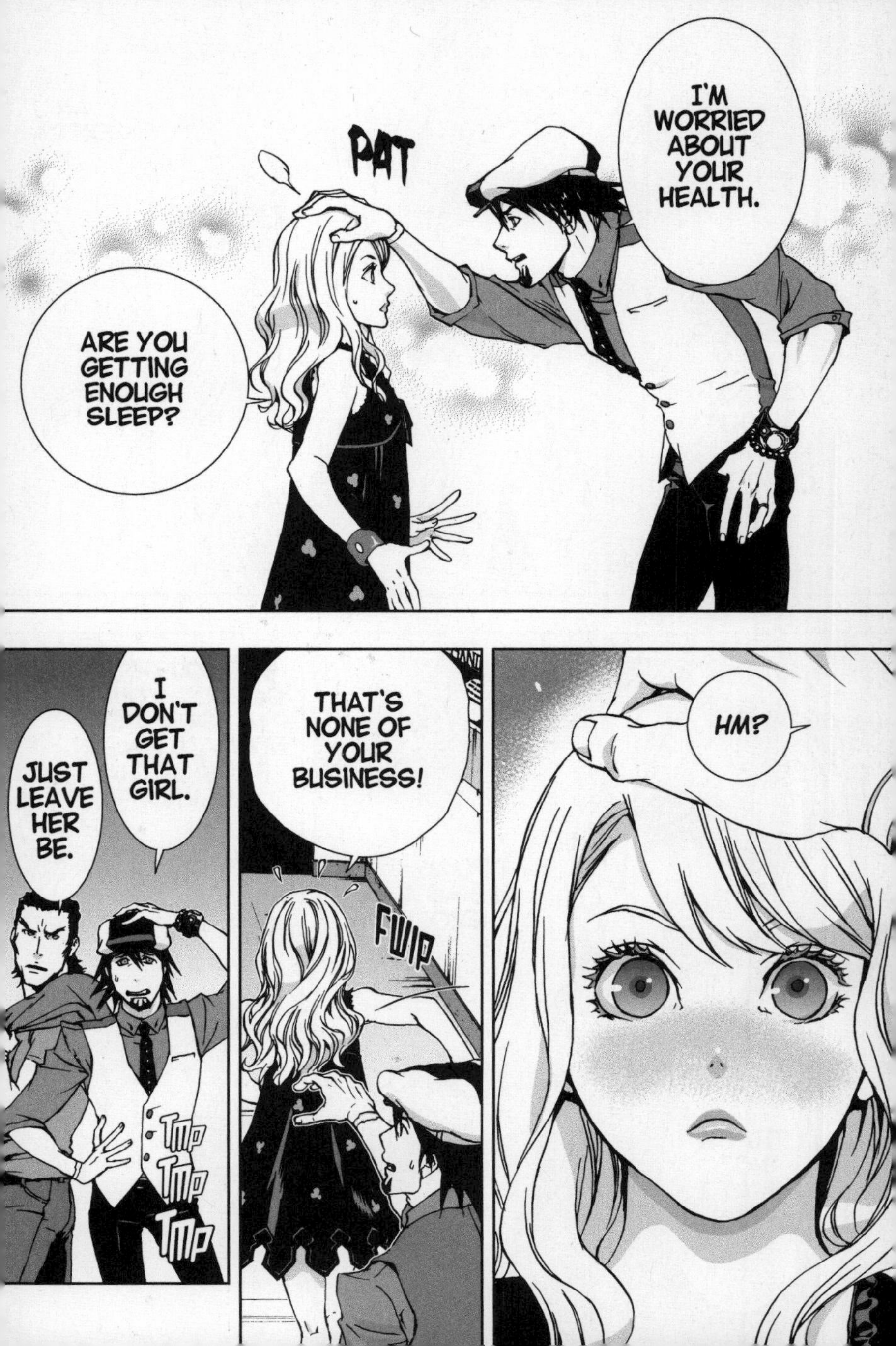
I'M WORRIED ABOUT YOUR HEALTH.
PAT
ARE YOU GETTING ENOUGH SLEEP?
HM?
THAT'S NONE OF YOUR BUSINESS!
FWIP
I DON'T GET THAT GIRL.
JUST LEAVE HER BE.
TMP
TMP
TMP

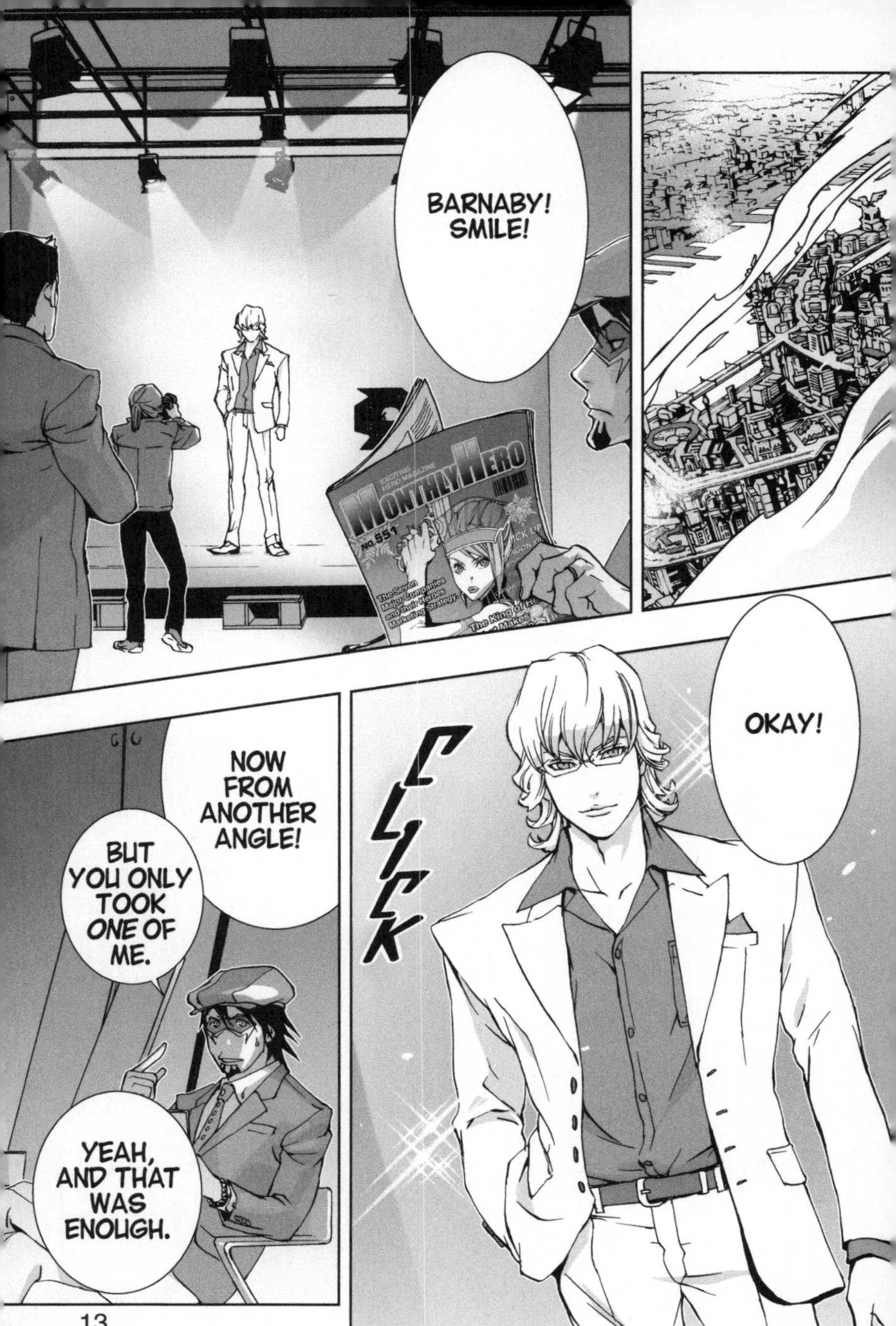
BARNABY! SMILE!
EXCITING HERO MAGAZINE
MONTHLY HERO
No. 551
The Seven Major Companies and their Heroes Marketing Strategy.
OKAY!
CLICK
NOW FROM ANOTHER ANGLE!
BUT YOU ONLY TOOK ONE OF ME.
YEAH, AND THAT WAS ENOUGH.

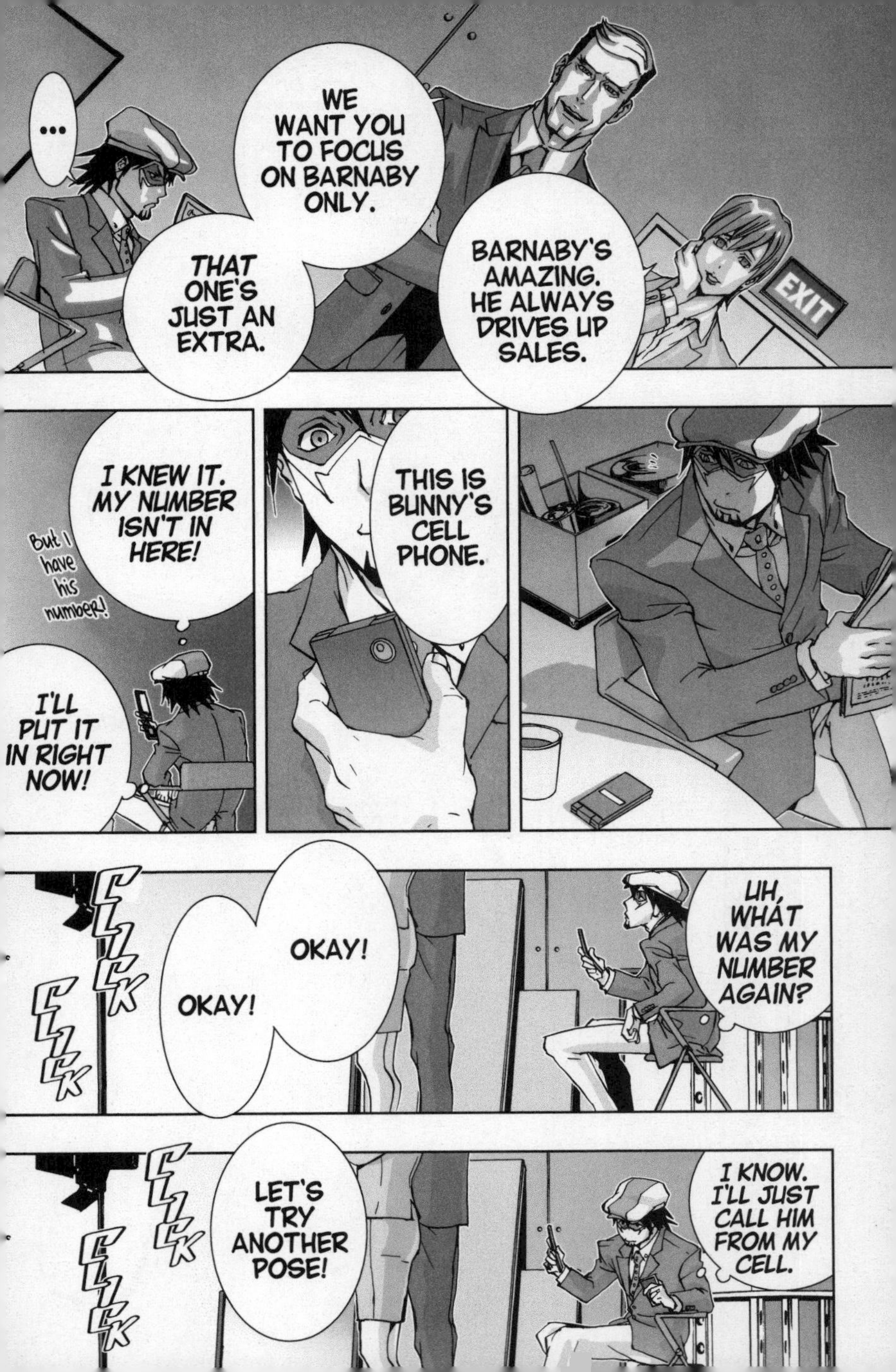
WE WANT YOU TO FOCUS ON BARNABY ONLY.
THAT ONE'S JUST AN EXTRA.
BARNABY'S AMAZING. HE ALWAYS DRIVES UP SALES.
...
EXIT
THIS IS BUNNY'S CELL PHONE.
I KNEW IT. MY NUMBER ISN'T IN HERE!
But I have his number!
I'LL PUT IT IN RIGHT NOW!
UH, WHAT WAS MY NUMBER AGAIN?
OKAY!
OKAY!
CLICK
CLICK
I KNOW. I'LL JUST CALL HIM FROM MY CELL.
LET'S TRY ANOTHER POSE!
CLICK
CLICK

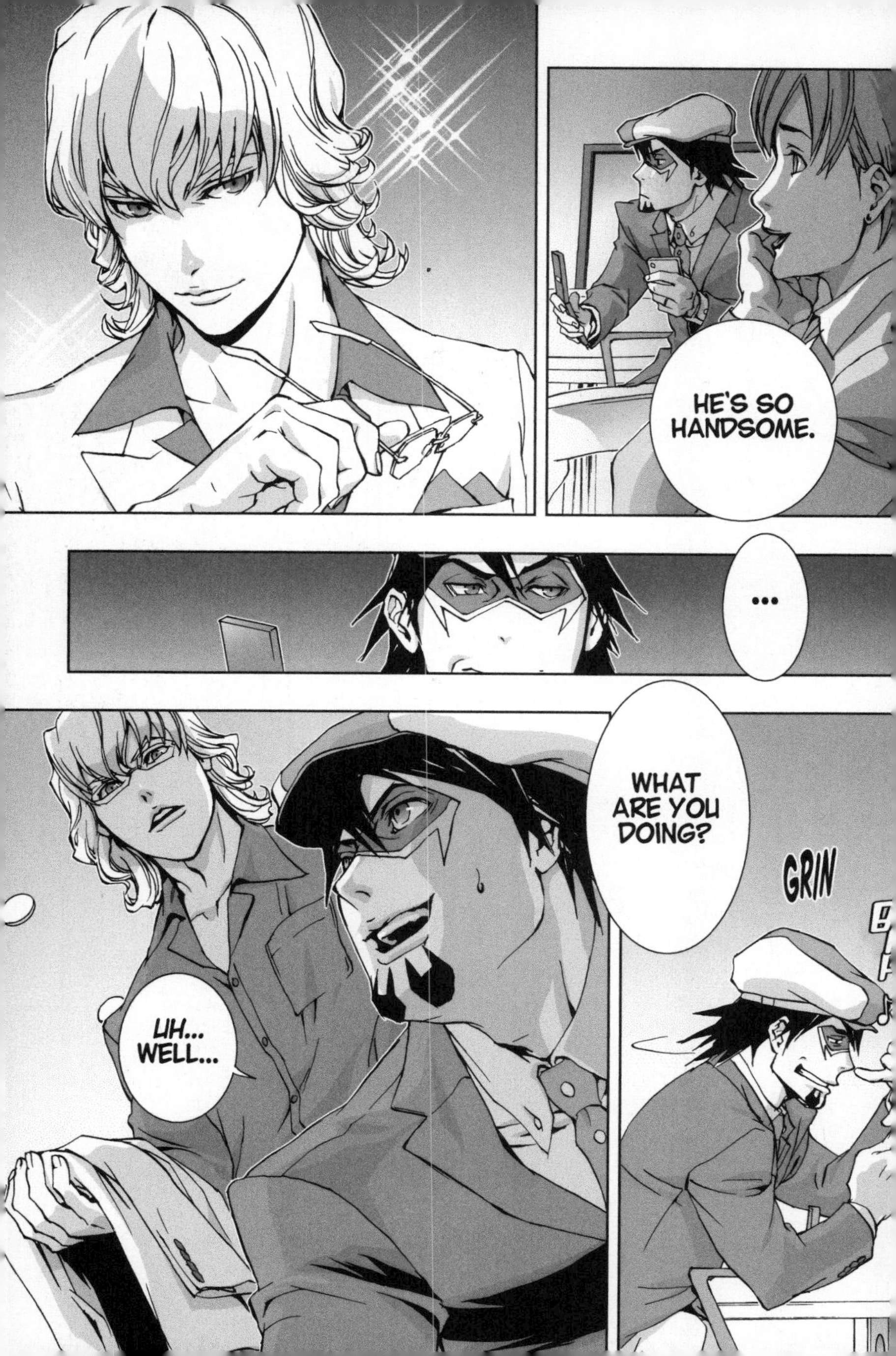
HE'S SO HANDSOME.
...
GRIN
WHAT ARE YOU DOING?
UH... WELL...

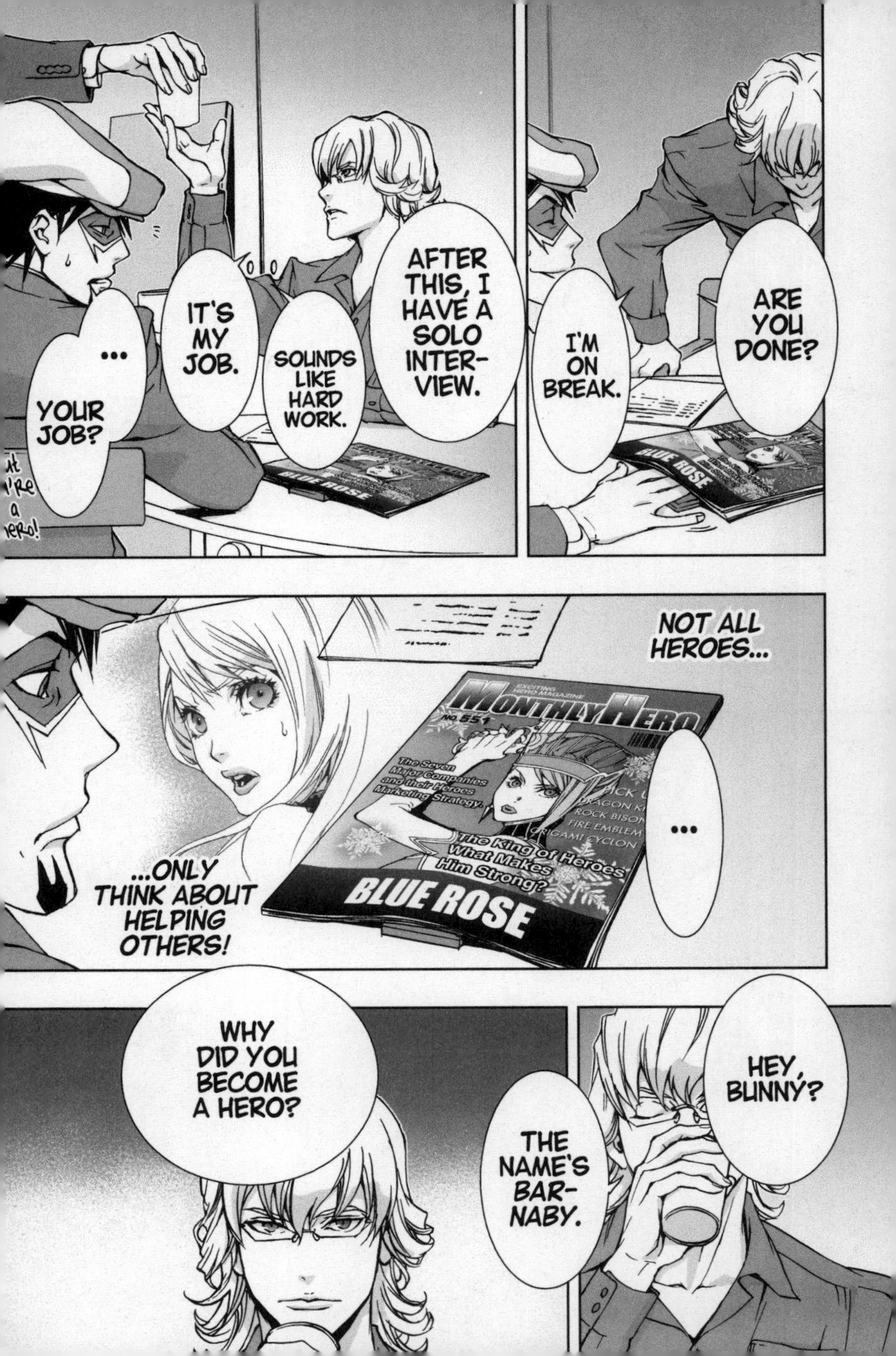
ARE YOU DONE?
I'M ON BREAK.
AFTER THIS, I HAVE A SOLO INTER-VIEW.
SOUNDS LIKE HARD WORK.
IT'S MY JOB.
... YOUR JOB?
NOT ALL HEROES...
...
EXCITING HERO MAGAZINE
MONTHLY HERO
NO.551
The Seven Major Companies and their Heroes Marketing Strategy.
PICK U
DRAGON KI
ROCK BISON
FIRE EMBLEM
ORIGAMI CYCLON
The King of Heroes What Makes Him Strong?
BLUE ROSE
...ONLY THINK ABOUT HELPING OTHERS!
HEY, BUNNY?
THE NAME'S BAR-NABY.
WHY DID YOU BECOME A HERO?

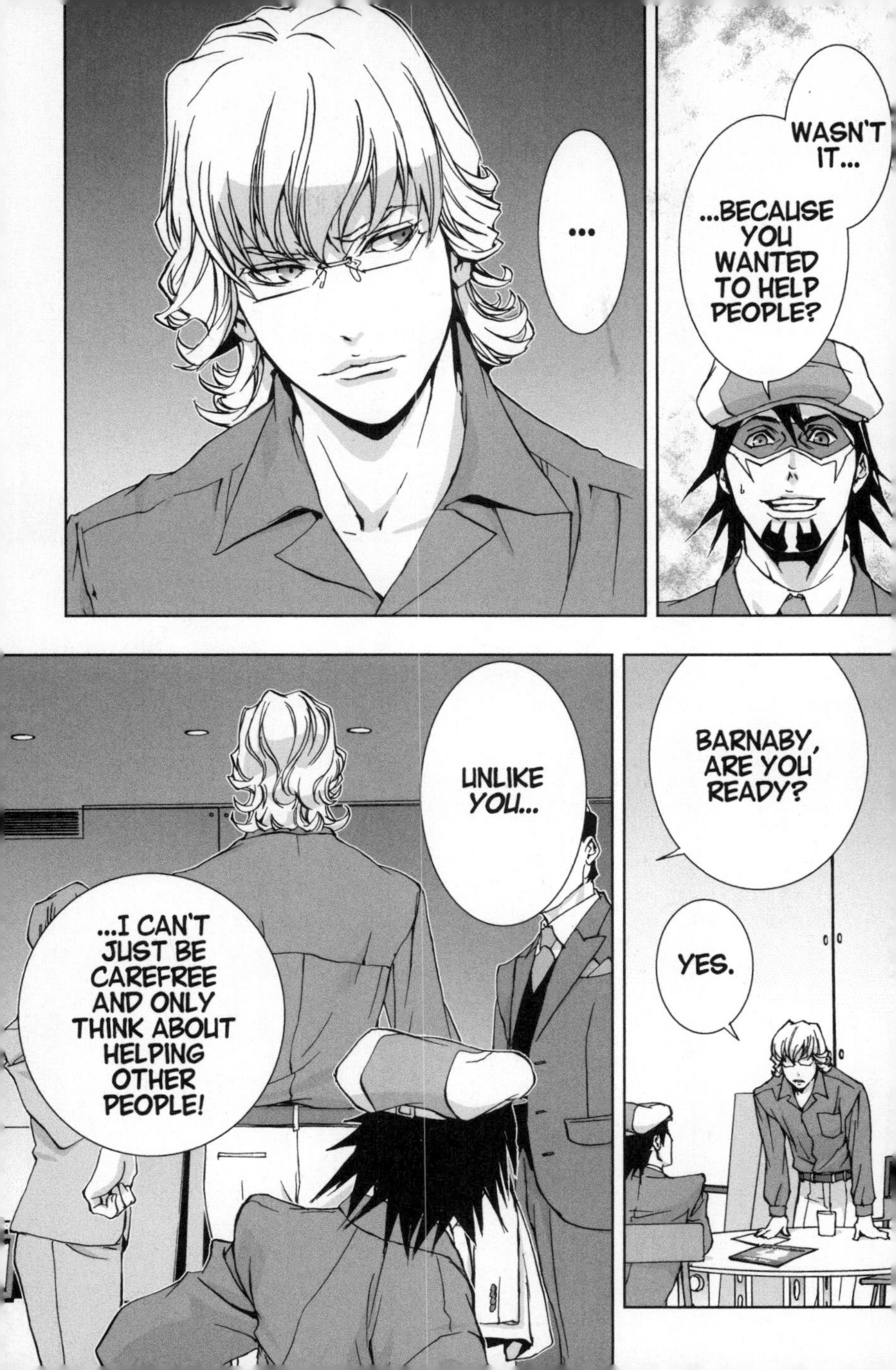

WASN'T IT...
...BECAUSE YOU WANTED TO HELP PEOPLE?
...
BARNABY, ARE YOU READY?
YES.
UNLIKE YOU...
...I CAN'T JUST BE CAREFREE AND ONLY THINK ABOUT HELPING OTHER PEOPLE!

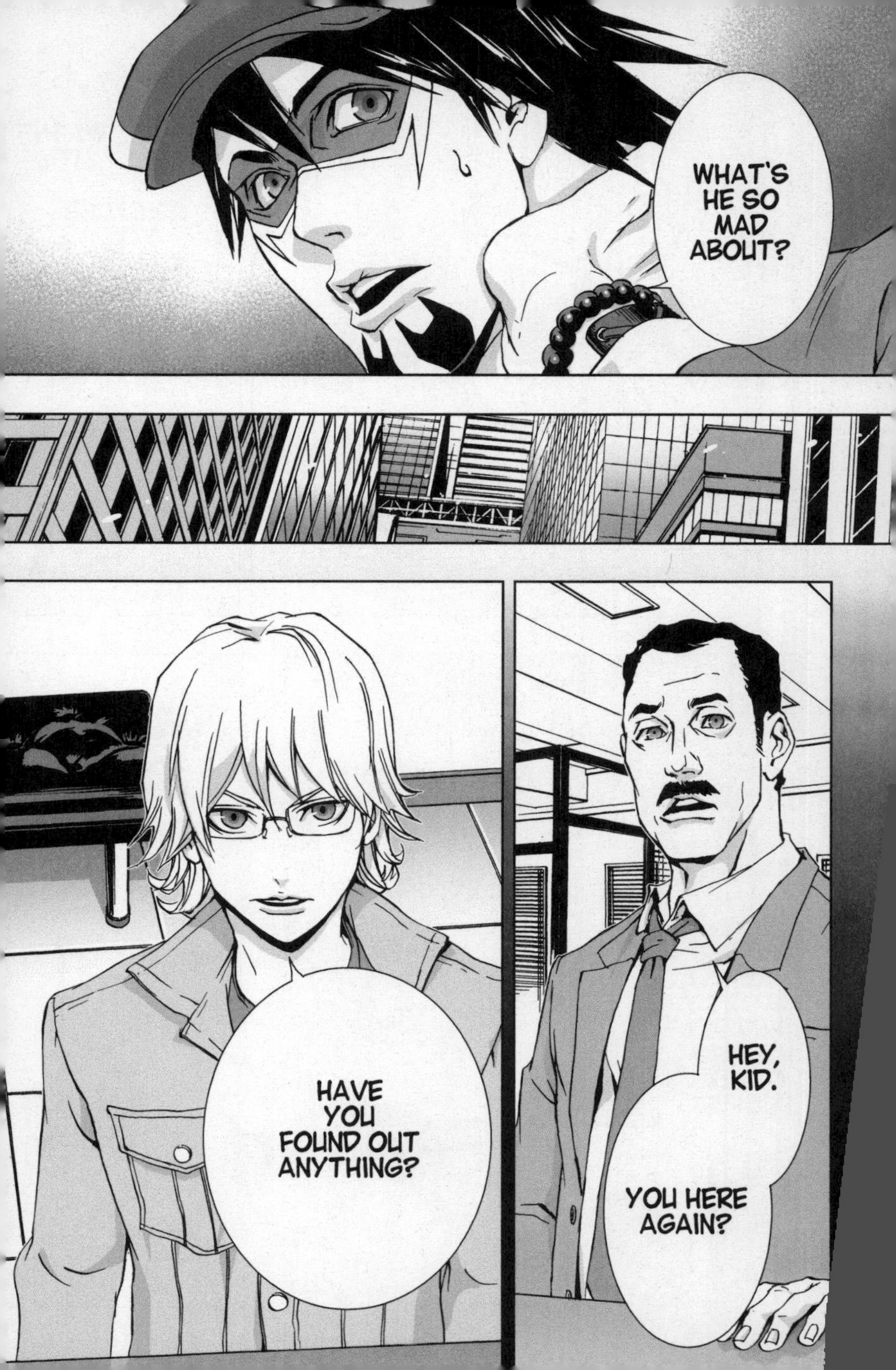
WHAT'S HE SO MAD ABOUT?
HEY, KID.
YOU HERE AGAIN?
HAVE YOU FOUND OUT ANYTHING?

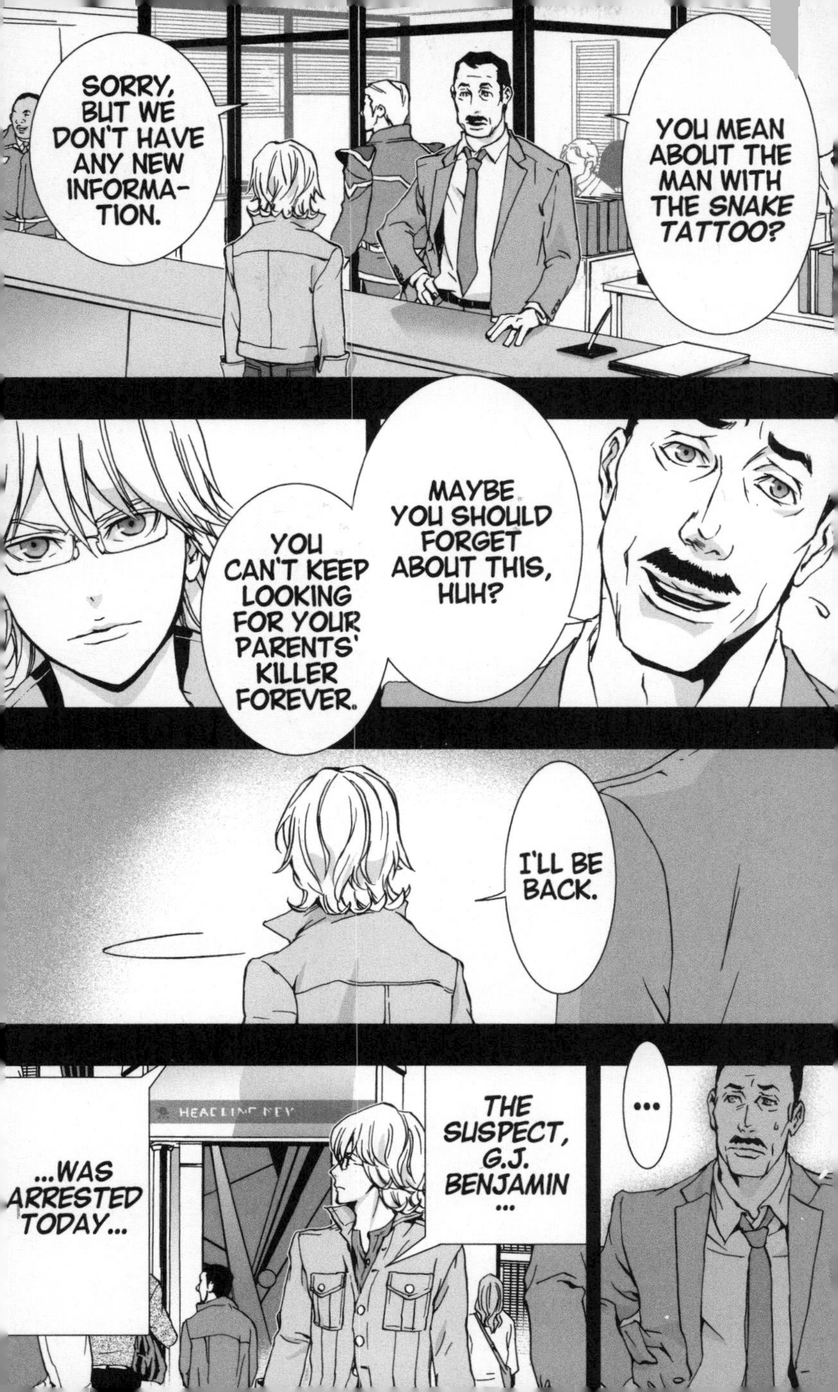
YOU MEAN ABOUT THE MAN WITH THE SNAKE TATTOO?
SORRY, BUT WE DON'T HAVE ANY NEW INFORMATION.
MAYBE YOU SHOULD FORGET ABOUT THIS, HUH?
YOU CAN'T KEEP LOOKING FOR YOUR PARENTS' KILLER FOREVER.
I'LL BE BACK.
...
THE SUSPECT, G.J. BENJAMIN ...
...WAS ARRESTED TODAY...

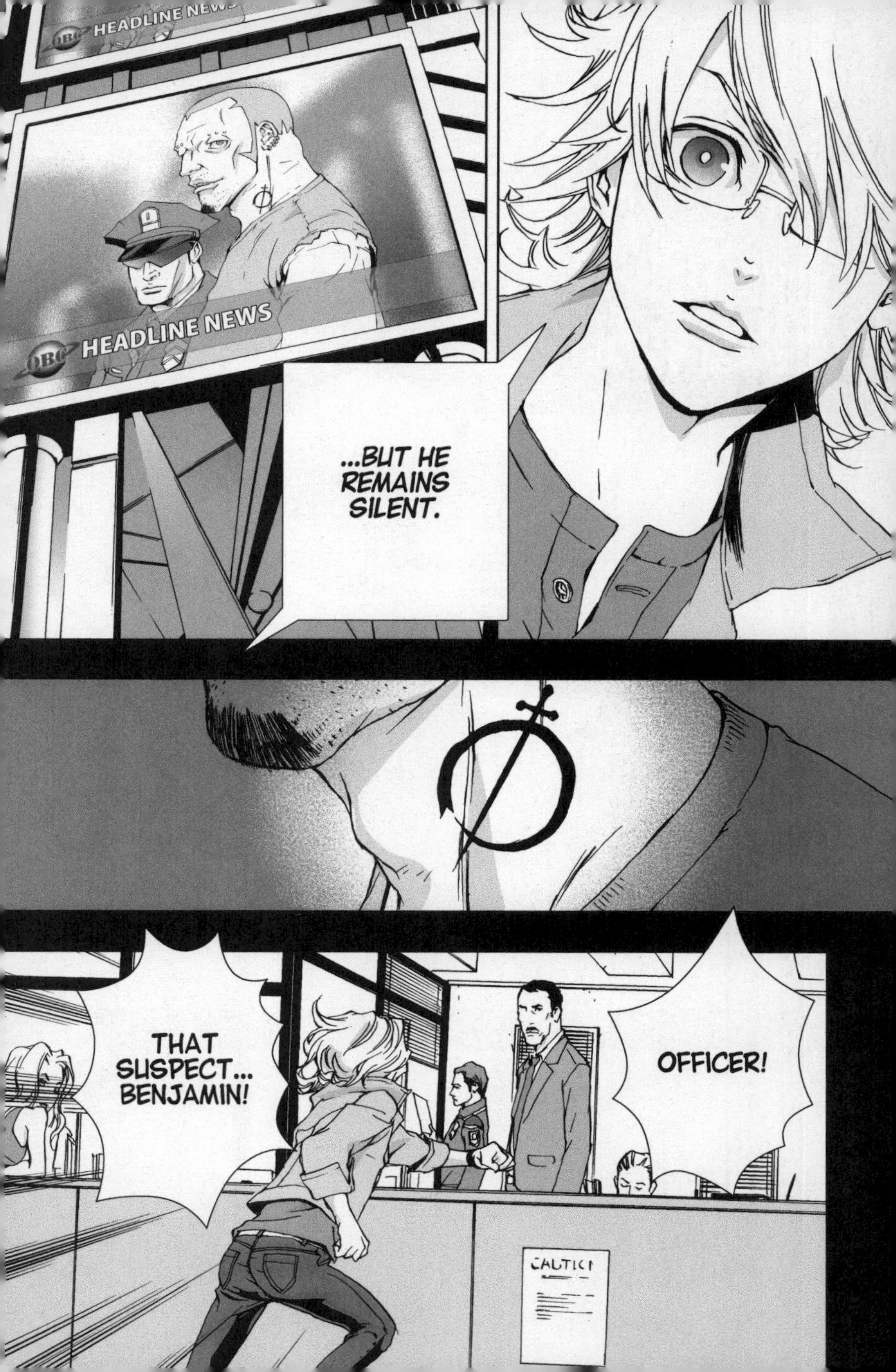
...BUT HE REMAINS SILENT.
HEADLINE NEWS
HEADLINE NEWS
OFFICER!
THAT SUSPECT... BENJAMIN!

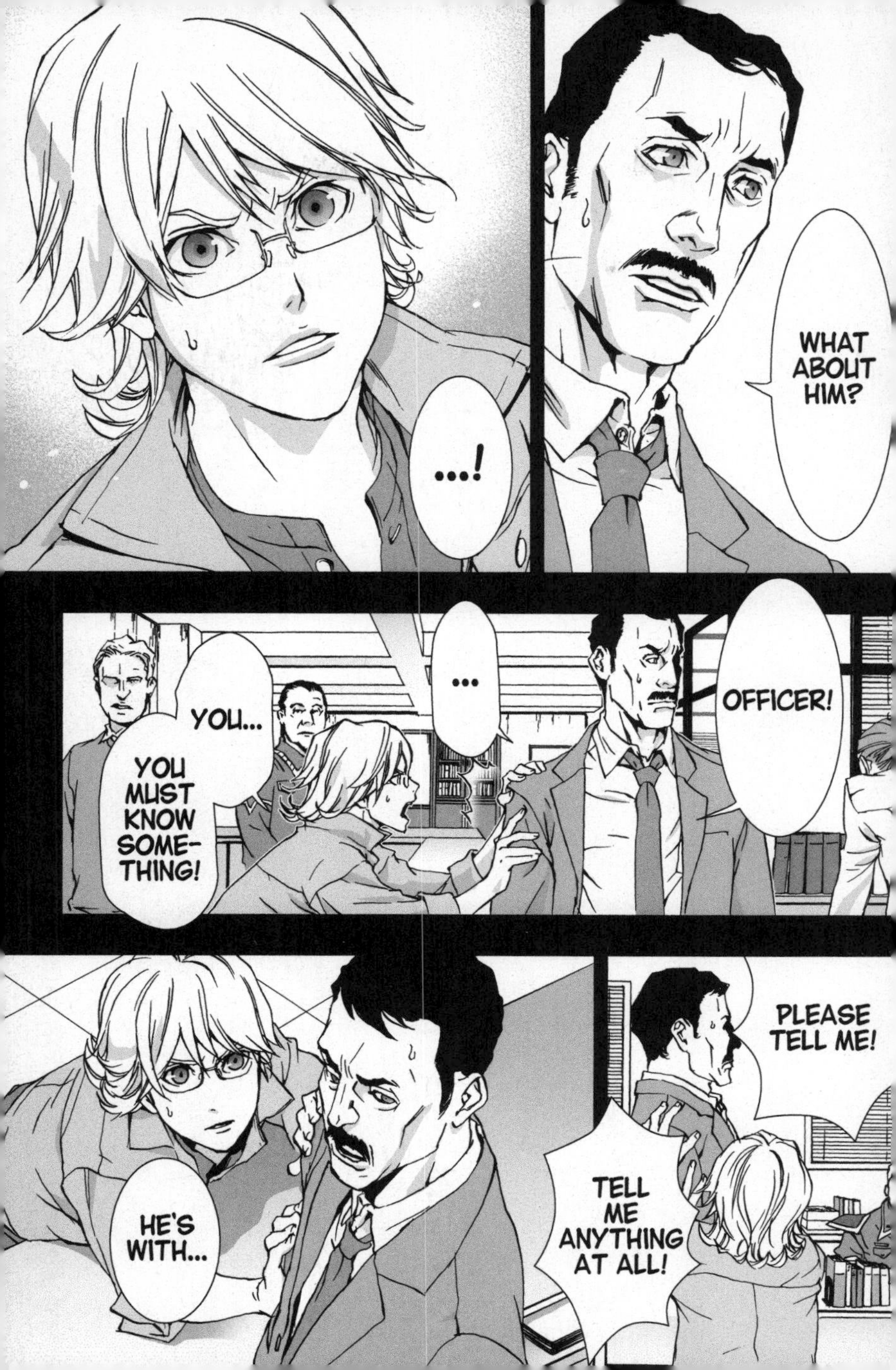
WHAT ABOUT HIM?
...!
OFFICER!
...
YOU...
YOU MUST KNOW SOME-THING!
PLEASE TELL ME!
TELL ME ANYTHING AT ALL!
HE'S WITH...

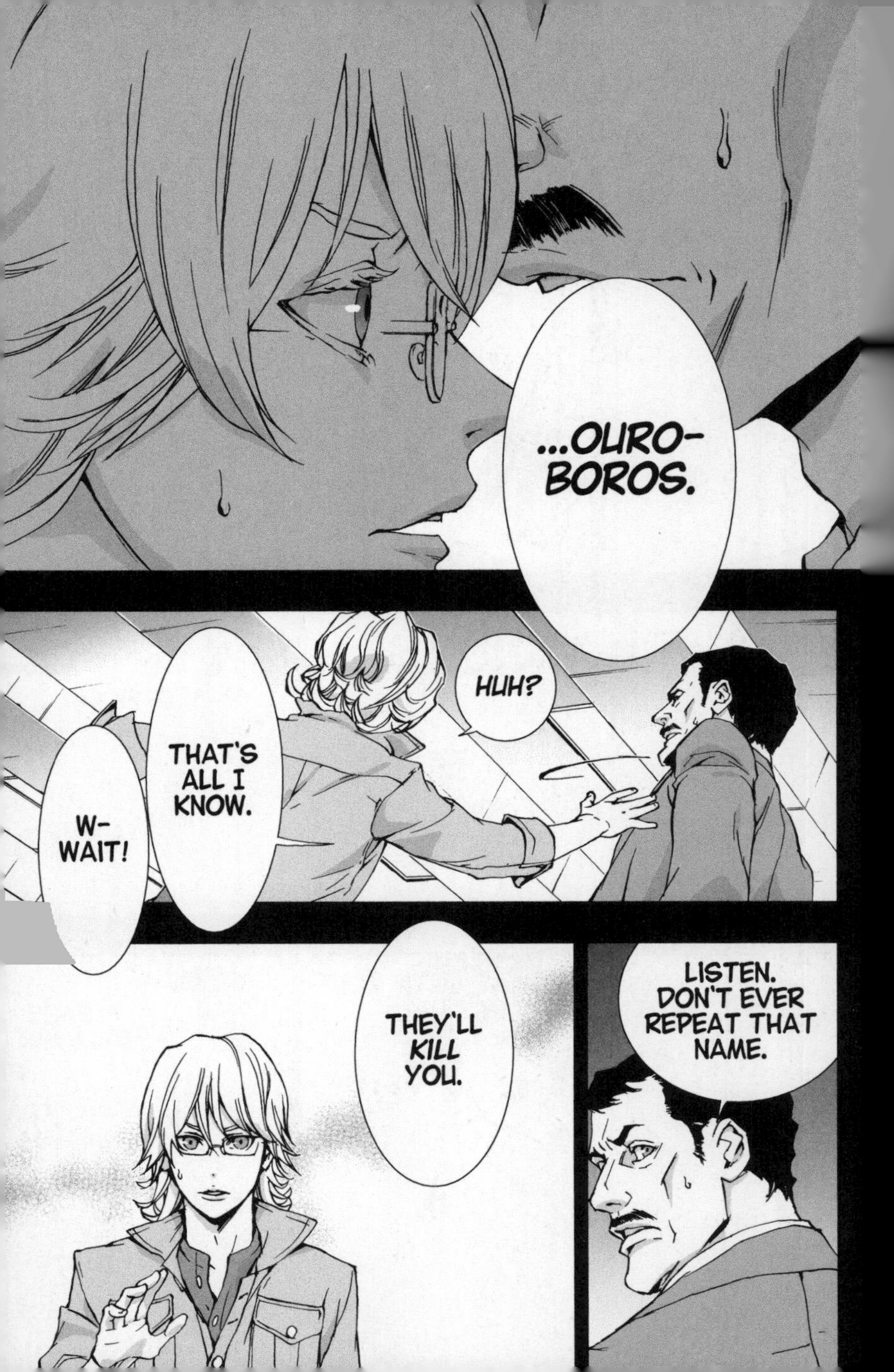
...OURO-BOROS.
HUH?
THAT'S ALL I KNOW.
W-WAIT!
LISTEN. DON'T EVER REPEAT THAT NAME.
THEY'LL KILL YOU.

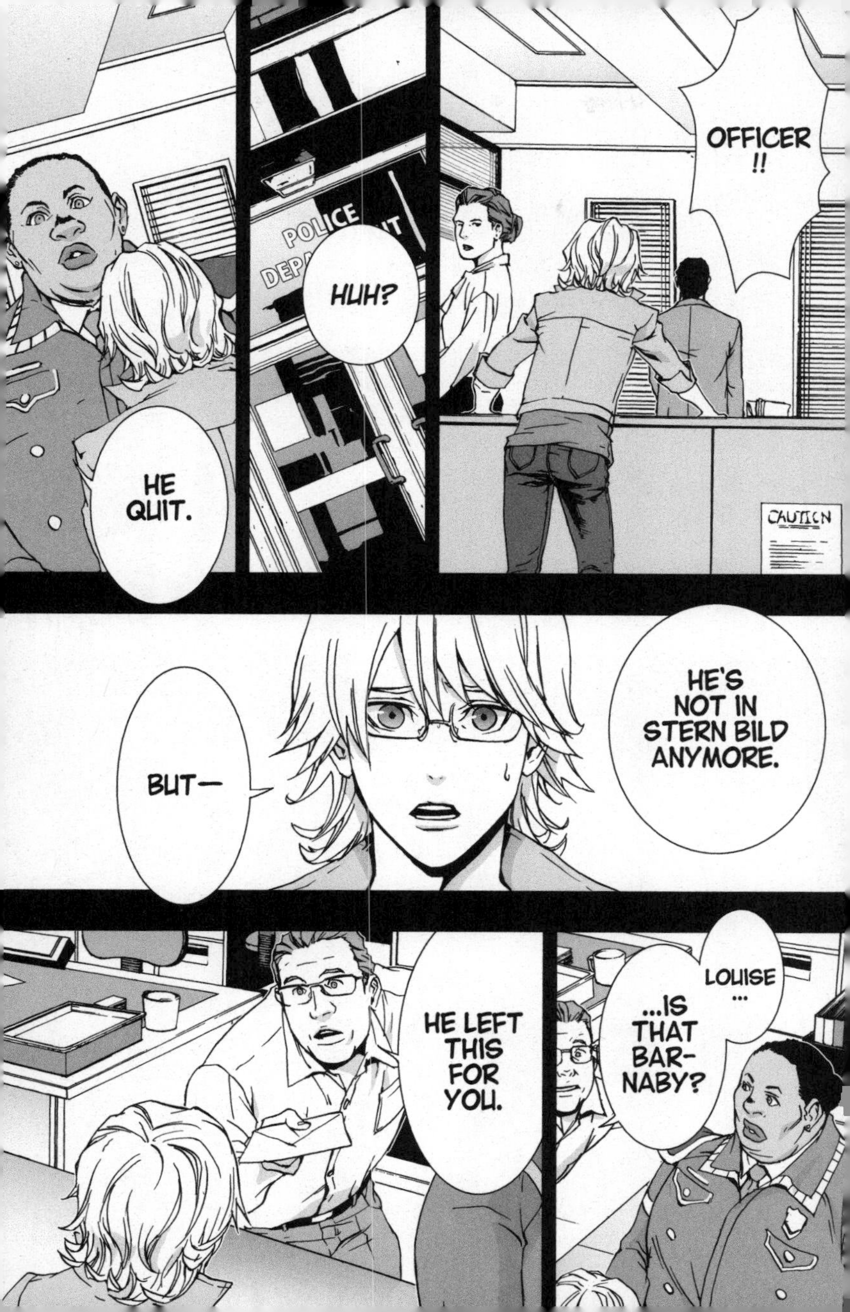
OFFICER !!
HUH?
HE QUIT.
HE'S NOT IN STERN BILD ANYMORE.
BUT—
LOUISE ...
...IS THAT BAR-NABY?
HE LEFT THIS FOR YOU.
POLICE DEPA
CAUTION

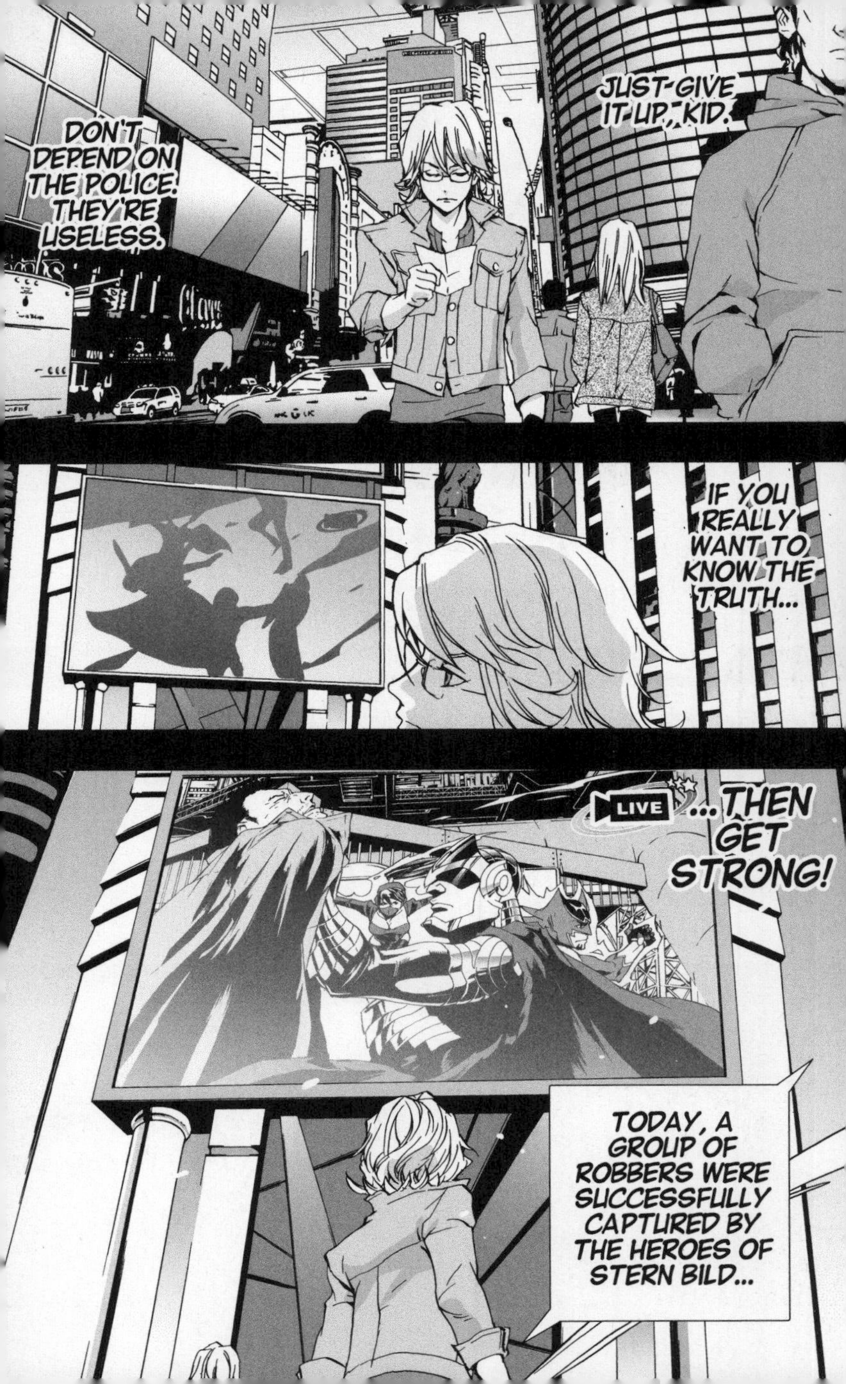
JUST GIVE IT UP, KID.
DON'T DEPEND ON THE POLICE. THEY'RE USELESS.
IF YOU REALLY WANT TO KNOW THE TRUTH...
LIVE
...THEN GET STRONG!
TODAY, A GROUP OF ROBBERS WERE SUCCESSFULLY CAPTURED BY THE HEROES OF STERN BILD...

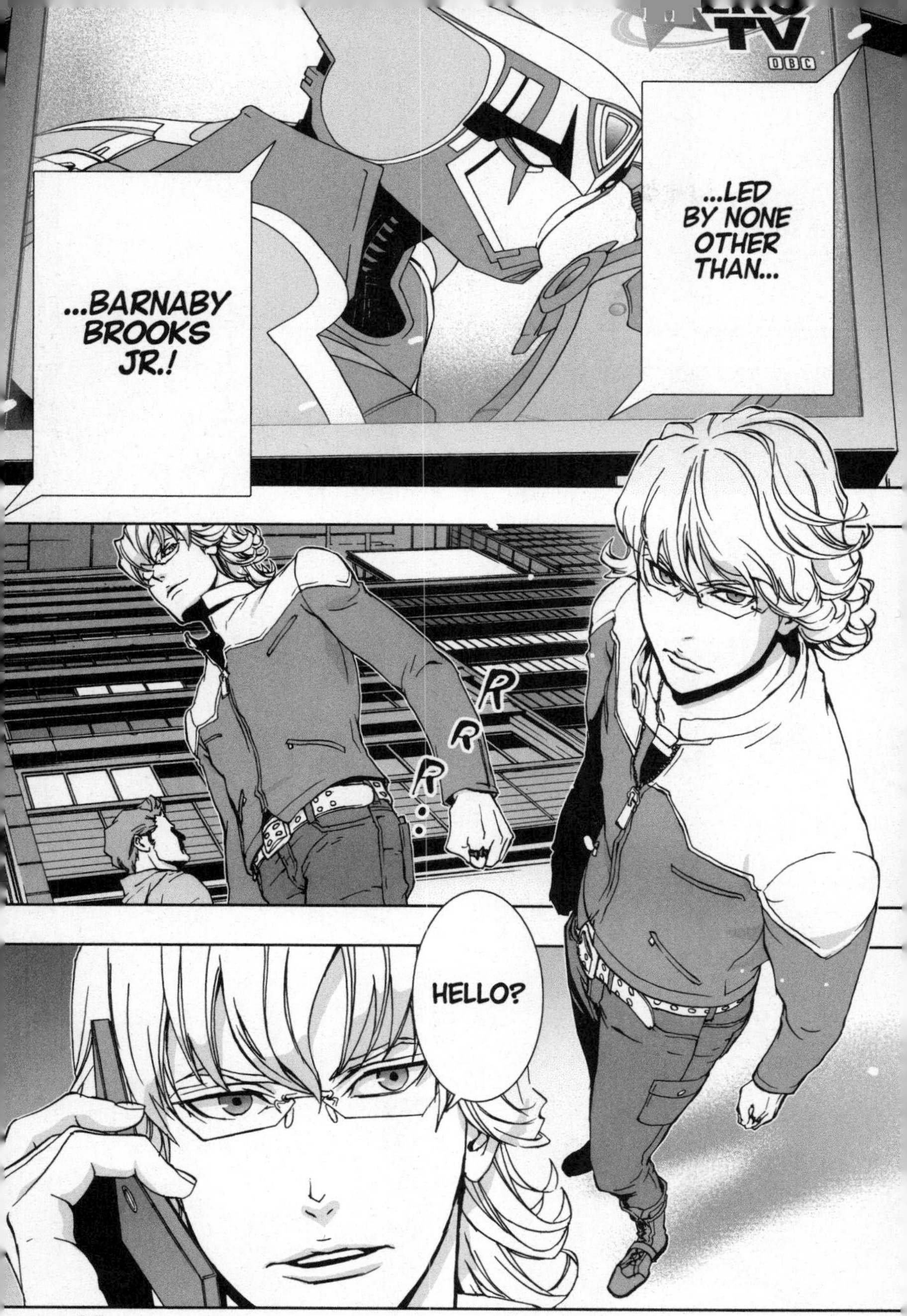
TV
OBC
...LED BY NONE OTHER THAN...
...BARNABY BROOKS JR.!
RRR...
HELLO?

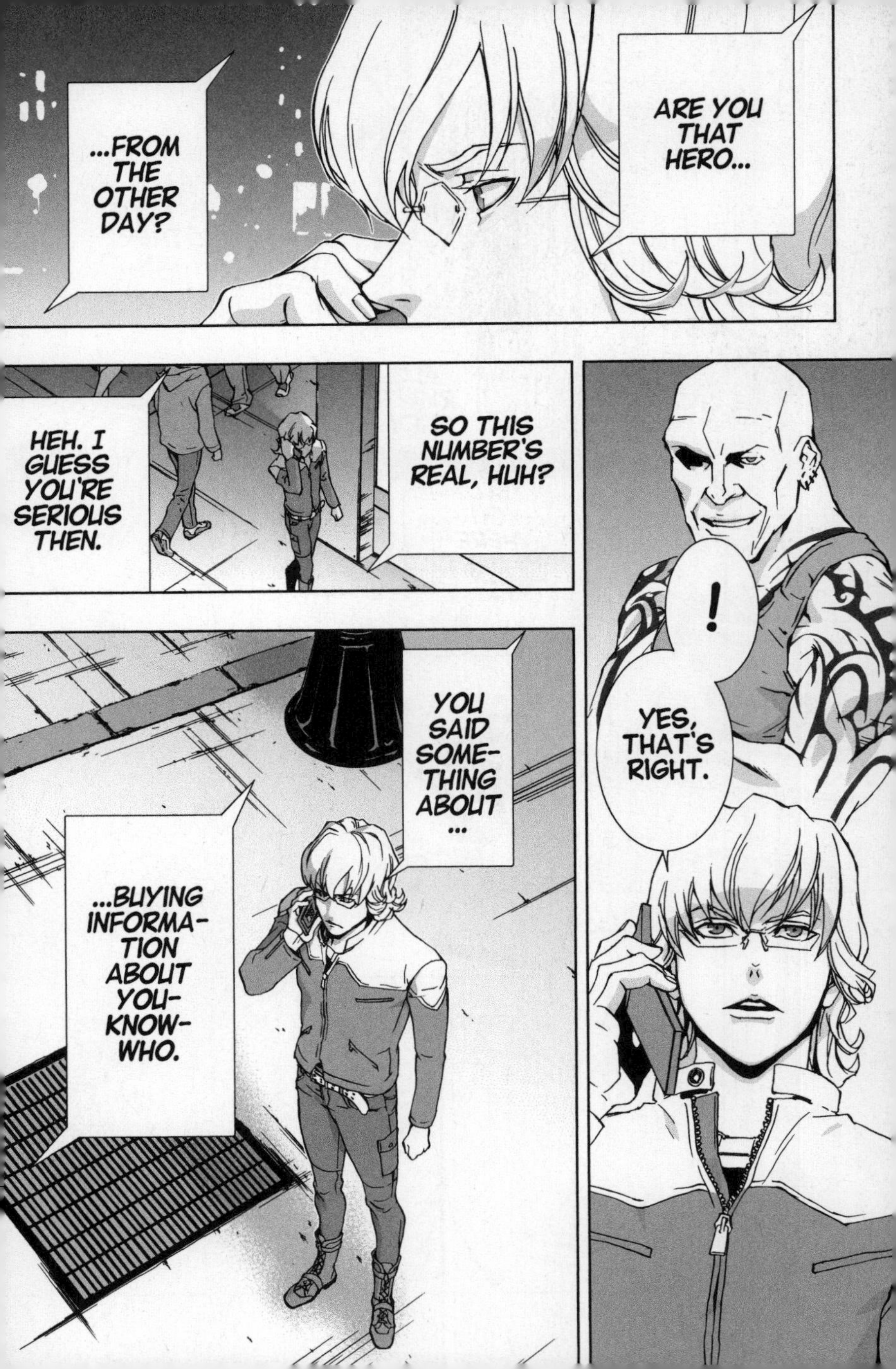
ARE YOU THAT HERO...
...FROM THE OTHER DAY?
!
YES, THAT'S RIGHT.
SO THIS NUMBER'S REAL, HUH?
HEH. I GUESS YOU'RE SERIOUS THEN.
YOU SAID SOME-THING ABOUT...
...BUYING INFORMA-TION ABOUT YOU-KNOW-WHO.

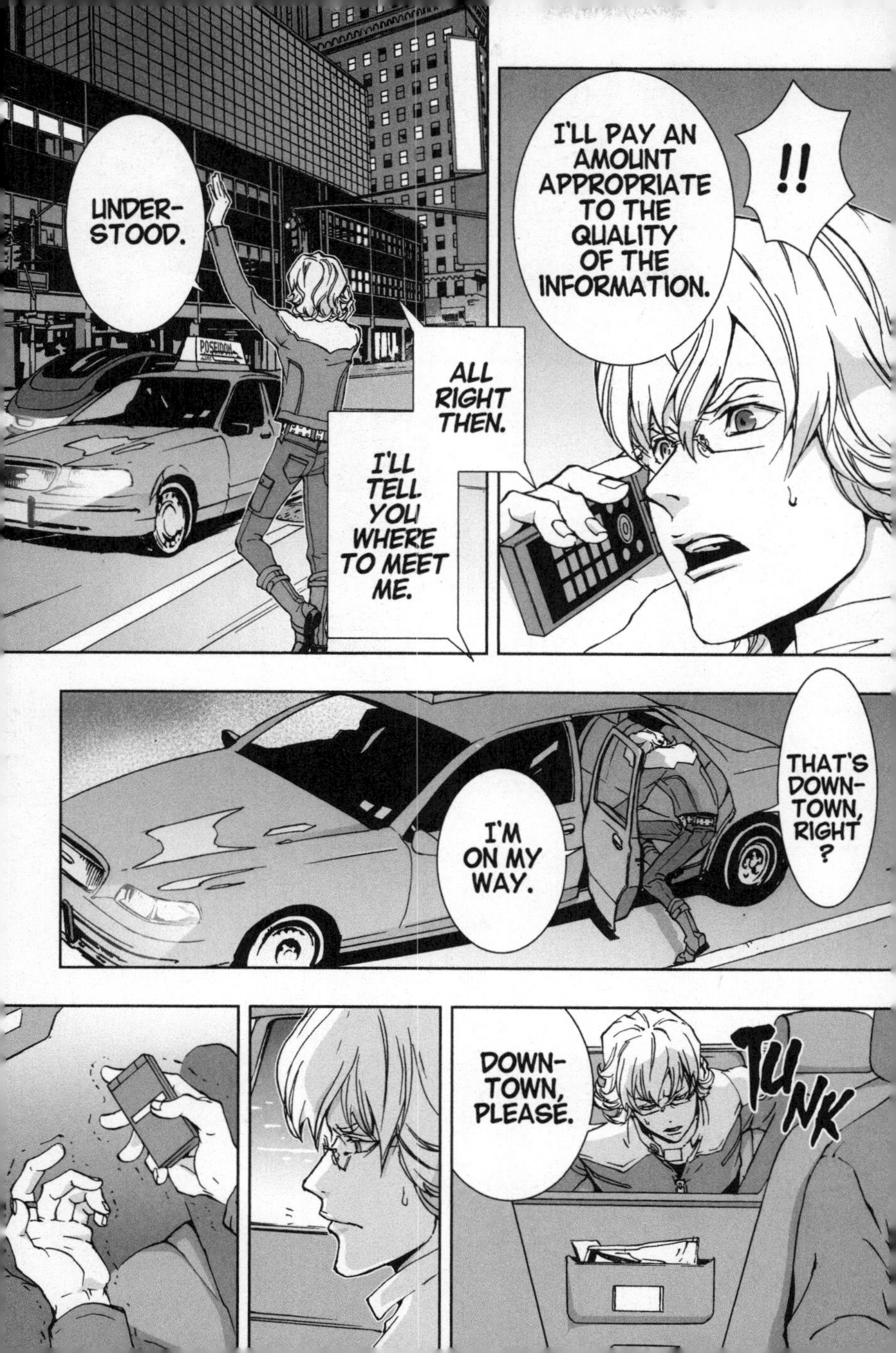
!!
I'LL PAY AN AMOUNT APPROPRIATE TO THE QUALITY OF THE INFORMATION.
ALL RIGHT THEN.
I'LL TELL YOU WHERE TO MEET ME.
UNDER-STOOD.
THAT'S DOWN-TOWN, RIGHT?
I'M ON MY WAY.
TUNK
DOWN-TOWN, PLEASE.

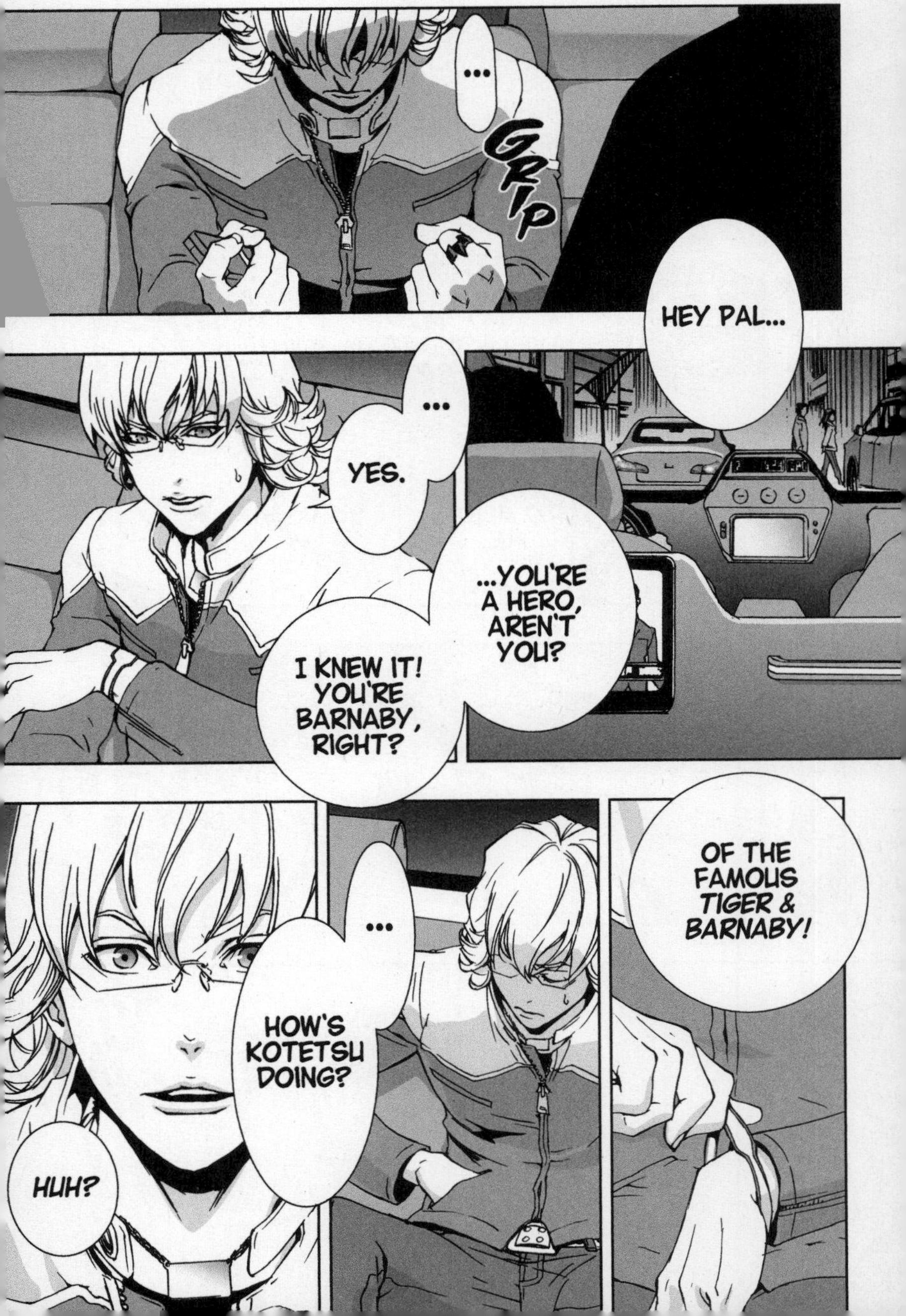
...
GRIP
HEY PAL...
...YOU'RE A HERO, AREN'T YOU?
...
YES.
I KNEW IT! YOU'RE BARNABY, RIGHT?
OF THE FAMOUS TIGER & BARNABY!
...
HOW'S KOTETSU DOING?
HUH?

I WORKED WITH KOTETSU UNTIL A LITTLE WHILE BACK.

AT TOP MAG. HE WORKED THERE BEFORE APOLLON.

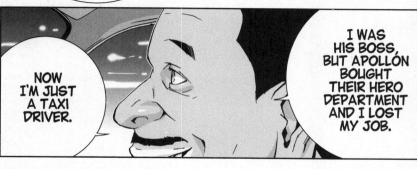

I WAS HIS BOSS, BUT APOLLON BOUGHT THEIR HERO DEPARTMENT AND I LOST MY JOB.

NOW I'M JUST A TAXI DRIVER.

YEAH...

I BET YOU KNOW...

...HOW NOSY KOTETSU CAN BE.

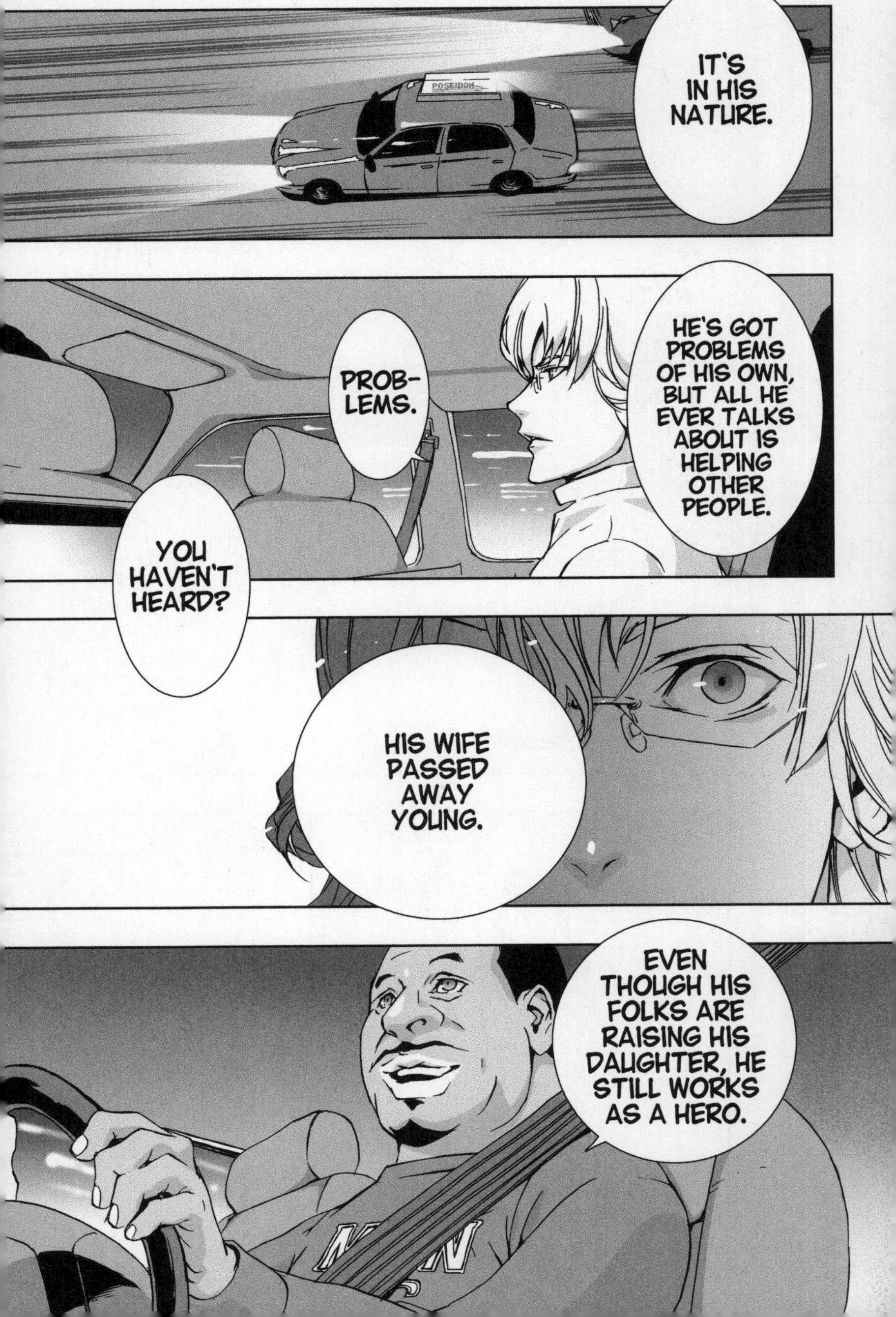
IT'S IN HIS NATURE.
POSEIDON
HE'S GOT PROBLEMS OF HIS OWN, BUT ALL HE EVER TALKS ABOUT IS HELPING OTHER PEOPLE.
PROB-LEMS.
YOU HAVEN'T HEARD?
HIS WIFE PASSED AWAY YOUNG.
EVEN THOUGH HIS FOLKS ARE RAISING HIS DAUGHTER, HE STILL WORKS AS A HERO.

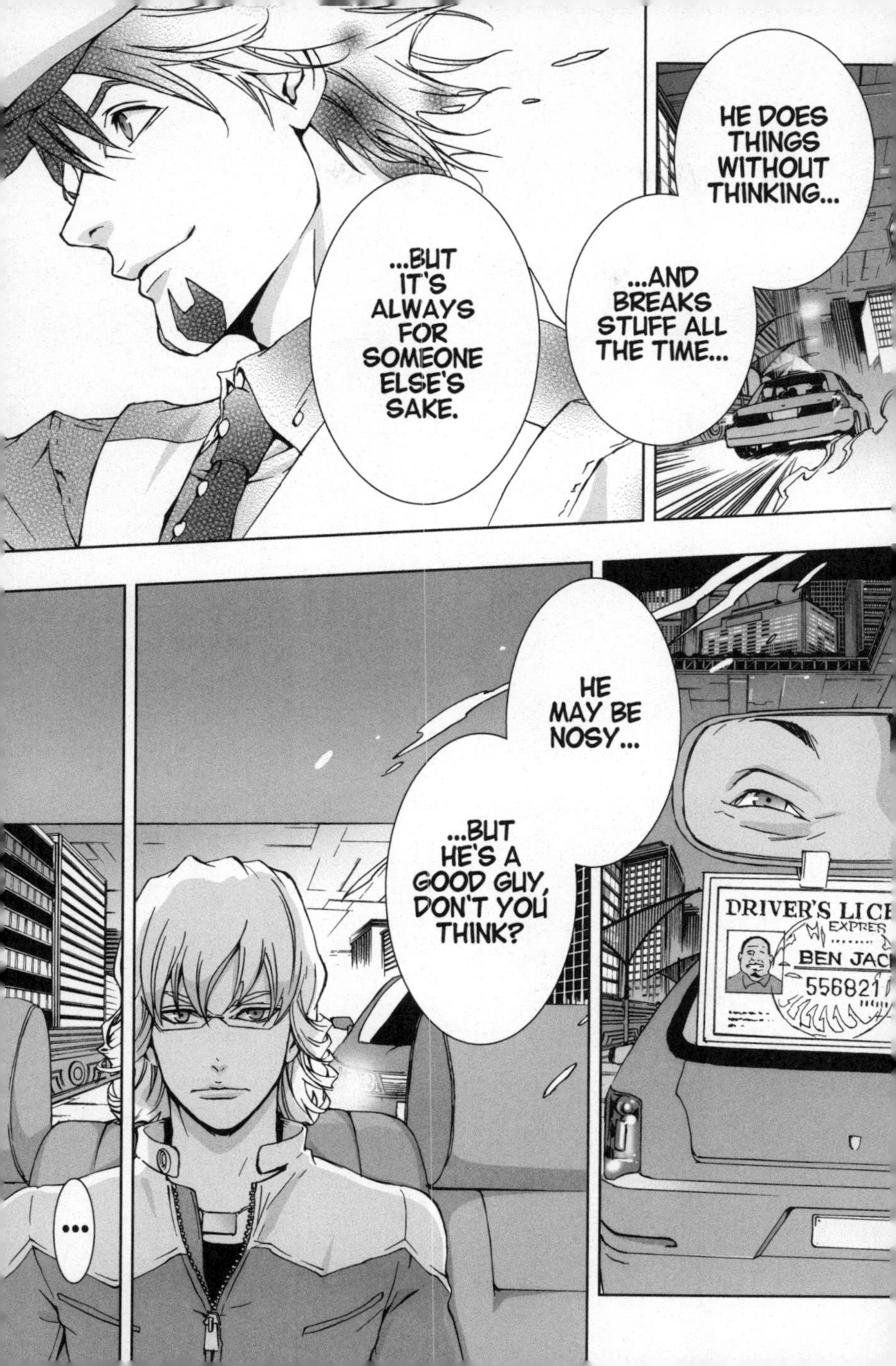
HE DOES THINGS WITHOUT THINKING...
...AND BREAKS STUFF ALL THE TIME...
...BUT IT'S ALWAYS FOR SOMEONE ELSE'S SAKE.
HE MAY BE NOSY...
...BUT HE'S A GOOD GUY, DON'T YOU THINK?
...

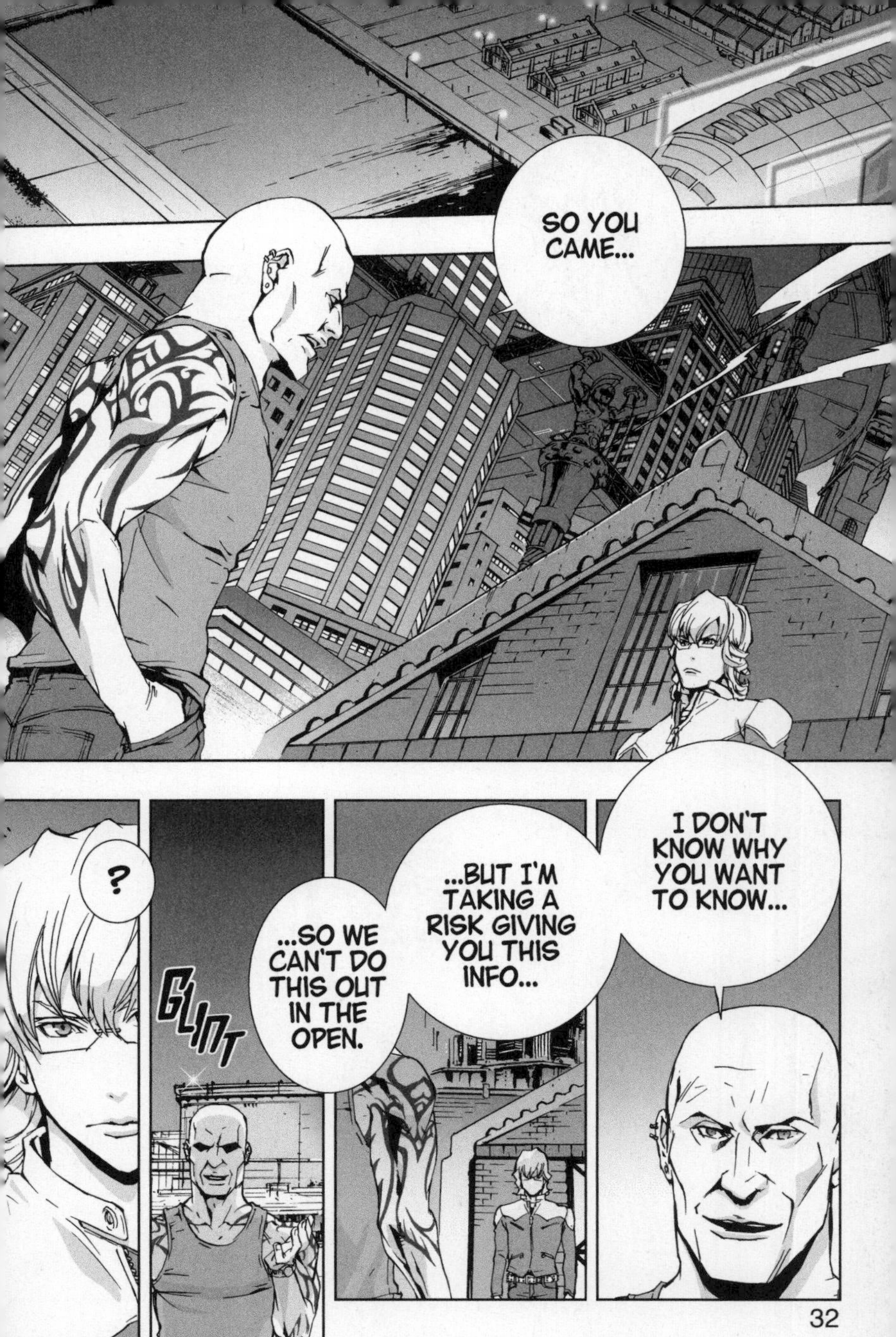
SO YOU CAME...
I DON'T KNOW WHY YOU WANT TO KNOW...
...BUT I'M TAKING A RISK GIVING YOU THIS INFO...
...SO WE CAN'T DO THIS OUT IN THE OPEN.
GLINT
?

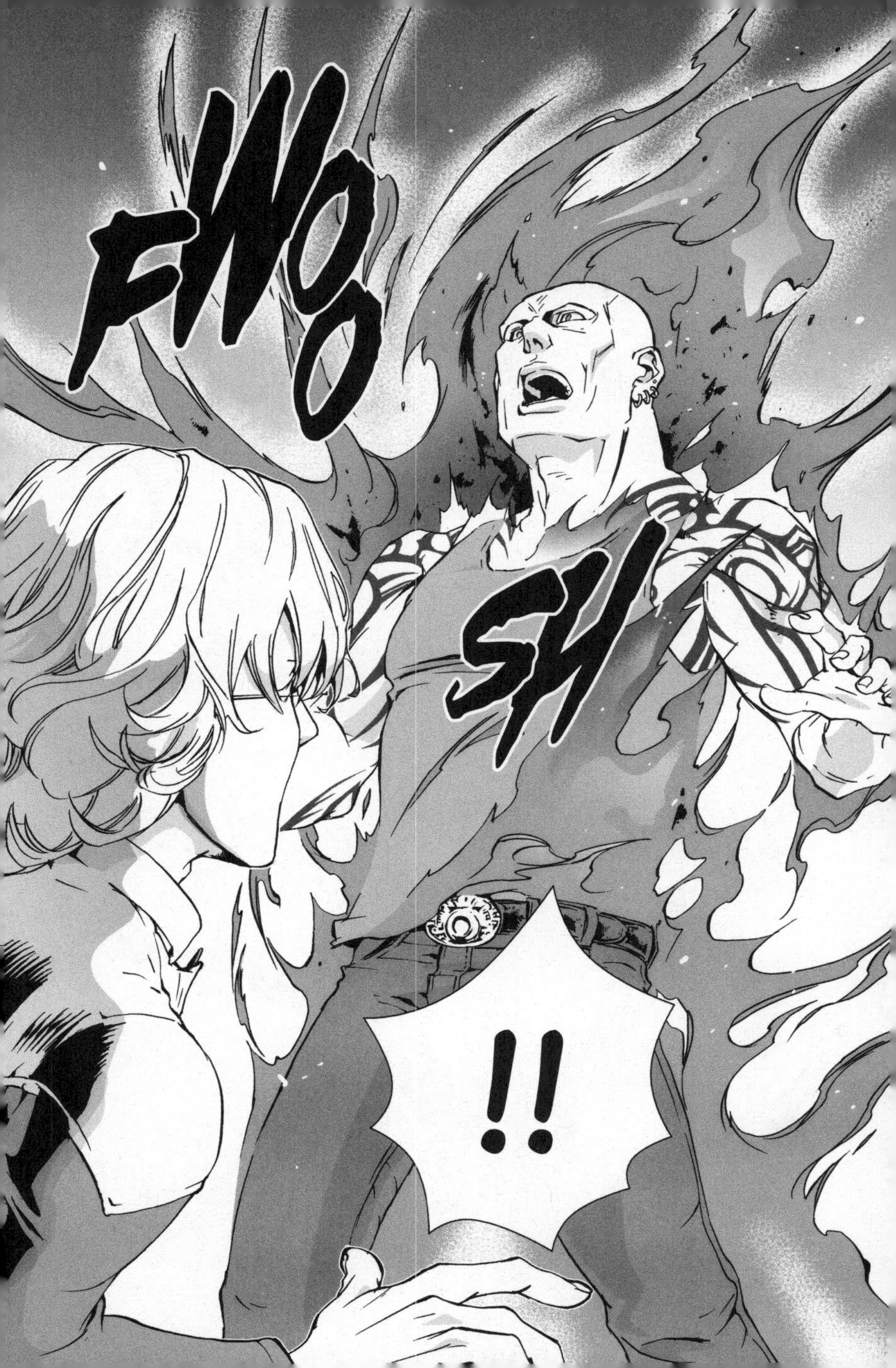
FWOO
SH
!!

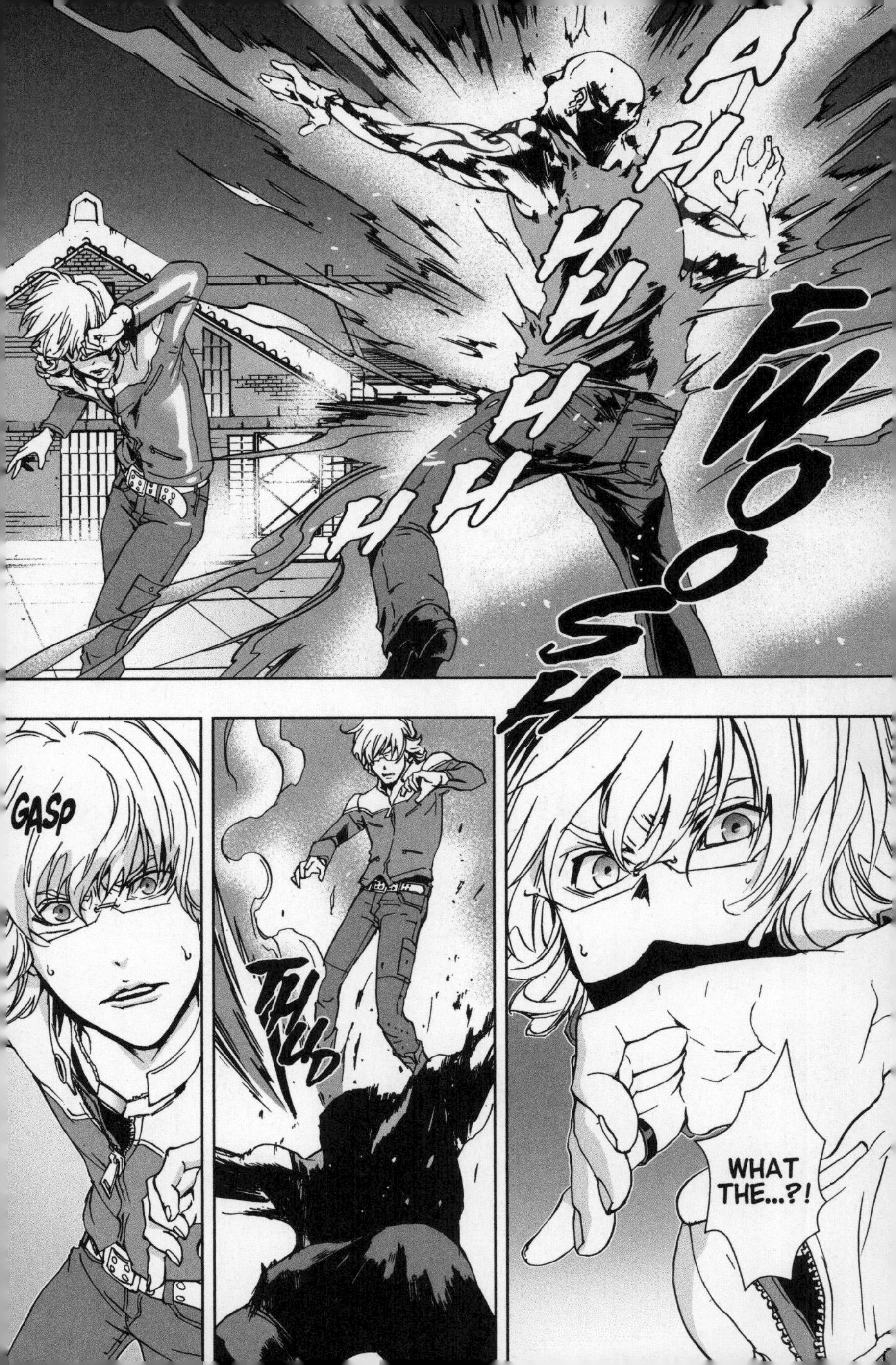
FWOOOSH
AHHHHHH
WHAT THE...?!
THUD
GASP

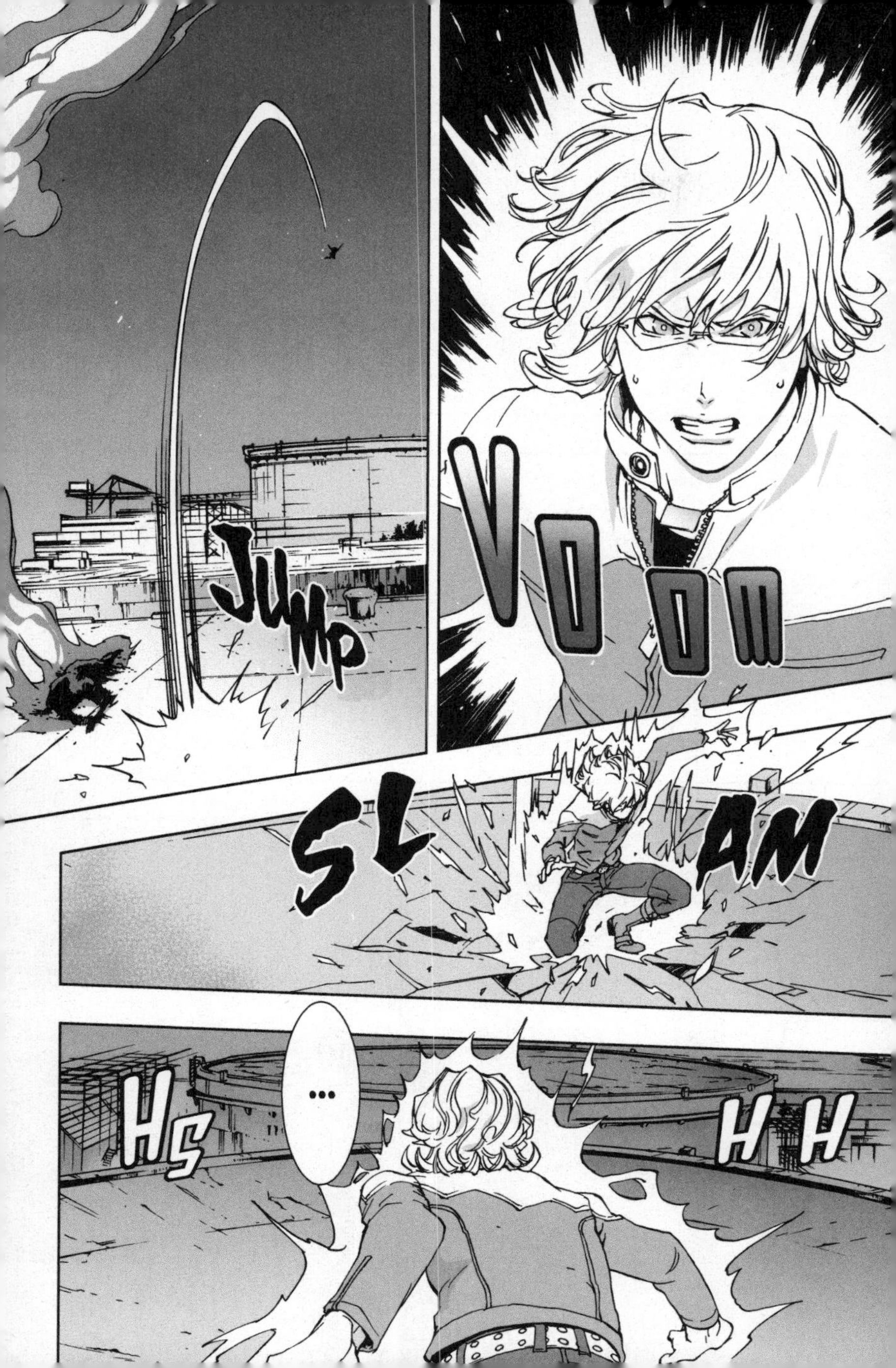
VROOM
JUMP
SLAM
H H
...
HS

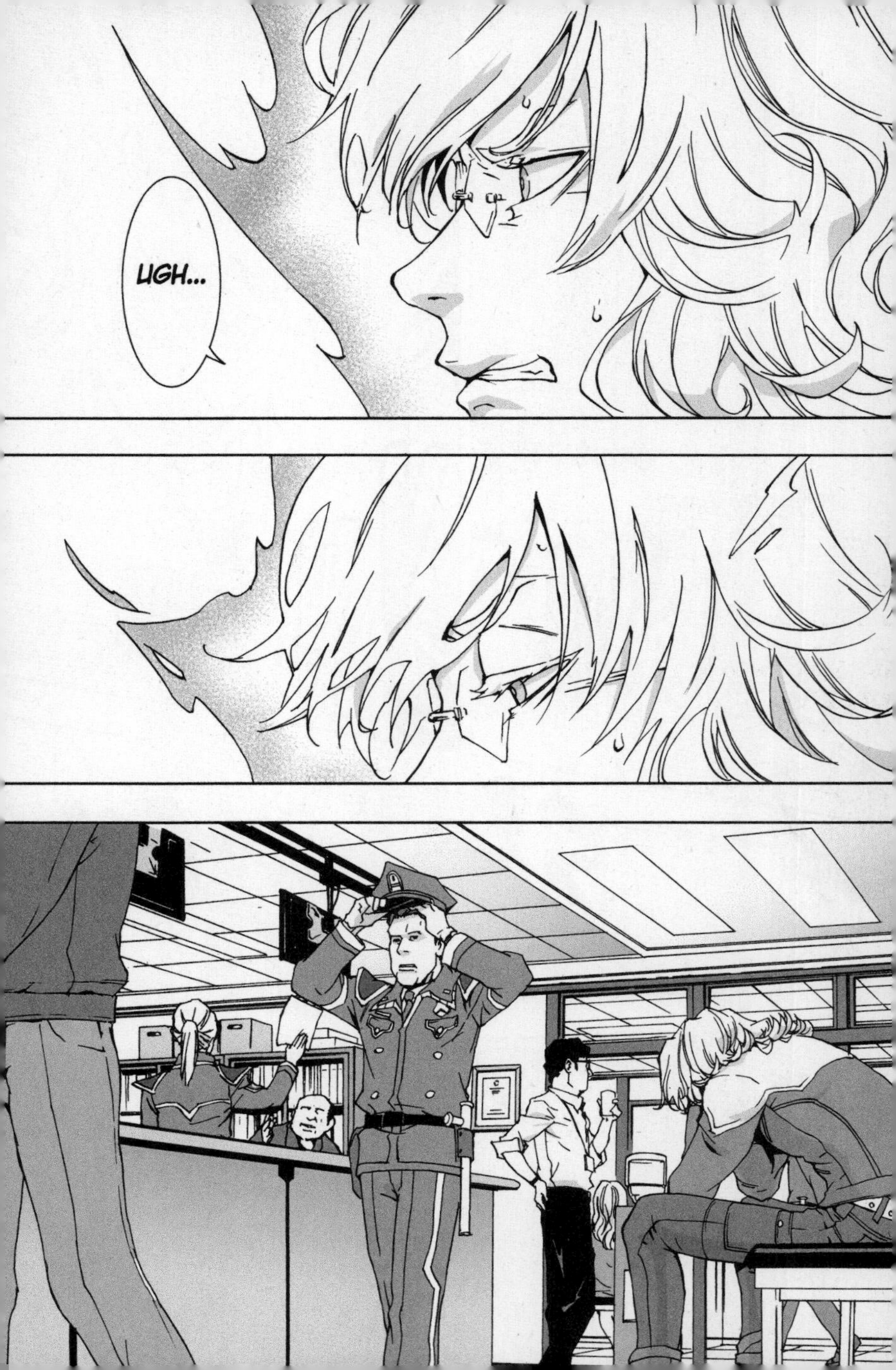
UGH...

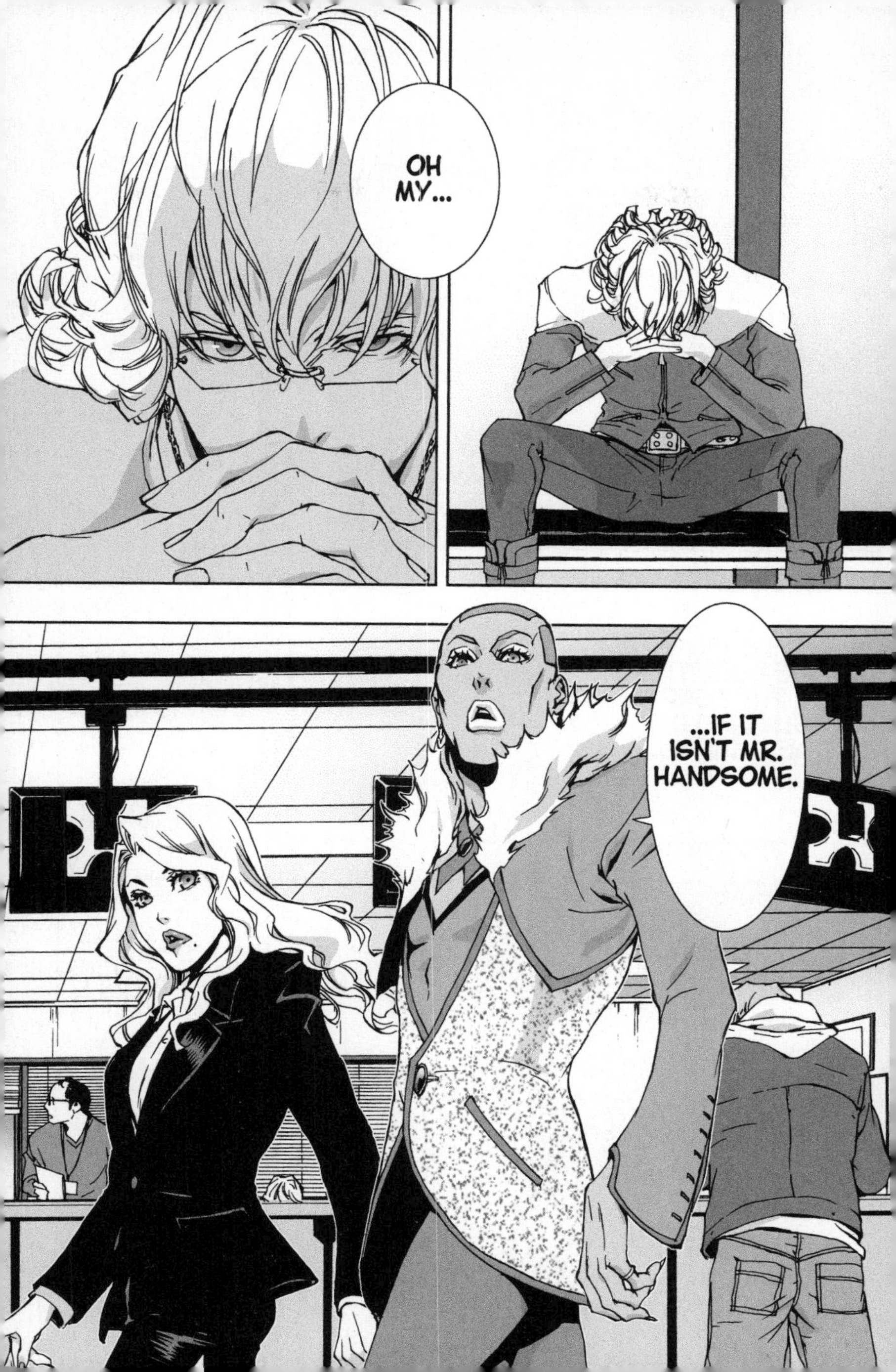
OH MY...
...IF IT ISN'T MR. HANDSOME.

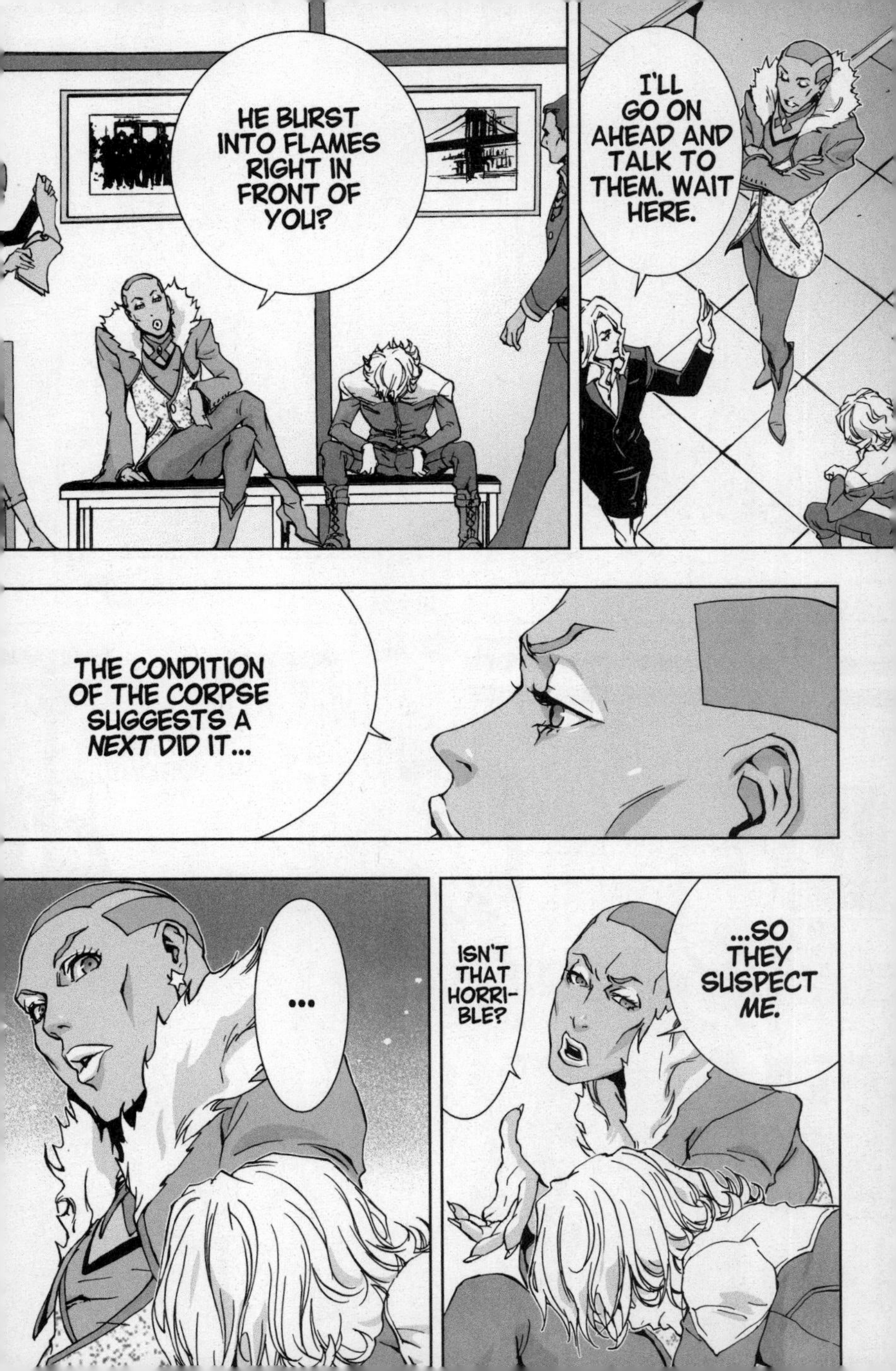
I'LL GO ON AHEAD AND TALK TO THEM. WAIT HERE.
HE BURST INTO FLAMES RIGHT IN FRONT OF YOU?
THE CONDITION OF THE CORPSE SUGGESTS A *NEXT* DID IT...
...SO THEY SUSPECT ME.
ISN'T THAT HORRI-BLE?
...

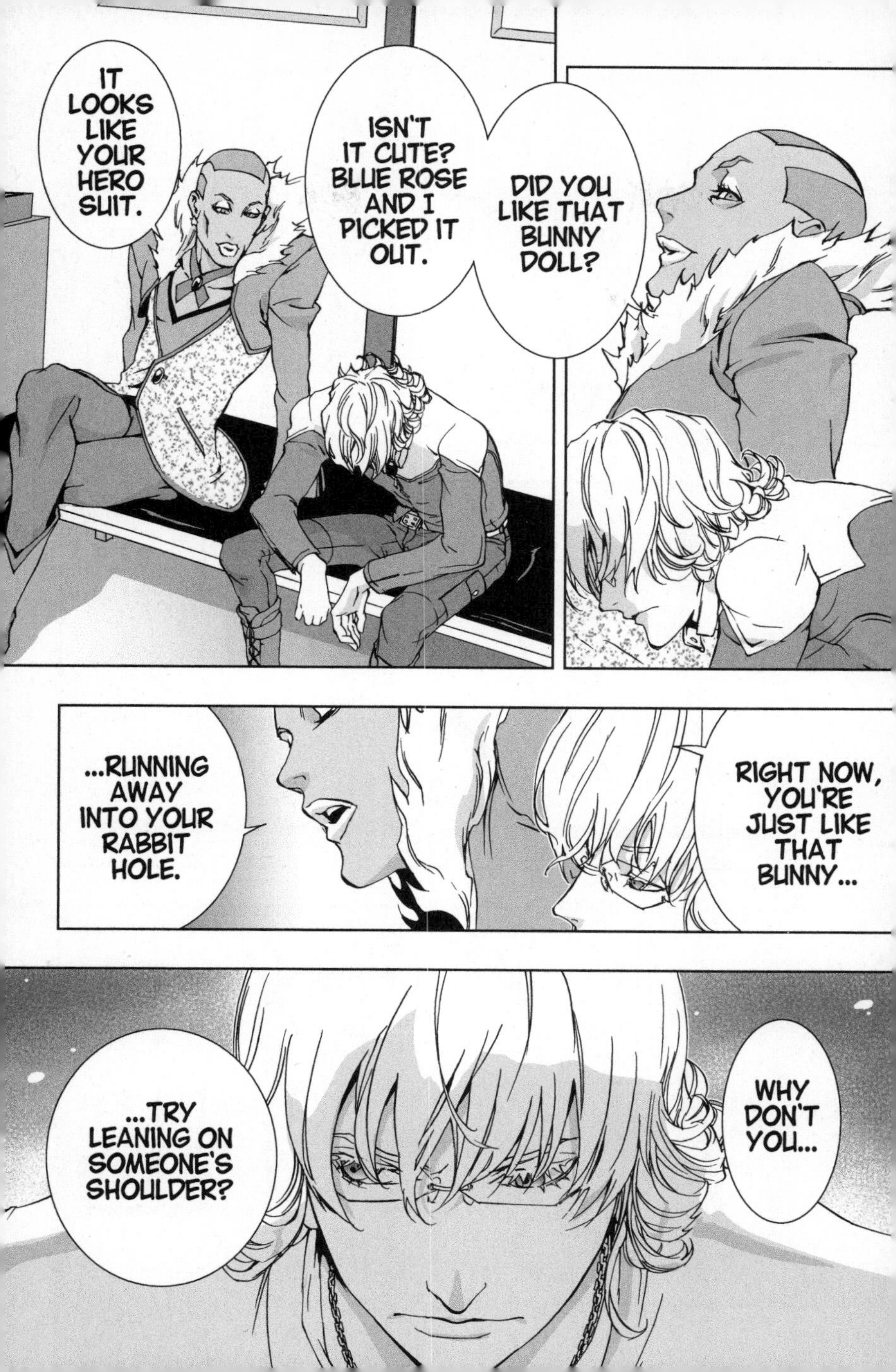
DID YOU LIKE THAT BUNNY DOLL?
ISN'T IT CUTE? BLUE ROSE AND I PICKED IT OUT.
IT LOOKS LIKE YOUR HERO SUIT.
RIGHT NOW, YOU'RE JUST LIKE THAT BUNNY...
...RUNNING AWAY INTO YOUR RABBIT HOLE.
WHY DON'T YOU...
...TRY LEANING ON SOMEONE'S SHOULDER?

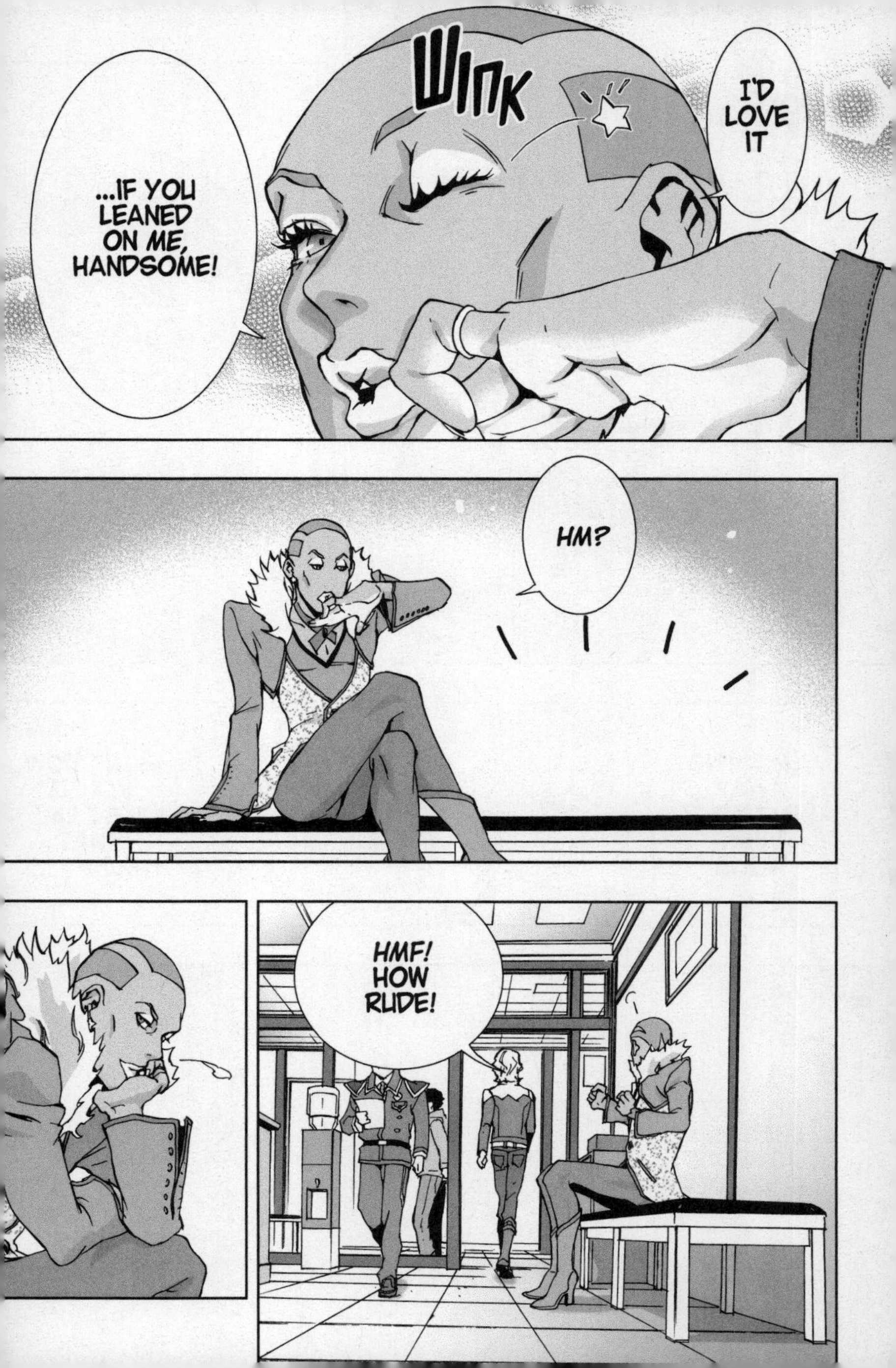
I'D LOVE IT
WINK
...IF YOU LEANED ON ME, HANDSOME!
HM?
HMF! HOW RUDE!

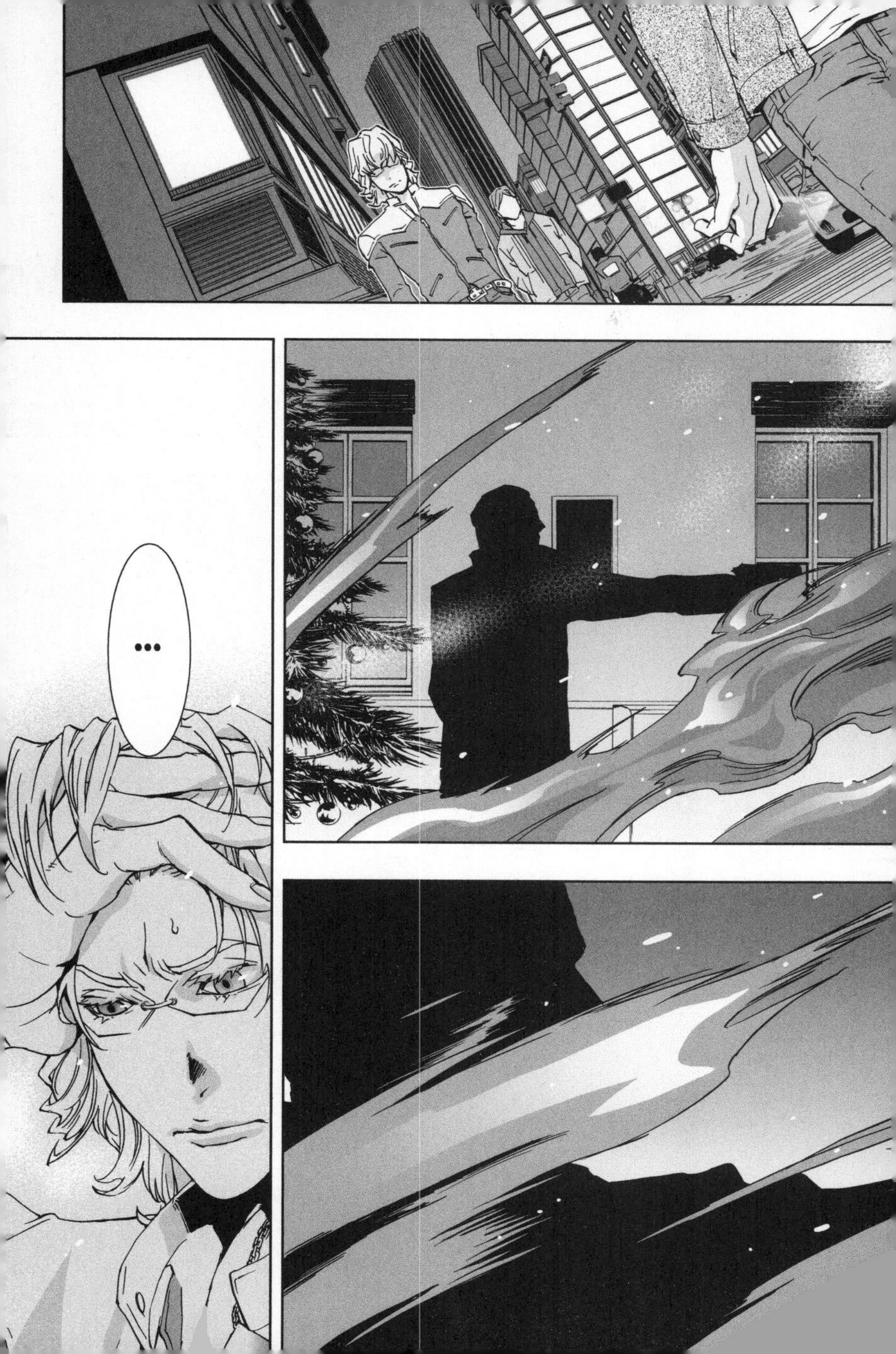
...

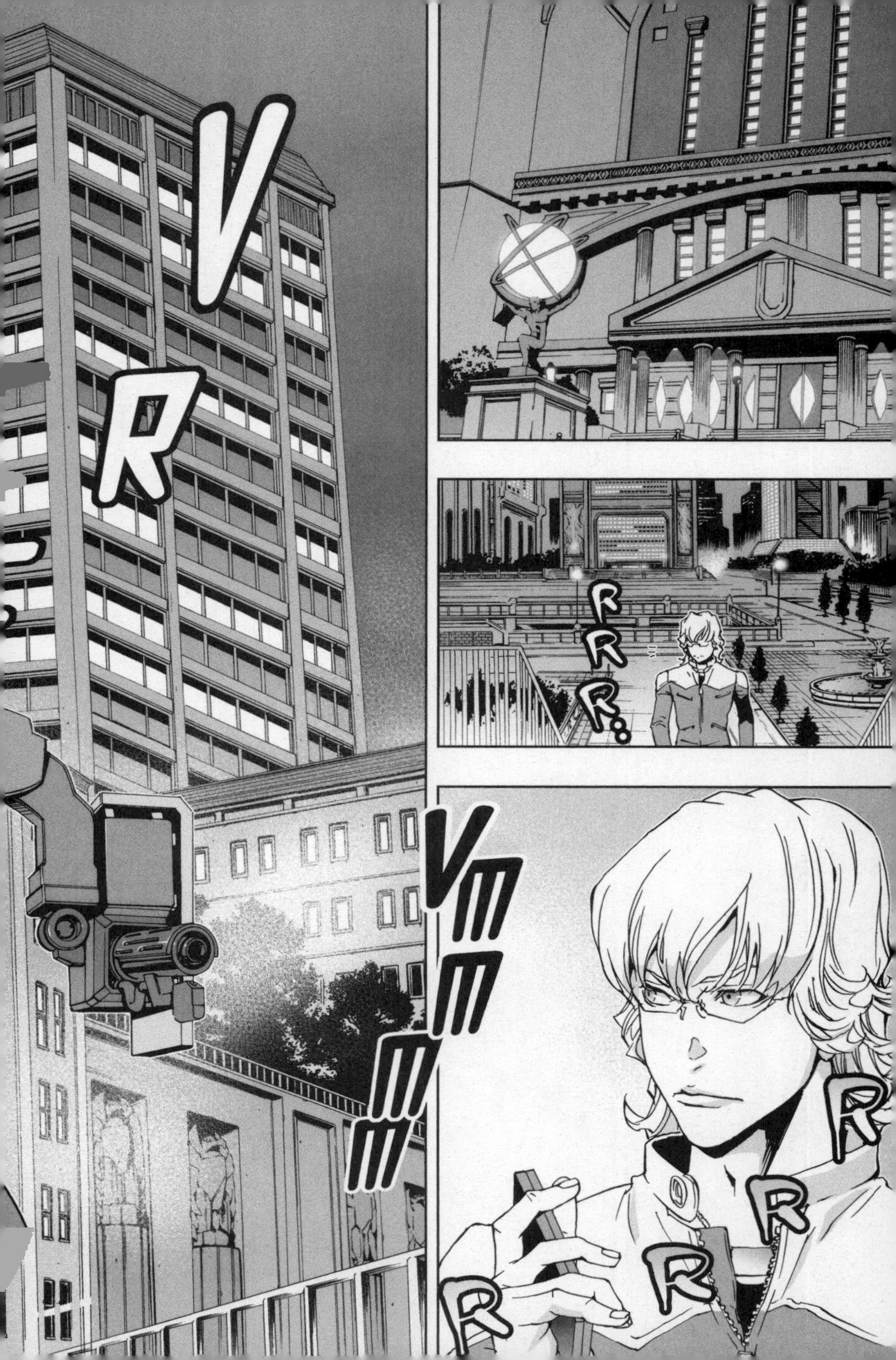
RRR..
RRRRR
VR
VMMMM

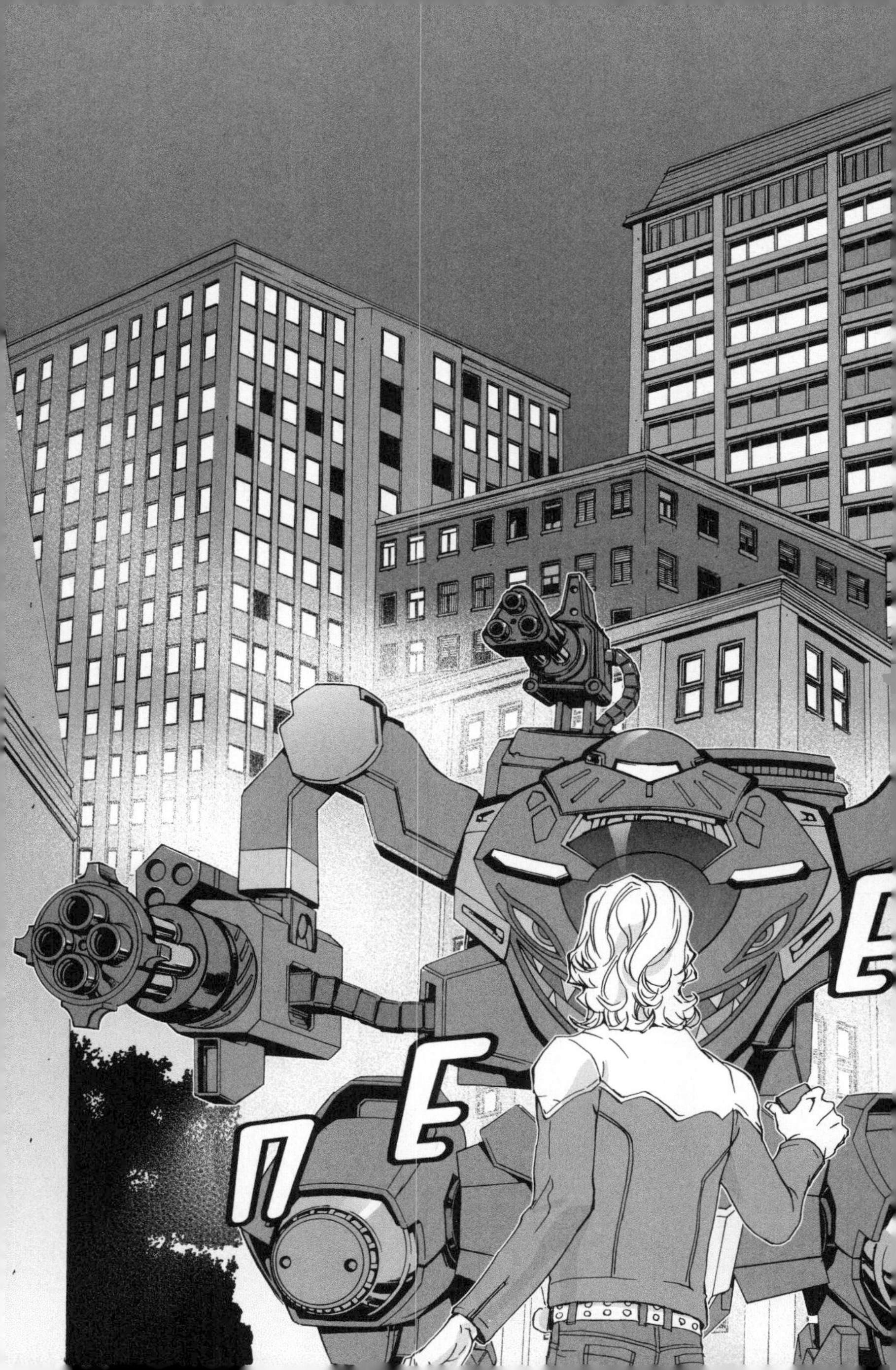

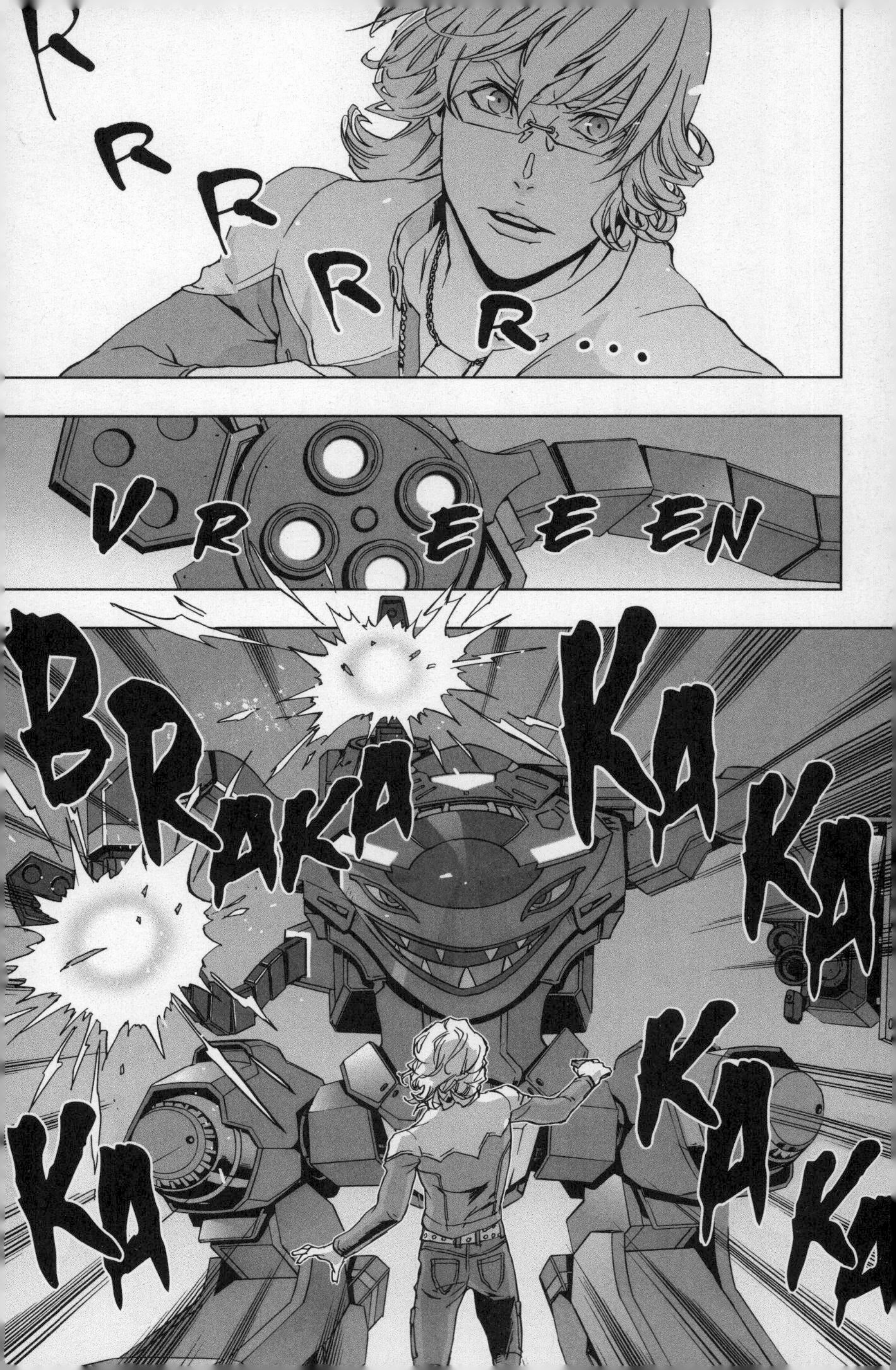
KRRRRR...
VREEEN
BRAKAKAKAKA
KAKAKA
KA

#11 Fire Is a Good Servant but a Bad Master, Part 2

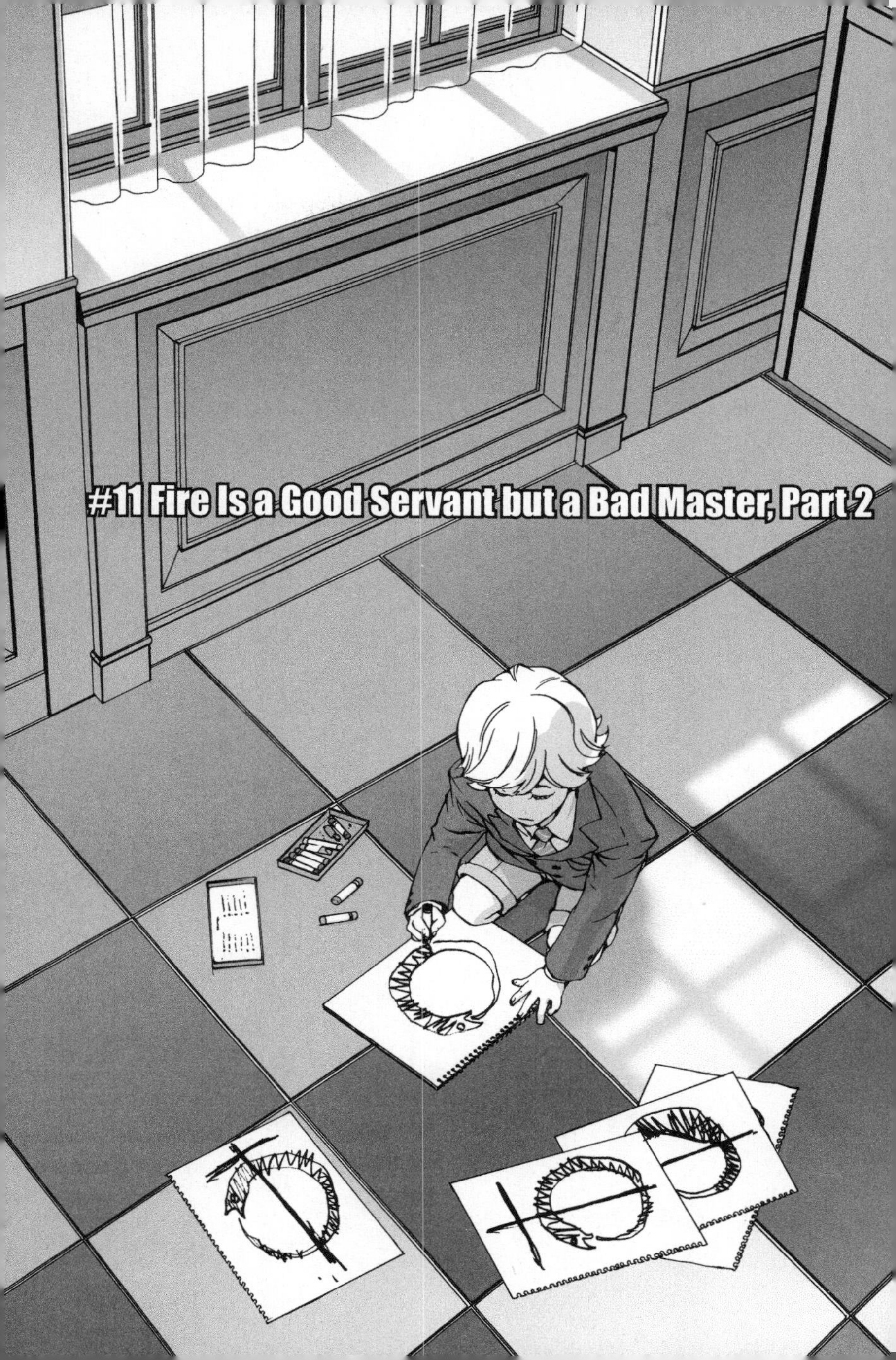

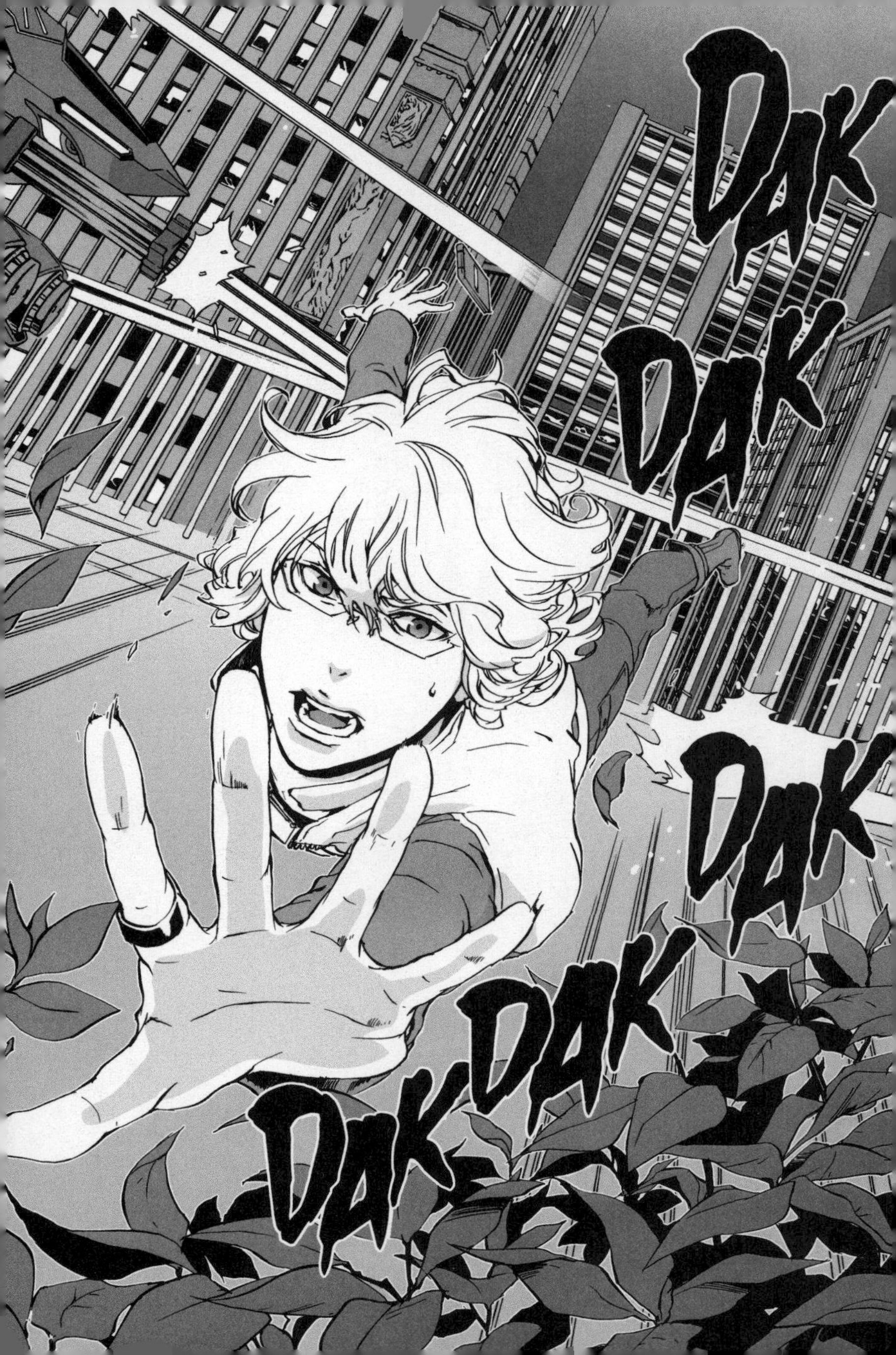
DAK
DAK
DAK
DAK
DAK
DAK

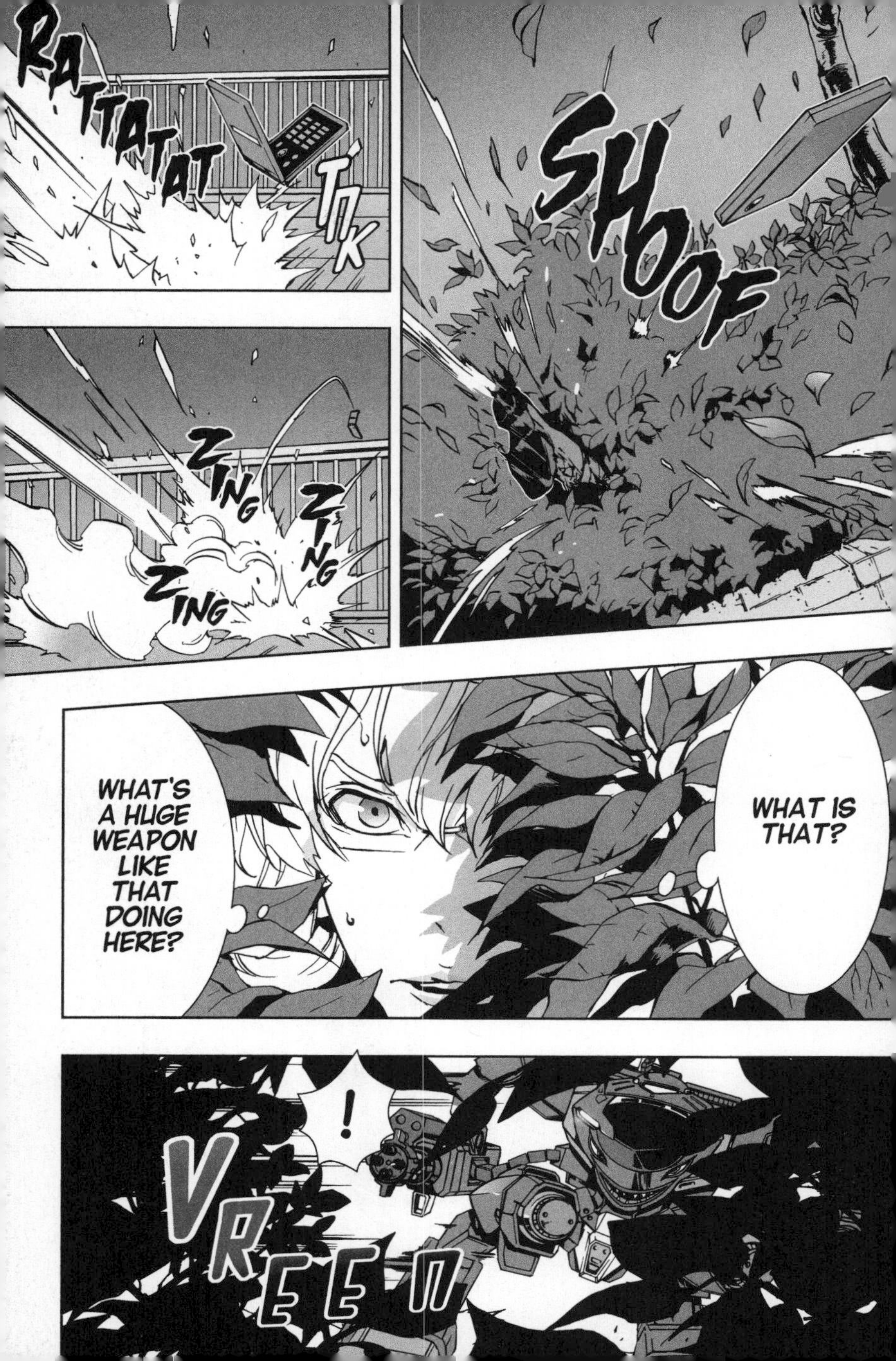
SHOOF
RATTATATAT
TINK
ZING
ZING
ZING
WHAT IS THAT?
WHAT'S A HUGE WEAPON LIKE THAT DOING HERE?
!
VREEN

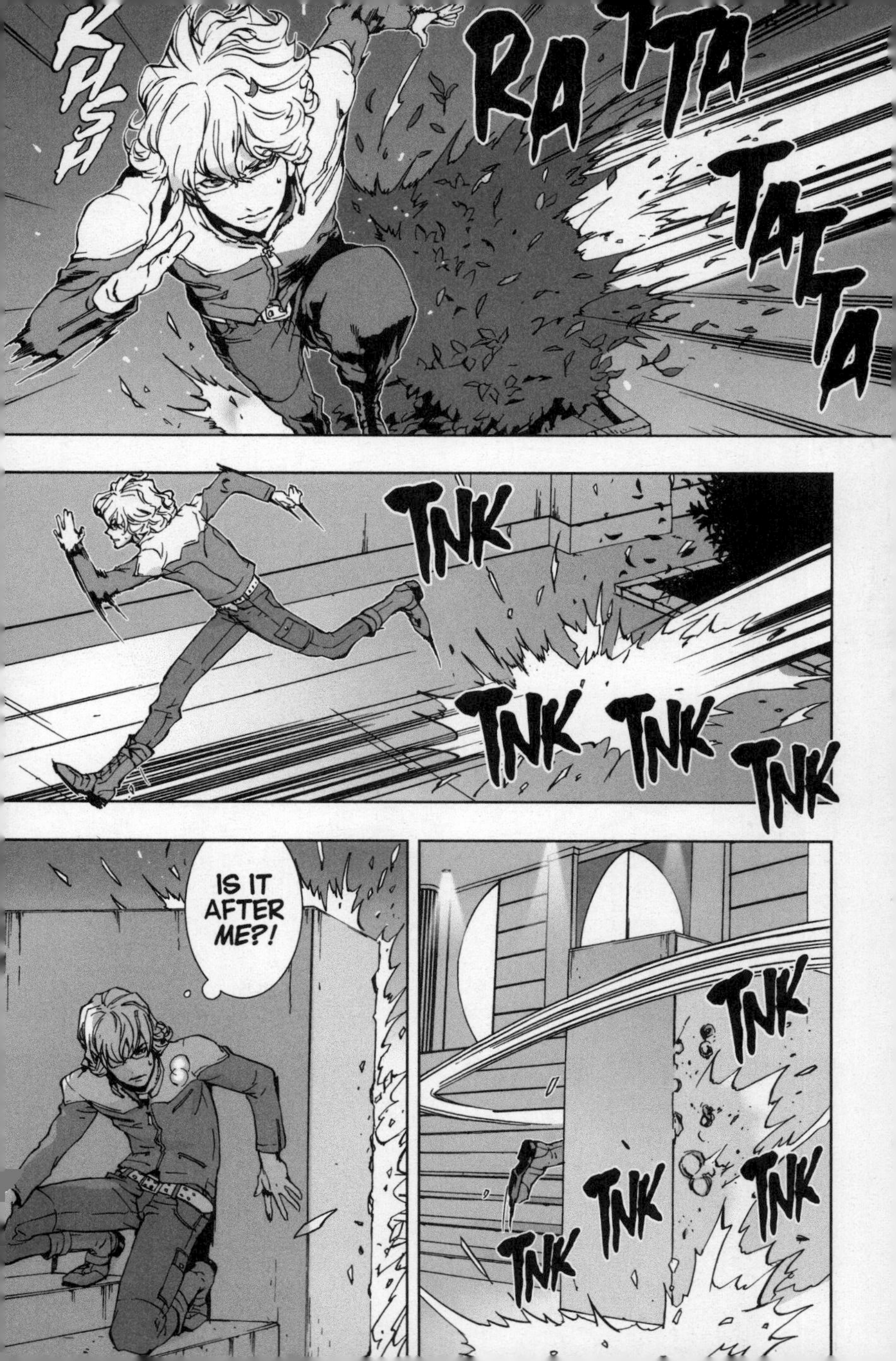
RA TTA
TATTA
TNK
TNK TNK TNK
TNK
TNK TNK TNK TNK
IS IT AFTER ME?!

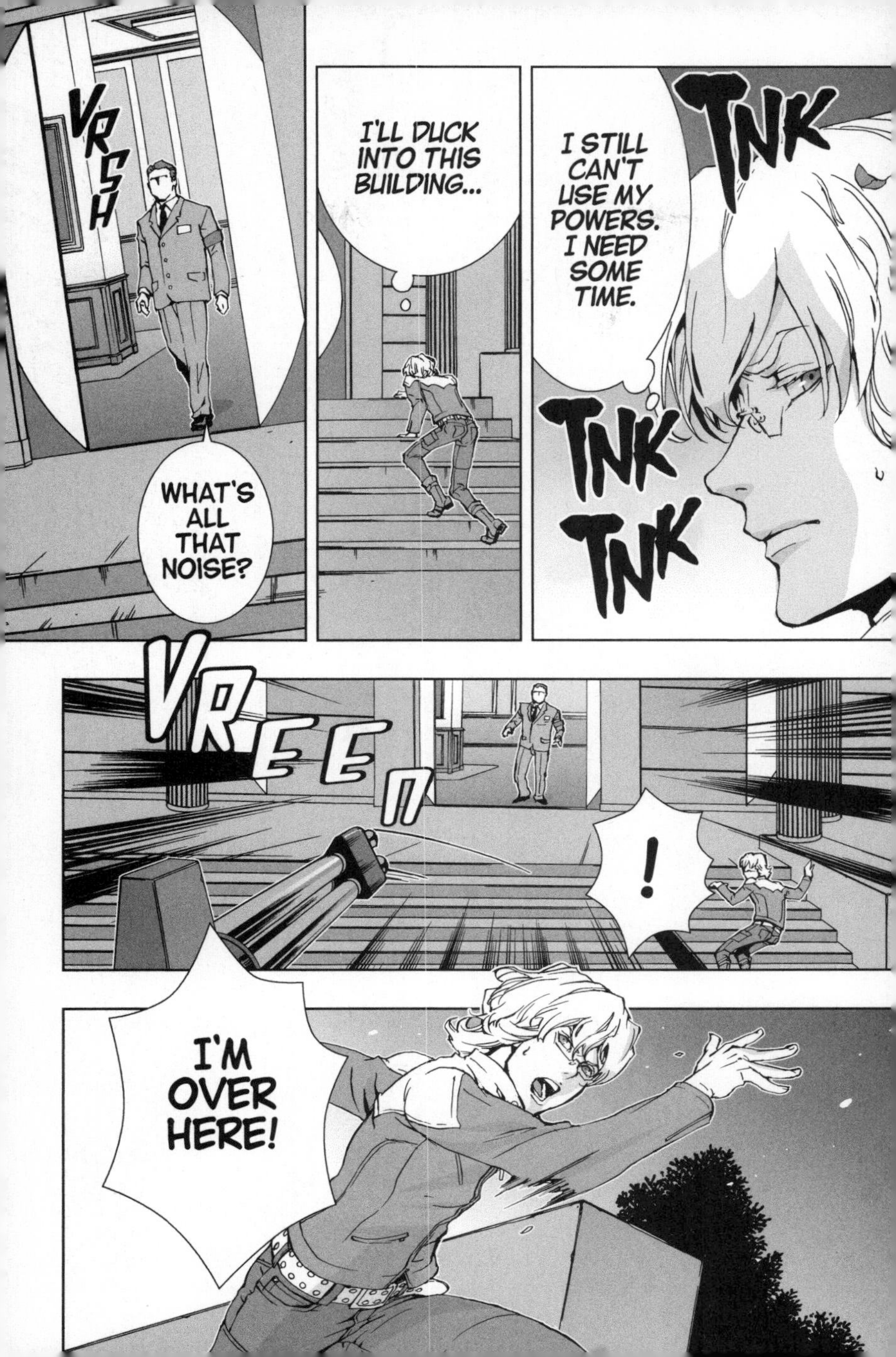
TNK
I STILL CAN'T USE MY POWERS. I NEED SOME TIME.
TNK
TNK
I'LL DUCK INTO THIS BUILDING...
VRSH
WHAT'S ALL THAT NOISE?
VREEEN
!
I'M OVER HERE!

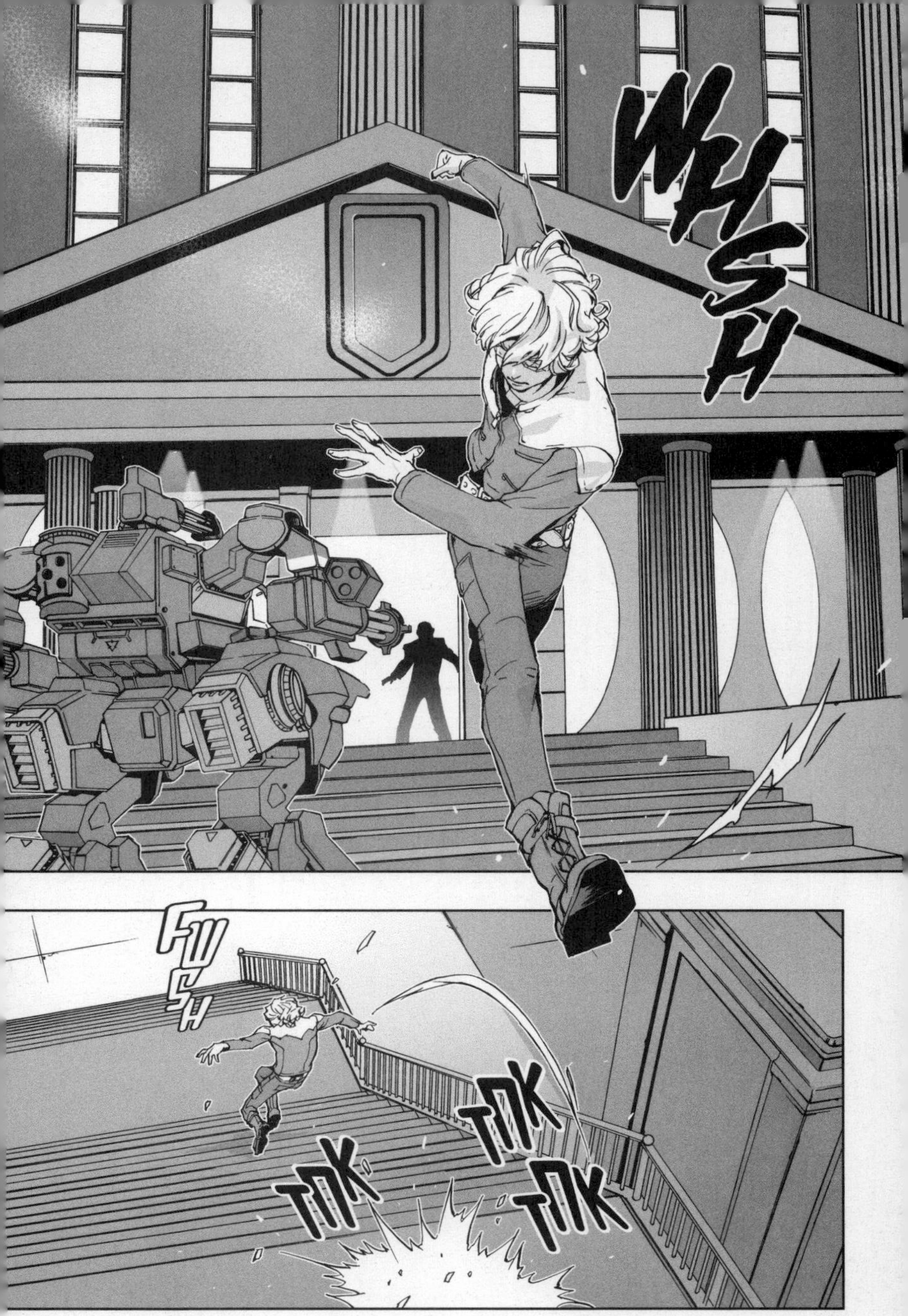
WHSH
FWSH
TNK TNK
TNK TNK

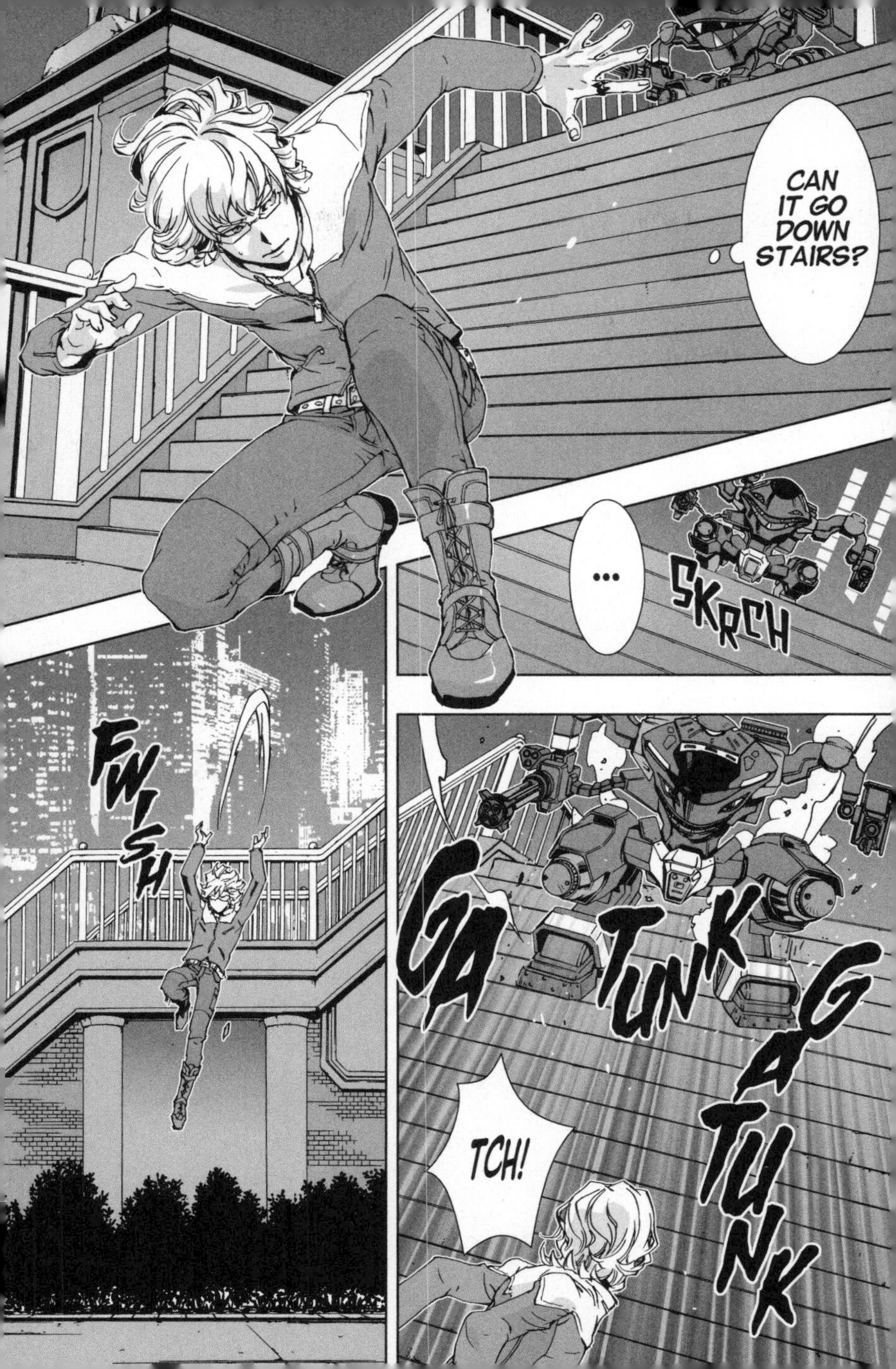

CAN IT GO DOWN STAIRS?
...
SKRCH
GA TUNK
GA TUNK
TCH!
FWISH

GATUNK

TOMP

VREED

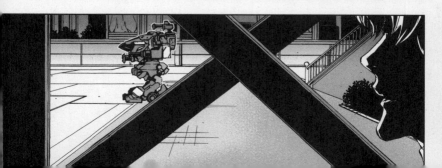

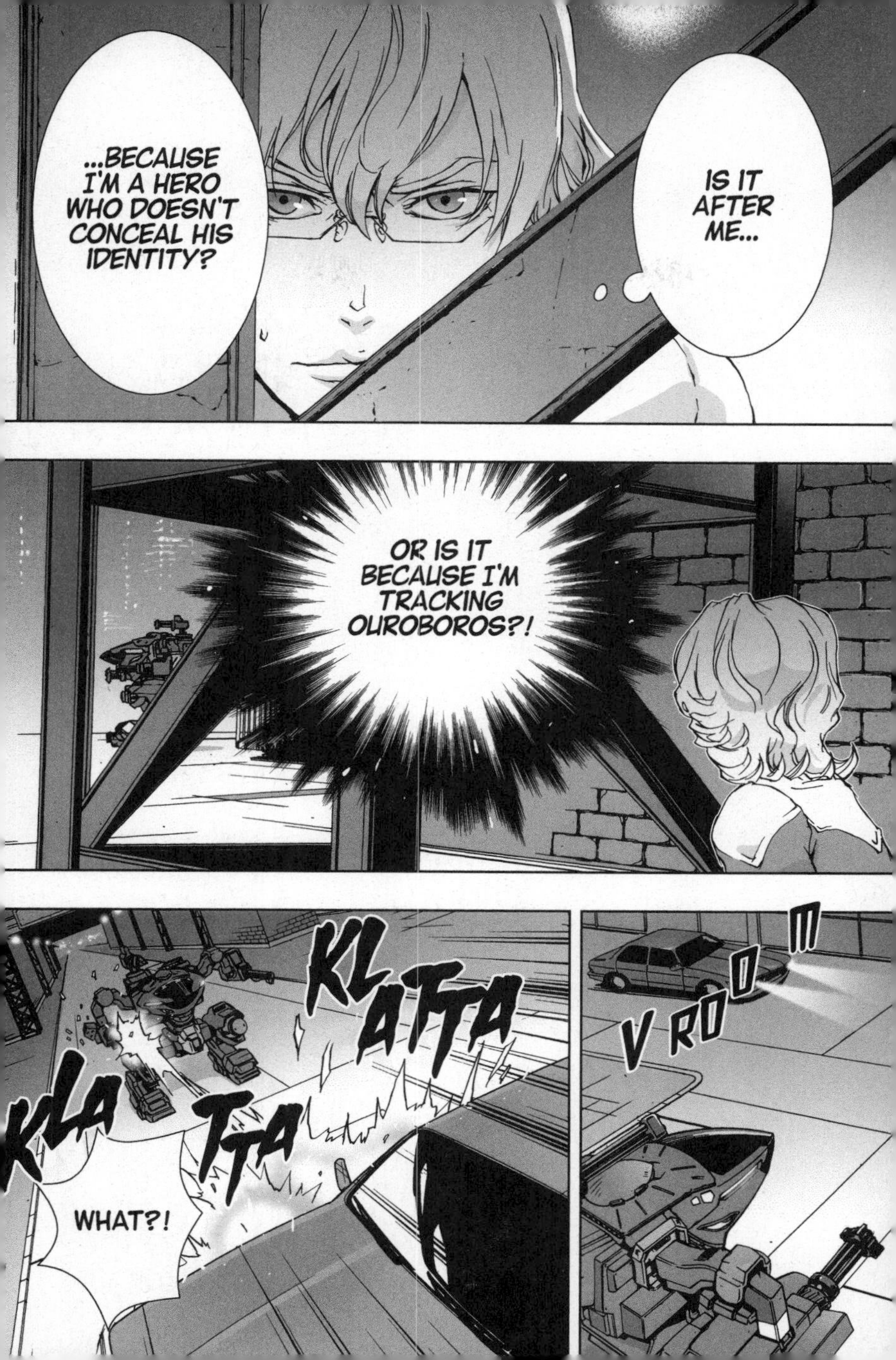
IS IT AFTER ME...
...BECAUSE I'M A HERO WHO DOESN'T CONCEAL HIS IDENTITY?
OR IS IT BECAUSE I'M TRACKING OUROBOROS?!
VROOOM
KLATTA
KLATTA
WHAT?!

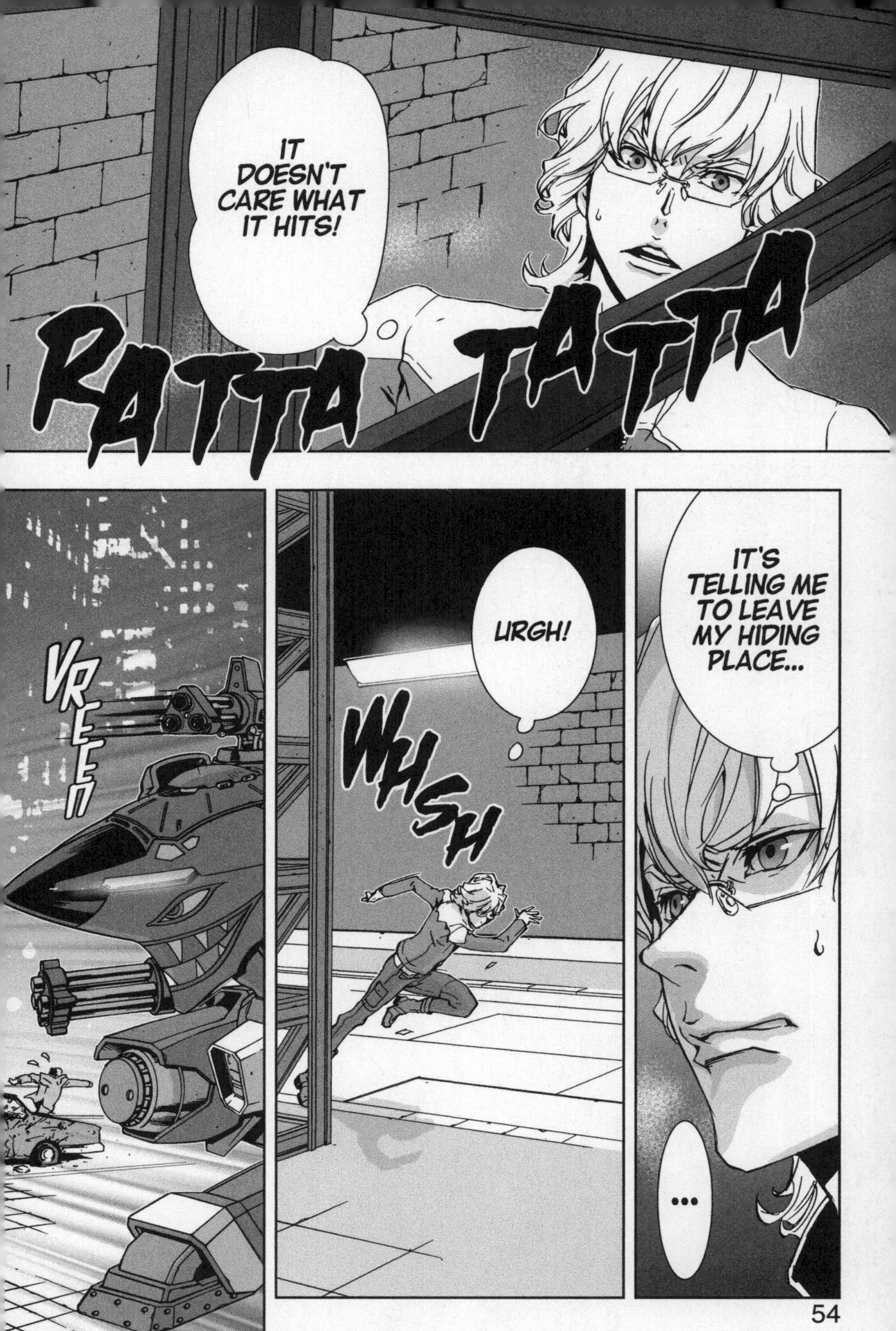
IT DOESN'T CARE WHAT IT HITS!
RATTA TATTA
IT'S TELLING ME TO LEAVE MY HIDING PLACE...
...
URGH!
WHSH
VREEEN

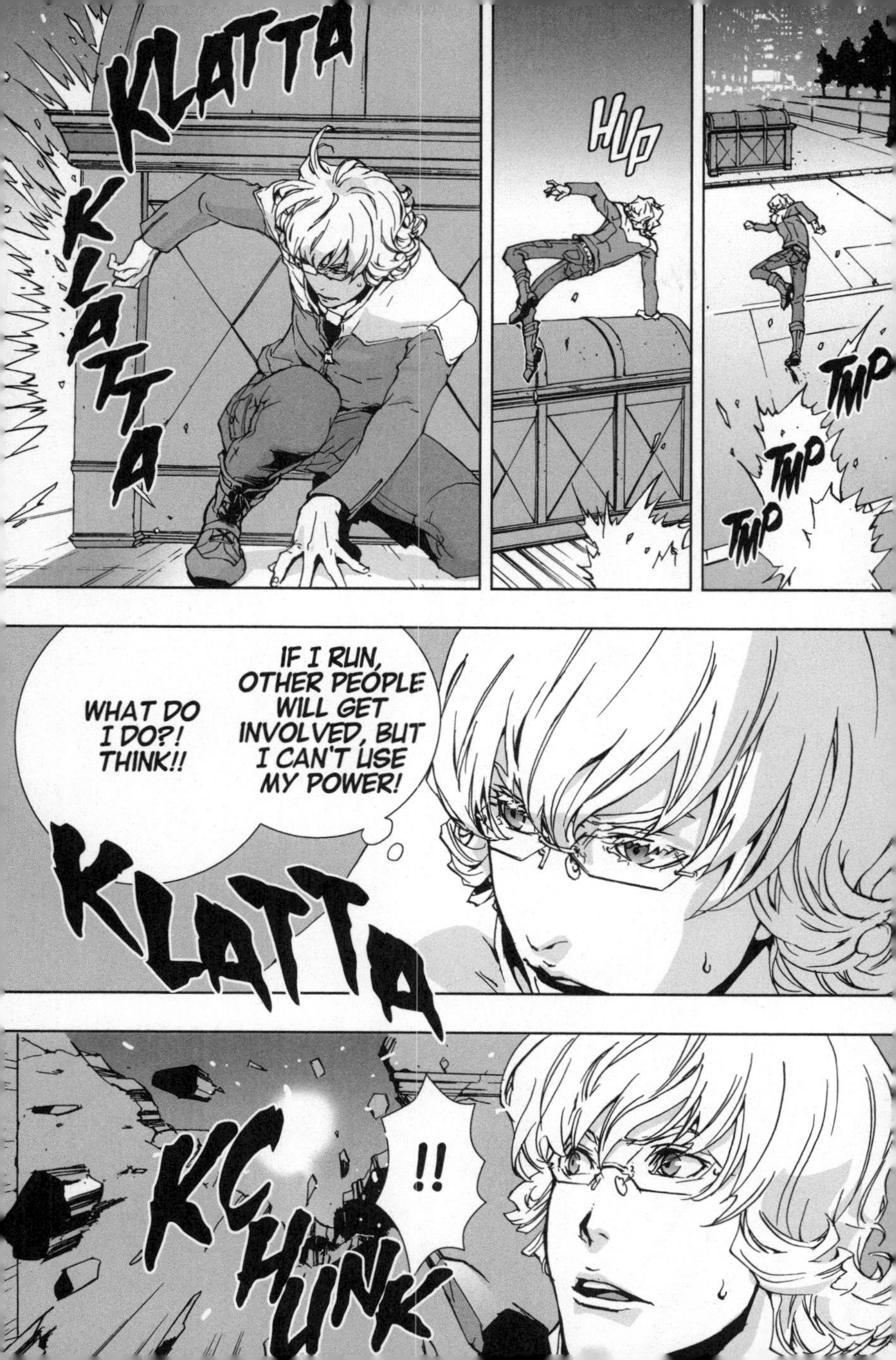
TMP
TMP
TMP
HUP
KLATTA
KLATTA
IF I RUN, OTHER PEOPLE WILL GET INVOLVED, BUT I CAN'T USE MY POWER!
WHAT DO I DO?! THINK!!
KLATTA
!!
KCHUNK

TNK TNK TNK TNK TNK TNK

THUNK ?

WAP

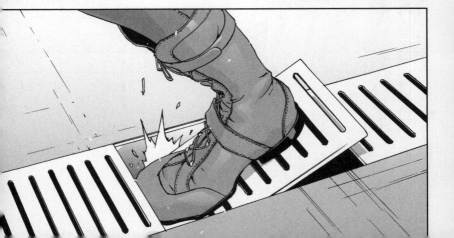

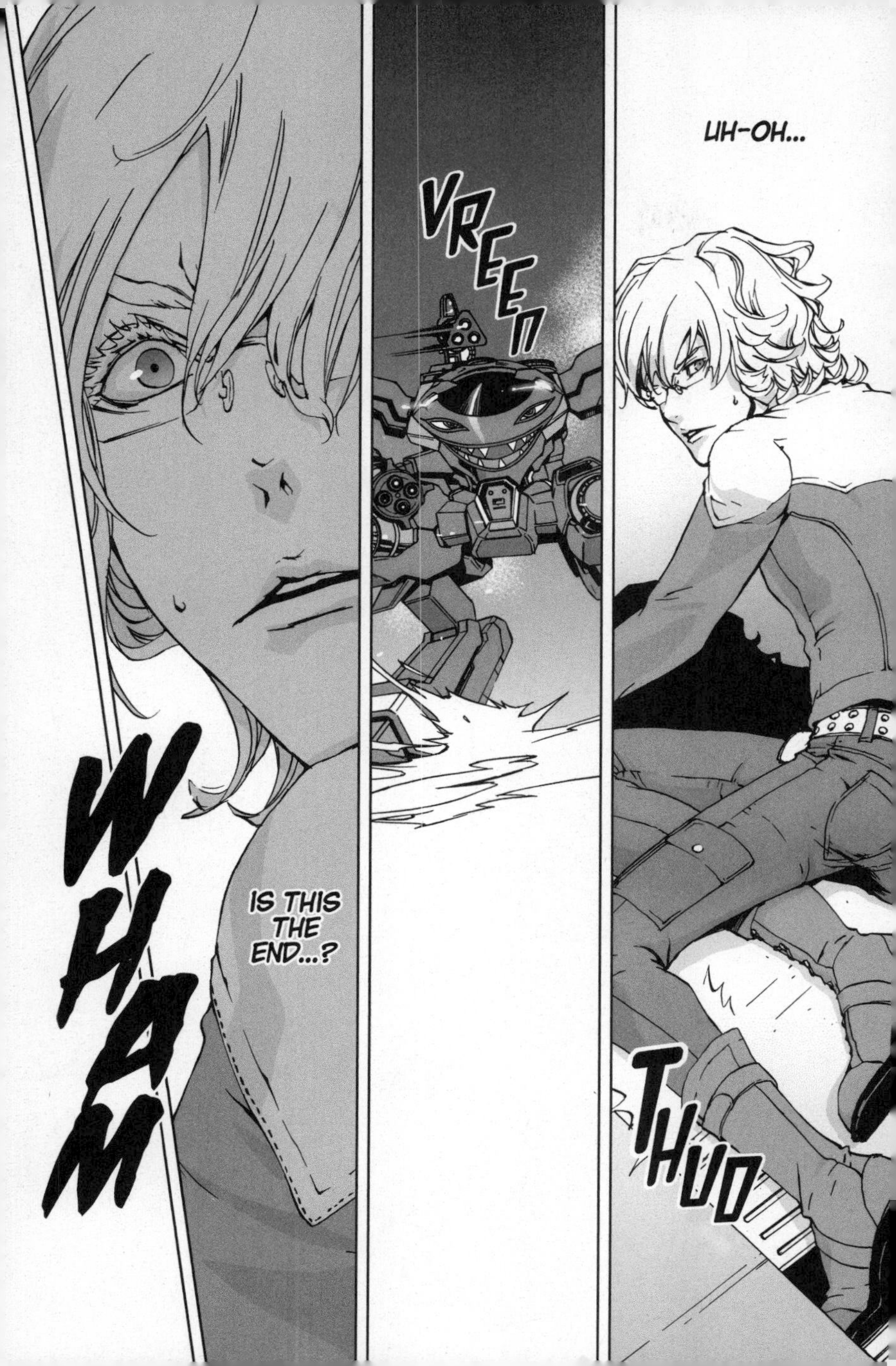
UH-OH...
THUD
VREEN
WHAM
IS THIS THE END...?

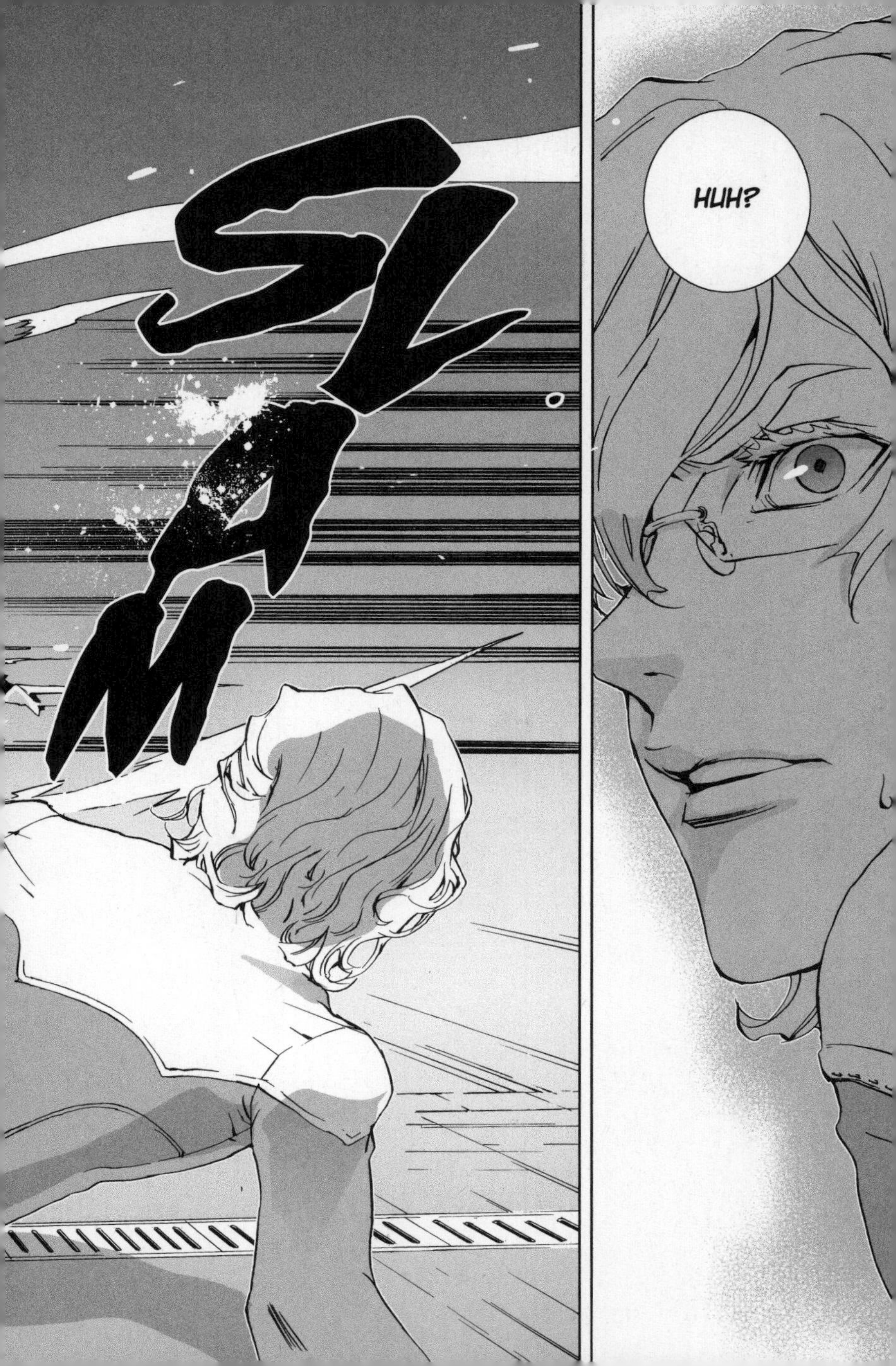
HUH?
SLAM

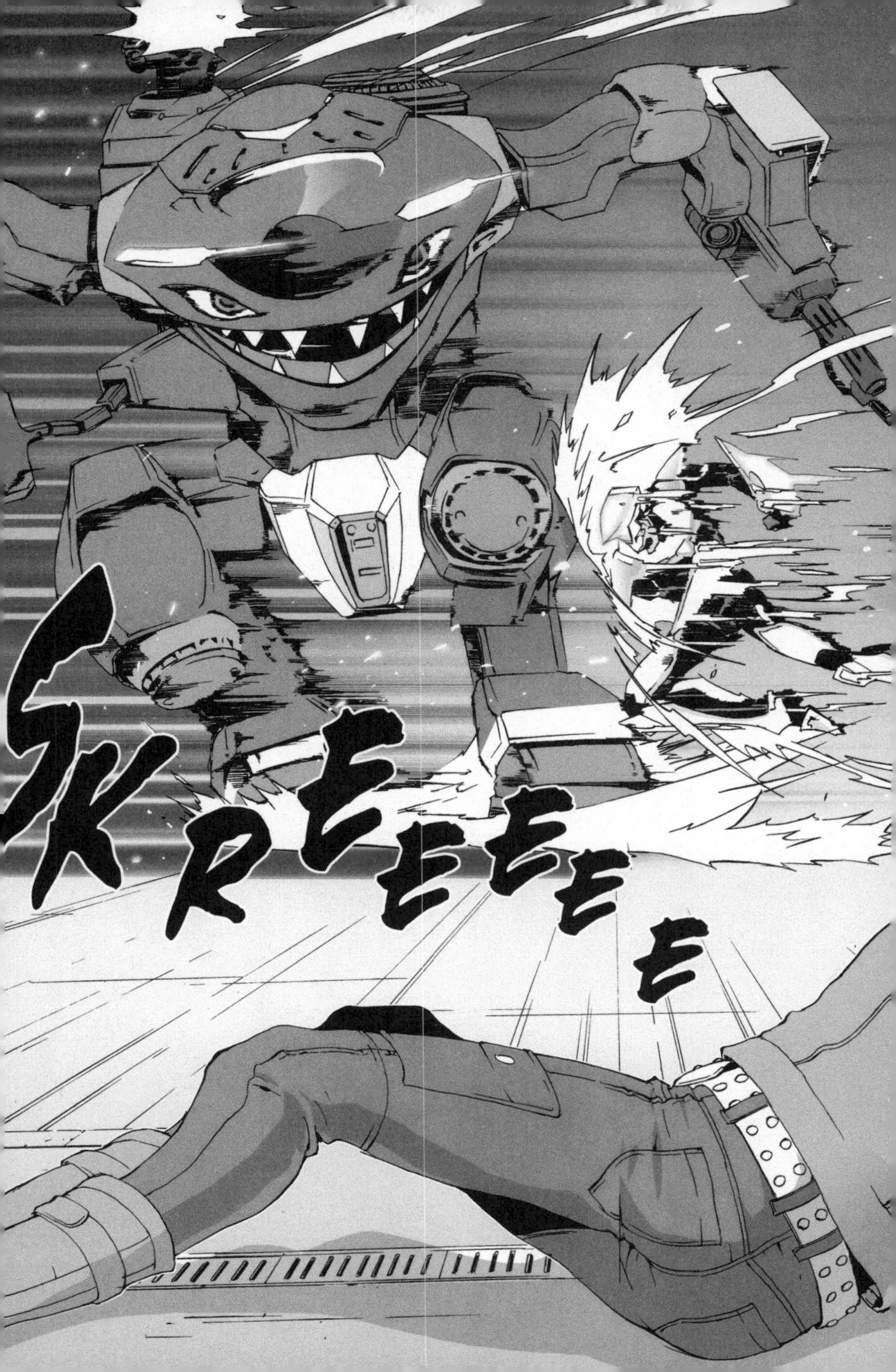
SKREEEEEE

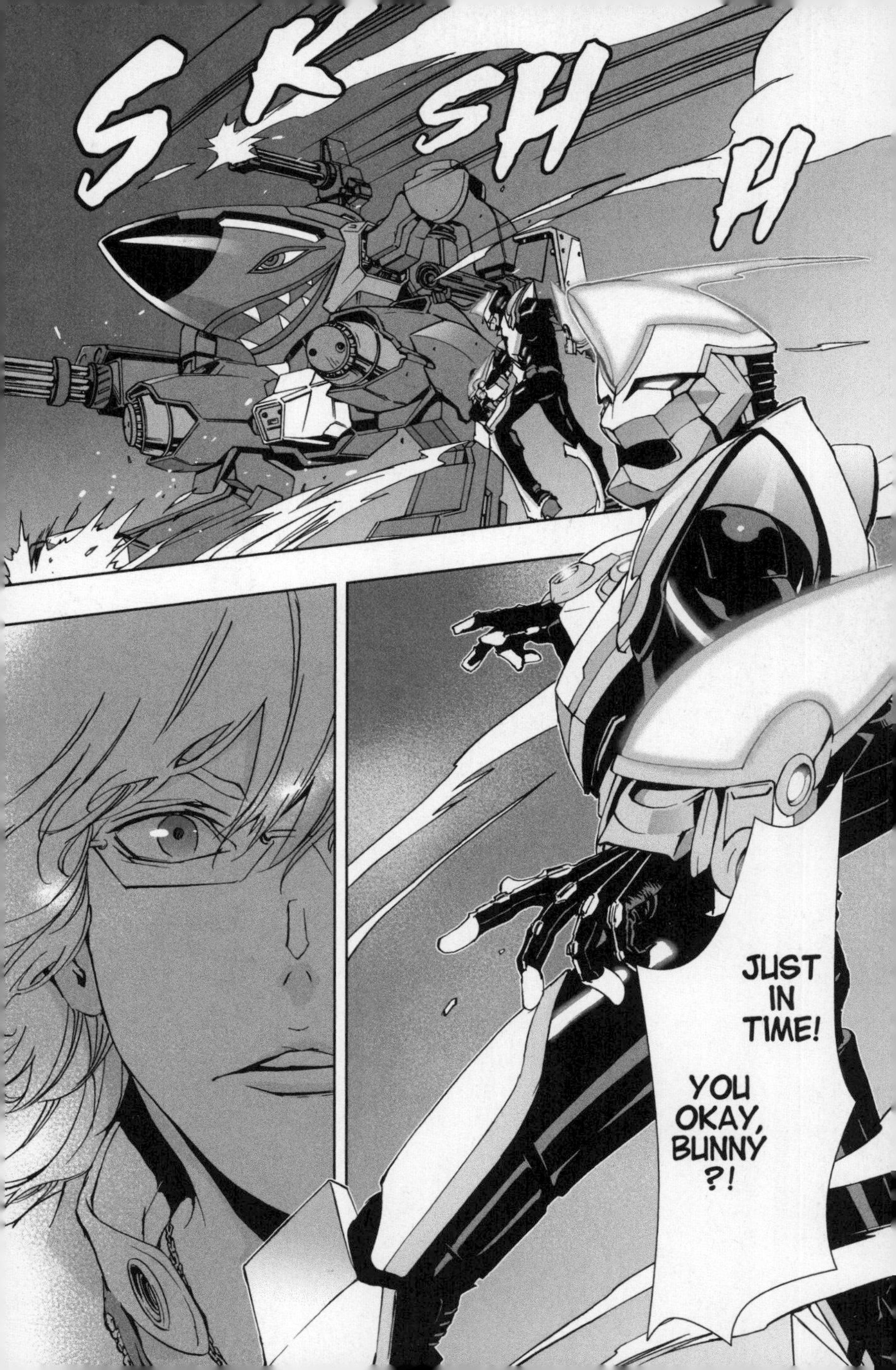
SKSHHH
JUST IN TIME!
YOU OKAY, BUNNY?!

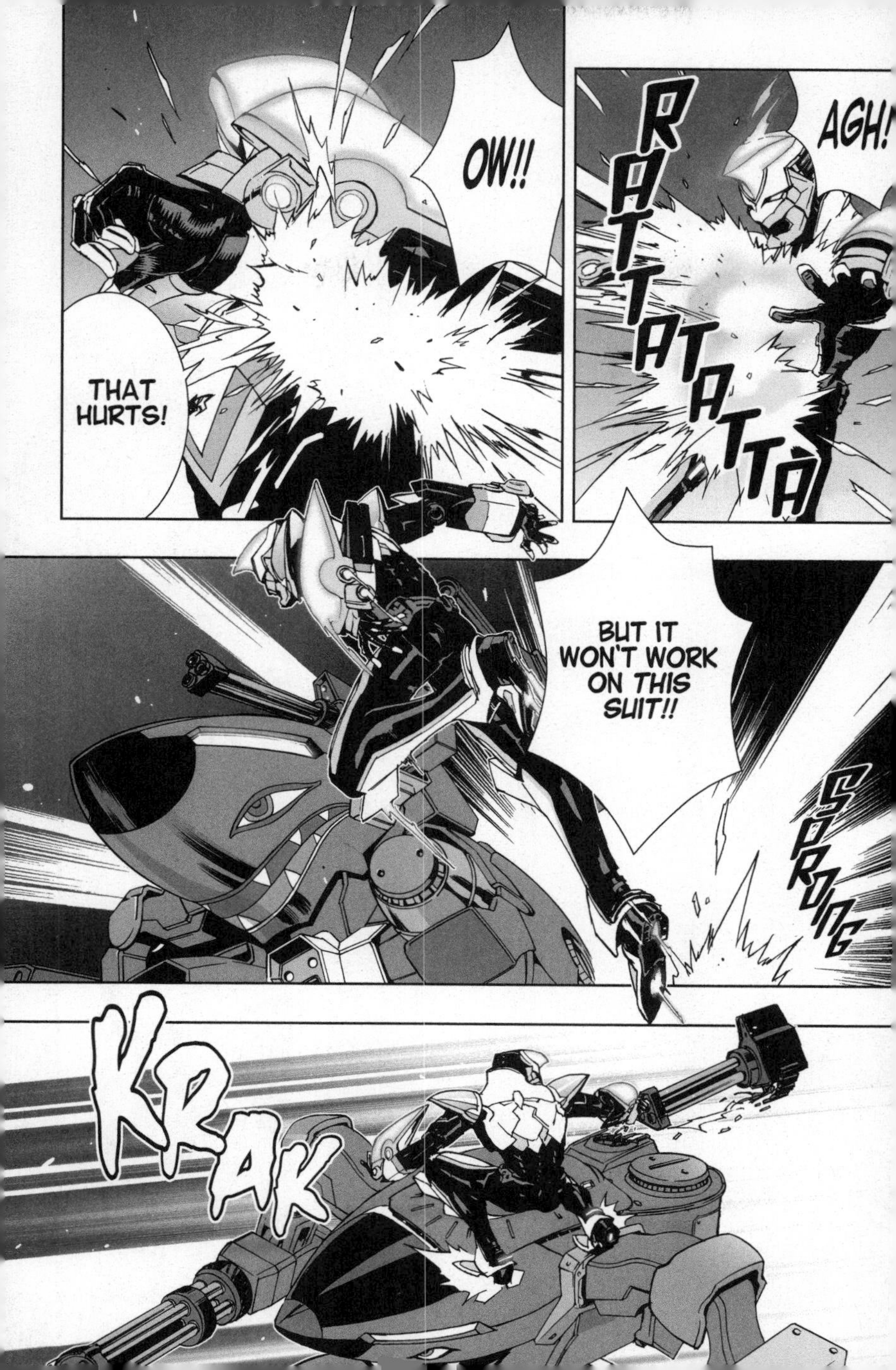
RATTATTATTA
AGH!
OW!!
THAT HURTS!
BUT IT WON'T WORK ON THIS SUIT!!
SPROING
KRAK

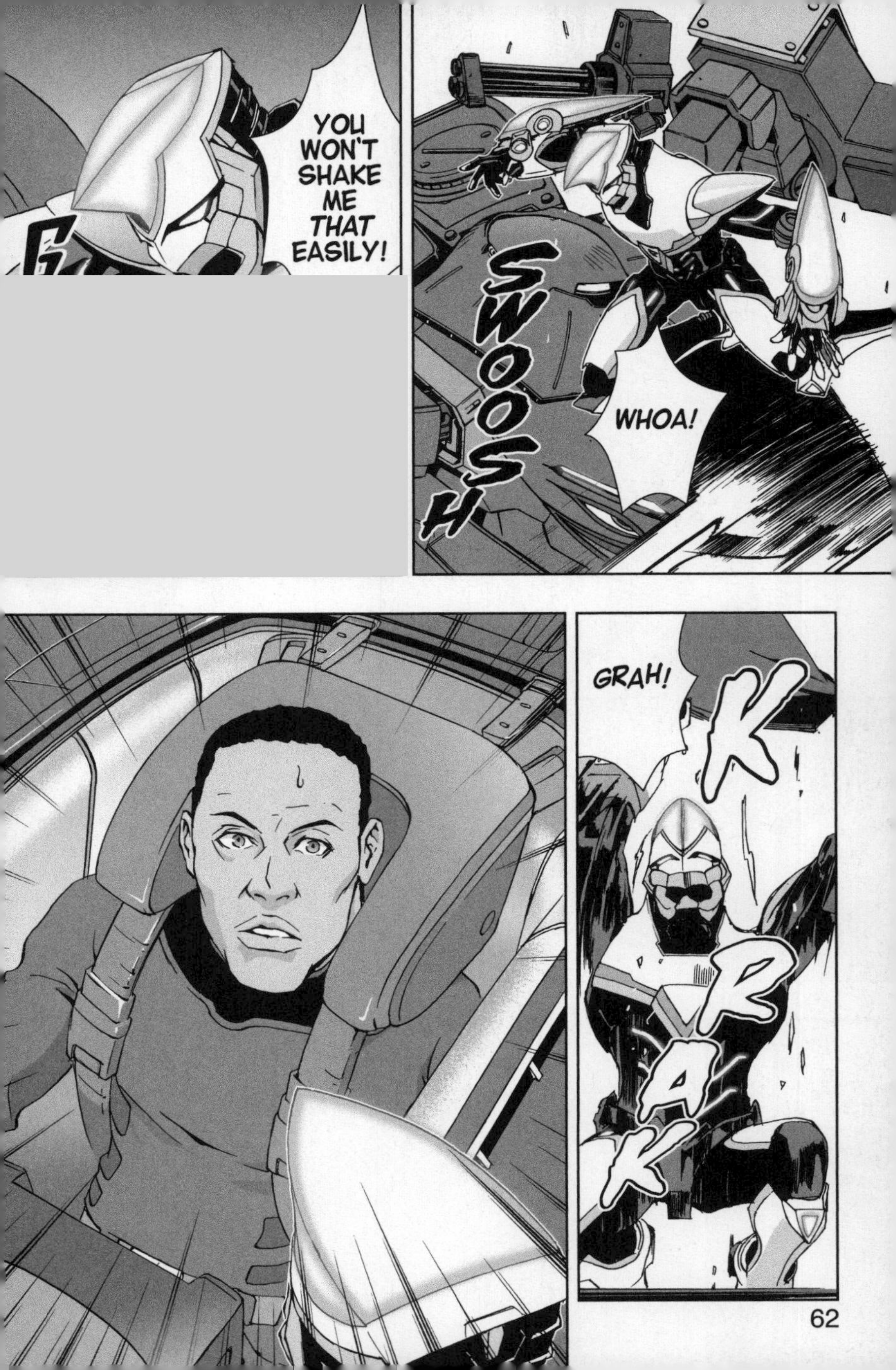
SWOOSH
WHOA!
YOU WON'T SHAKE ME THAT EASILY!
GRAH!
KRAK

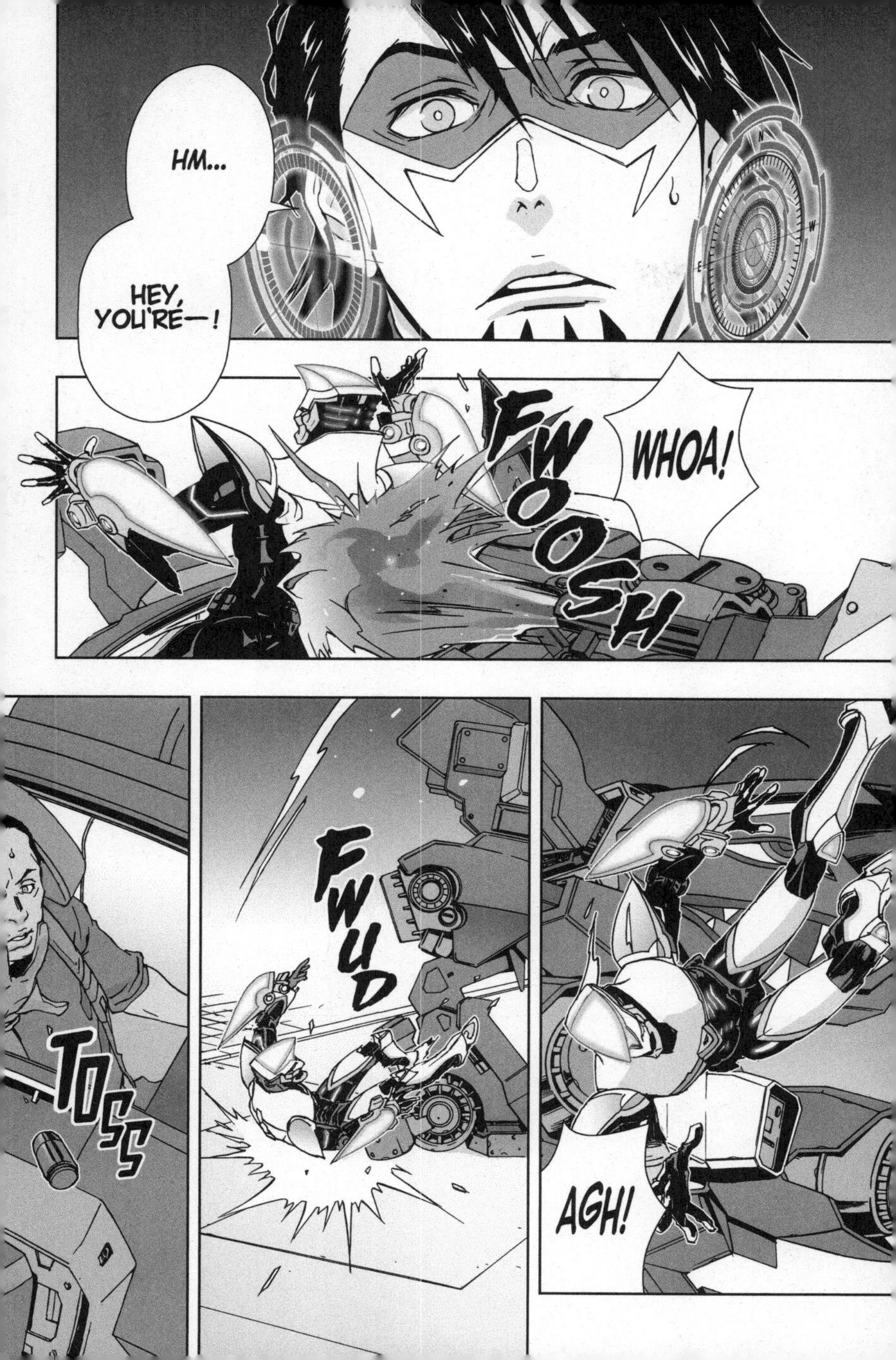
HM...
HEY, YOU'RE—!
WHOA!
FWOOOSH
AGH!
FWUD
TOSS

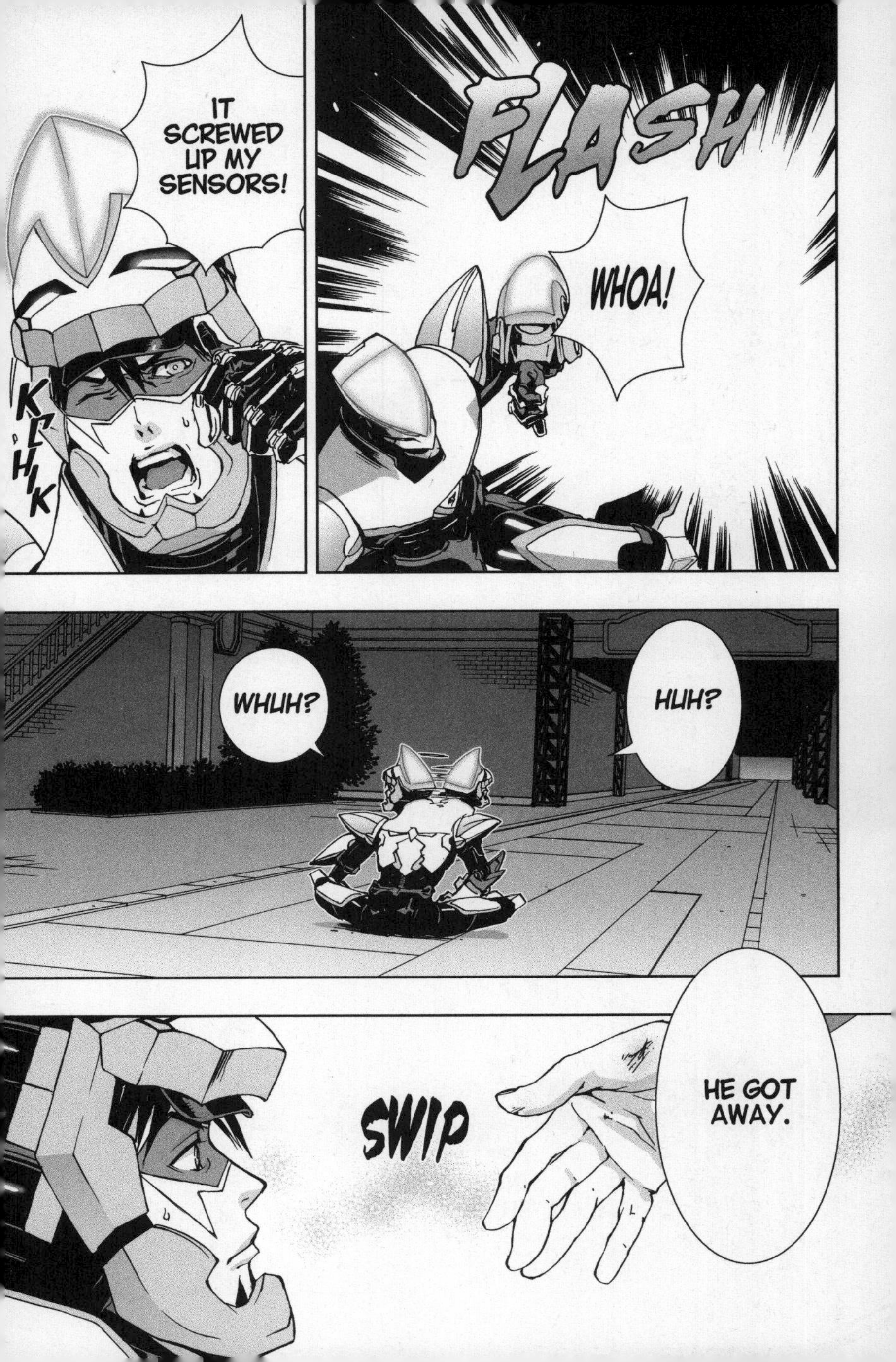
FLASH
WHOA!
IT SCREWED UP MY SENSORS!
KCHIK
HUH?
WHUH?
HE GOT AWAY.
SWIP

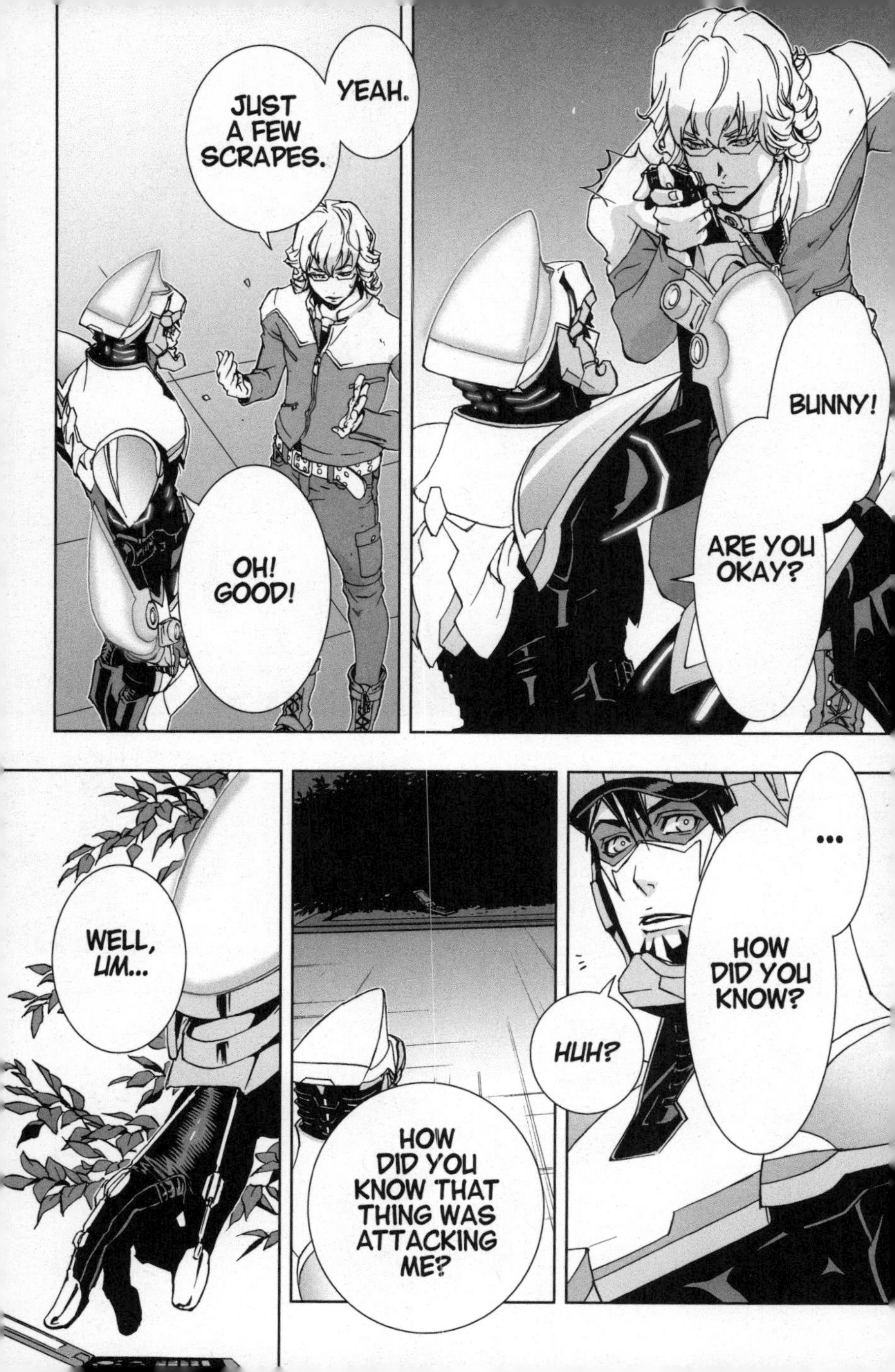
BUNNY!
ARE YOU OKAY?
YEAH.
JUST A FEW SCRAPES.
OH! GOOD!
...
HOW DID YOU KNOW?
HUH?
HOW DID YOU KNOW THAT THING WAS ATTACKING ME?
WELL, UM...

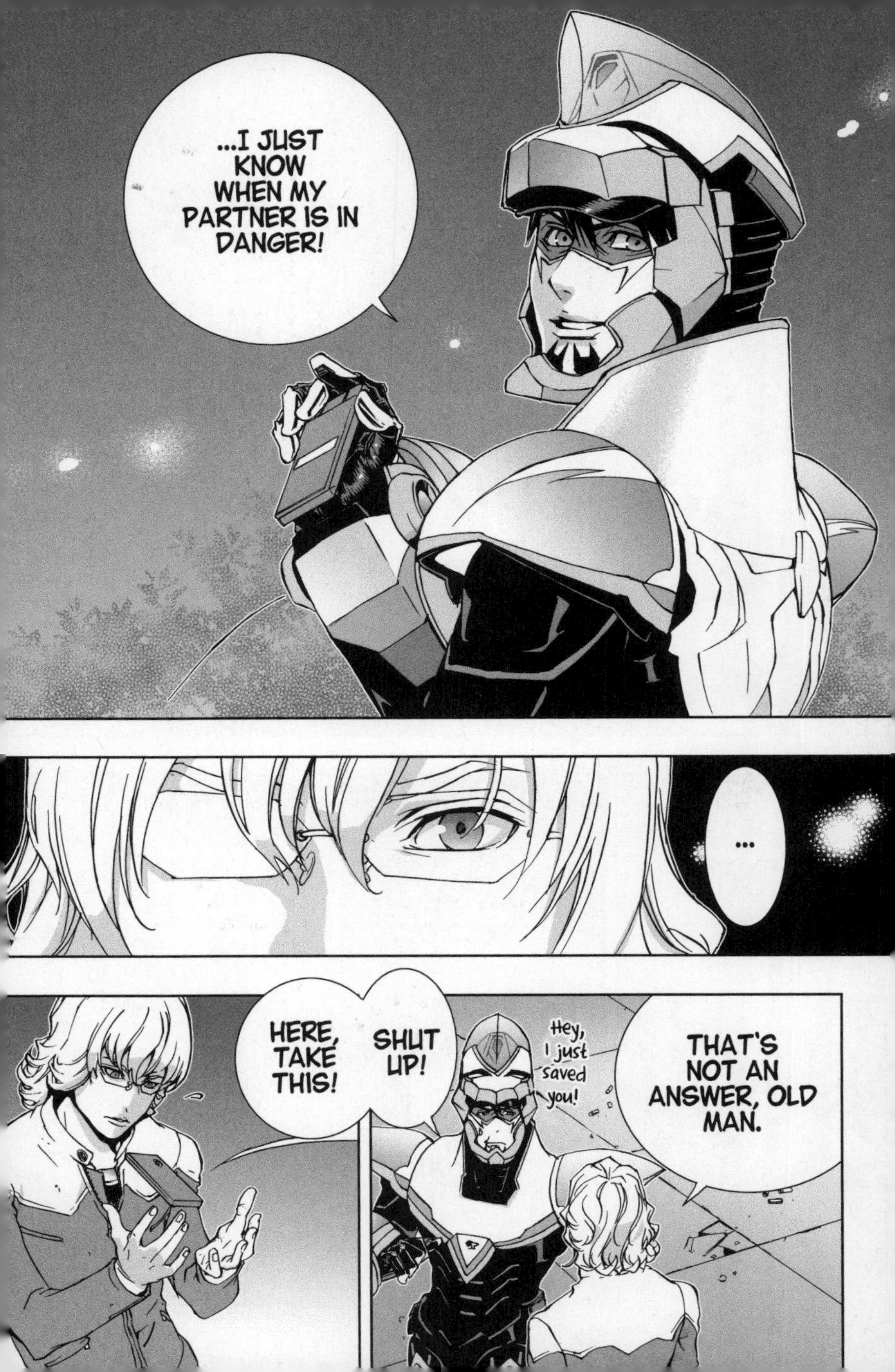
...I JUST KNOW WHEN MY PARTNER IS IN DANGER!
...
THAT'S NOT AN ANSWER, OLD MAN.
Hey, I just saved you!
SHUT UP!
HERE, TAKE THIS!

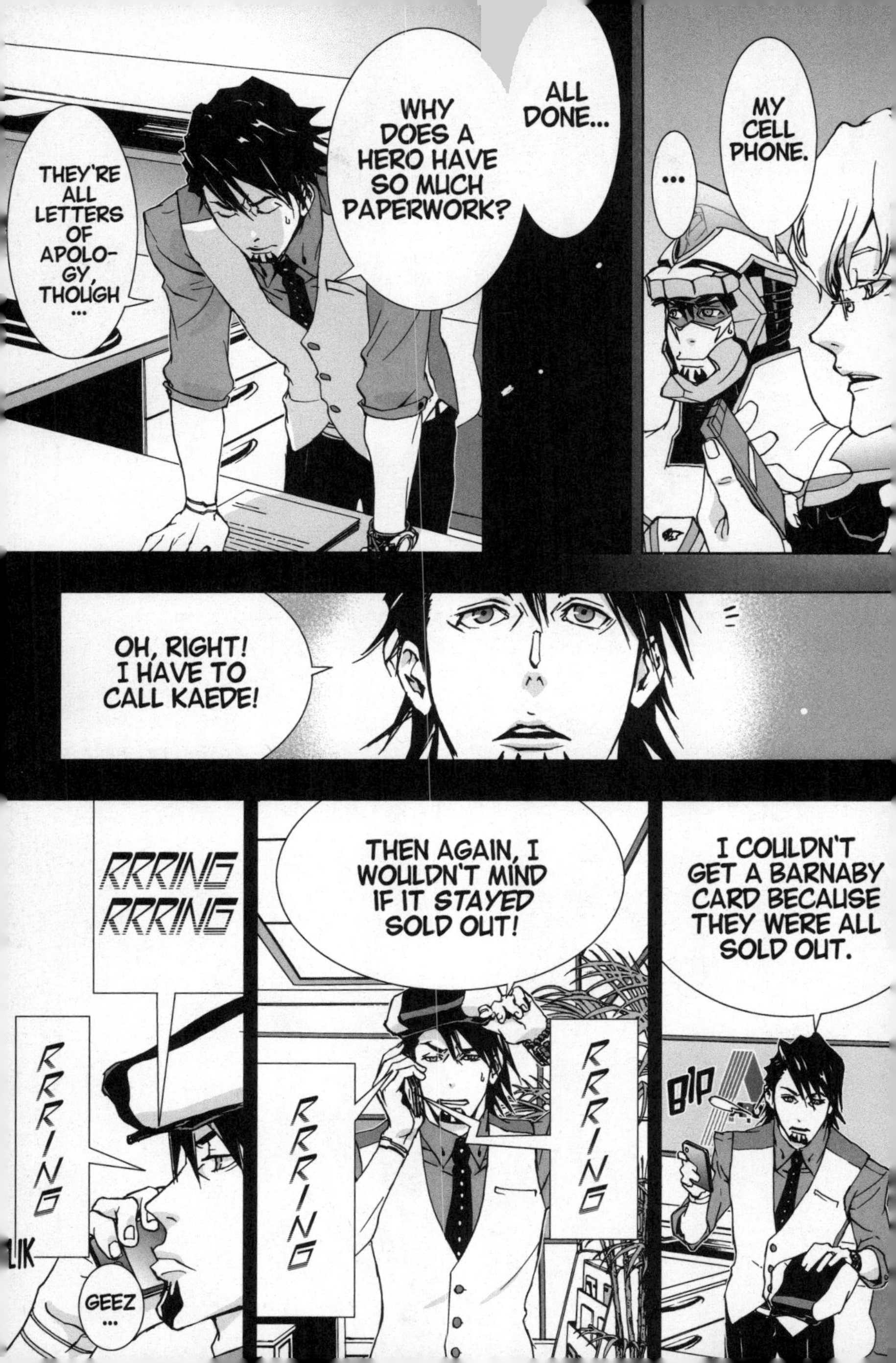

MY CELL PHONE.
...
ALL DONE...
WHY DOES A HERO HAVE SO MUCH PAPERWORK?
THEY'RE ALL LETTERS OF APOLOGY, THOUGH...
OH, RIGHT! I HAVE TO CALL KAEDE!
I COULDN'T GET A BARNABY CARD BECAUSE THEY WERE ALL SOLD OUT.
BIP
THEN AGAIN, I WOULDN'T MIND IF IT STAYED SOLD OUT!
RRRING
RRRING
RRRING RRRING
RRRING
LIK
GEEZ...

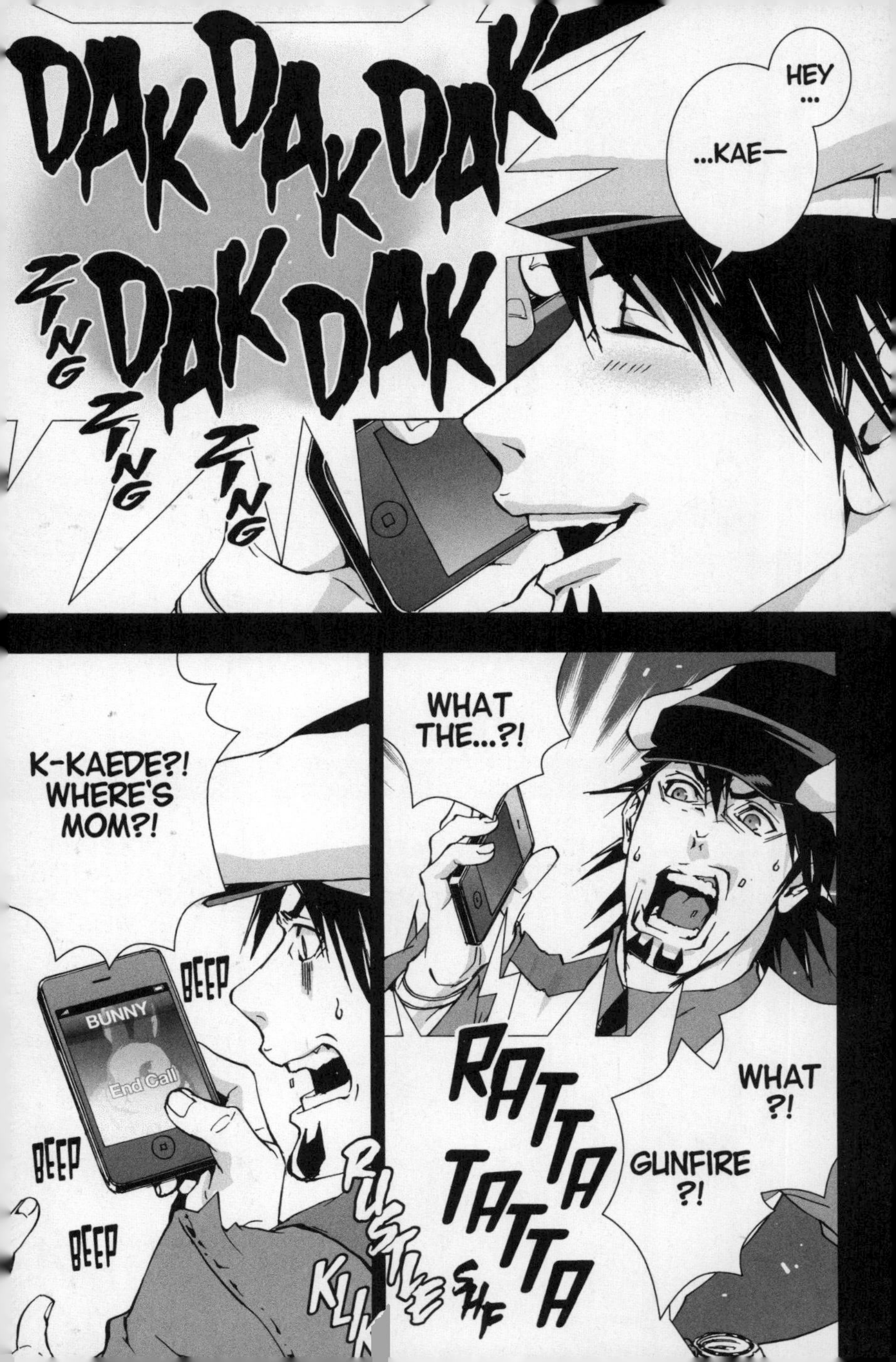
HEY ...
...KAE—
DAK DAK DAK
DAK DAK
ZING
ZING
ZING
ZING
WHAT THE...?!
WHAT ?!
GUNFIRE ?!
RATTA TATTA TATTA
SHF
K-KAEDE?! WHERE'S MOM?!
BEEP
BUNNY
End Call
BEEP
BEEP
RUSTLE
KLIK

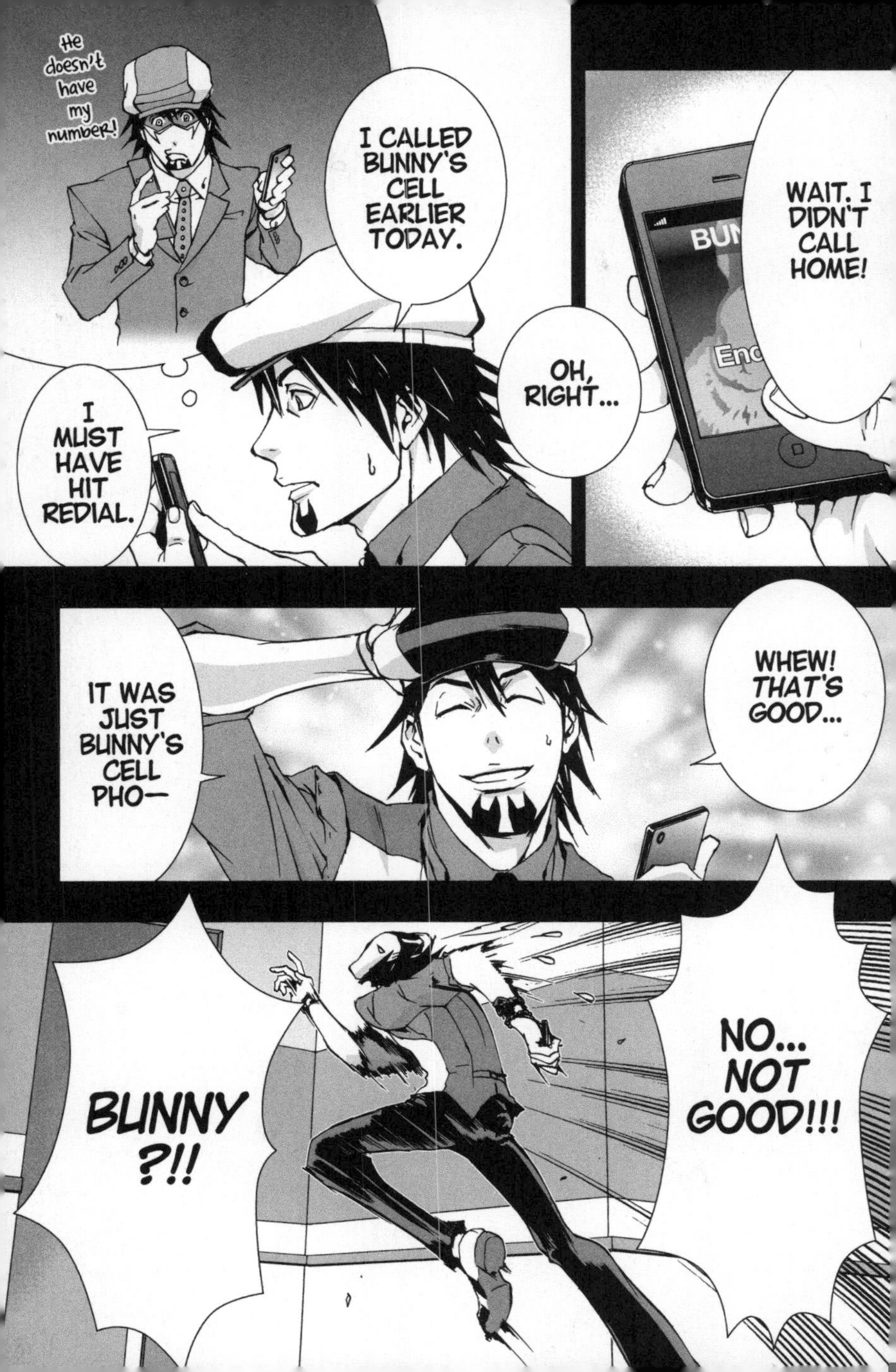
WAIT. I DIDN'T CALL HOME!
I CALLED BUNNY'S CELL EARLIER TODAY.
He doesn't have my number!
OH, RIGHT...
I MUST HAVE HIT REDIAL.
WHEW! *THAT'S* GOOD...
IT WAS JUST BUNNY'S CELL PHO—
NO... *NOT* GOOD!!!
BUNNY ?!!

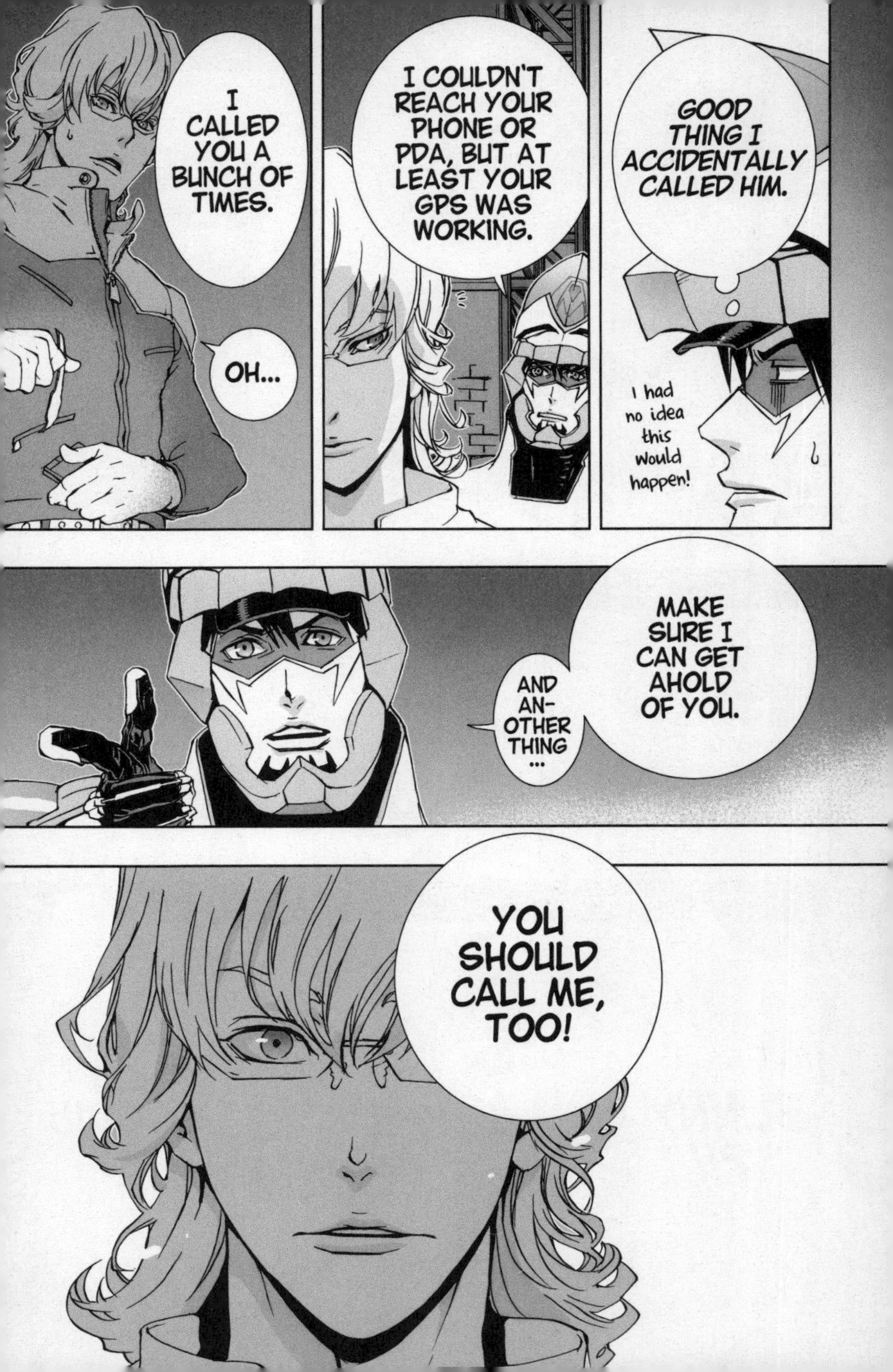
GOOD THING I ACCIDENTALLY CALLED HIM.
I had no idea this would happen!
I COULDN'T REACH YOUR PHONE OR PDA, BUT AT LEAST YOUR GPS WAS WORKING.
I CALLED YOU A BUNCH OF TIMES.
OH...
MAKE SURE I CAN GET AHOLD OF YOU.
AND AN-OTHER THING...
YOU SHOULD CALL ME, TOO!

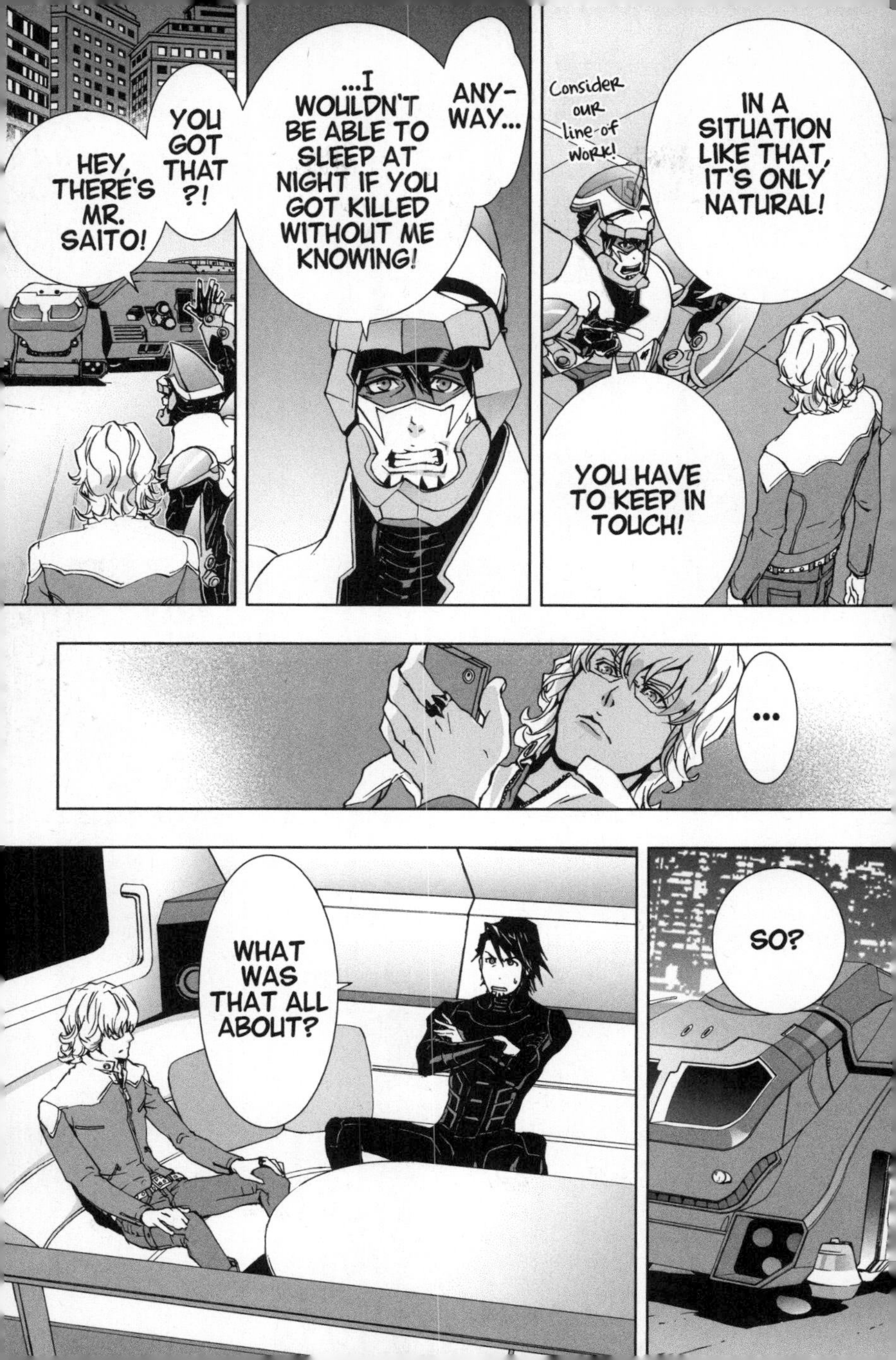
IN A SITUATION LIKE THAT, IT'S ONLY NATURAL!
Consider our line-of WORK!
YOU HAVE TO KEEP IN TOUCH!
ANY-WAY...
...I WOULDN'T BE ABLE TO SLEEP AT NIGHT IF YOU GOT KILLED WITHOUT ME KNOWING!
YOU GOT THAT ?!
HEY, THERE'S MR. SAITO!
...
SO?
WHAT WAS THAT ALL ABOUT?

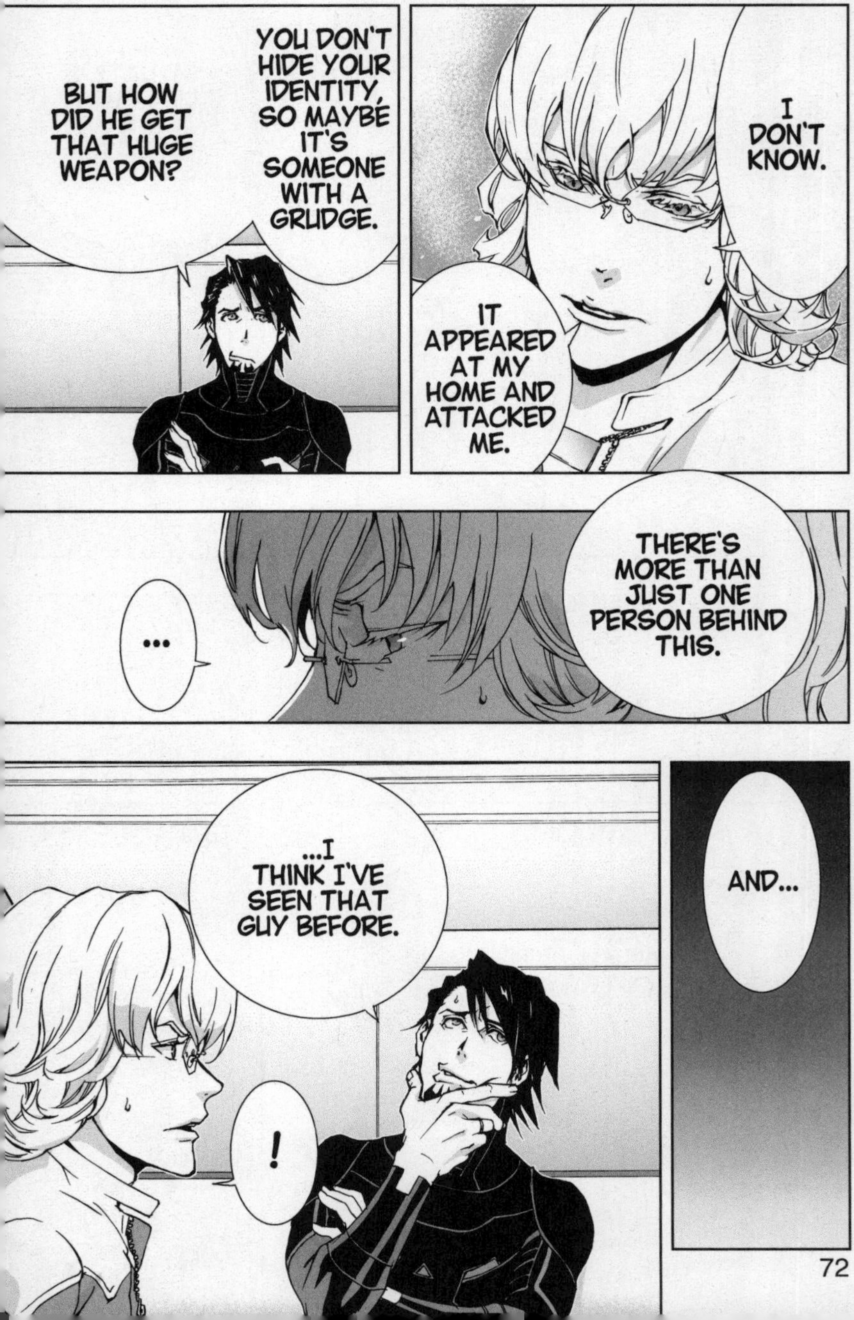
I DON'T KNOW.
IT APPEARED AT MY HOME AND ATTACKED ME.
YOU DON'T HIDE YOUR IDENTITY, SO MAYBE IT'S SOMEONE WITH A GRUDGE.
BUT HOW DID HE GET THAT HUGE WEAPON?
THERE'S MORE THAN JUST ONE PERSON BEHIND THIS.
...
AND...
...I THINK I'VE SEEN THAT GUY BEFORE.
!

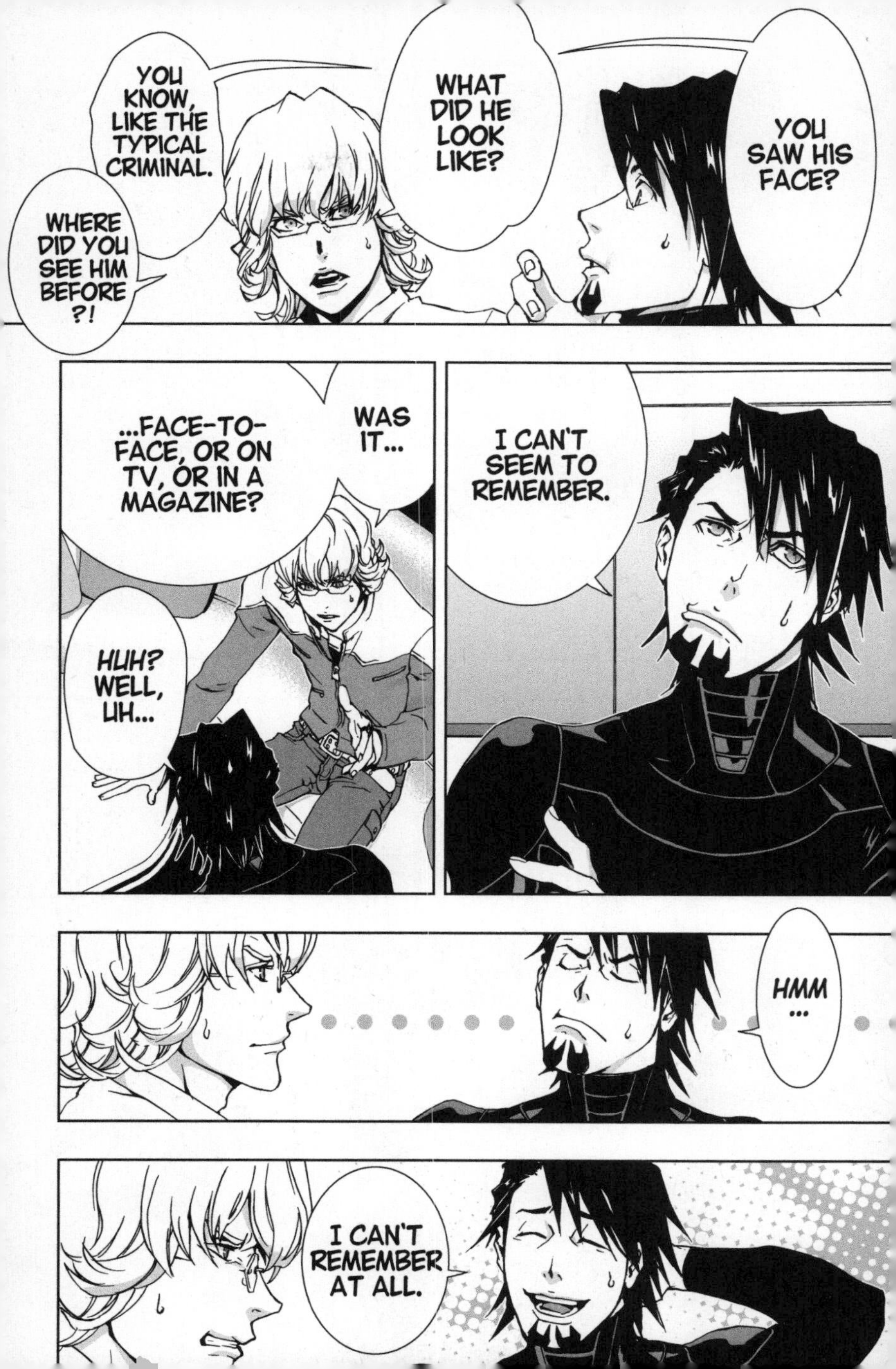
YOU SAW HIS FACE?
WHAT DID HE LOOK LIKE?
YOU KNOW, LIKE THE TYPICAL CRIMINAL.
WHERE DID YOU SEE HIM BEFORE?!
I CAN'T SEEM TO REMEMBER.
WAS IT...
...FACE-TO-FACE, OR ON TV, OR IN A MAGAZINE?
HUH? WELL, UH...
HMM...
I CAN'T REMEMBER AT ALL.

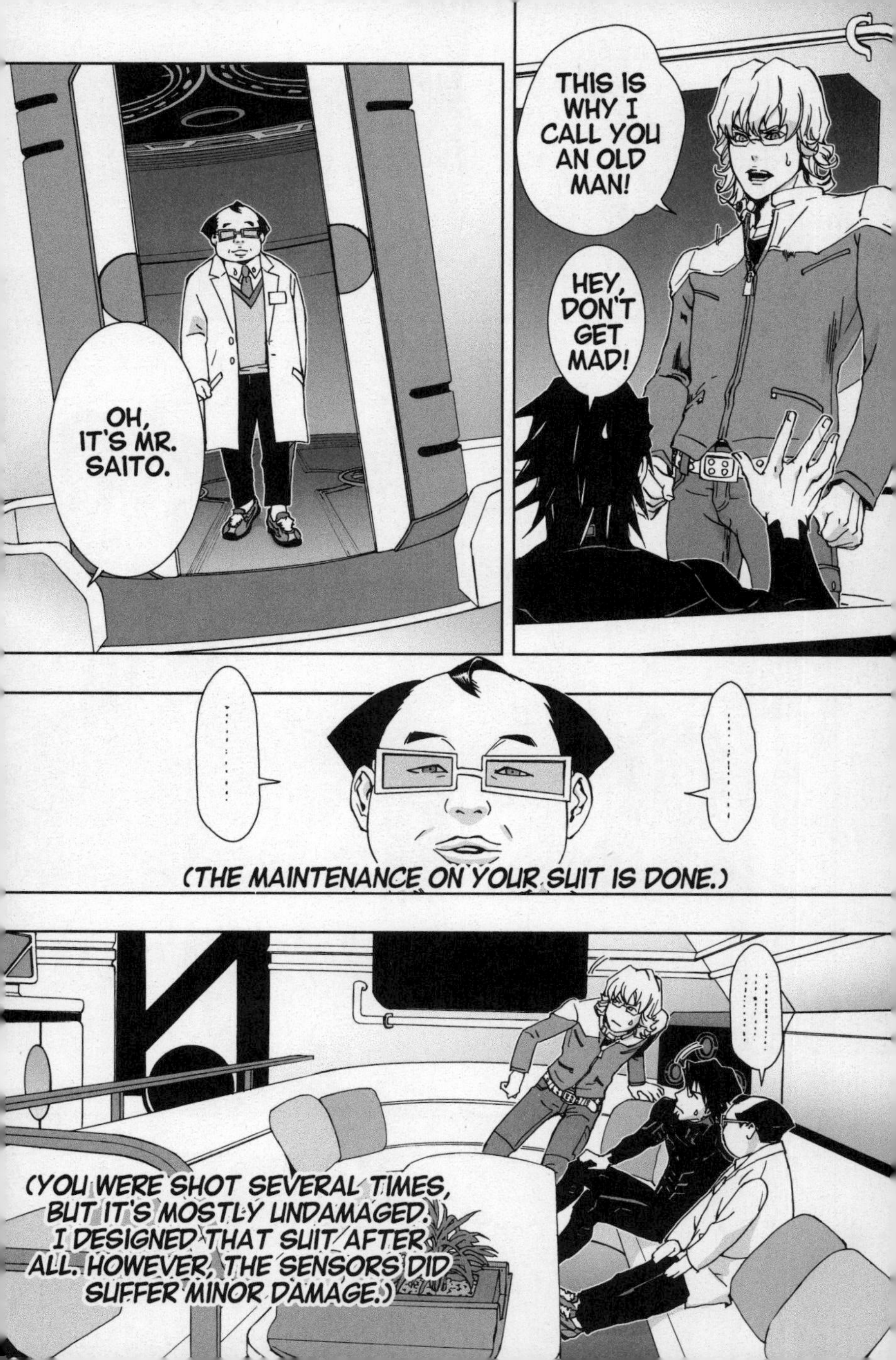
THIS IS WHY I CALL YOU AN OLD MAN!
HEY, DON'T GET MAD!
OH, IT'S MR. SAITO.
......
......
(THE MAINTENANCE ON YOUR SUIT IS DONE.)
......
(YOU WERE SHOT SEVERAL TIMES, BUT IT'S MOSTLY UNDAMAGED. I DESIGNED THAT SUIT AFTER ALL. HOWEVER, THE SENSORS DID SUFFER MINOR DAMAGE.)

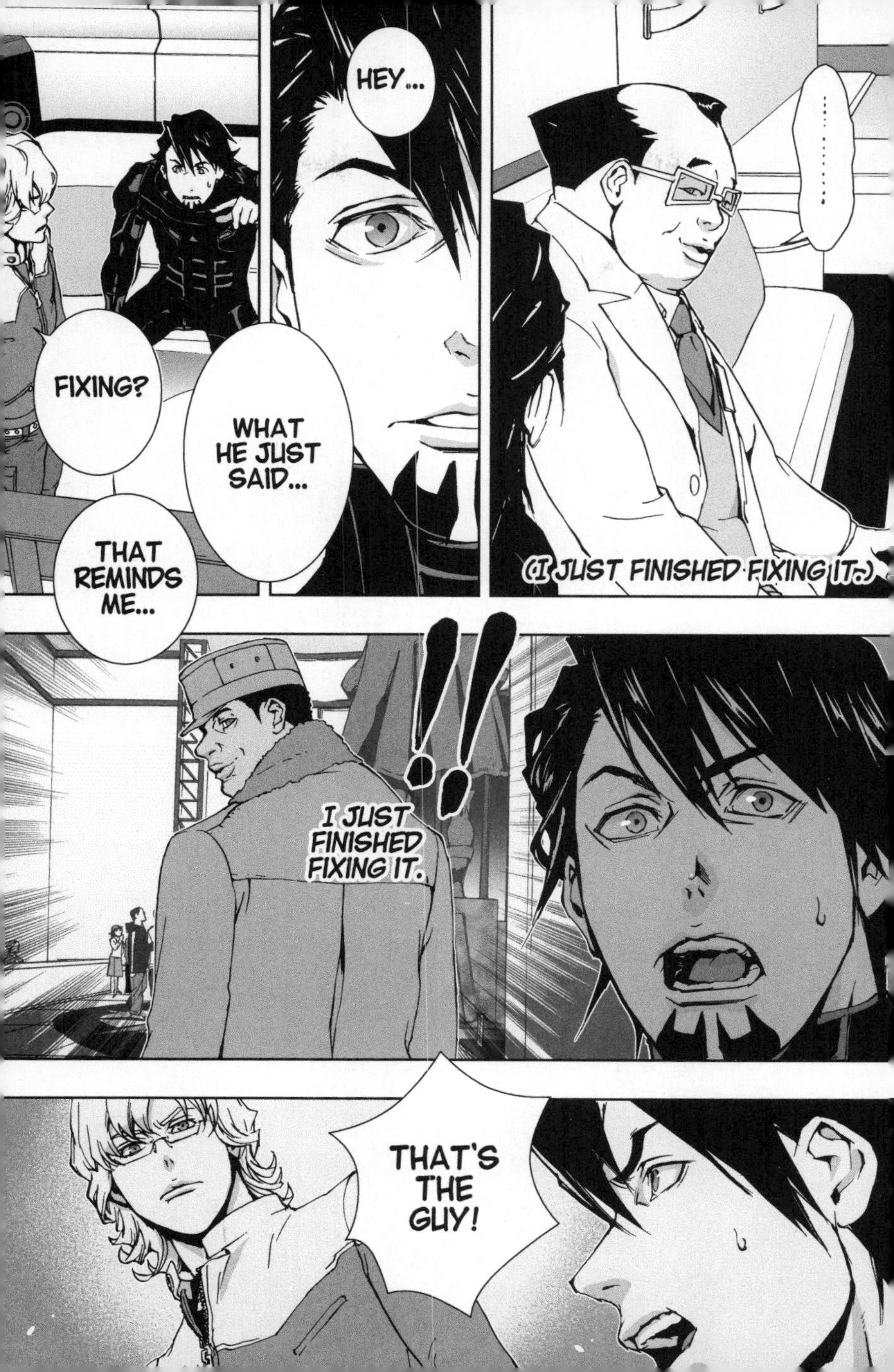

......
(I JUST FINISHED FIXING IT.)
HEY...
WHAT HE JUST SAID...
THAT REMINDS ME...
FIXING?
!!
I JUST FINISHED FIXING IT.
THAT'S THE GUY!

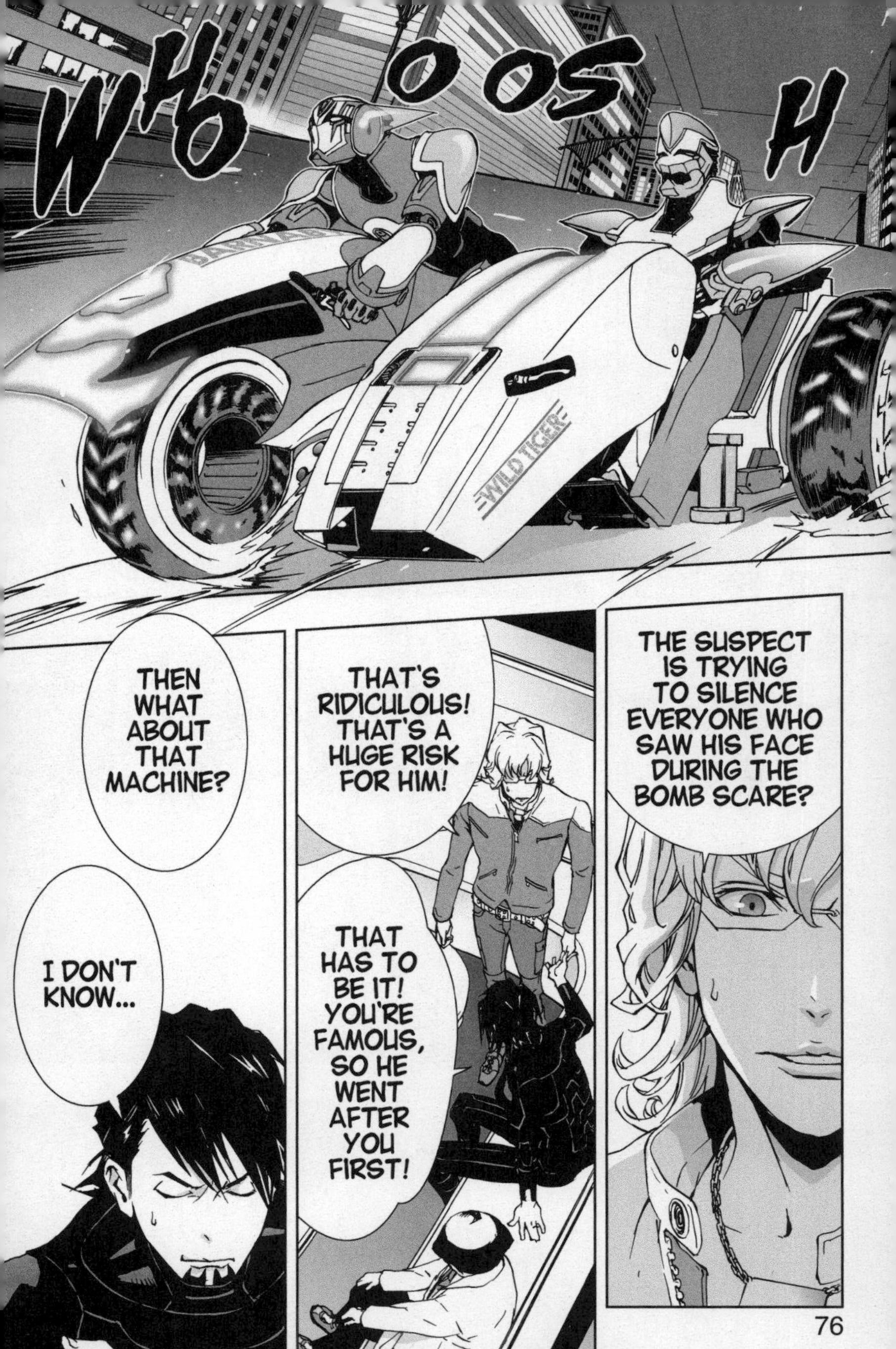
WHOOOSH
BARNABY
WILD TIGER
THE SUSPECT IS TRYING TO SILENCE EVERYONE WHO SAW HIS FACE DURING THE BOMB SCARE?
THAT'S RIDICULOUS! THAT'S A HUGE RISK FOR HIM!
THAT HAS TO BE IT! YOU'RE FAMOUS, SO HE WENT AFTER YOU FIRST!
THEN WHAT ABOUT THAT MACHINE?
I DON'T KNOW...

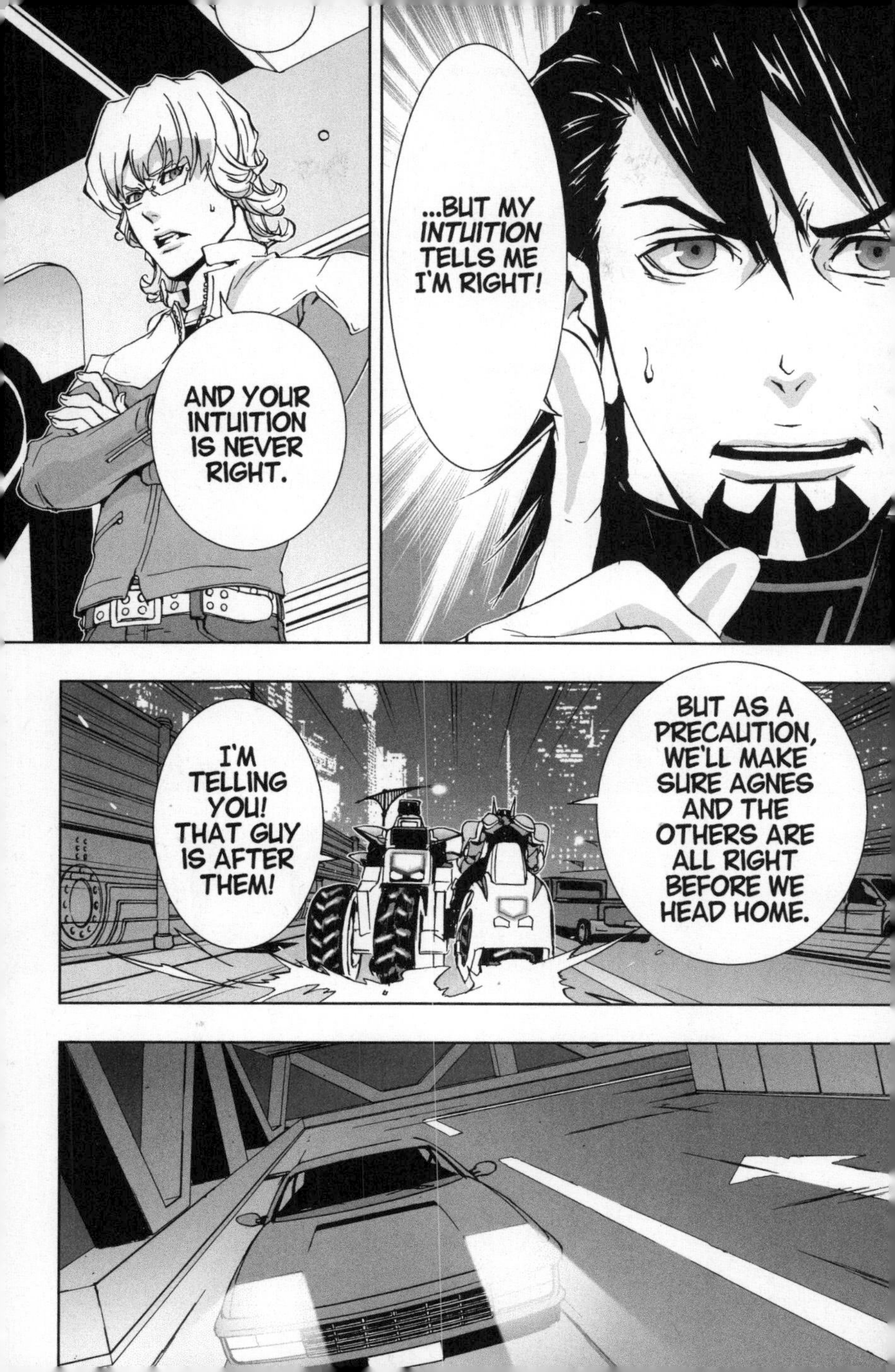

...BUT MY INTUITION TELLS ME I'M RIGHT!
AND YOUR INTUITION IS NEVER RIGHT.
BUT AS A PRECAUTION, WE'LL MAKE SURE AGNES AND THE OTHERS ARE ALL RIGHT BEFORE WE HEAD HOME.
I'M TELLING YOU! THAT GUY IS AFTER THEM!

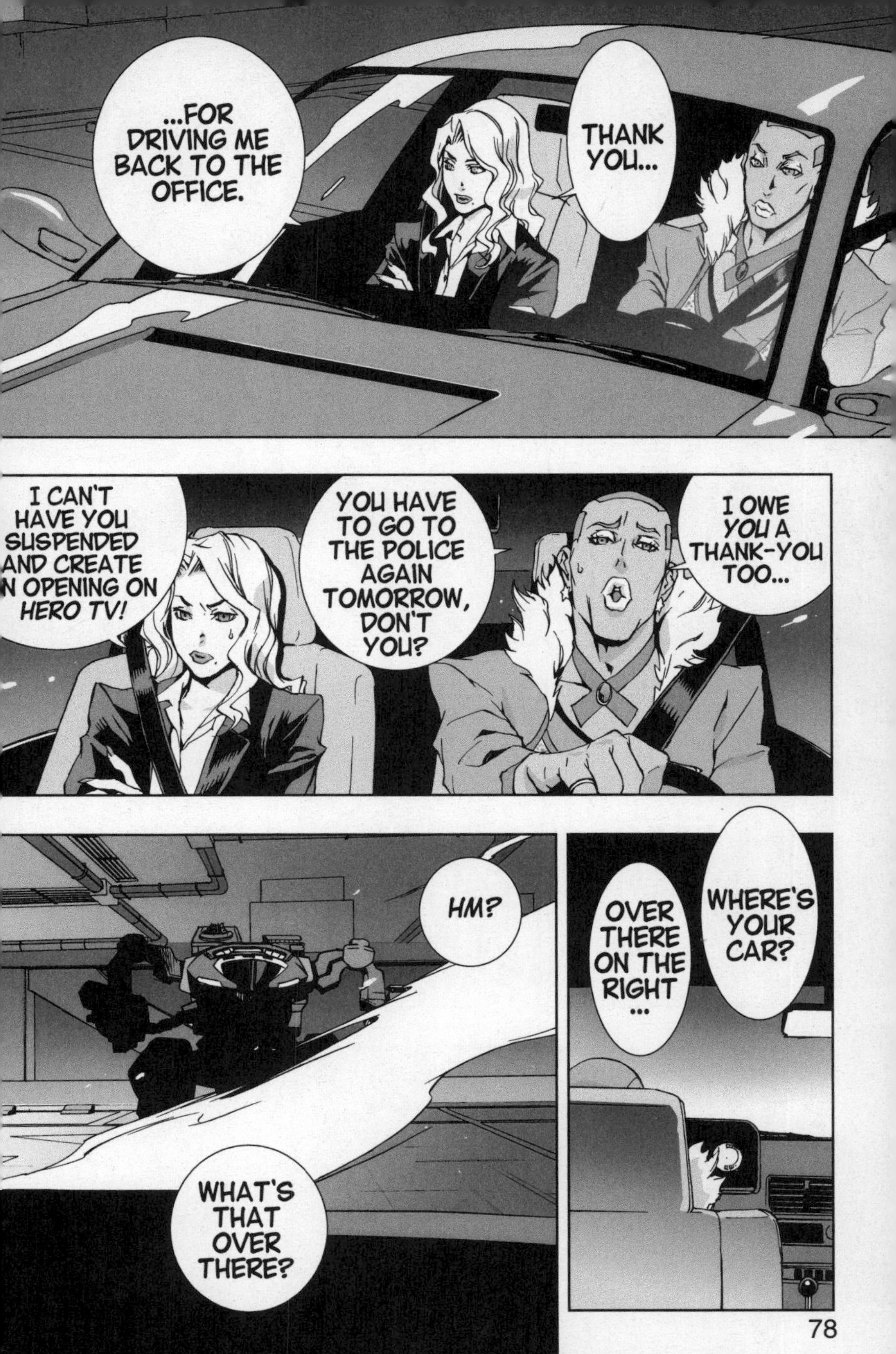
THANK YOU...
...FOR DRIVING ME BACK TO THE OFFICE.
I OWE YOU A THANK-YOU TOO...
YOU HAVE TO GO TO THE POLICE AGAIN TOMORROW, DON'T YOU?
I CAN'T HAVE YOU SUSPENDED AND CREATE N OPENING ON HERO TV!
WHERE'S YOUR CAR?
OVER THERE ON THE RIGHT ...
HM?
WHAT'S THAT OVER THERE?

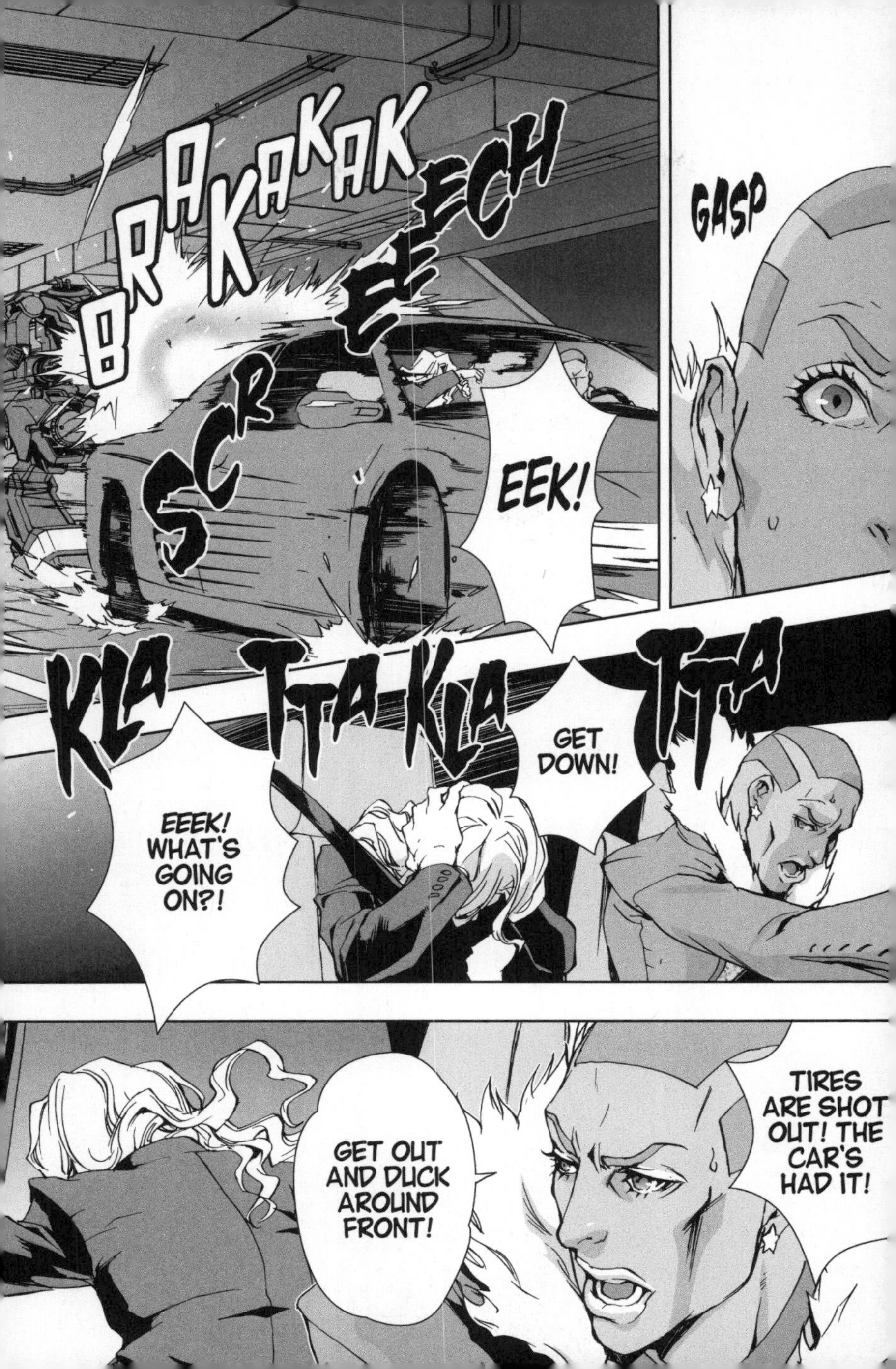
GASP
BRAKAKAK
SCREEECH
EEK!
KLATTA KLATTA
GET DOWN!
EEEK! WHAT'S GOING ON?!
TIRES ARE SHOT OUT! THE CAR'S HAD IT!
GET OUT AND DUCK AROUND FRONT!

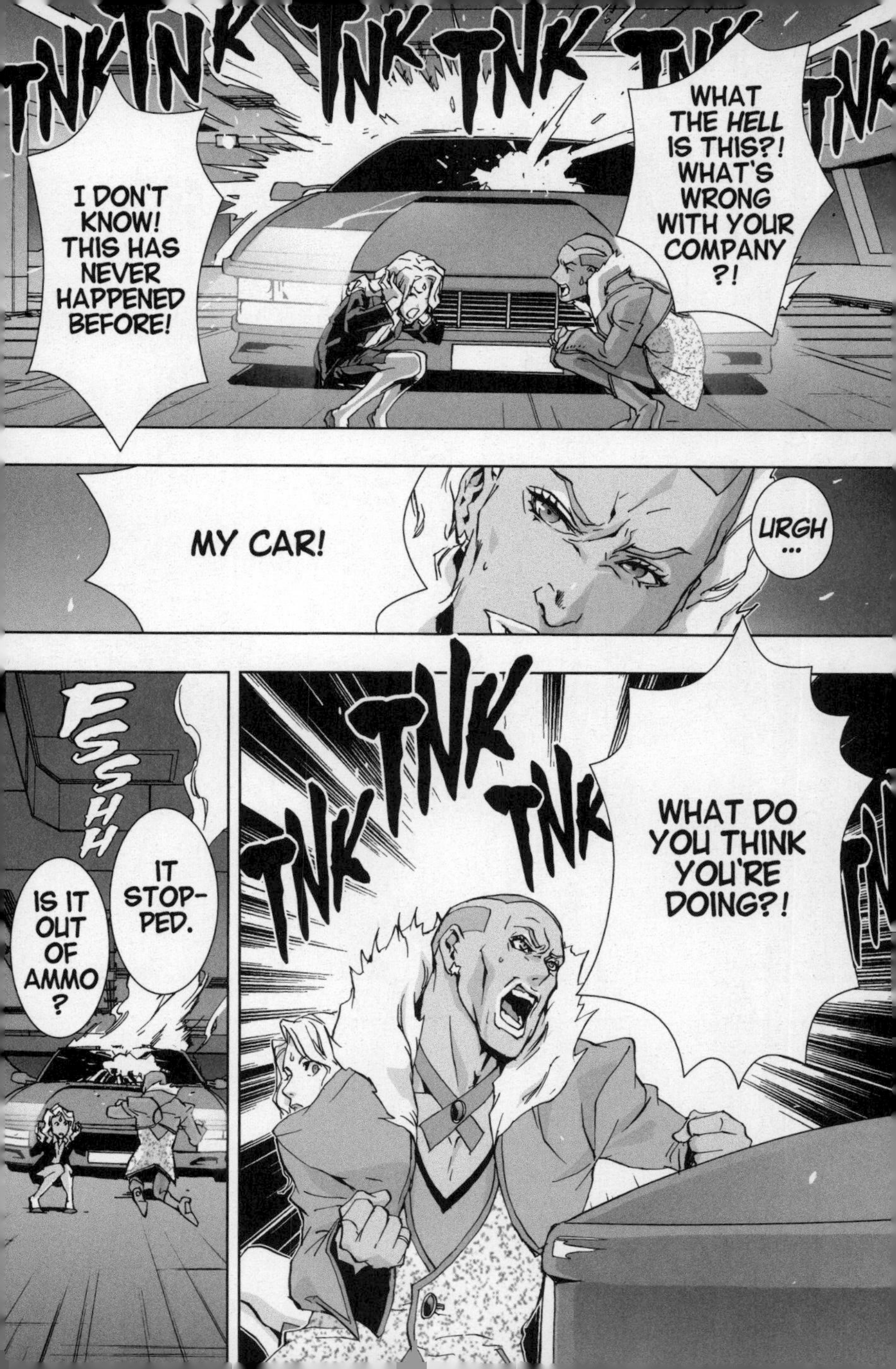
TNK TNK TNK TNK TNK TNK
WHAT THE HELL IS THIS?! WHAT'S WRONG WITH YOUR COMPANY?!
I DON'T KNOW! THIS HAS NEVER HAPPENED BEFORE!
URGH...
MY CAR!
TNK TNK TNK TNK
WHAT DO YOU THINK YOU'RE DOING?!
FSSHH
IT STOP-PED.
IS IT OUT OF AMMO?

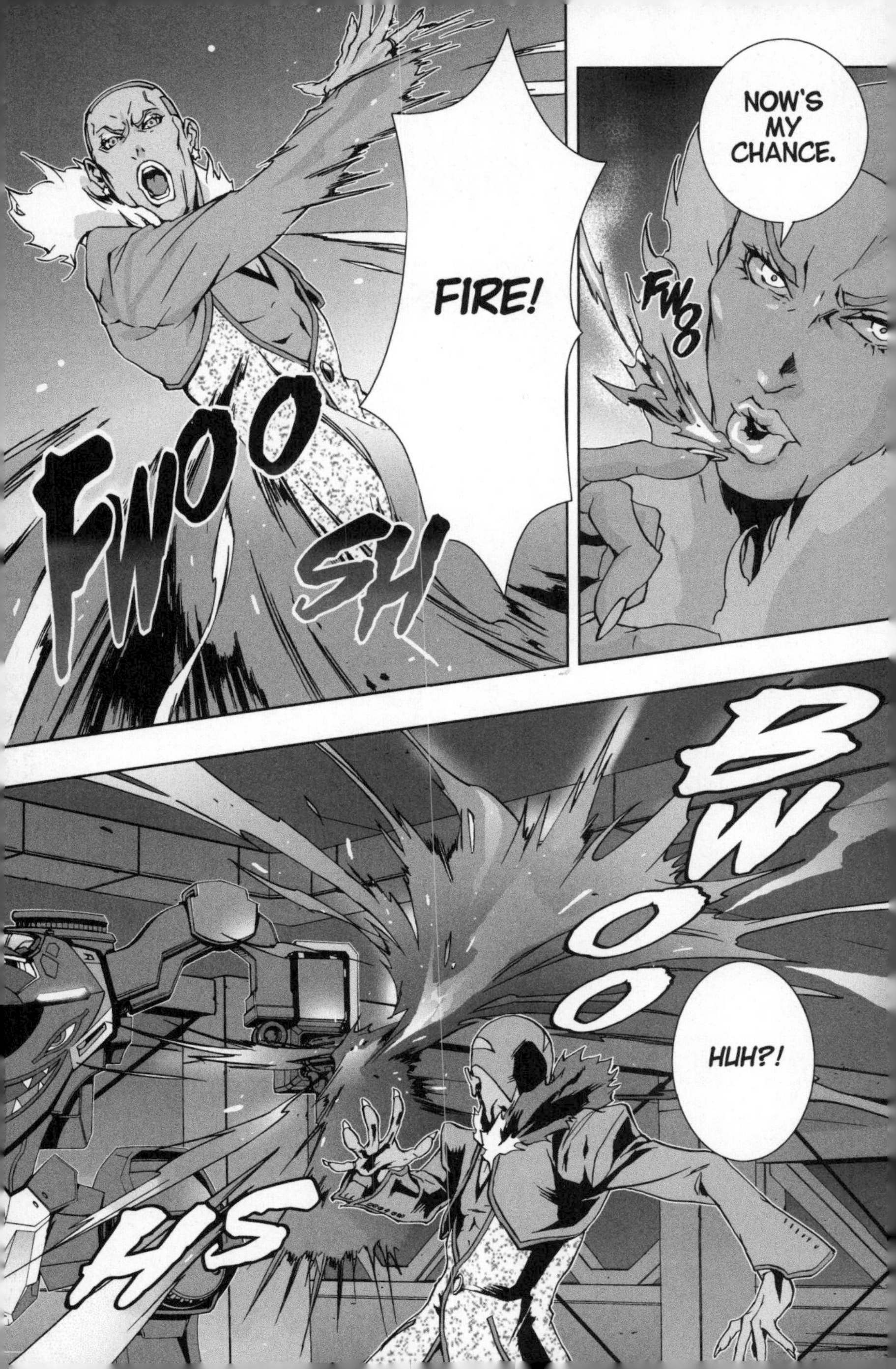
NOW'S MY CHANCE.
FWOO
FIRE!
FWOOSH
BWOOO
HUH?!
HIS

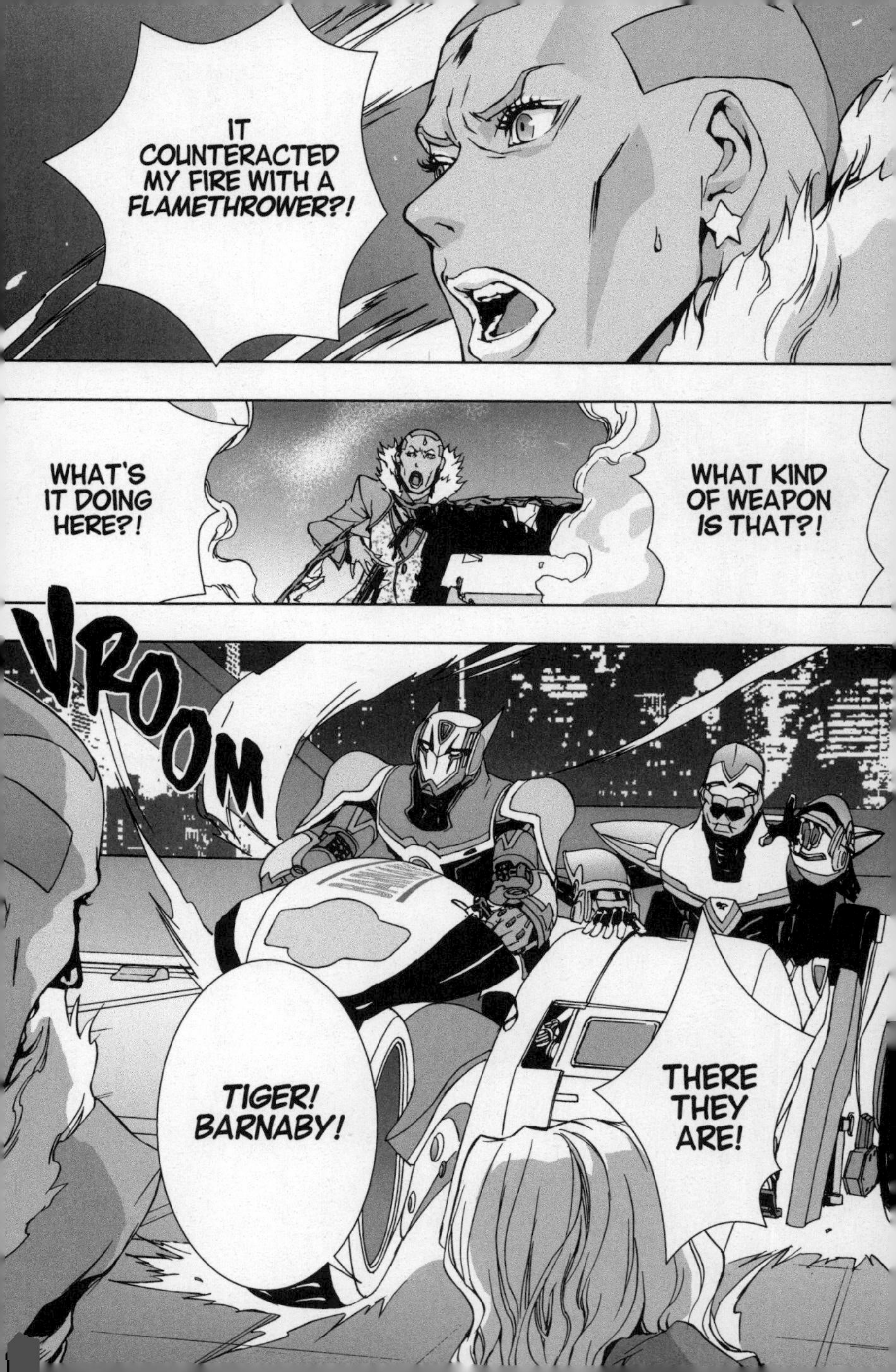

IT COUNTERACTED MY FIRE WITH A FLAMETHROWER?!
WHAT KIND OF WEAPON IS THAT?!
WHAT'S IT DOING HERE?!
VROOM
THERE THEY ARE!
TIGER! BARNABY!

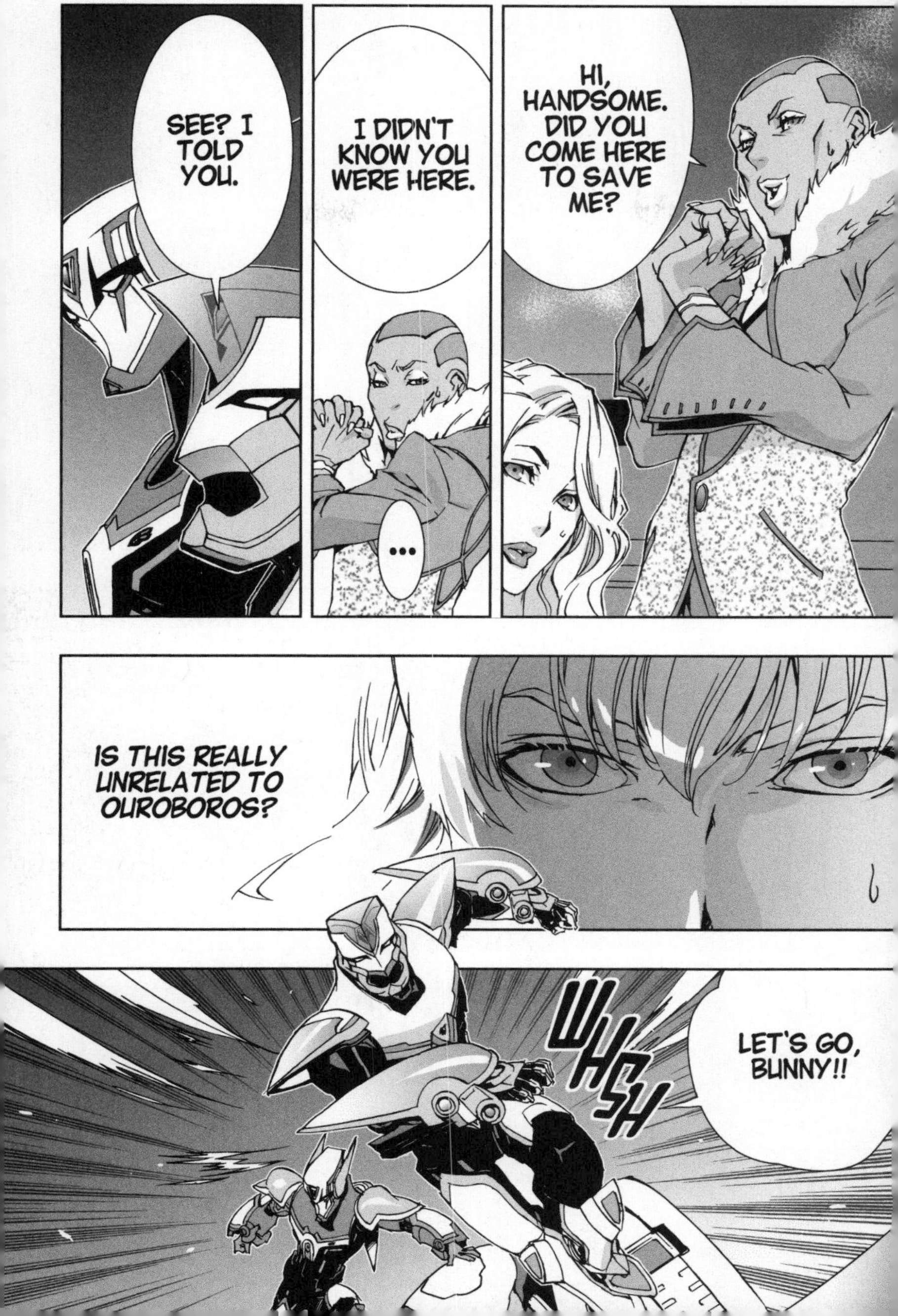
HI, HANDSOME. DID YOU COME HERE TO SAVE ME?
I DIDN'T KNOW YOU WERE HERE.
...
SEE? I TOLD YOU.
IS THIS REALLY UNRELATED TO OUROBOROS?
LET'S GO, BUNNY!!
WHSH

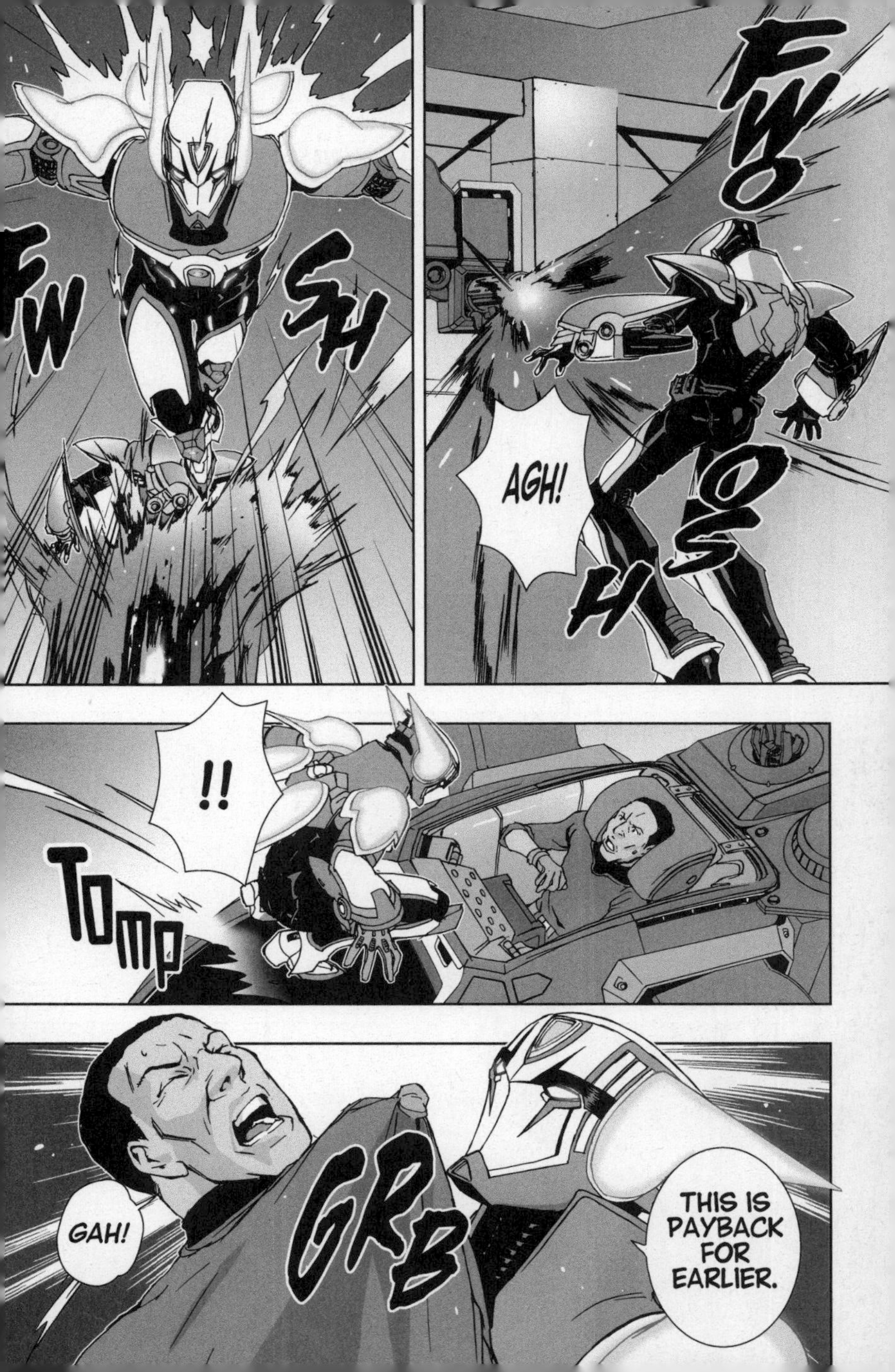
FWOOSH
AGH!
FWSH
!!
TOMP
THIS IS PAYBACK FOR EARLIER.
GRB
GAH!

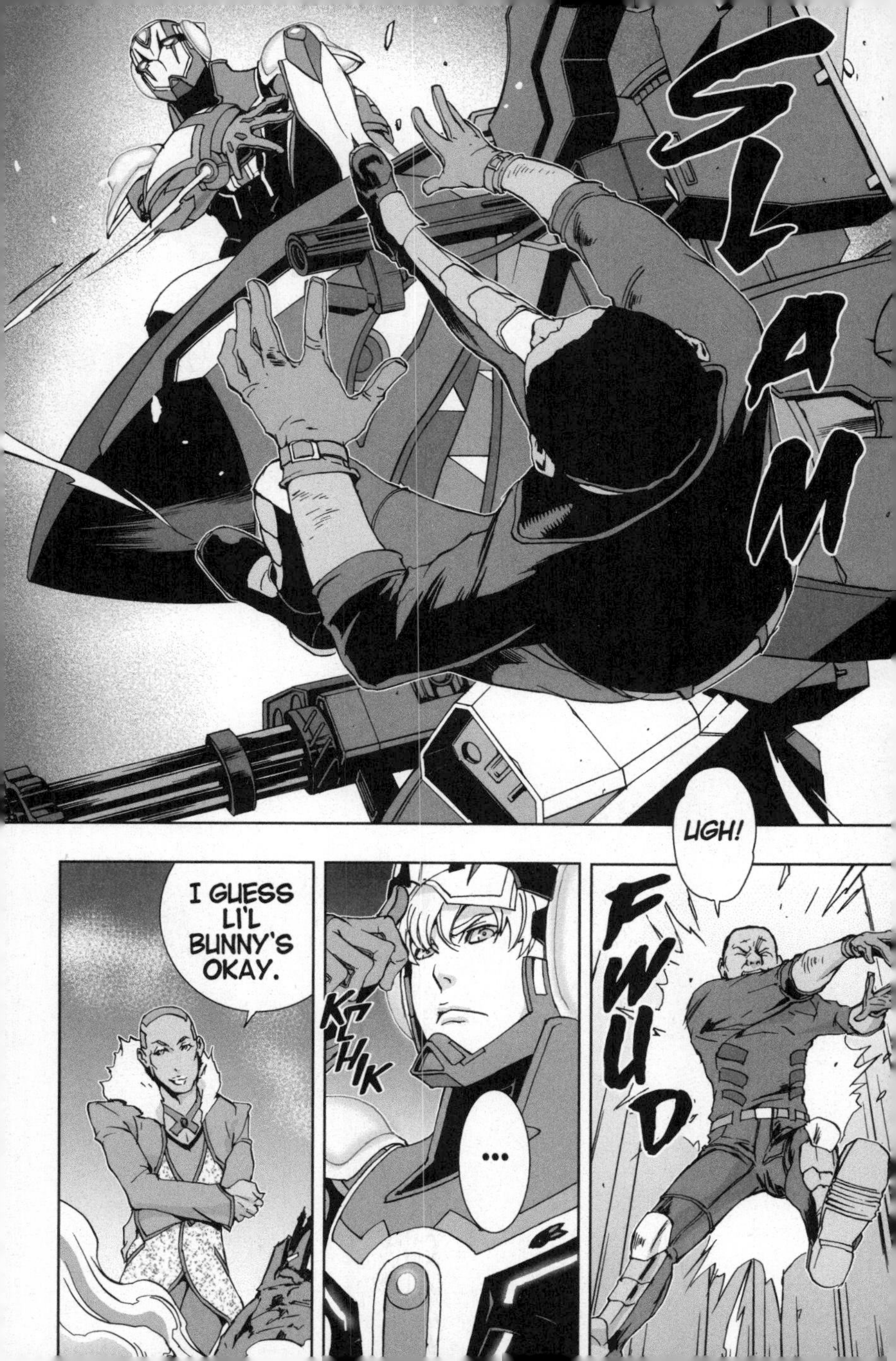
SLAM
UGH!
FWUD
KCHIK
...
I GUESS LI'L BUNNY'S OKAY.

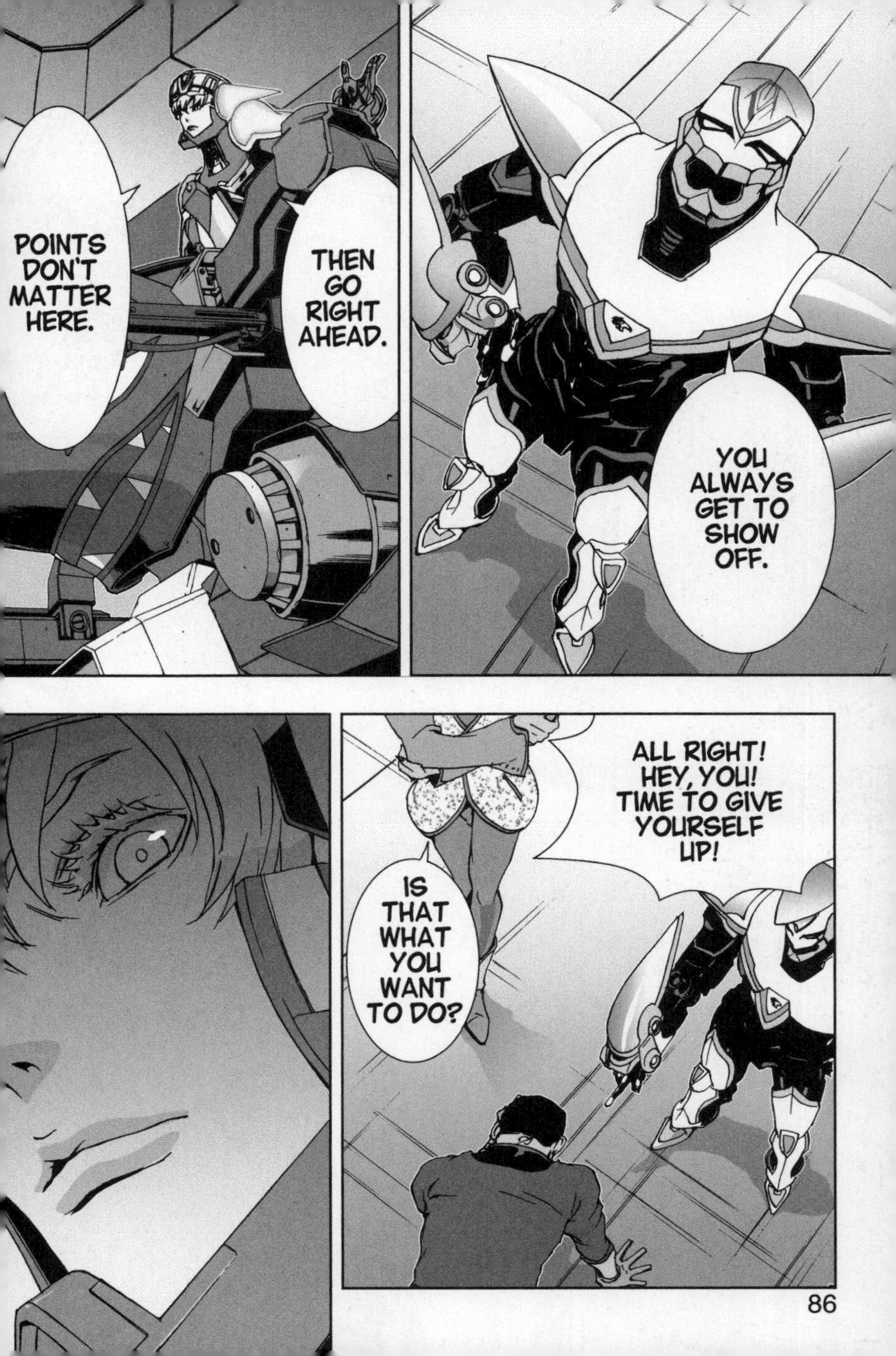
YOU ALWAYS GET TO SHOW OFF.
THEN GO RIGHT AHEAD.
POINTS DON'T MATTER HERE.
ALL RIGHT! HEY, YOU! TIME TO GIVE YOURSELF UP!
IS THAT WHAT YOU WANT TO DO?

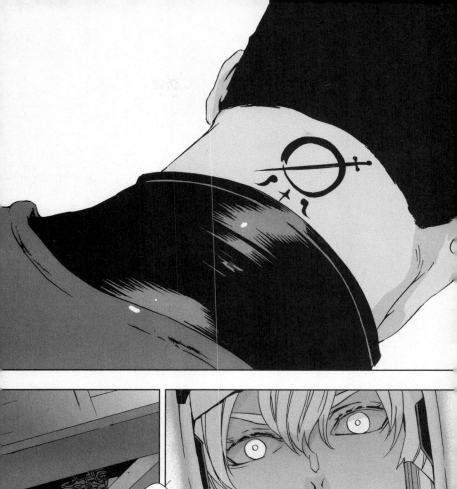

OURO...
BOROS
...

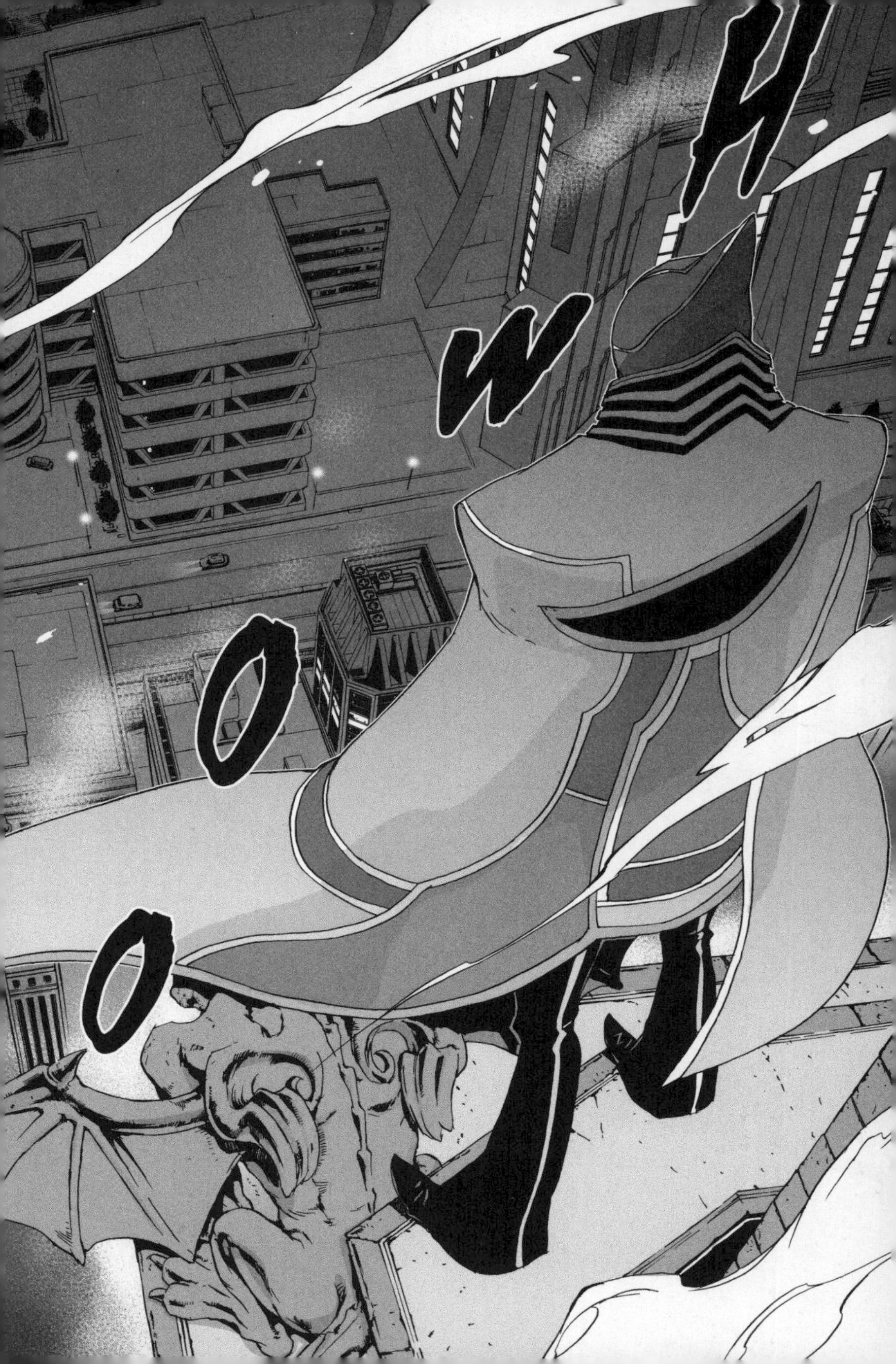
HWOO

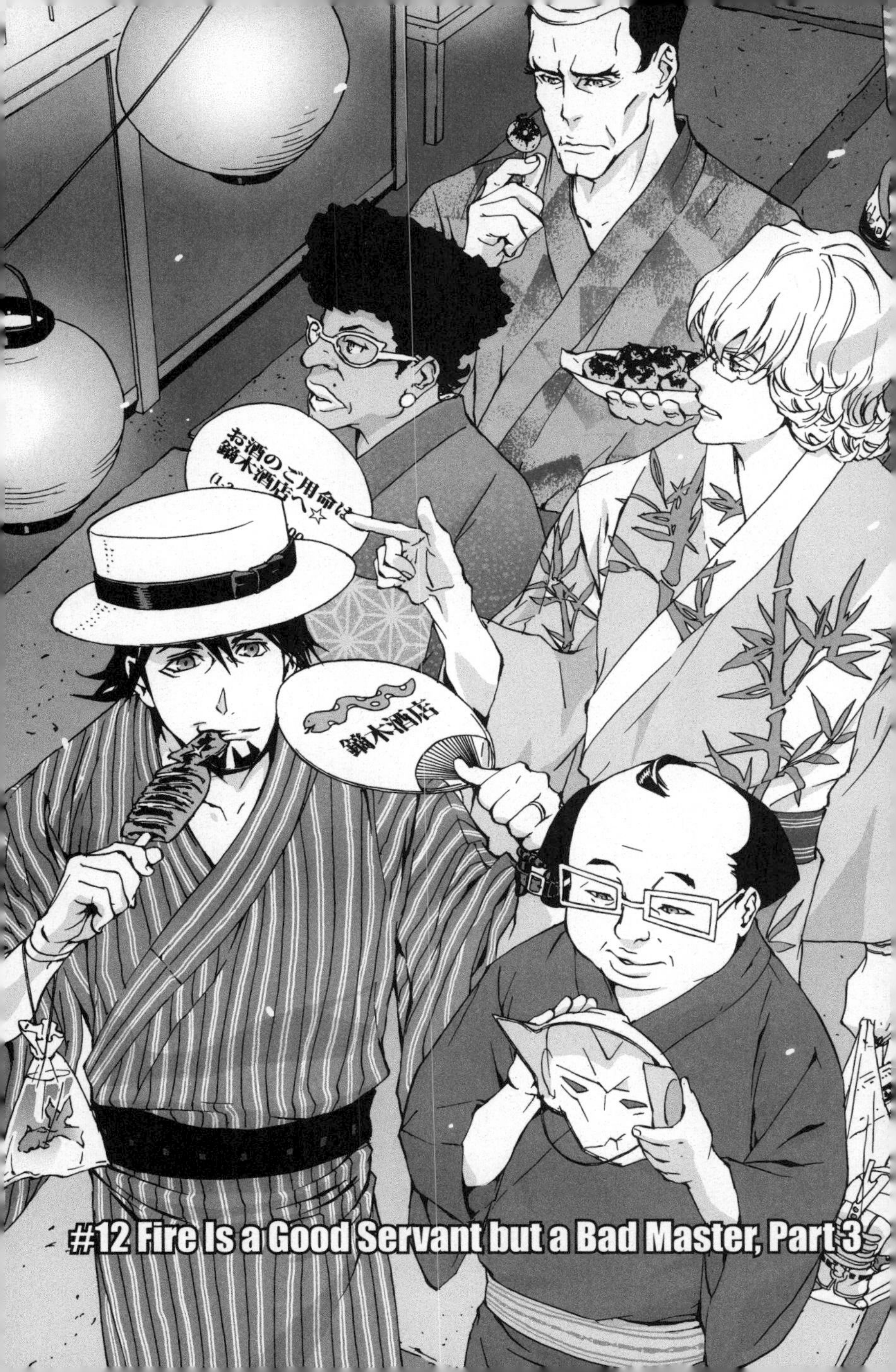
お酒のご用命は
鏑木酒店へ☆
鏑木酒店

#12 Fire Is a Good Servant but a Bad Master, Part 3

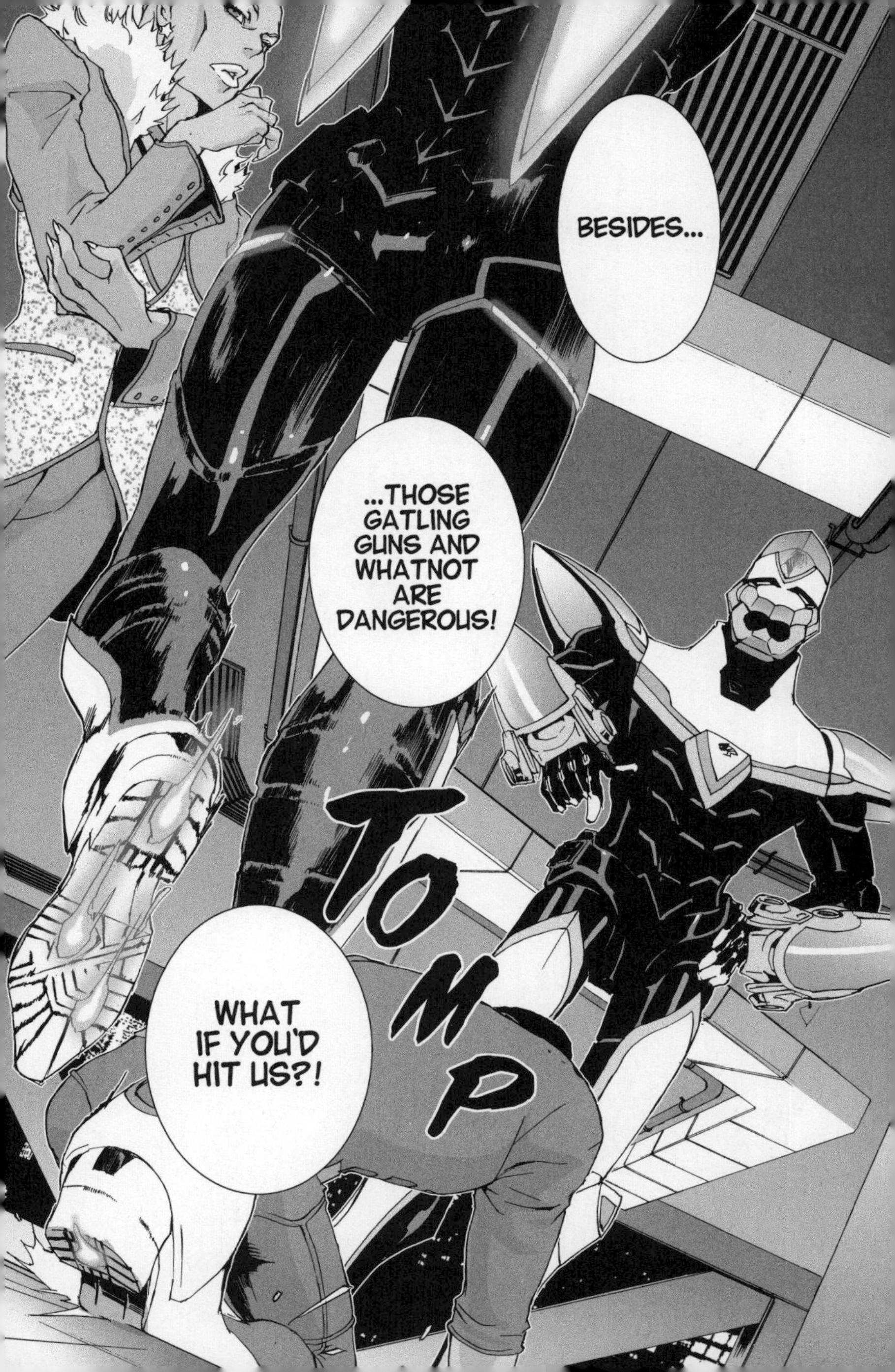
BESIDES...
...THOSE GATLING GUNS AND WHATNOT ARE DANGEROUS!
TOMP
WHAT IF YOU'D HIT US?!

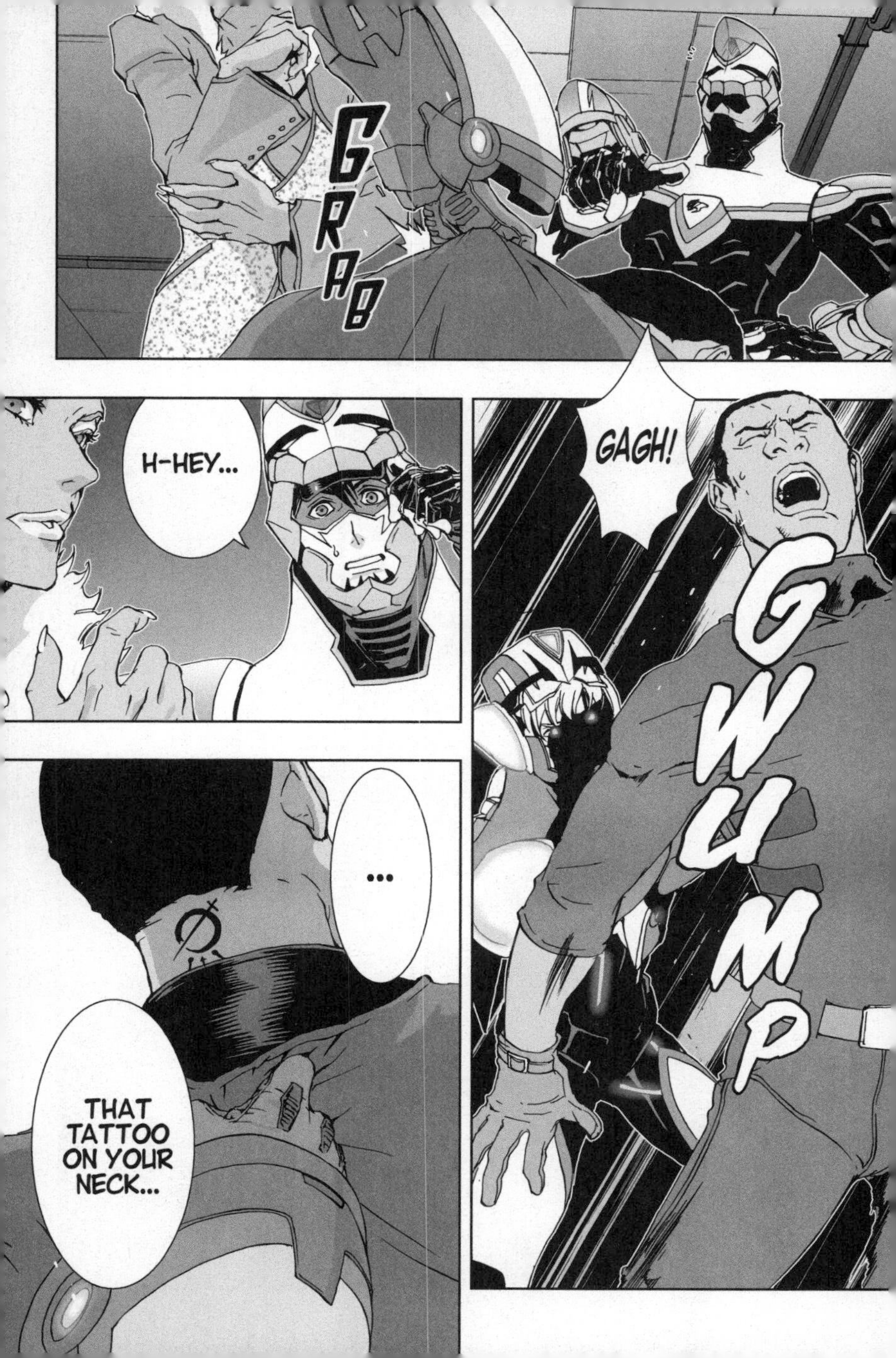
GRAB
GAGH!
GWUMP
H-HEY...
...
THAT TATTOO ON YOUR NECK...

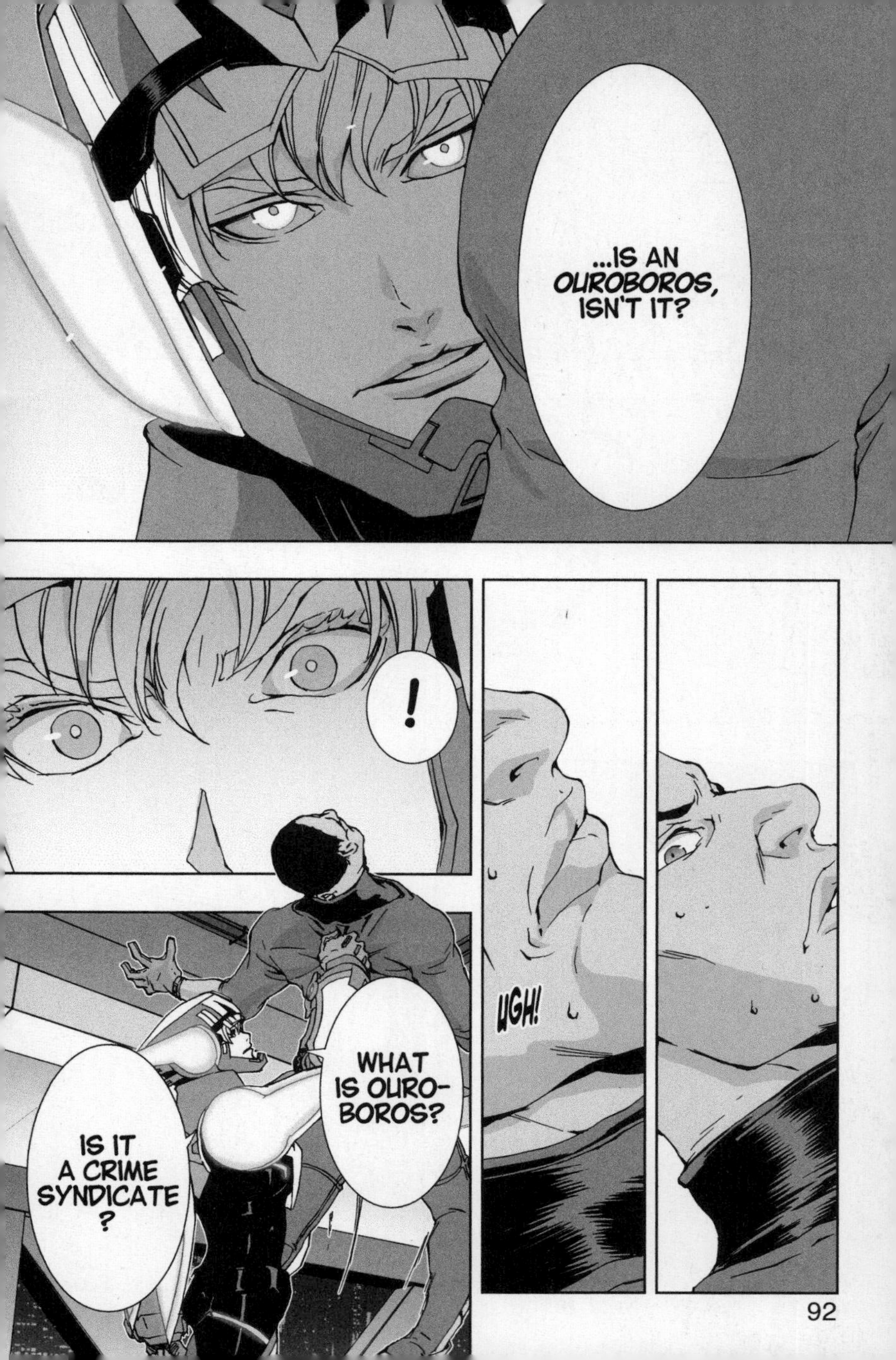
...IS AN OUROBOROS, ISN'T IT?
UGH!
!
WHAT IS OURO-BOROS?
IS IT A CRIME SYNDICATE?

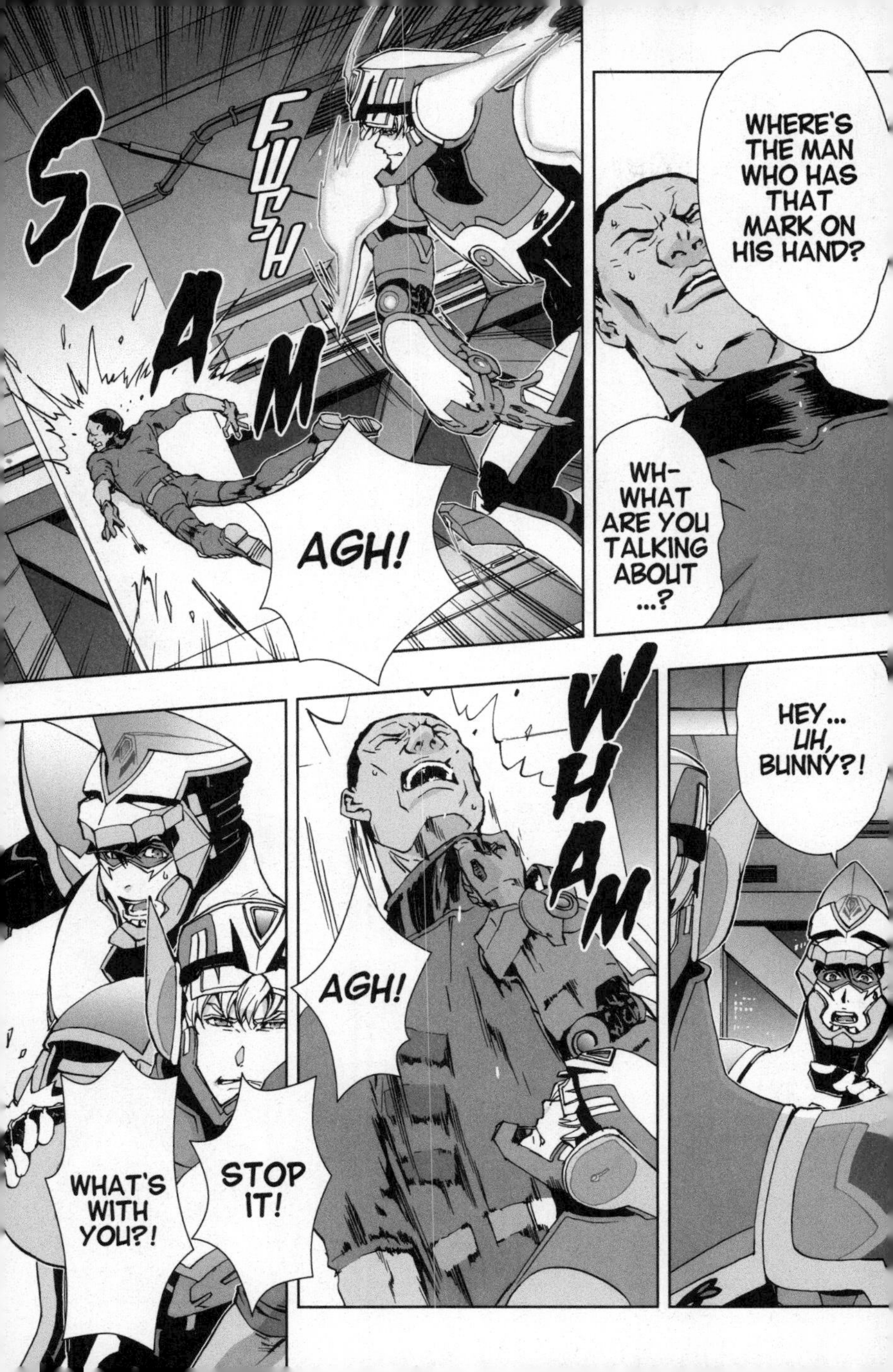
WHERE'S THE MAN WHO HAS THAT MARK ON HIS HAND?
WH- WHAT ARE YOU TALKING ABOUT ...?
FWSH
SLAM
AGH!
HEY... UH, BUNNY?!
WHAM
AGH!
STOP IT!
WHAT'S WITH YOU?!

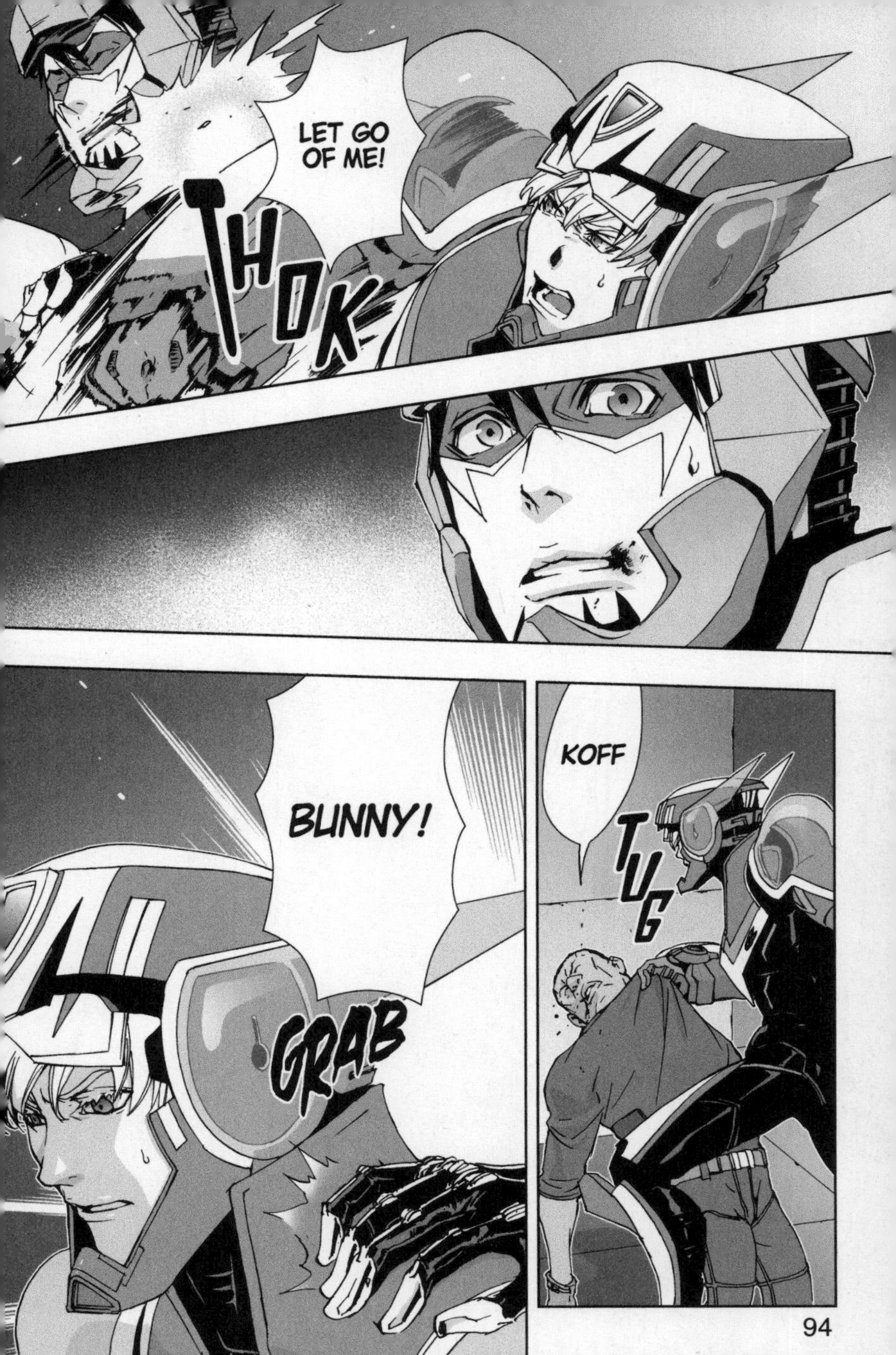
LET GO OF ME!
THOK
KOFF
TUG
BUNNY!
GRAB

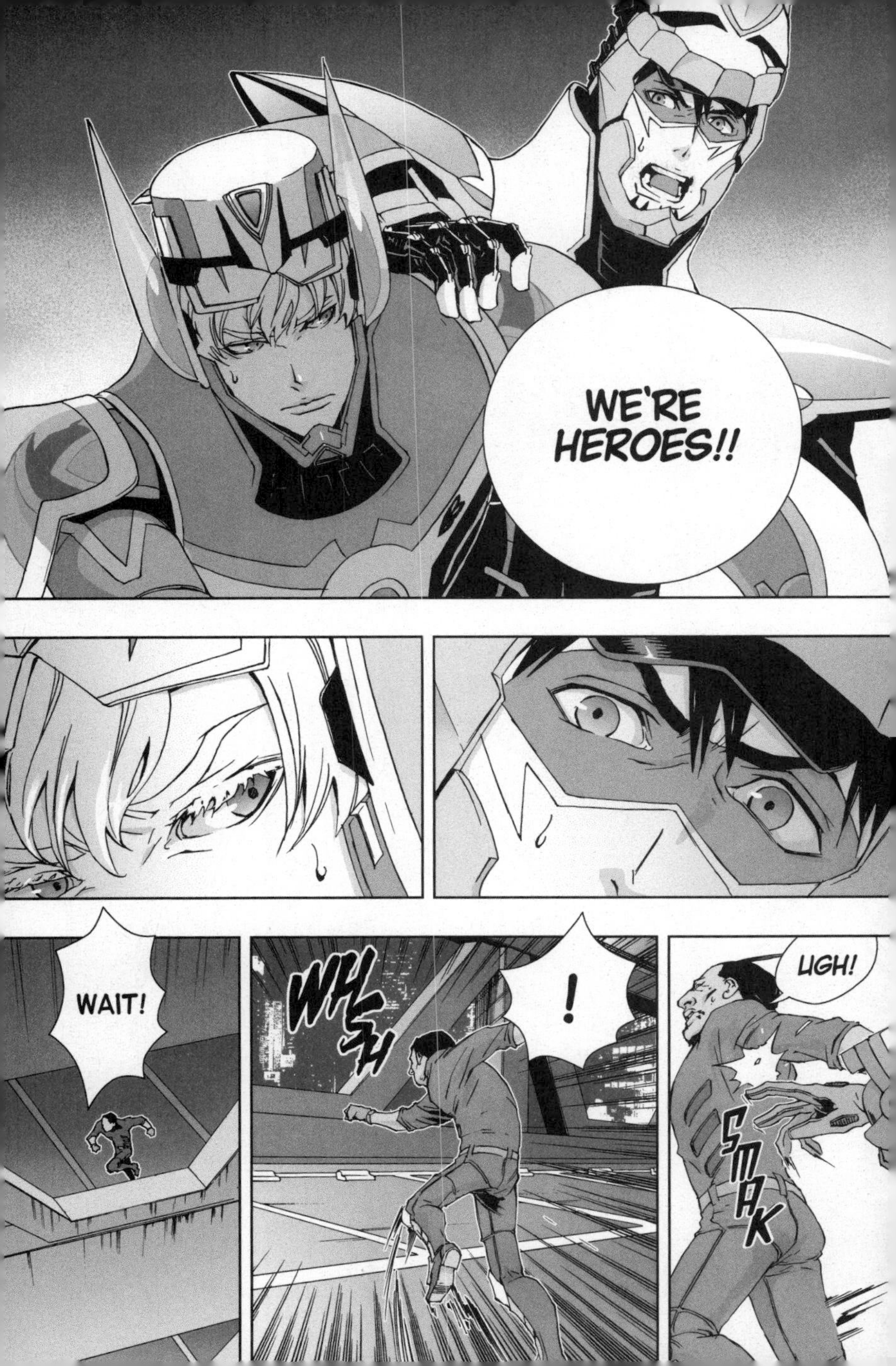
WE'RE HEROES!!
UGH!
SMAK
!
WHSH
WAIT!

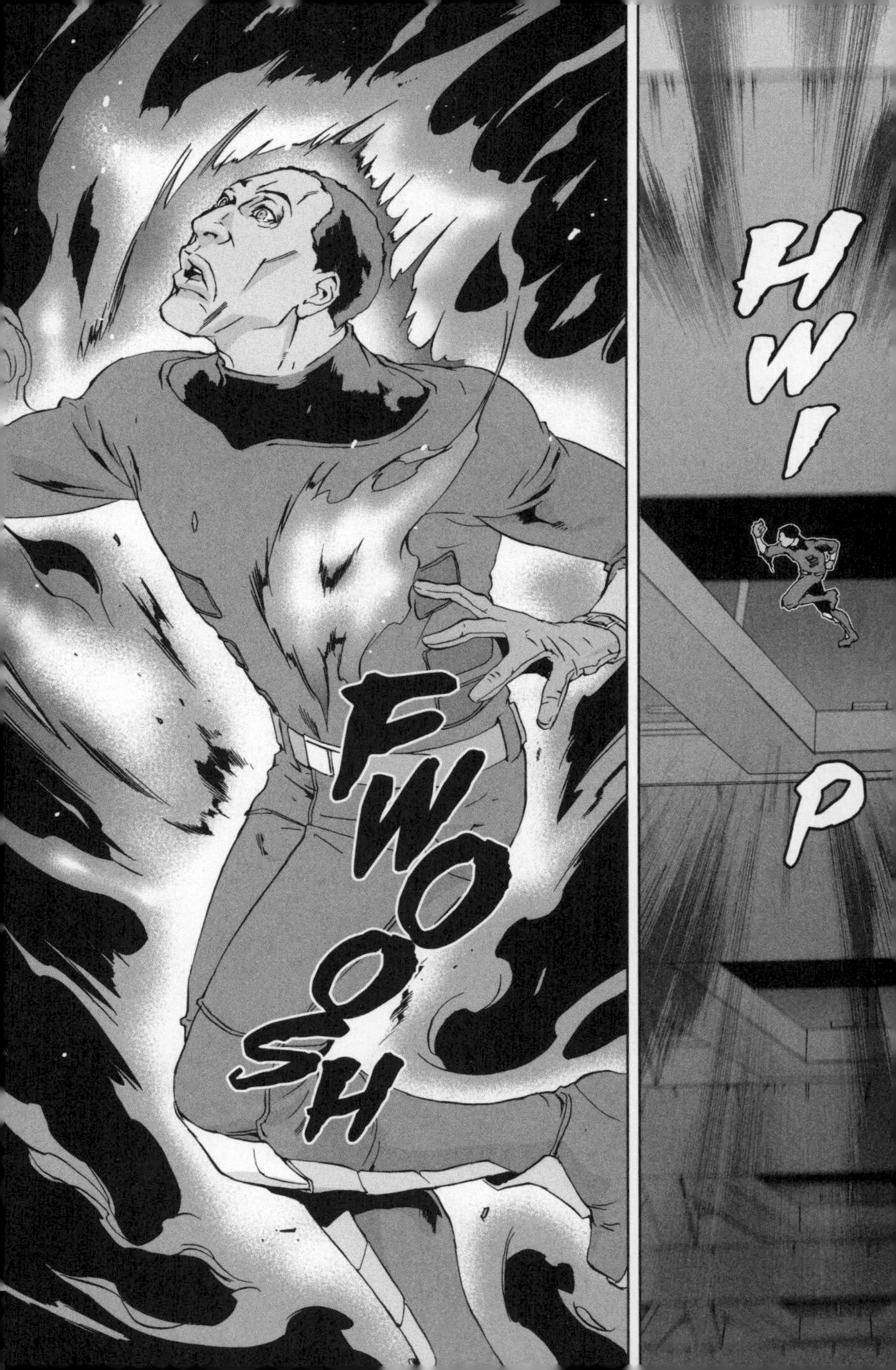
HWIP
FWOOSH

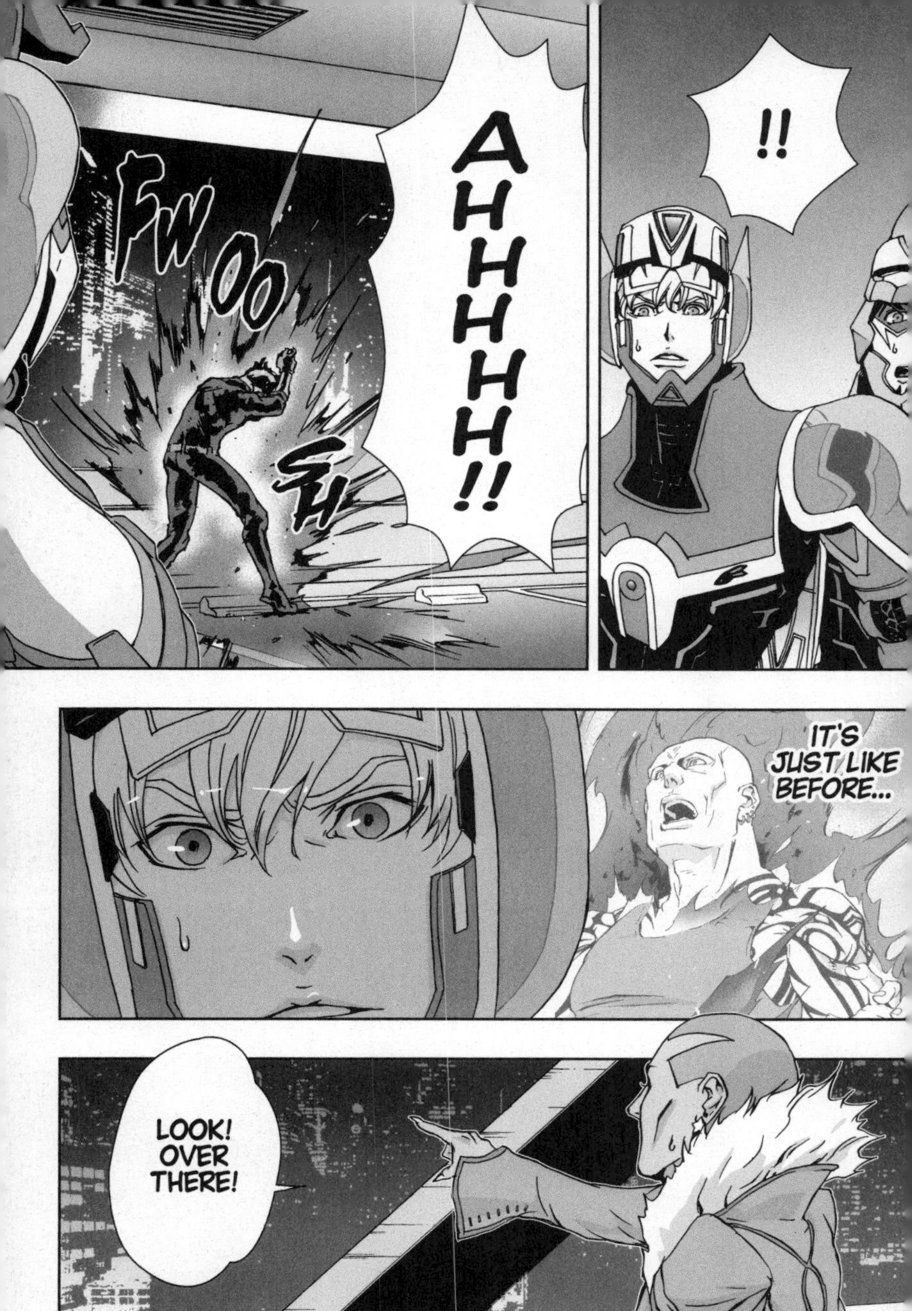
!!
AHHHHH!!
FWOO
SH
IT'S JUST LIKE BEFORE...
LOOK! OVER THERE!

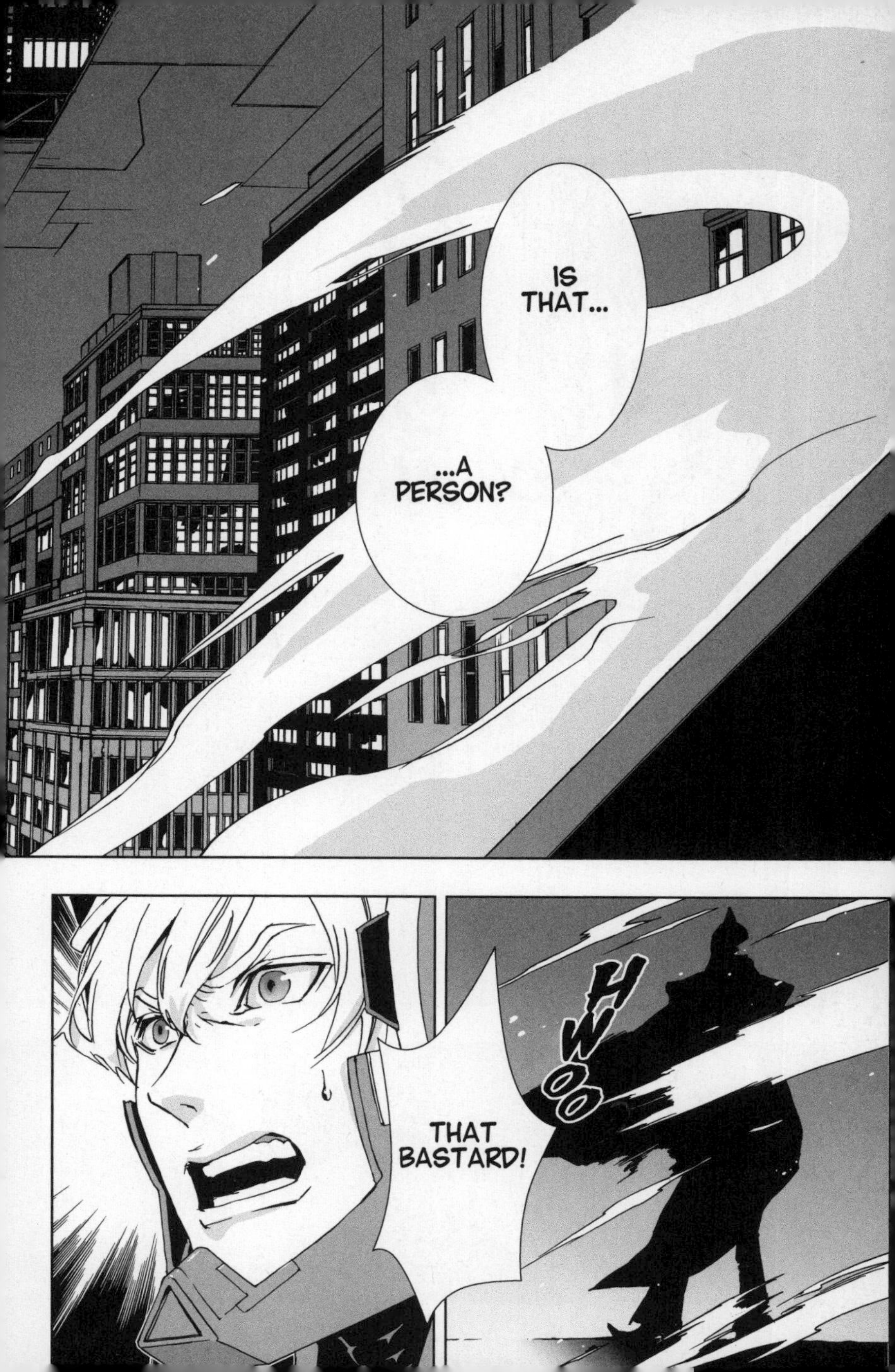
IS THAT...
...A PERSON?
HWOO
THAT BASTARD!

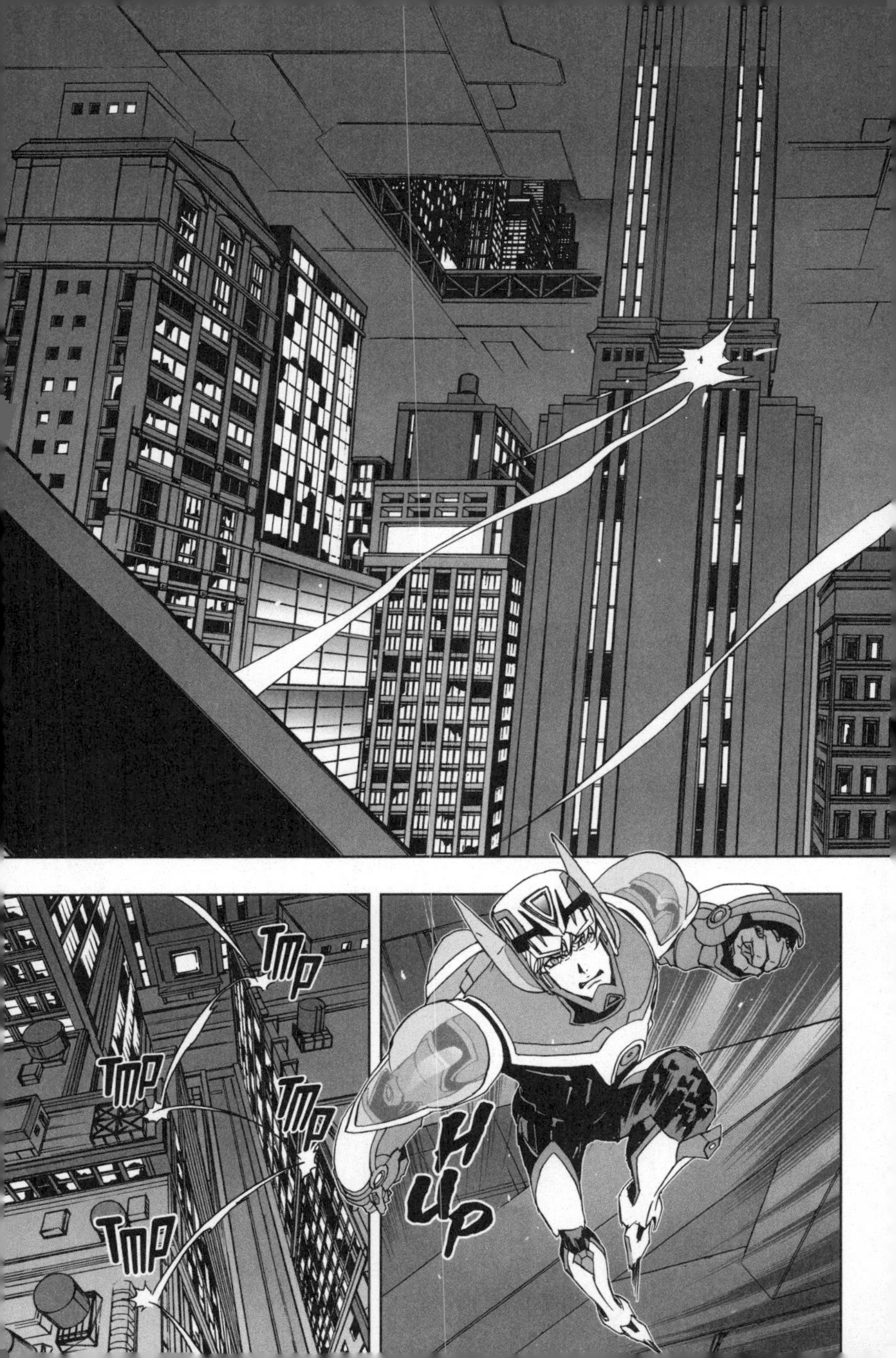
HUP
TMP
TMP
TMP
TMP

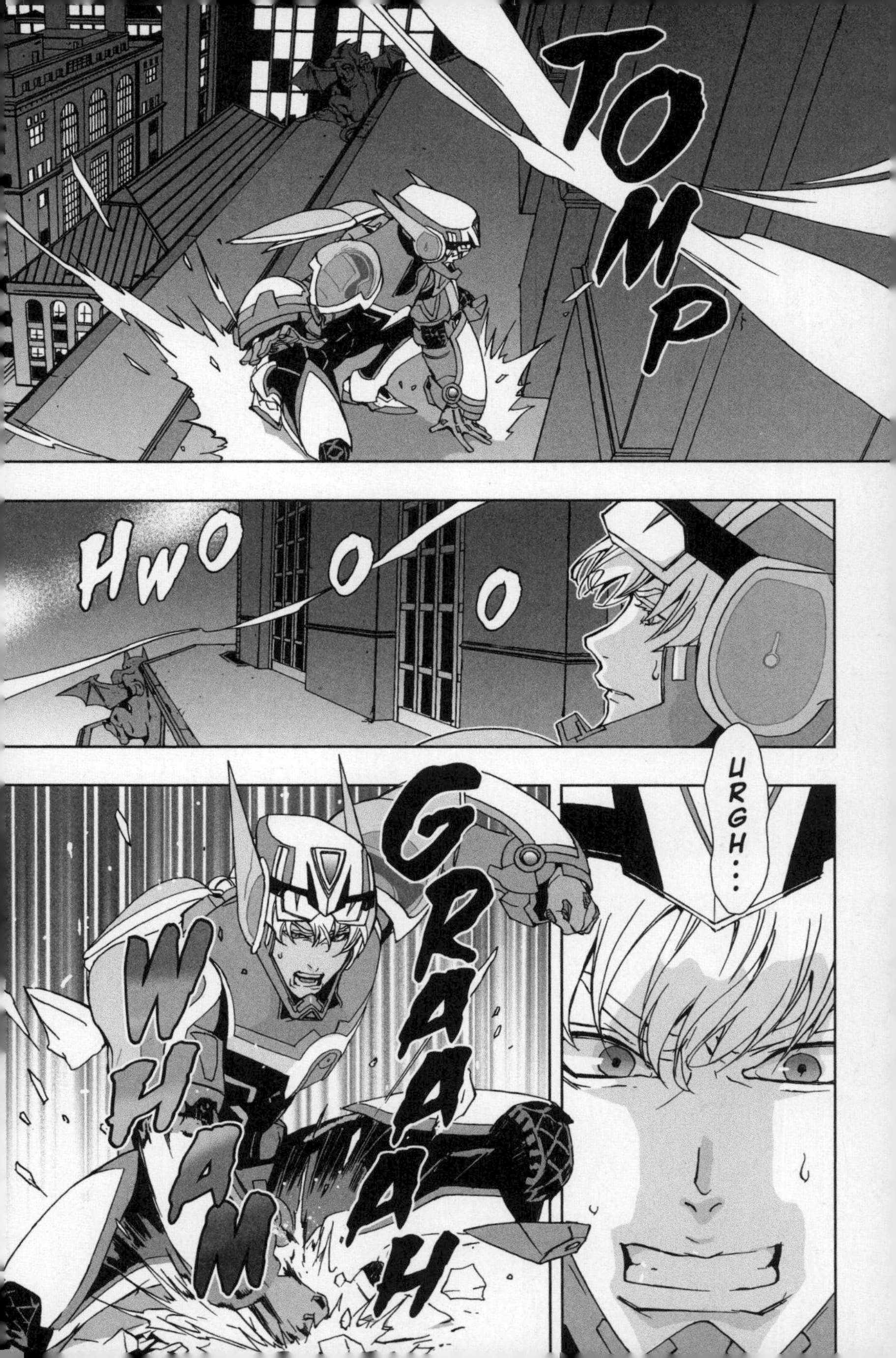
TOMP
HWOOO
URGH...
GRAAAAH
WHAM

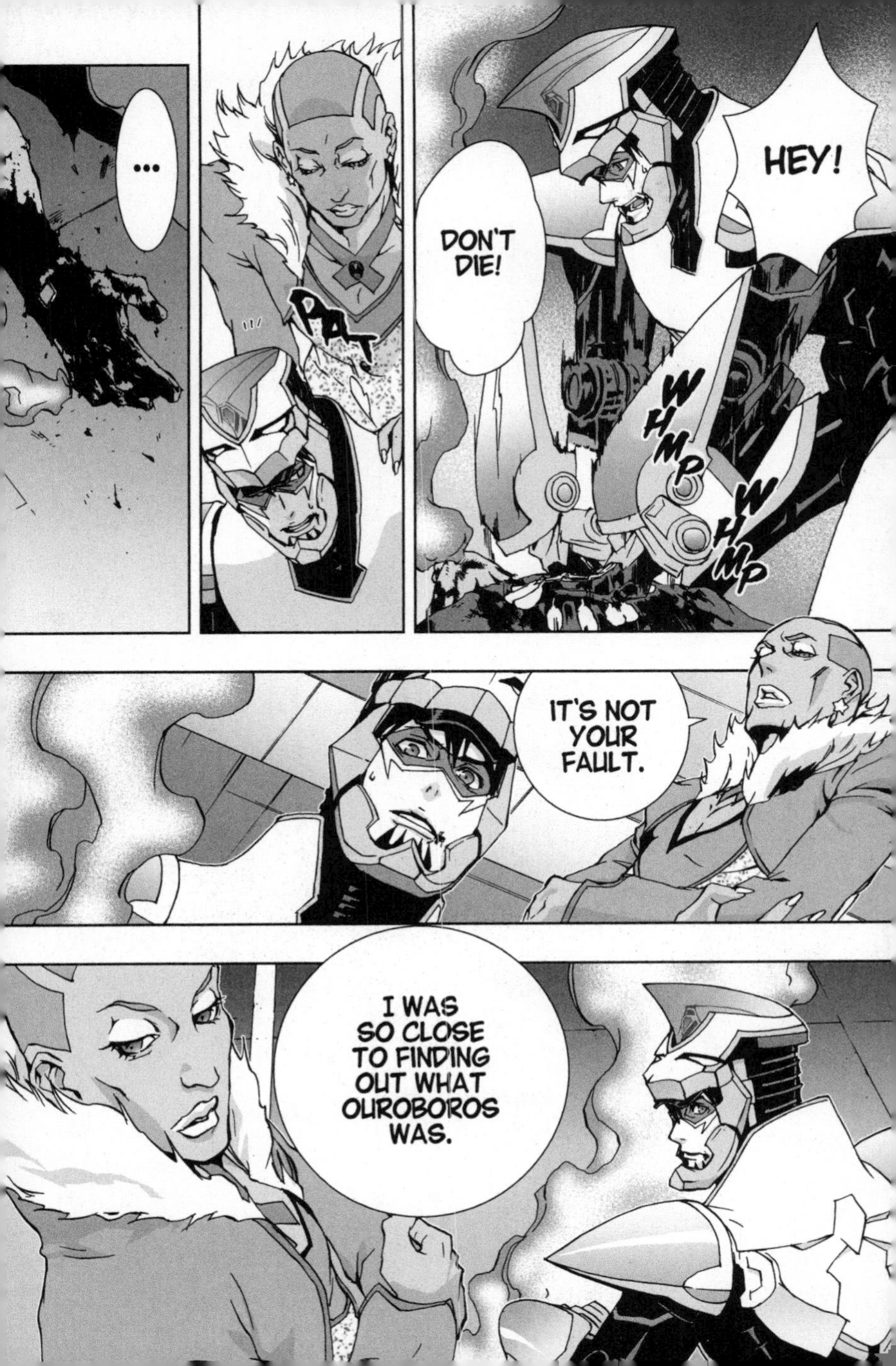
HEY!
DON'T DIE!
WHMP
WHMP
PAT
...
IT'S NOT YOUR FAULT.
I WAS SO CLOSE TO FINDING OUT WHAT OUROBOROS WAS.

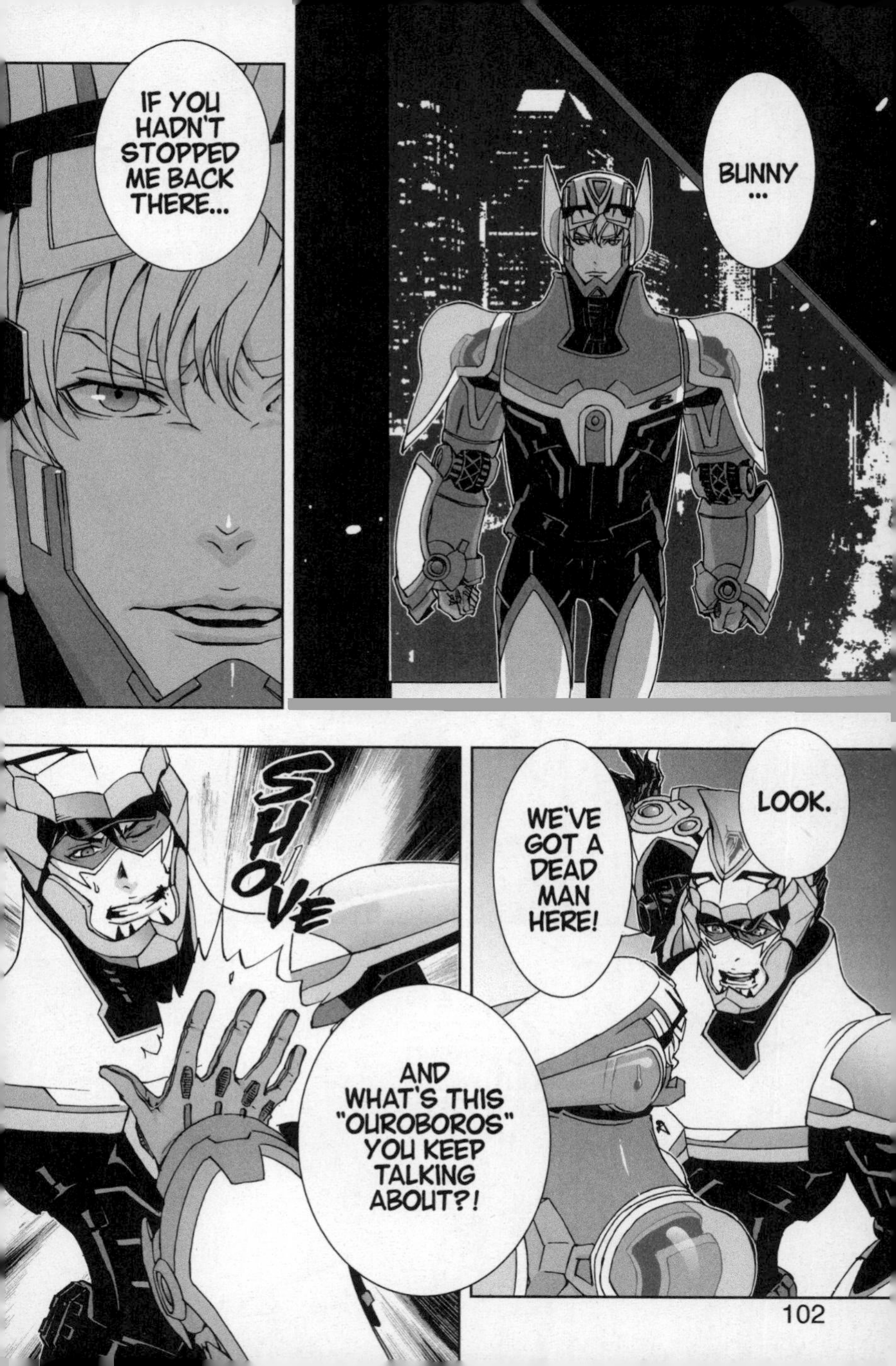
BUNNY...
IF YOU HADN'T STOPPED ME BACK THERE...
LOOK.
WE'VE GOT A DEAD MAN HERE!
SHOVE
AND WHAT'S THIS "OUROBOROS" YOU KEEP TALKING ABOUT?!

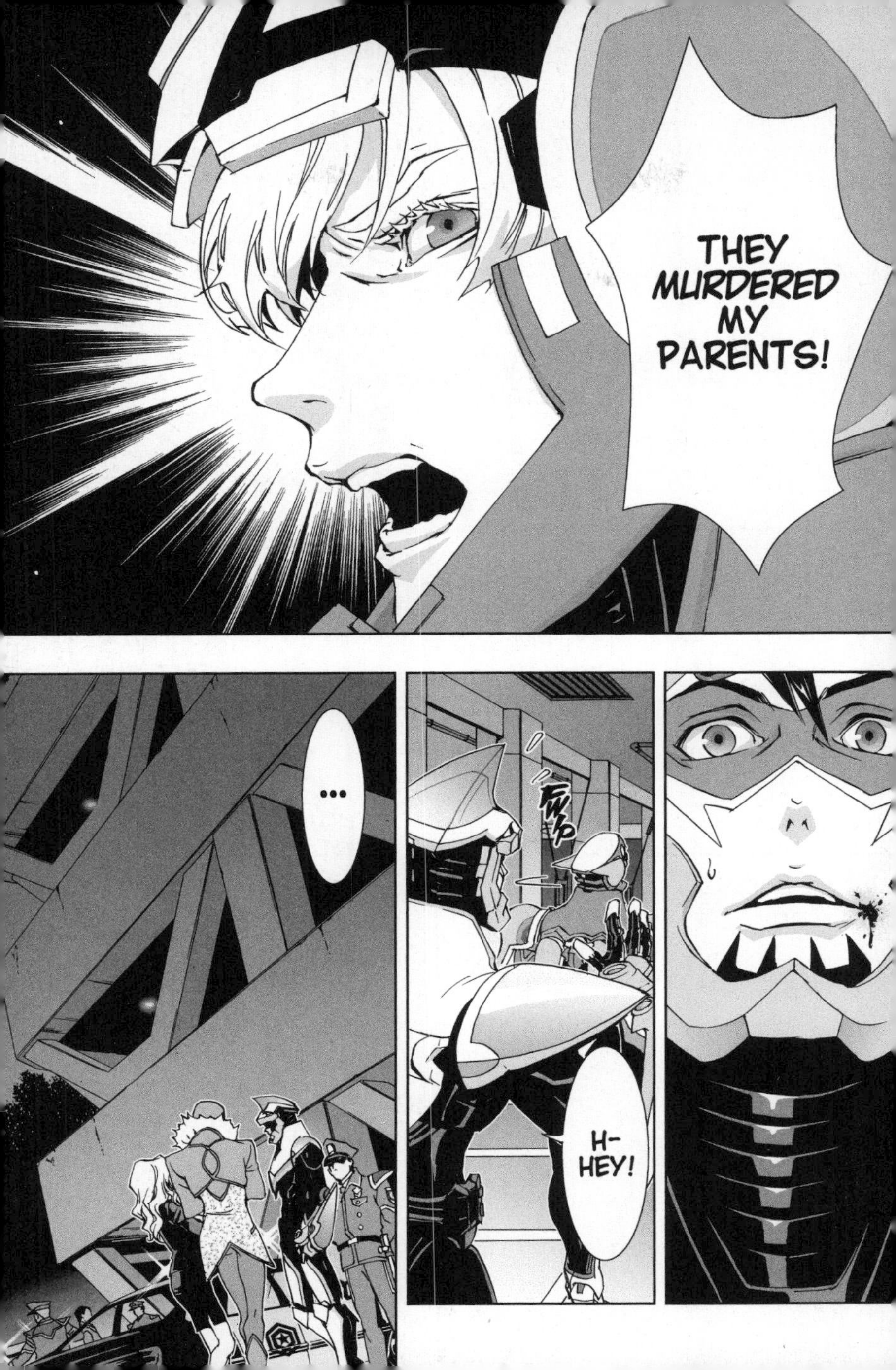
THEY MURDERED MY PARENTS!
FWIP
H- HEY!
...

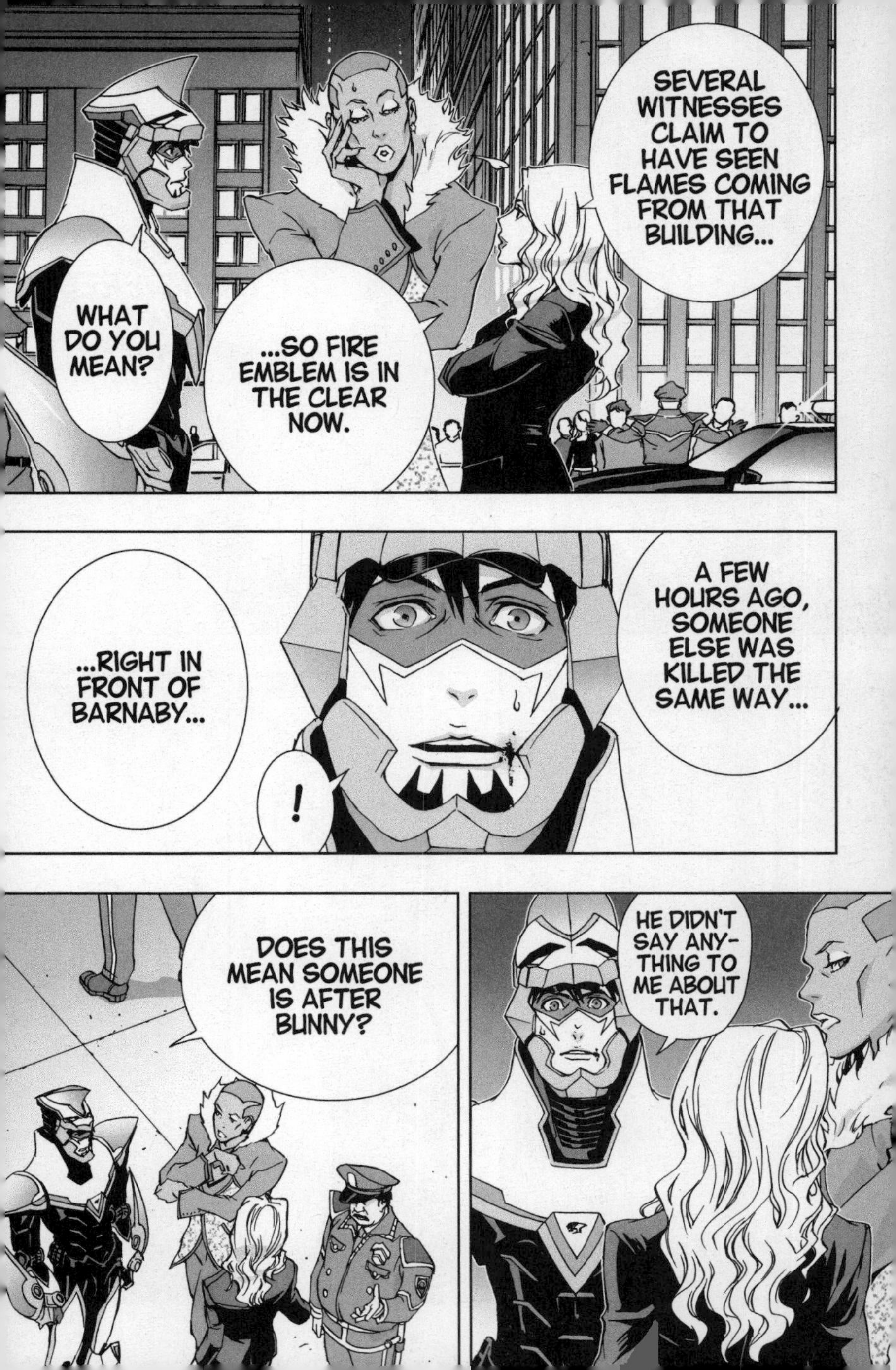
SEVERAL WITNESSES CLAIM TO HAVE SEEN FLAMES COMING FROM THAT BUILDING...
...SO FIRE EMBLEM IS IN THE CLEAR NOW.
WHAT DO YOU MEAN?
A FEW HOURS AGO, SOMEONE ELSE WAS KILLED THE SAME WAY...
...RIGHT IN FRONT OF BARNABY...
!
HE DIDN'T SAY ANY-THING TO ME ABOUT THAT.
DOES THIS MEAN SOMEONE IS AFTER BUNNY?

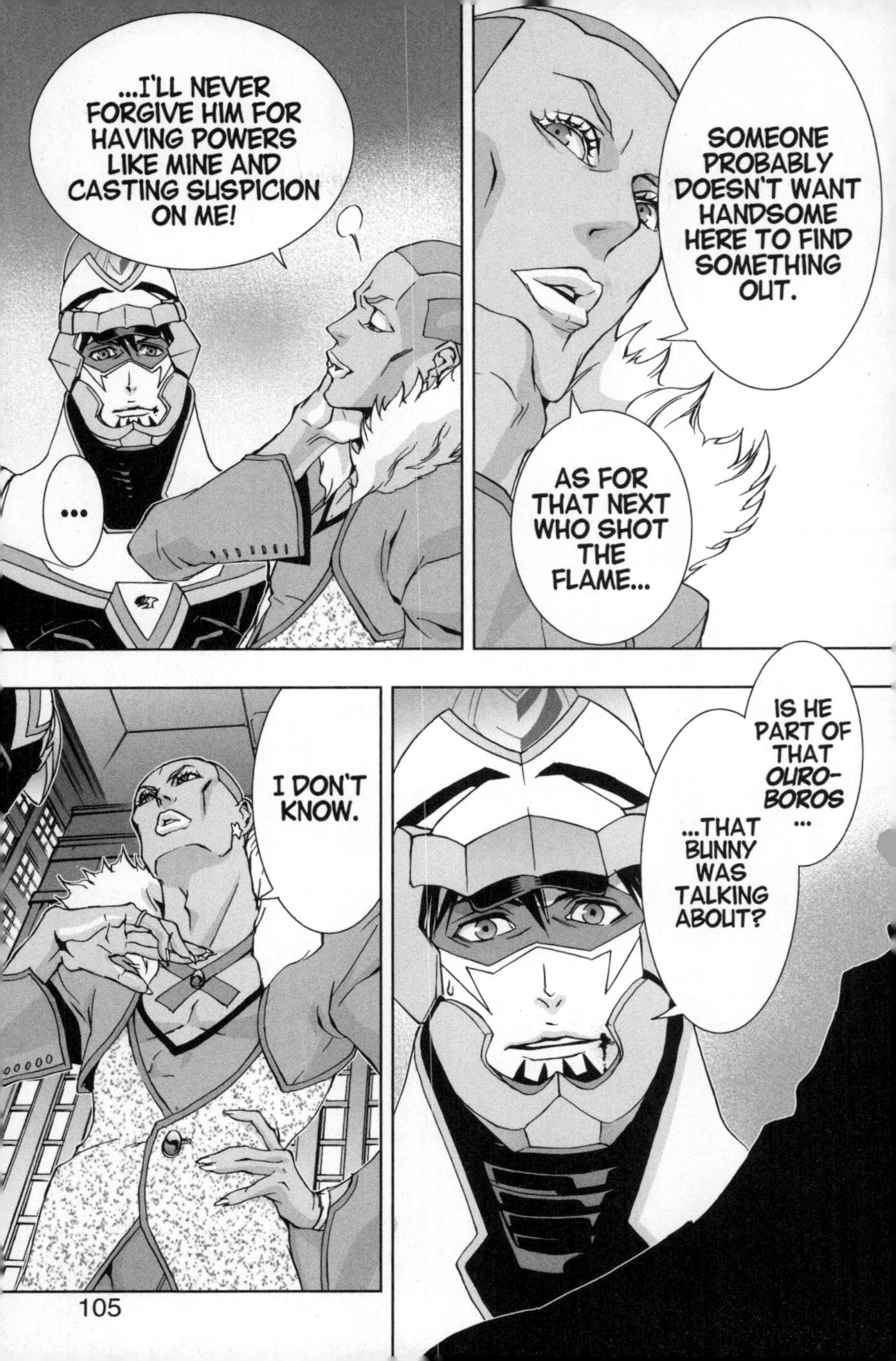
SOMEONE PROBABLY DOESN'T WANT HANDSOME HERE TO FIND SOMETHING OUT.
AS FOR THAT NEXT WHO SHOT THE FLAME...
...I'LL NEVER FORGIVE HIM FOR HAVING POWERS LIKE MINE AND CASTING SUSPICION ON ME!
...
IS HE PART OF THAT OURO-BOROS ...
...THAT BUNNY WAS TALKING ABOUT?
I DON'T KNOW.

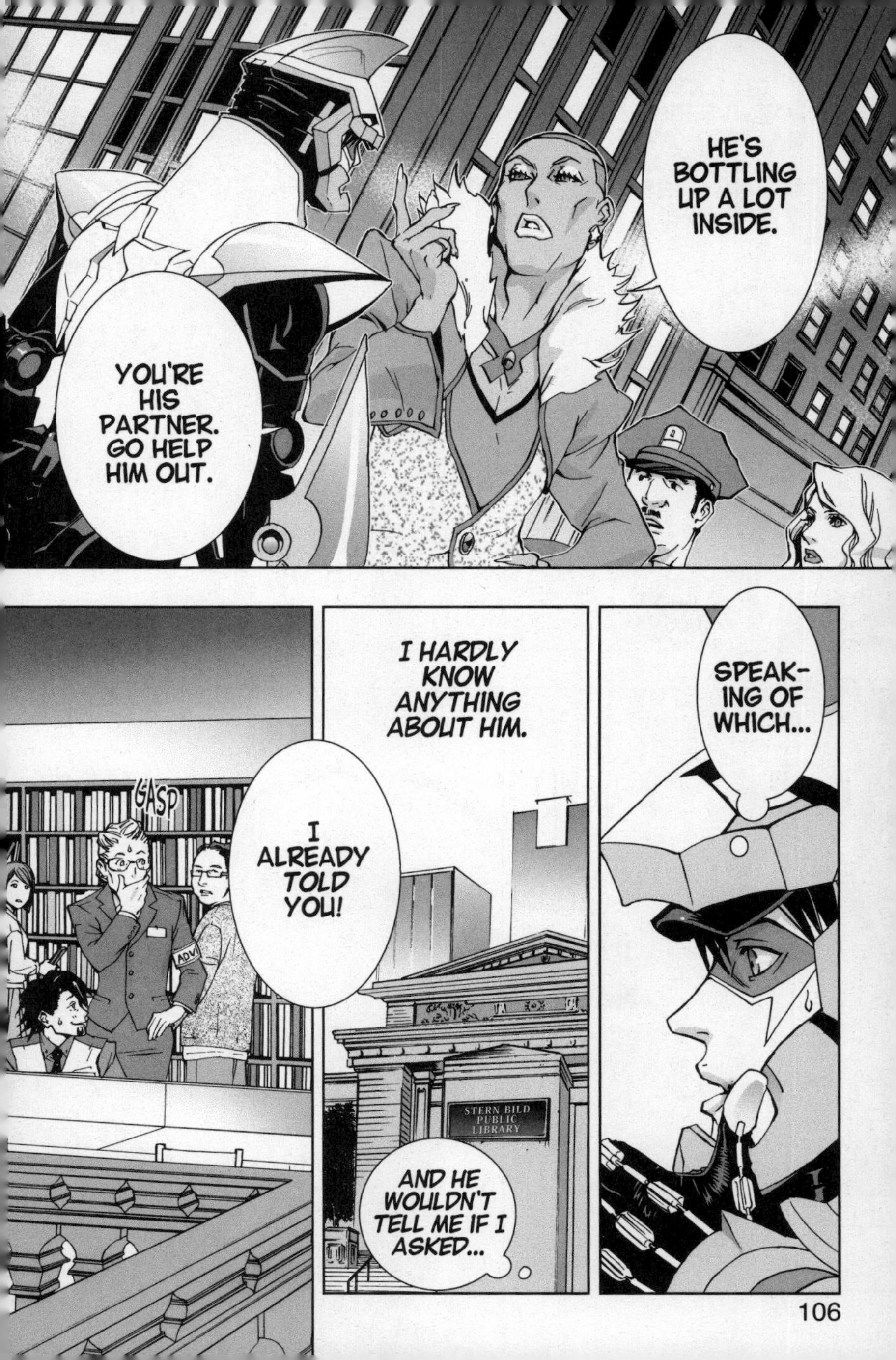
HE'S BOTTLING UP A LOT INSIDE.
YOU'RE HIS PARTNER. GO HELP HIM OUT.
SPEAK-ING OF WHICH...
I HARDLY KNOW ANYTHING ABOUT HIM.
I ALREADY TOLD YOU!
STERN BILD PUBLIC LIBRARY
AND HE WOULDN'T TELL ME IF I ASKED...
GASP
ADV

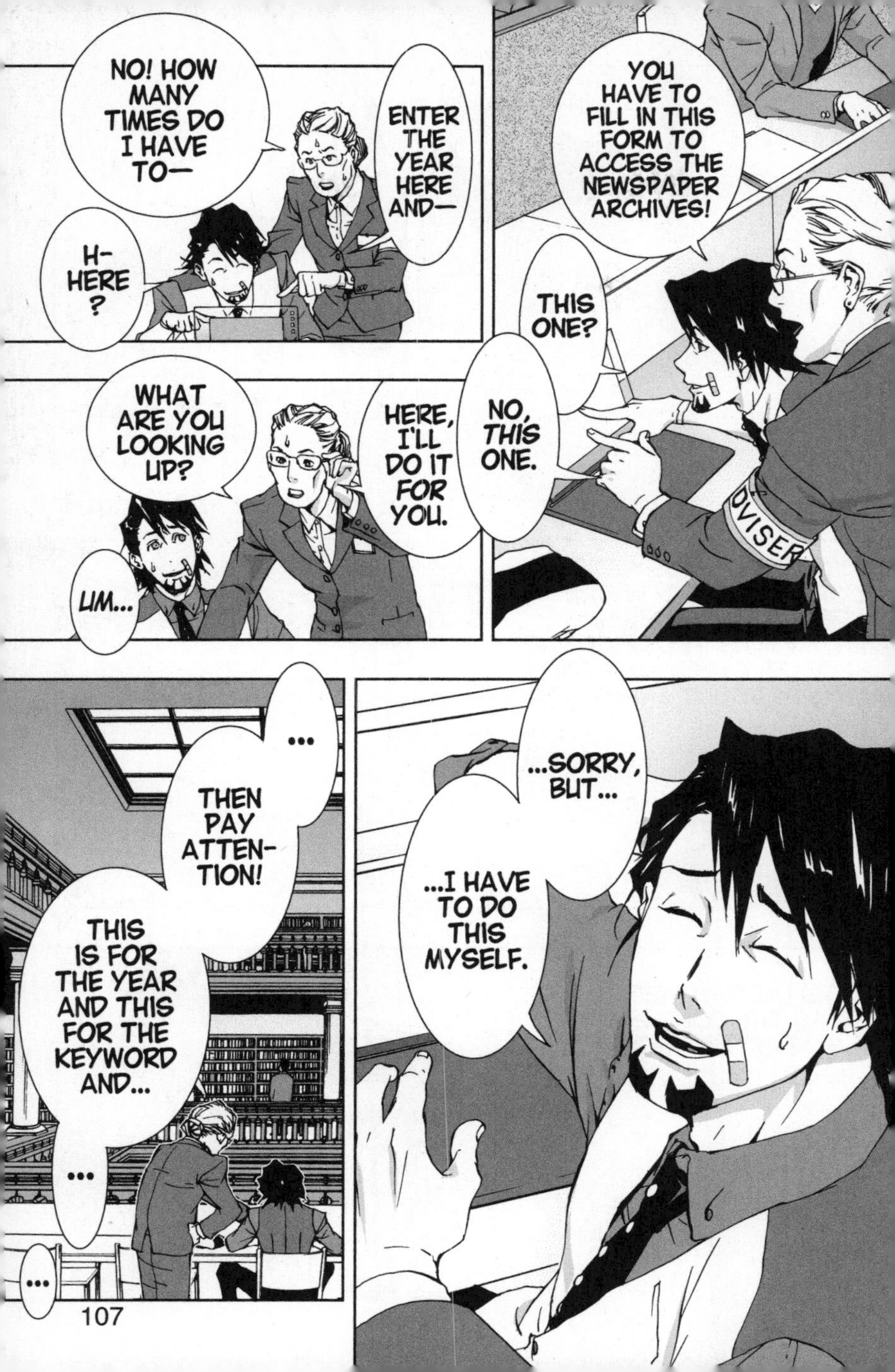
YOU HAVE TO FILL IN THIS FORM TO ACCESS THE NEWSPAPER ARCHIVES!
THIS ONE?
NO, THIS ONE.
DVISER
ENTER THE YEAR HERE AND—
NO! HOW MANY TIMES DO I HAVE TO—
H-HERE?
HERE, I'LL DO IT FOR YOU.
WHAT ARE YOU LOOKING UP?
UM...
...SORRY, BUT...
...I HAVE TO DO THIS MYSELF.
...
THEN PAY ATTEN-TION!
THIS IS FOR THE YEAR AND THIS FOR THE KEYWORD AND...
...
...

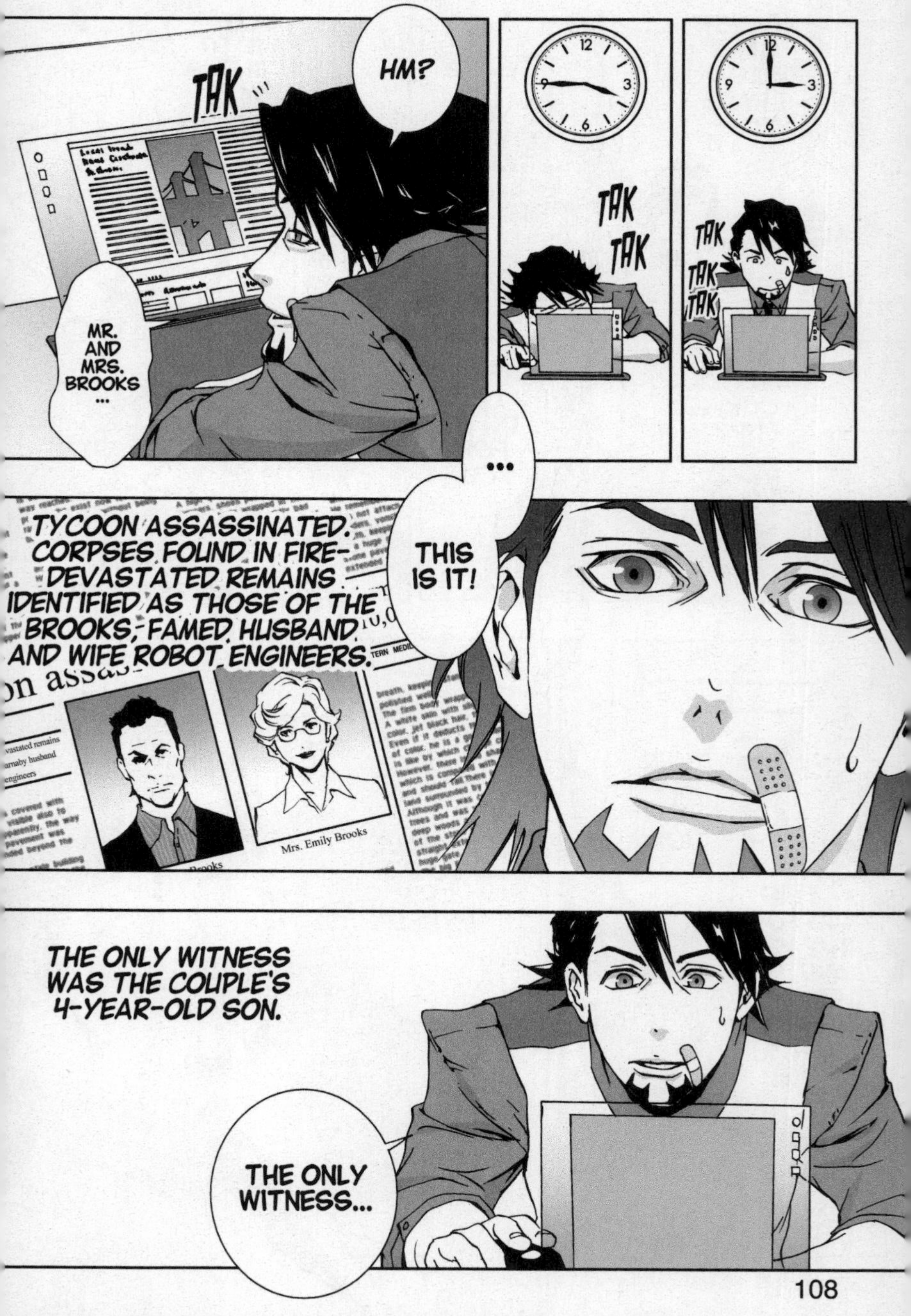

TAK TAK TAK
TAK TAK
TAK
HM?
MR. AND MRS. BROOKS...
...
THIS IS IT!
TYCOON ASSASSINATED. CORPSES FOUND IN FIRE-DEVASTATED REMAINS IDENTIFIED AS THOSE OF THE BROOKS, FAMED HUSBAND AND WIFE ROBOT ENGINEERS.
Mrs. Emily Brooks
THE ONLY WITNESS WAS THE COUPLE'S 4-YEAR-OLD SON.
THE ONLY WITNESS...

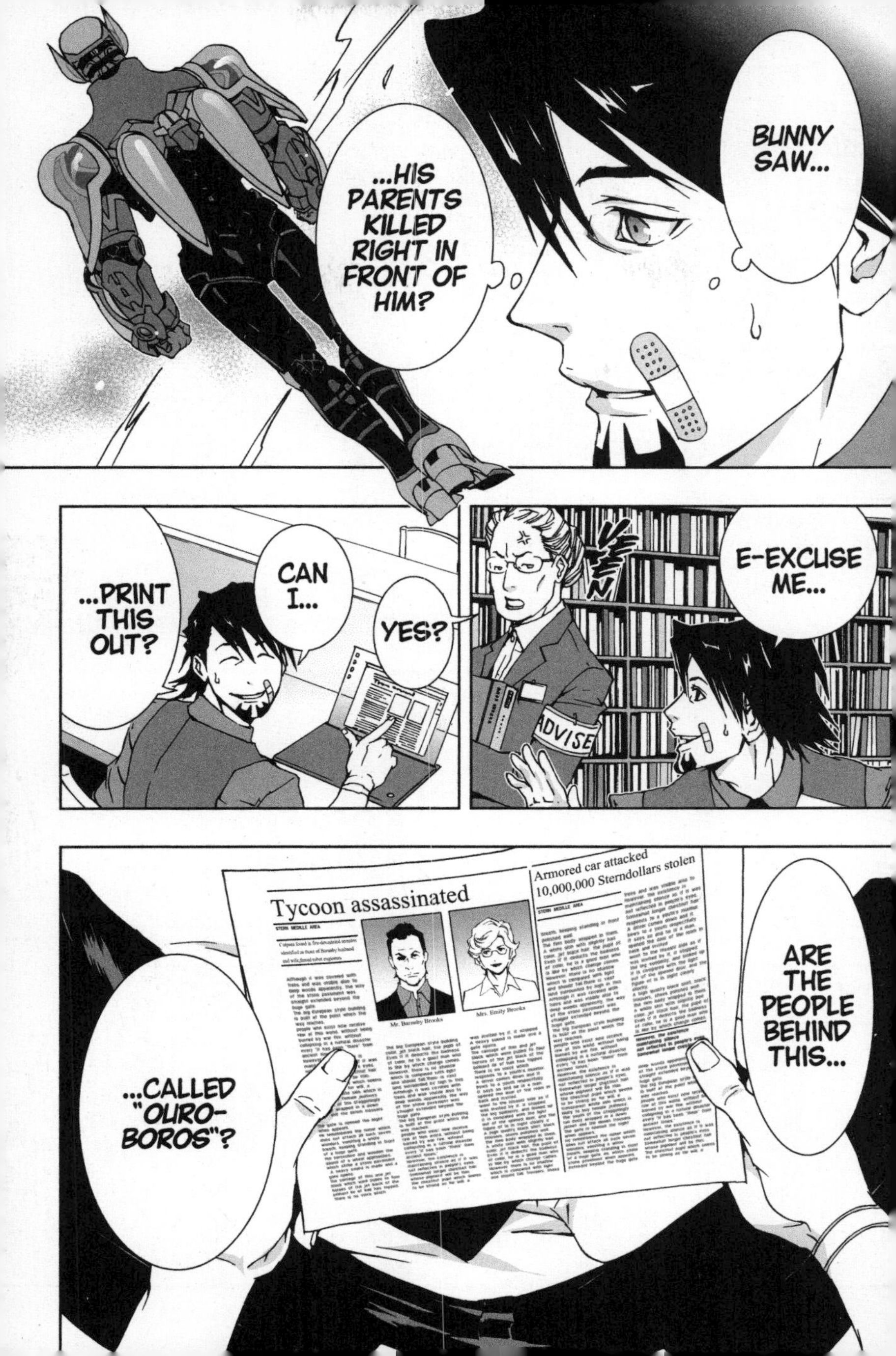
BUNNY SAW...
...HIS PARENTS KILLED RIGHT IN FRONT OF HIM?
E-EXCUSE ME...
VEIN
ADVISE
YES?
CAN I...
...PRINT THIS OUT?
ARE THE PEOPLE BEHIND THIS...
...CALLED "OURO-BOROS"?
Armored car attacked
10,000,000 Sterndollars stolen
Tycoon assassinated
Mr. Barnaby Brooks
Mrs. Emily Brooks

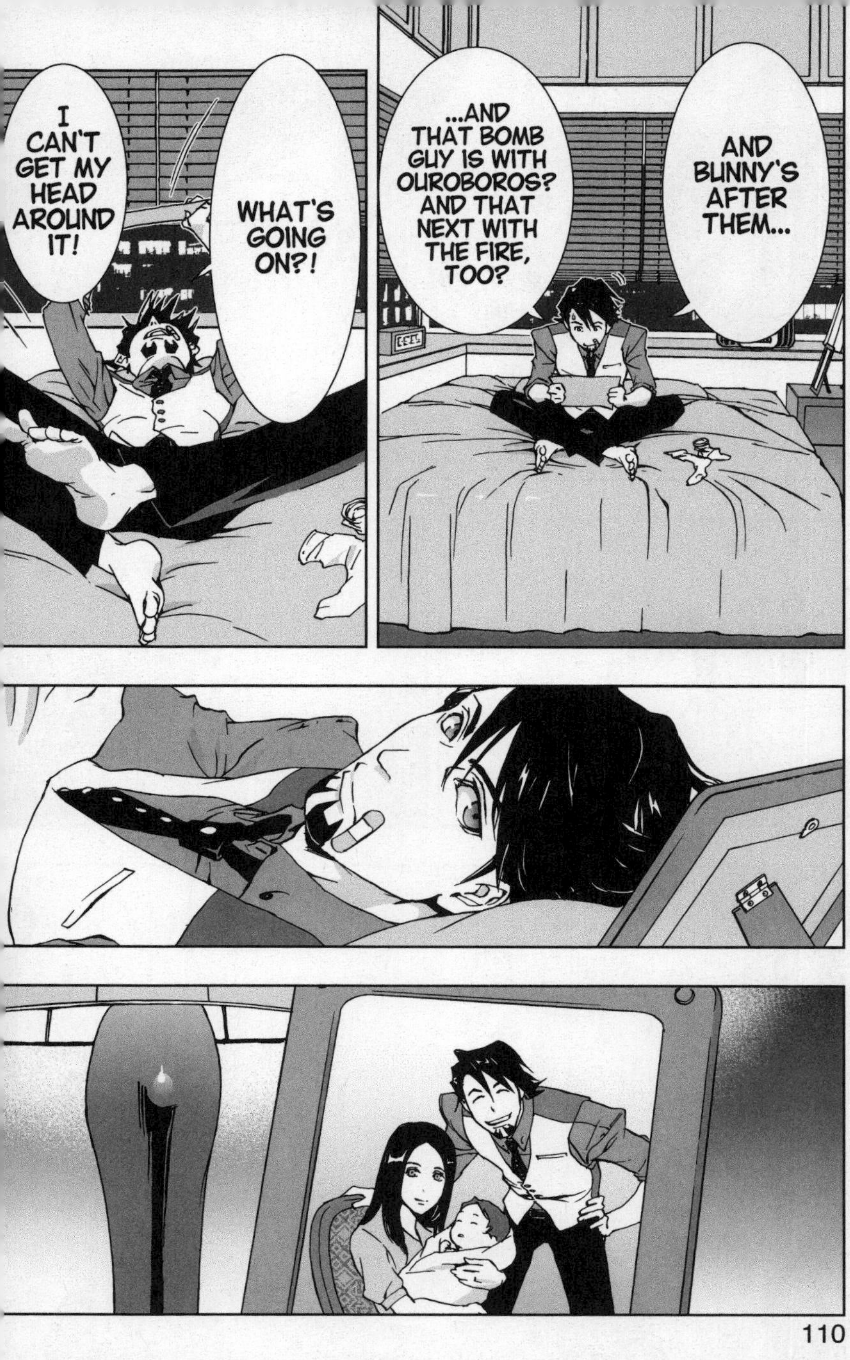
AND BUNNY'S AFTER THEM...
...AND THAT BOMB GUY IS WITH OUROBOROS? AND THAT NEXT WITH THE FIRE, TOO?
WHAT'S GOING ON?!
I CAN'T GET MY HEAD AROUND IT!

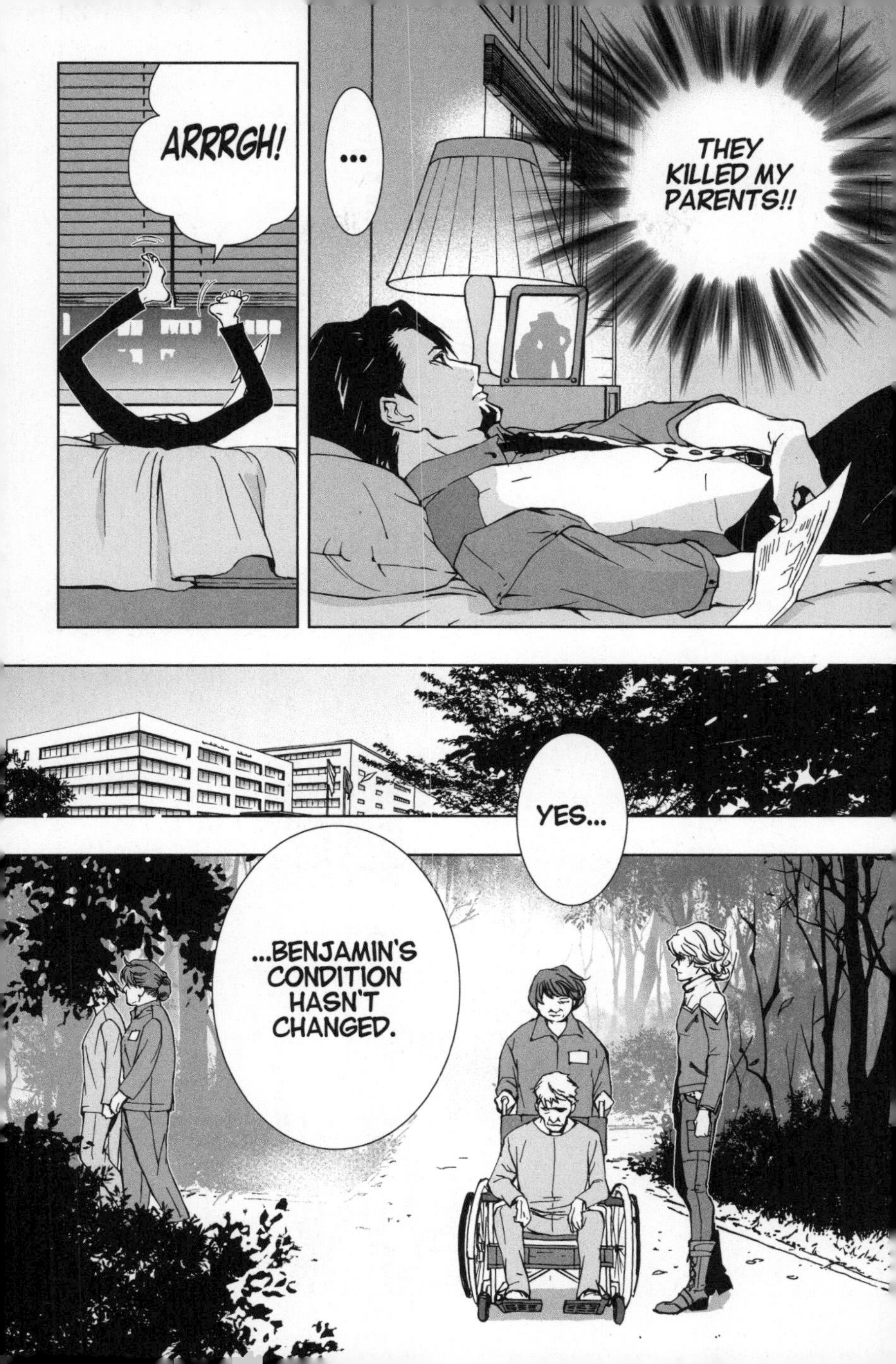
THEY KILLED MY PARENTS!!
...
ARRRGH!
YES...
...BENJAMIN'S CONDITION HASN'T CHANGED.

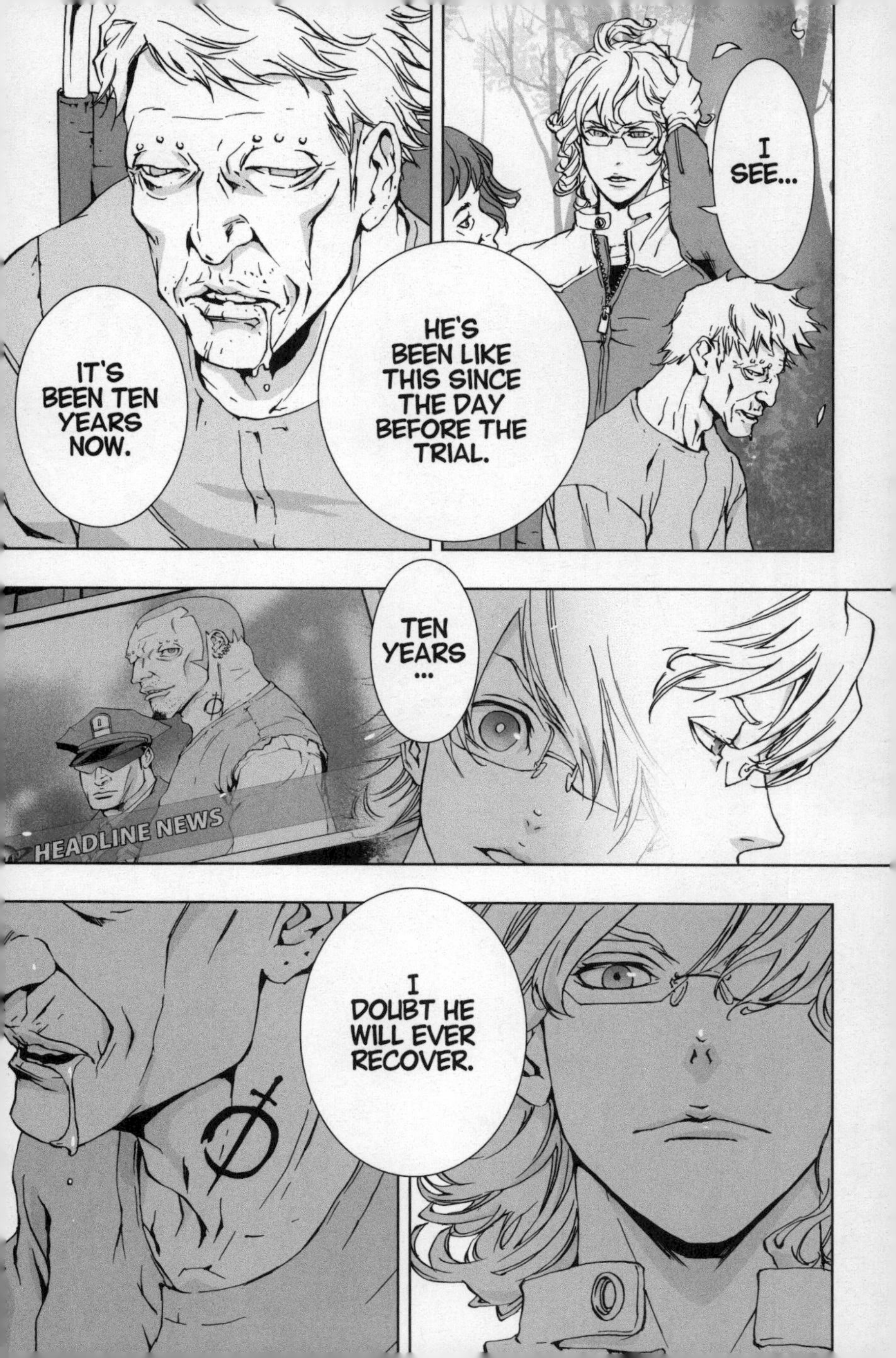
I SEE...
HE'S BEEN LIKE THIS SINCE THE DAY BEFORE THE TRIAL.
IT'S BEEN TEN YEARS NOW.
TEN YEARS ...
HEADLINE NEWS
I DOUBT HE WILL EVER RECOVER.

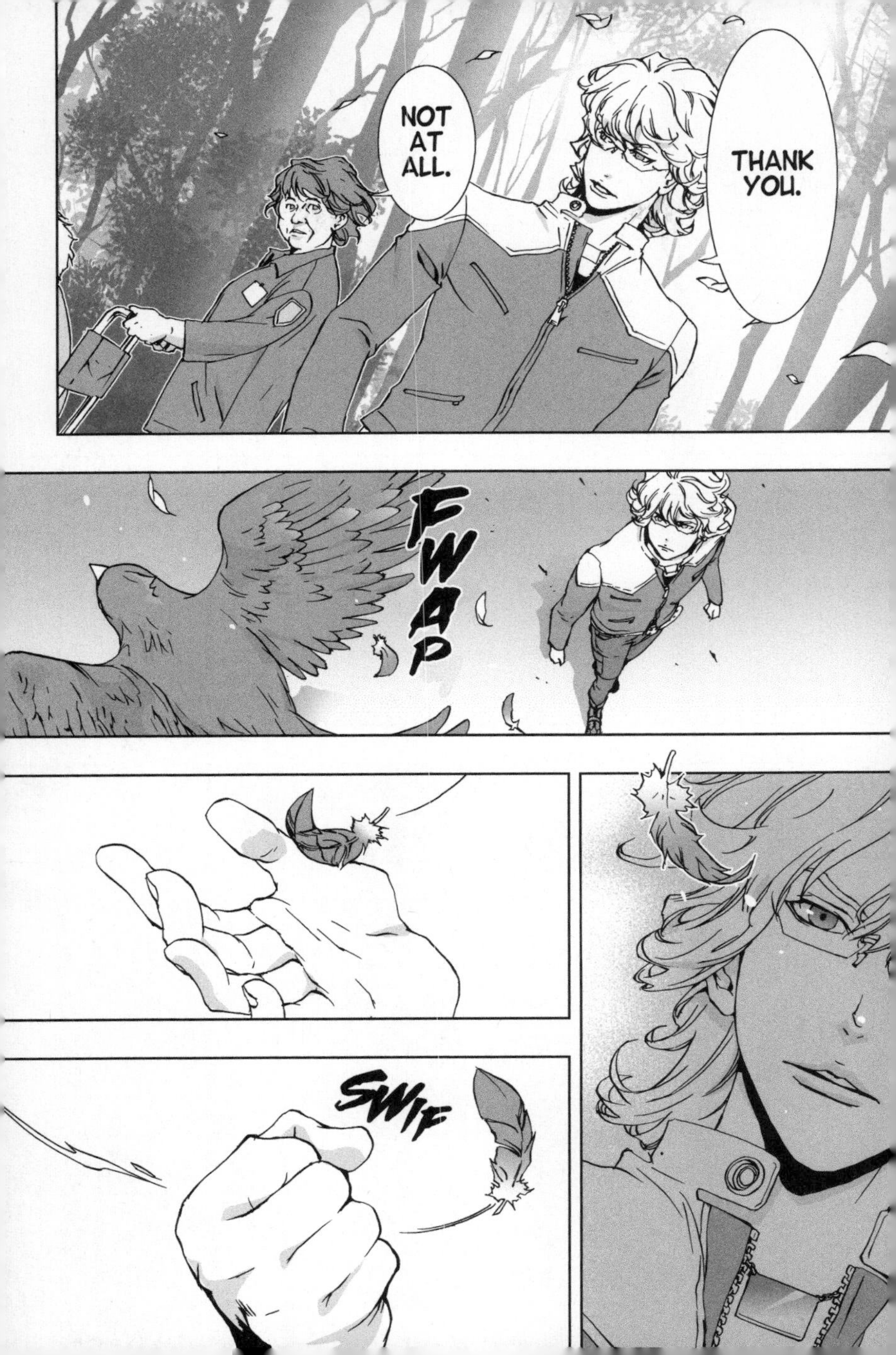
THANK YOU.
NOT AT ALL.
FWAP
SWIF

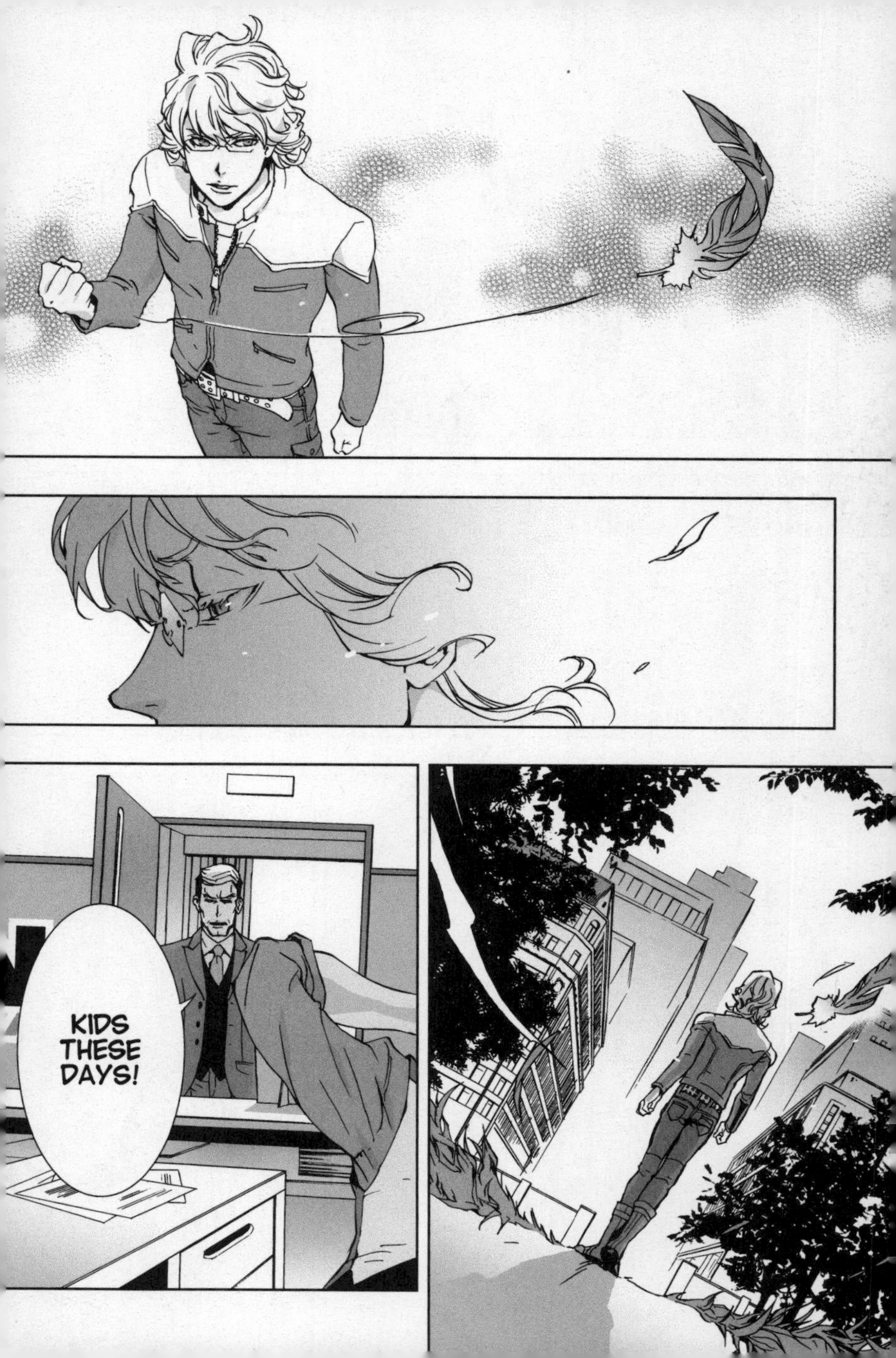
KIDS THESE DAYS!

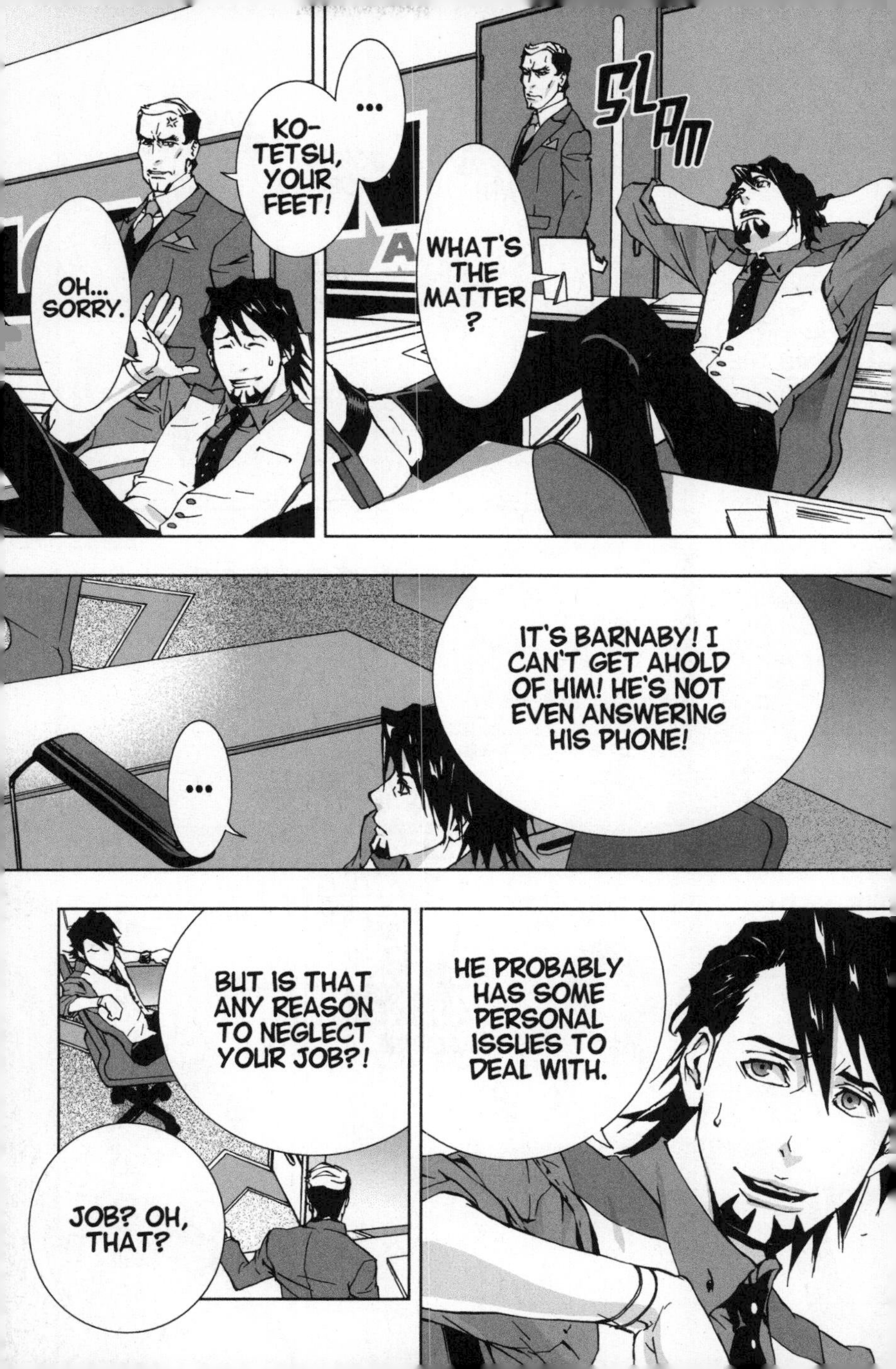
SLAM
WHAT'S THE MATTER?
...
KO-TETSU, YOUR FEET!
OH... SORRY.
IT'S BARNABY! I CAN'T GET AHOLD OF HIM! HE'S NOT EVEN ANSWERING HIS PHONE!
...
HE PROBABLY HAS SOME PERSONAL ISSUES TO DEAL WITH.
BUT IS THAT ANY REASON TO NEGLECT YOUR JOB?!
JOB? OH, THAT?

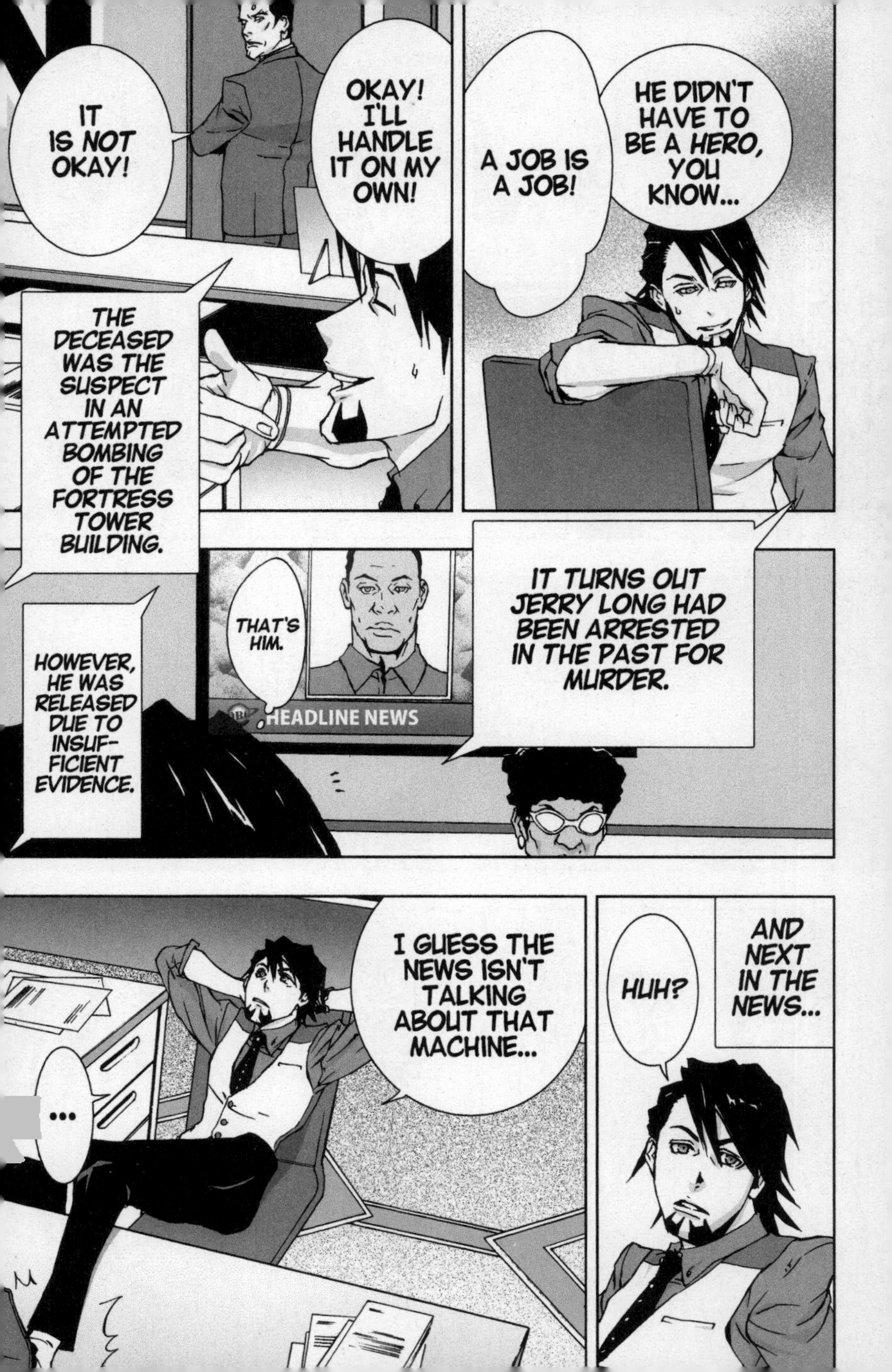
HE DIDN'T HAVE TO BE A HERO, YOU KNOW...
A JOB IS A JOB!
OKAY! I'LL HANDLE IT ON MY OWN!
IT IS NOT OKAY!
IT TURNS OUT JERRY LONG HAD BEEN ARRESTED IN THE PAST FOR MURDER.
THE DECEASED WAS THE SUSPECT IN AN ATTEMPTED BOMBING OF THE FORTRESS TOWER BUILDING.
HEADLINE NEWS
THAT'S HIM.
HOWEVER, HE WAS RELEASED DUE TO INSUF-FICIENT EVIDENCE.
AND NEXT IN THE NEWS...
HUH?
I GUESS THE NEWS ISN'T TALKING ABOUT THAT MACHINE...
...

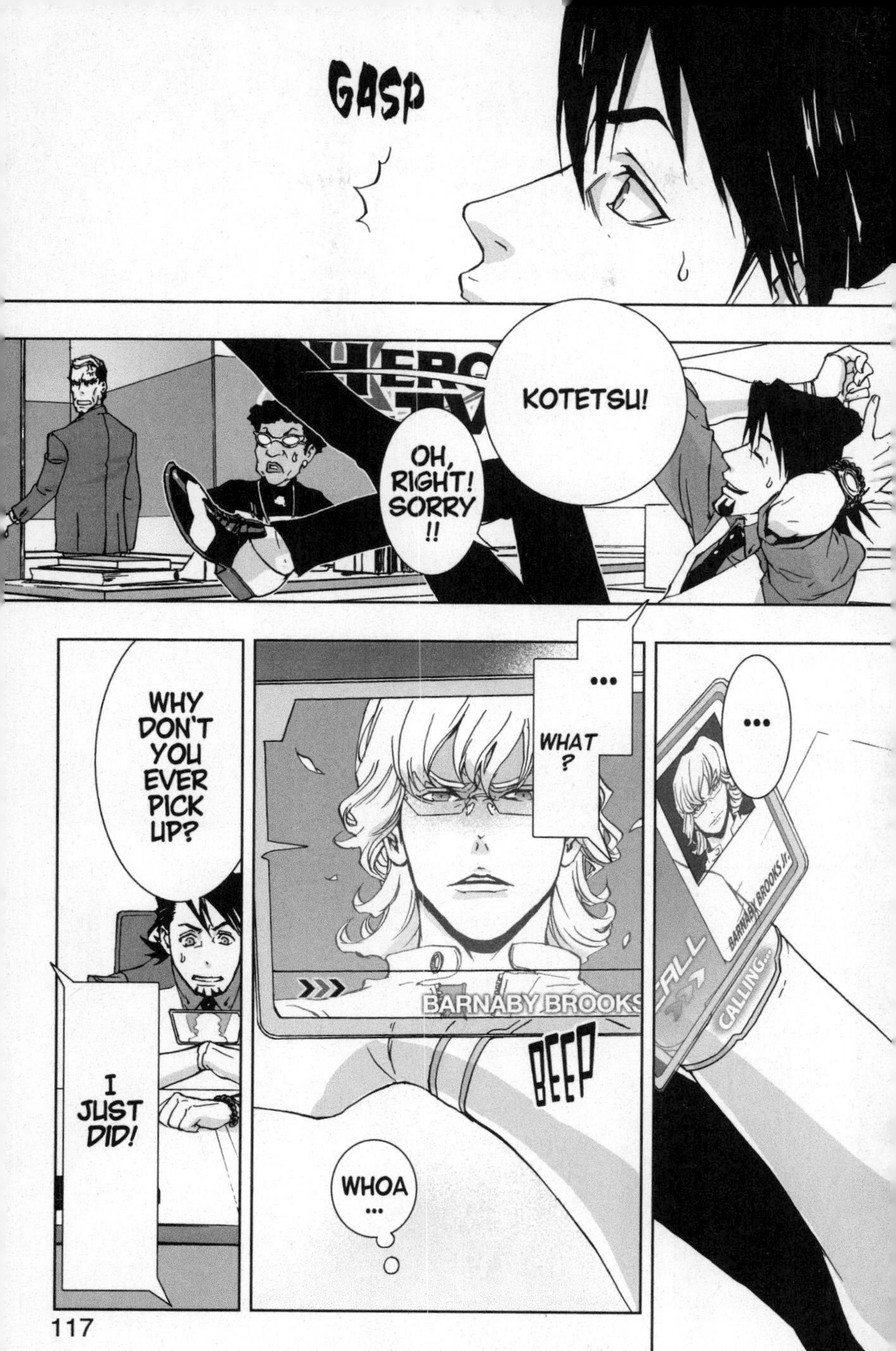
GASP
KOTETSU!
OH, RIGHT! SORRY!!
...
BARNABY BROOKS Jr.
CALL
CALLING...
...
WHAT?
BARNABY BROOKS
BEEP
WHOA...
WHY DON'T YOU EVER PICK UP?
I JUST DID!

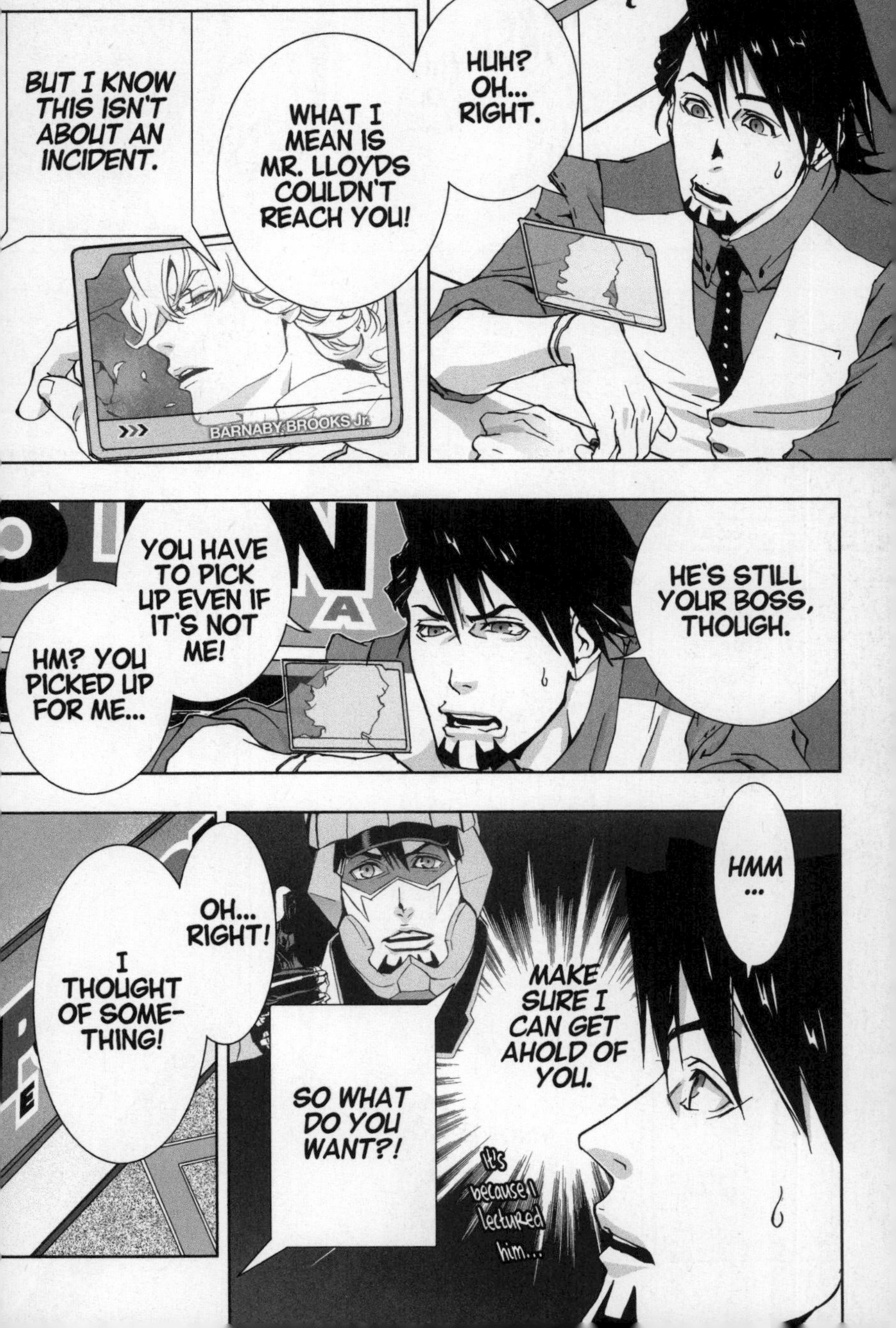

HUH? OH... RIGHT.
WHAT I MEAN IS MR. LLOYDS COULDN'T REACH YOU!
BUT I KNOW THIS ISN'T ABOUT AN INCIDENT.
BARNABY BROOKS Jr.
HE'S STILL YOUR BOSS, THOUGH.
YOU HAVE TO PICK UP EVEN IF IT'S NOT ME!
HM? YOU PICKED UP FOR ME...
HMM ...
MAKE SURE I CAN GET AHOLD OF YOU.
It's because I lectured him...
SO WHAT DO YOU WANT?!
OH... RIGHT!
I THOUGHT OF SOME-THING!

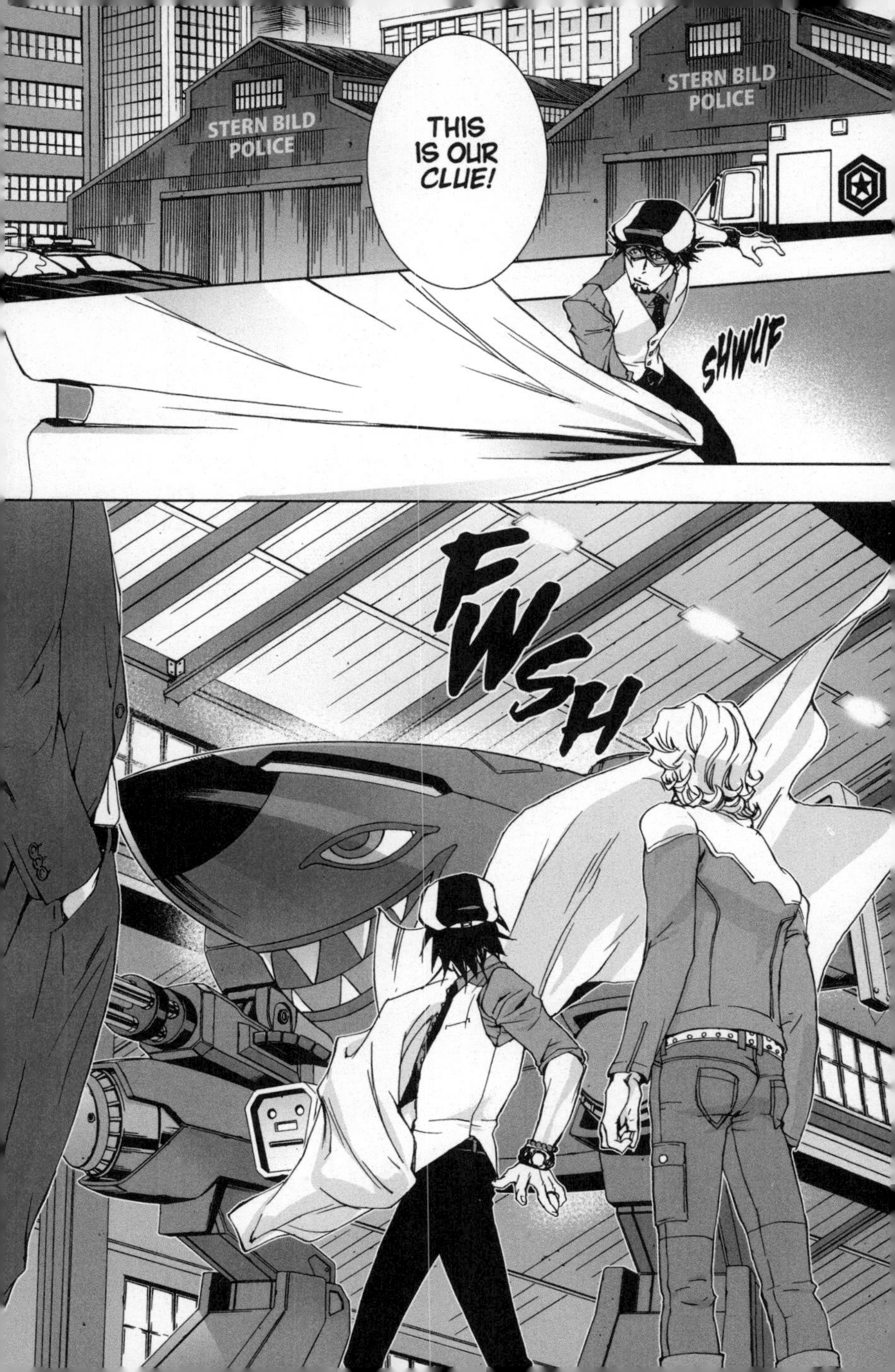
STERN BILD POLICE
THIS IS OUR CLUE!
STERN BILD POLICE
SHWUF
FWSH

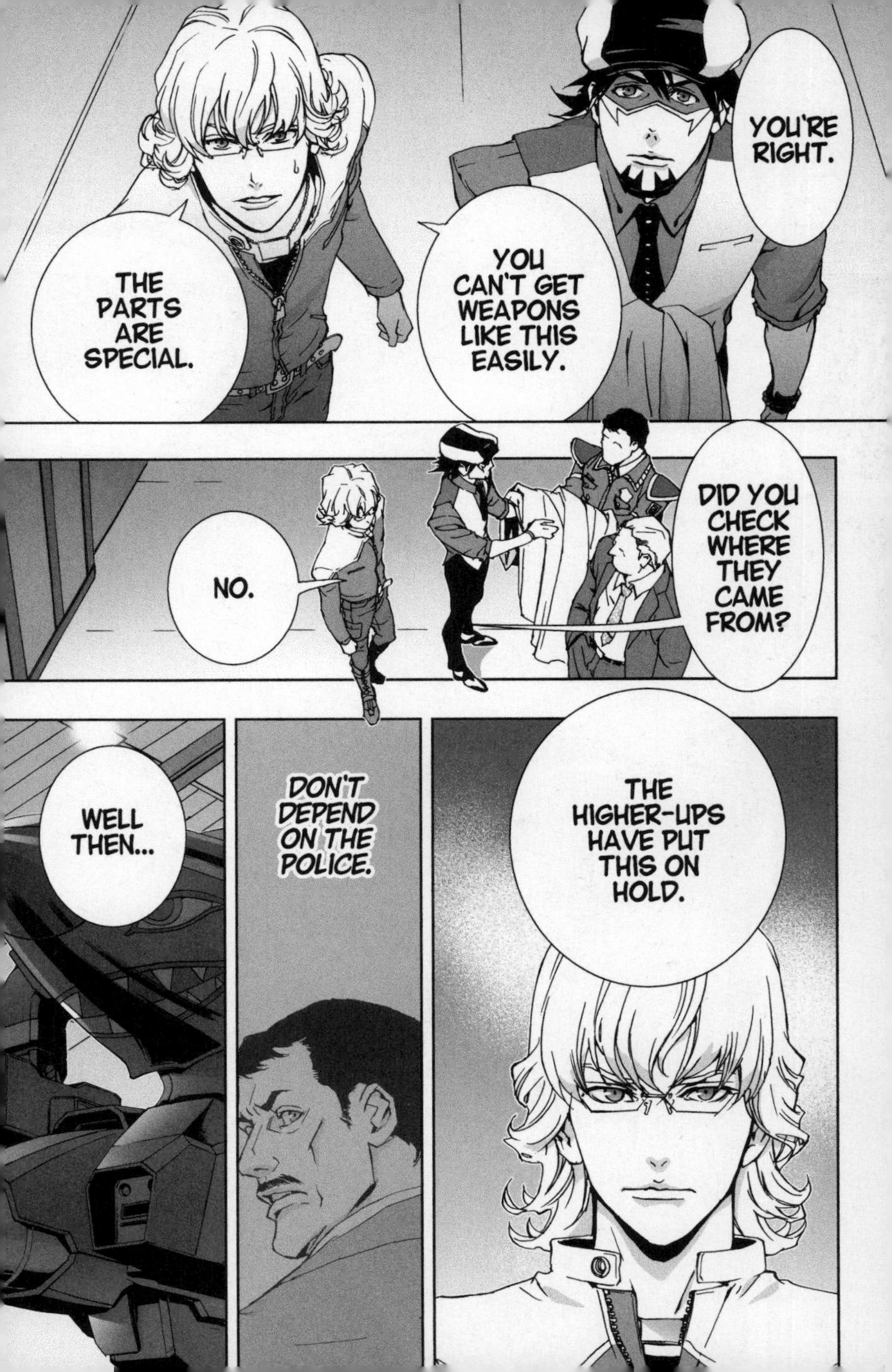
YOU'RE RIGHT.
YOU CAN'T GET WEAPONS LIKE THIS EASILY.
THE PARTS ARE SPECIAL.
DID YOU CHECK WHERE THEY CAME FROM?
NO.
THE HIGHER-UPS HAVE PUT THIS ON HOLD.
DON'T DEPEND ON THE POLICE.
WELL THEN...

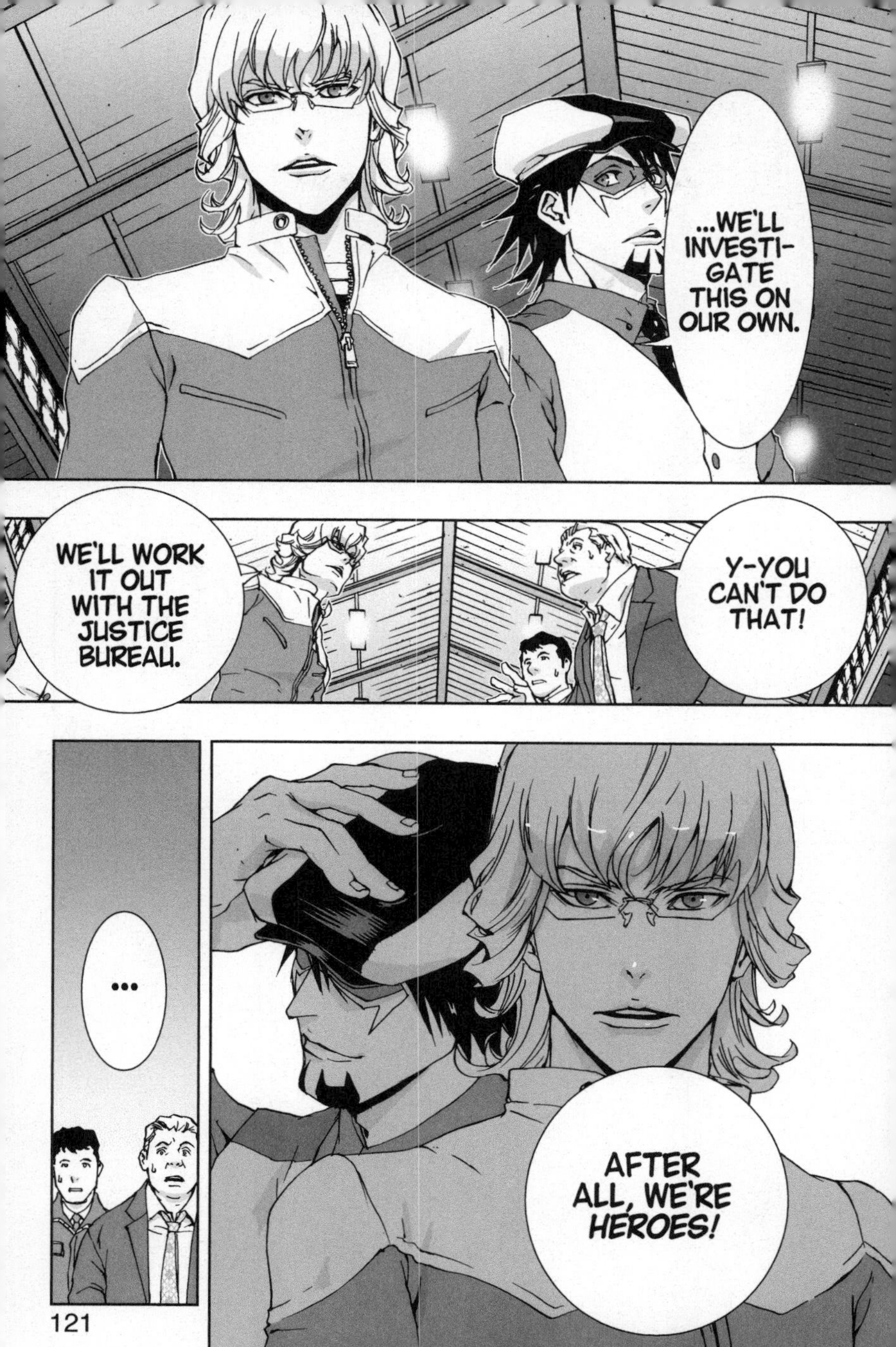
...WE'LL INVESTI-GATE THIS ON OUR OWN.
Y-YOU CAN'T DO THAT!
WE'LL WORK IT OUT WITH THE JUSTICE BUREAU.
AFTER ALL, WE'RE HEROES!
...

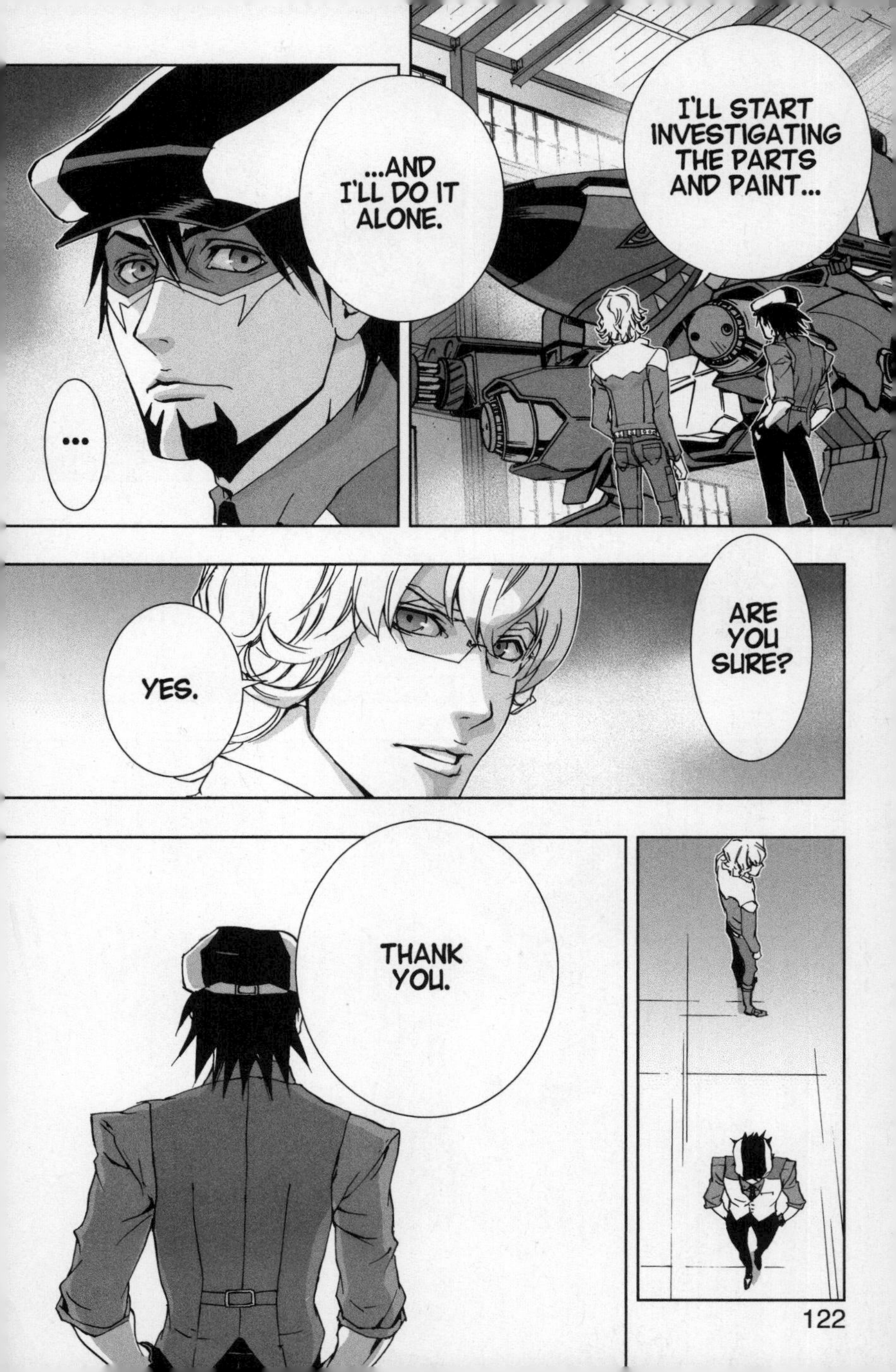
I'LL START INVESTIGATING THE PARTS AND PAINT...
...AND I'LL DO IT ALONE.
...
ARE YOU SURE?
YES.
THANK YOU.

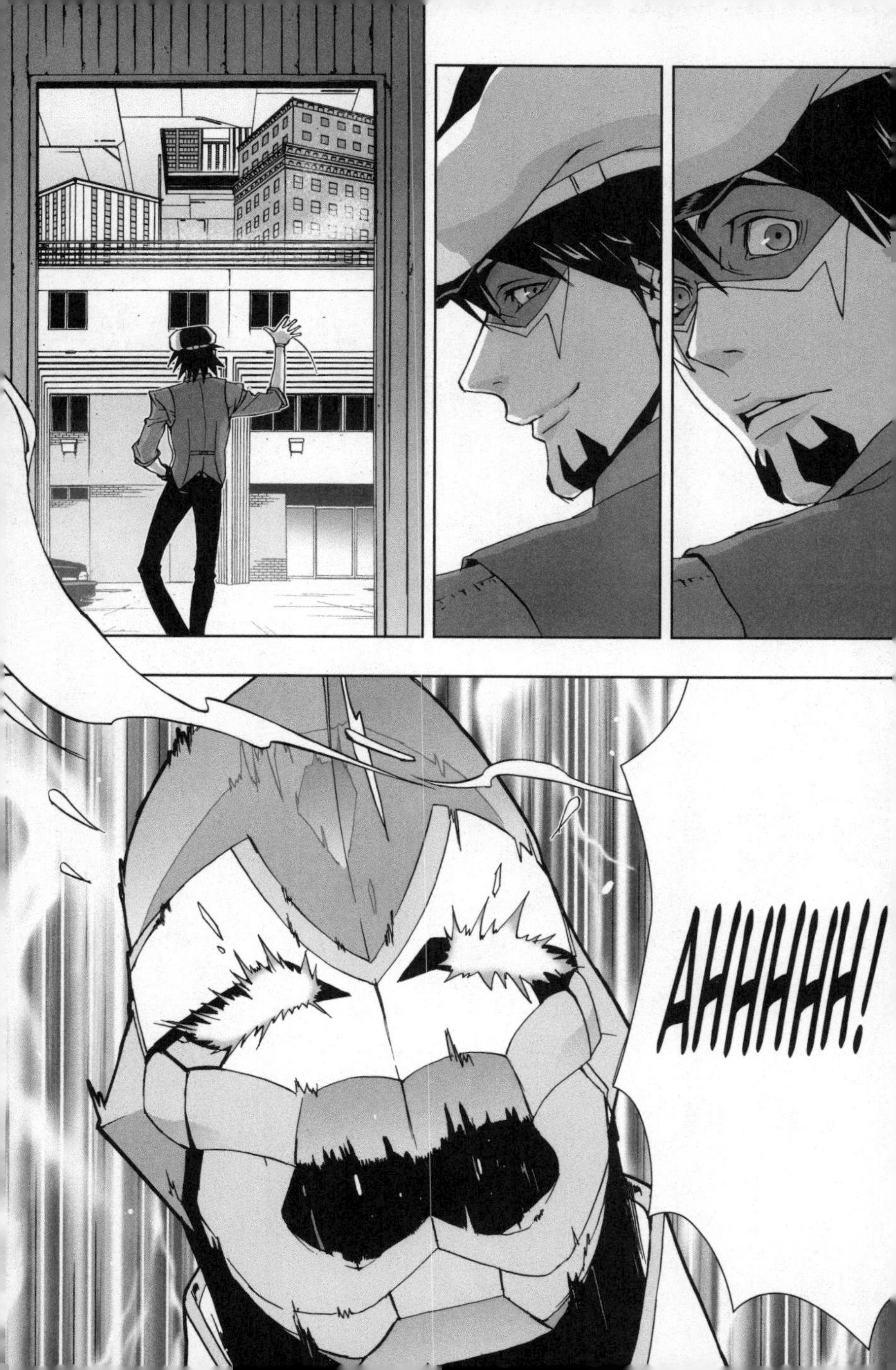
AHHHHH!

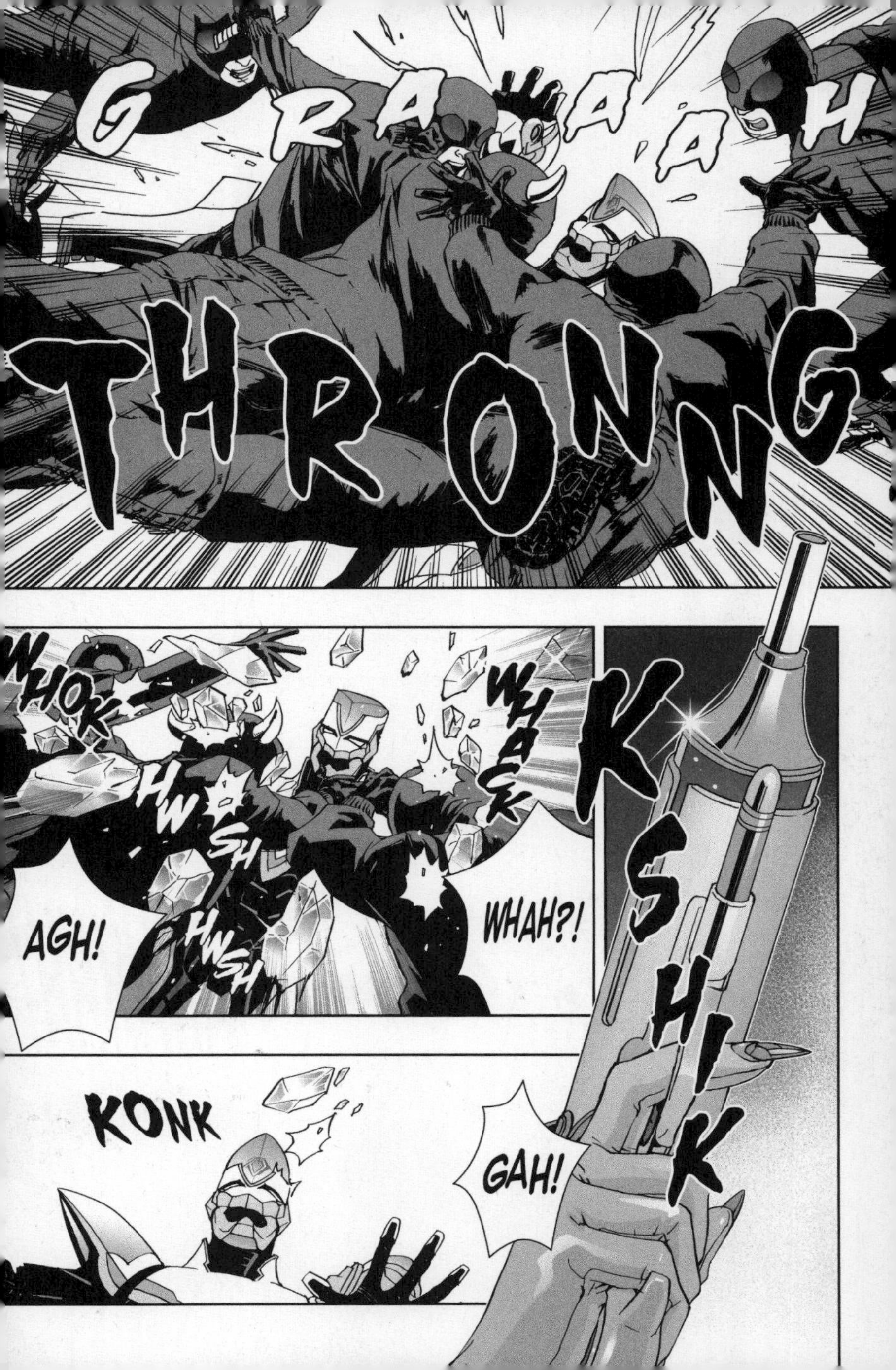
GRAAAH
THRONNG
KSHIK
WHACK
WHOK
HWSH
WHAH?!
HWSH
AGH!
GAH!
KONK

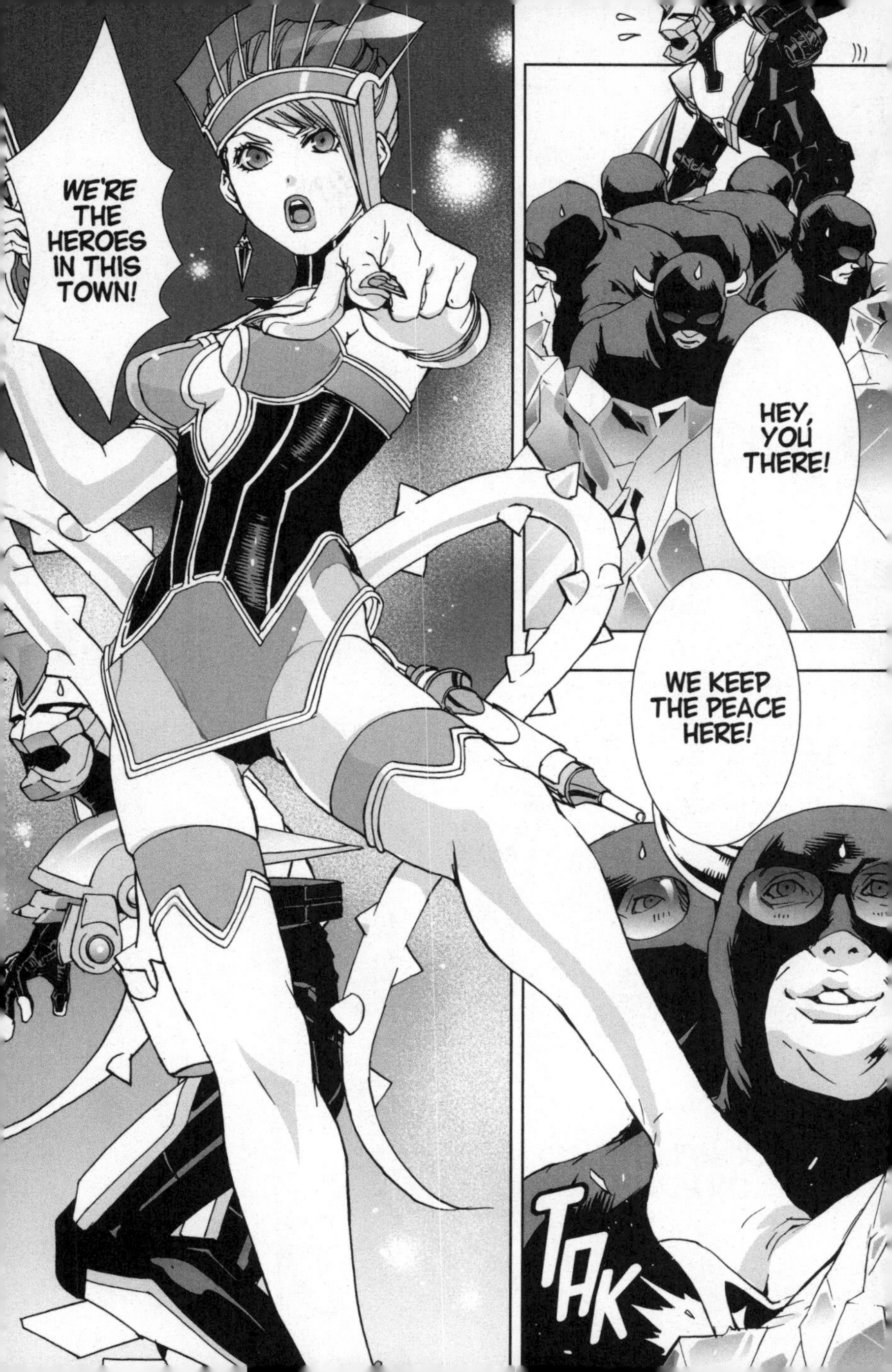
HEY, YOU THERE!
WE KEEP THE PEACE HERE!
TAK
WE'RE THE HEROES IN THIS TOWN!

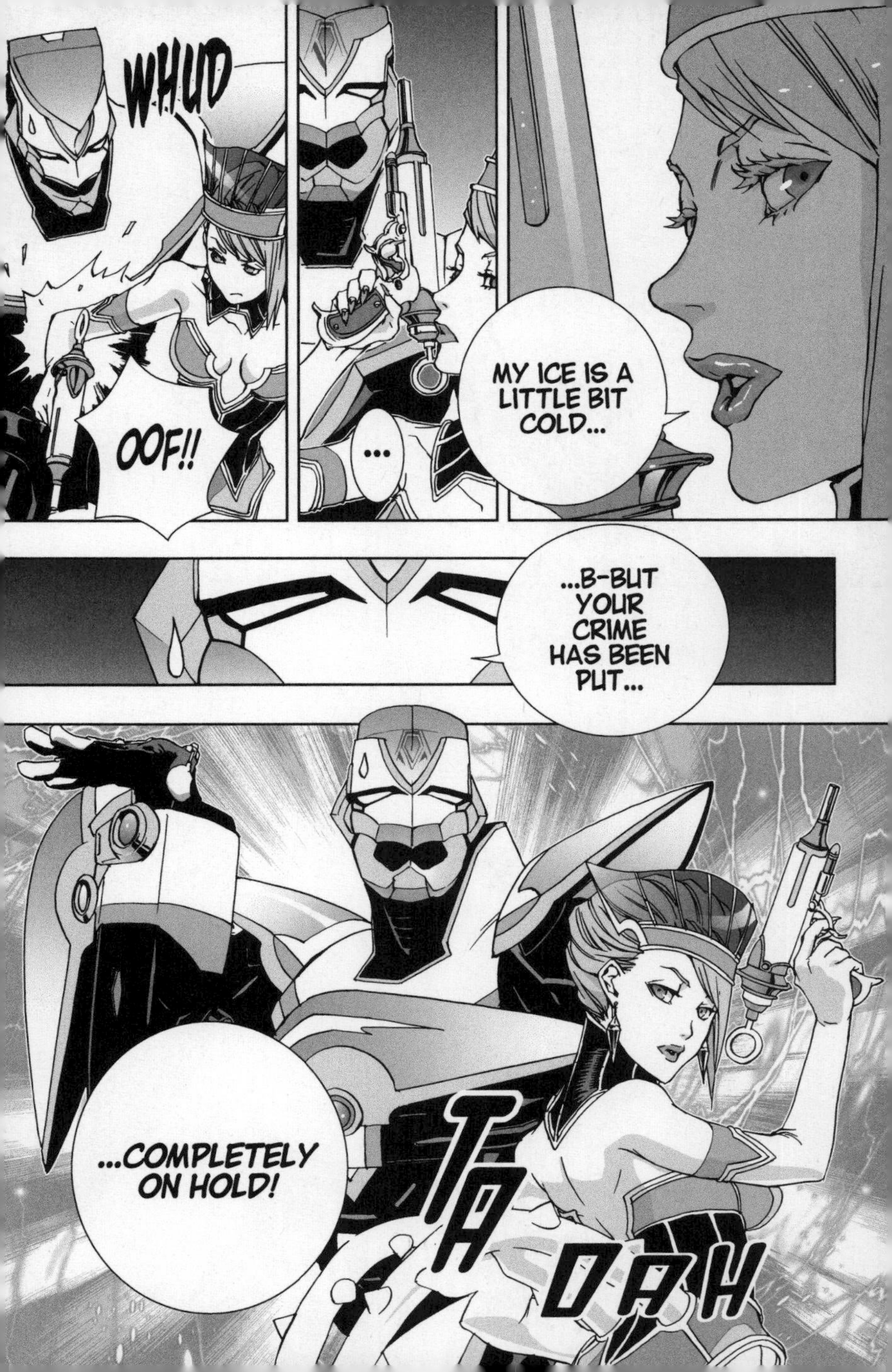
MY ICE IS A LITTLE BIT COLD...
...
WHUD
OOF!!
...B-BUT YOUR CRIME HAS BEEN PUT...
...COMPLETELY ON HOLD!
TA DAH

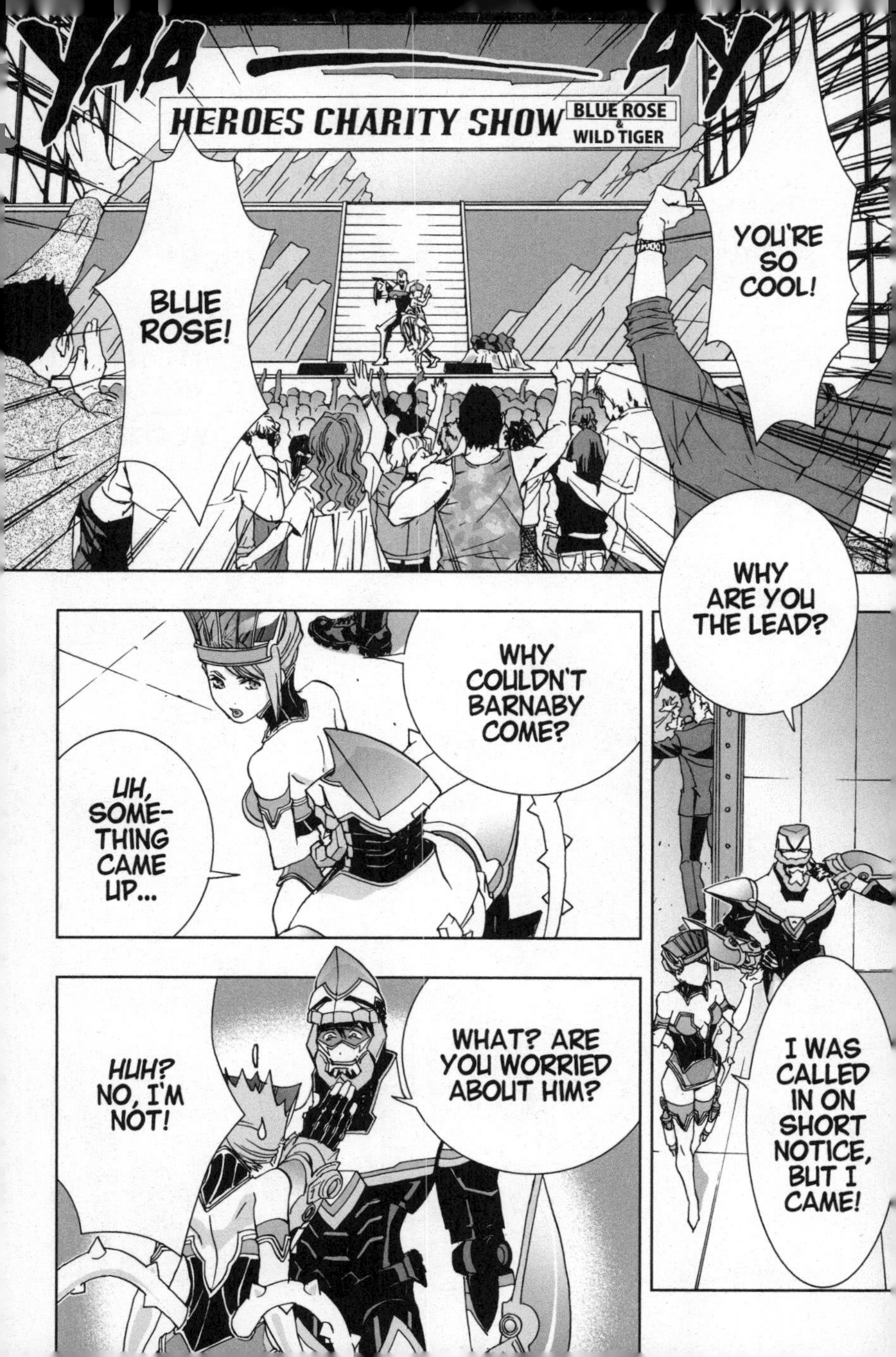
YAA——AY
HEROES CHARITY SHOW
BLUE ROSE & WILD TIGER
YOU'RE SO COOL!
BLUE ROSE!
WHY ARE YOU THE LEAD?
I WAS CALLED IN ON SHORT NOTICE, BUT I CAME!
WHY COULDN'T BARNABY COME?
UH, SOME-THING CAME UP...
WHAT? ARE YOU WORRIED ABOUT HIM?
HUH? NO, I'M NOT!

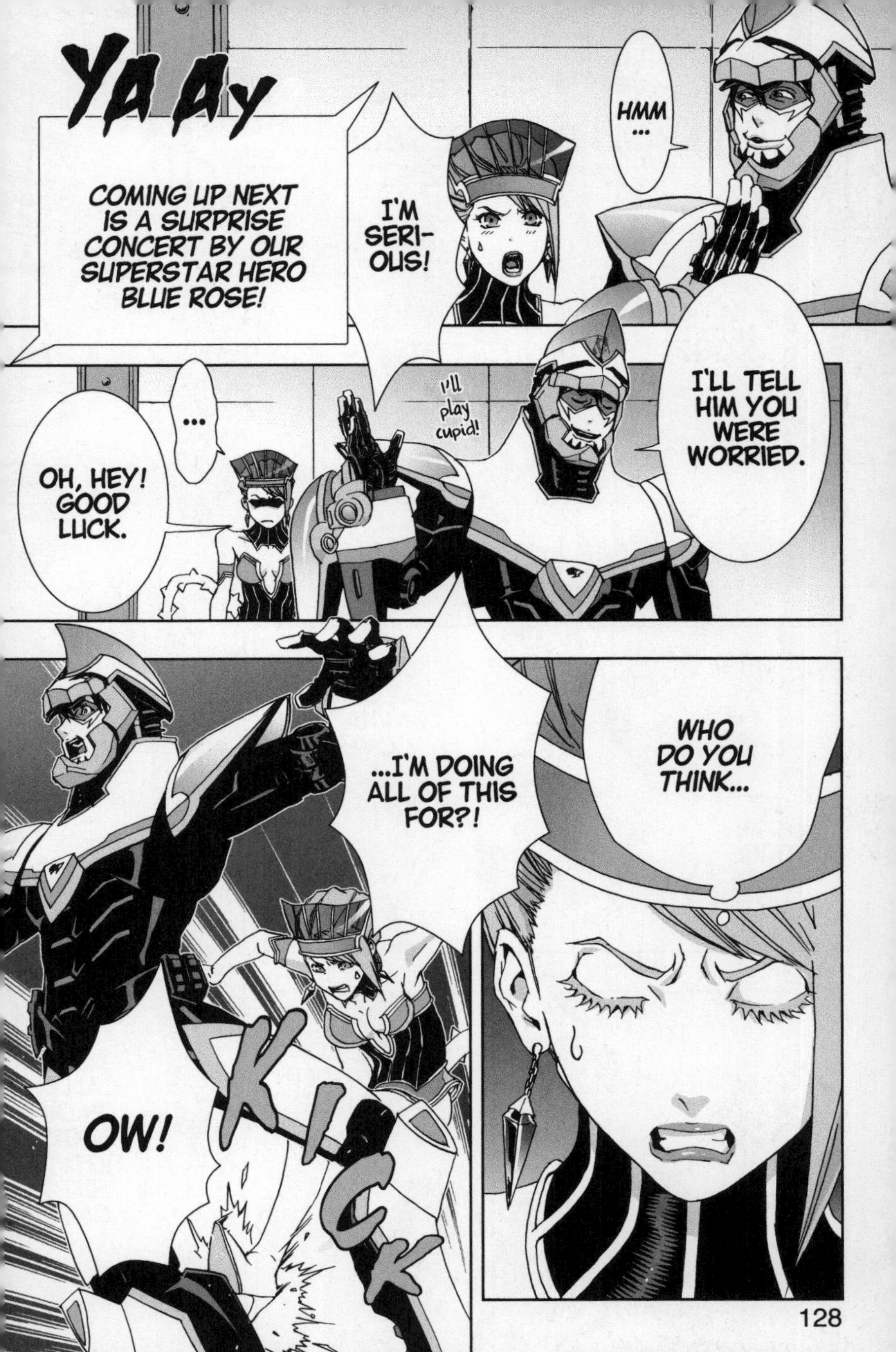
HMM...
I'M SERIOUS!
YA AY
COMING UP NEXT IS A SURPRISE CONCERT BY OUR SUPERSTAR HERO BLUE ROSE!
I'LL TELL HIM YOU WERE WORRIED.
I'll play cupid!
...
OH, HEY! GOOD LUCK.
WHO DO YOU THINK...
...I'M DOING ALL OF THIS FOR?!
KICK
OW!

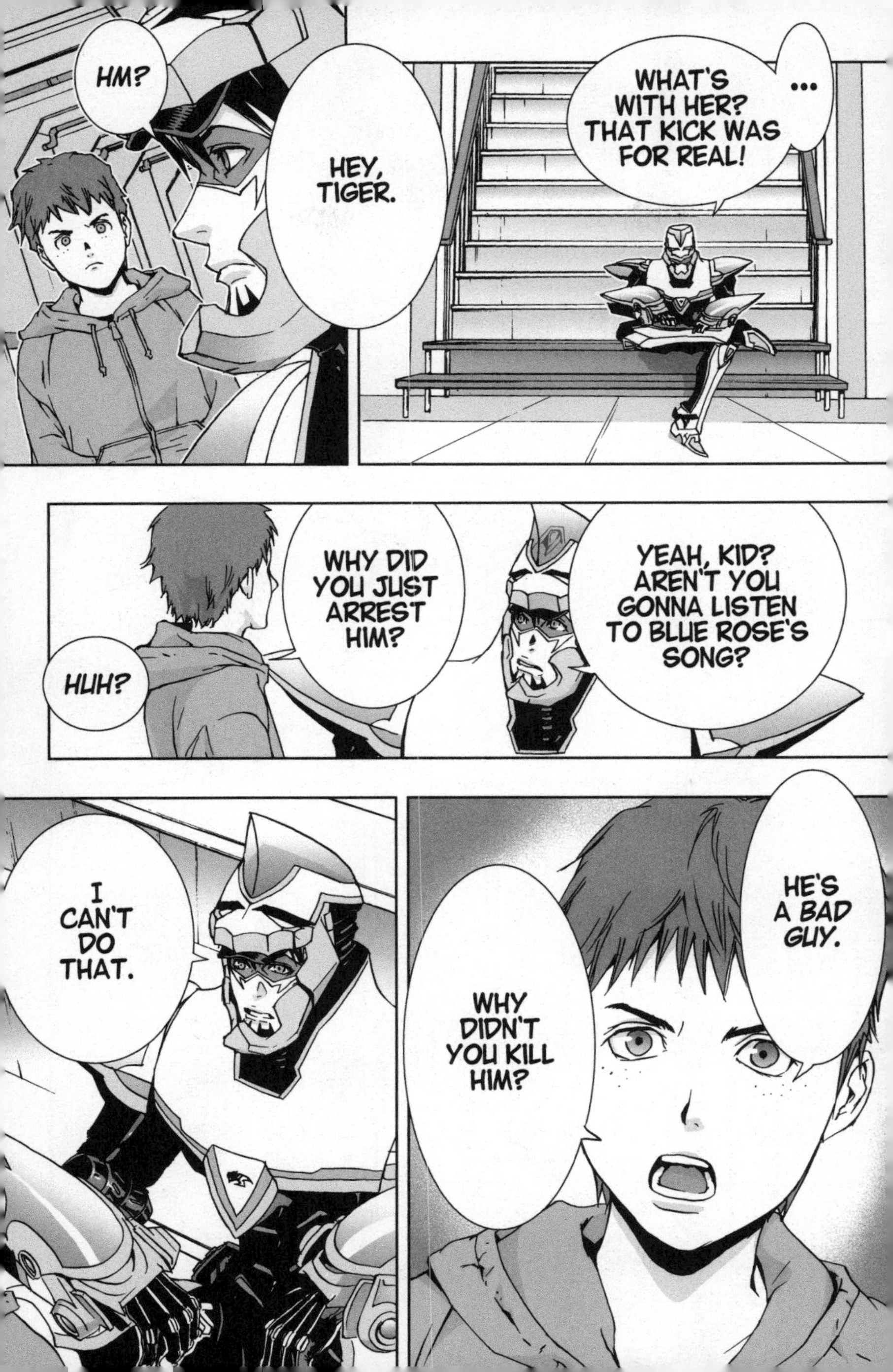
...
WHAT'S WITH HER? THAT KICK WAS FOR REAL!
HEY, TIGER.
HM?
YEAH, KID? AREN'T YOU GONNA LISTEN TO BLUE ROSE'S SONG?
WHY DID YOU JUST ARREST HIM?
HUH?
HE'S A BAD GUY.
WHY DIDN'T YOU KILL HIM?
I CAN'T DO THAT.

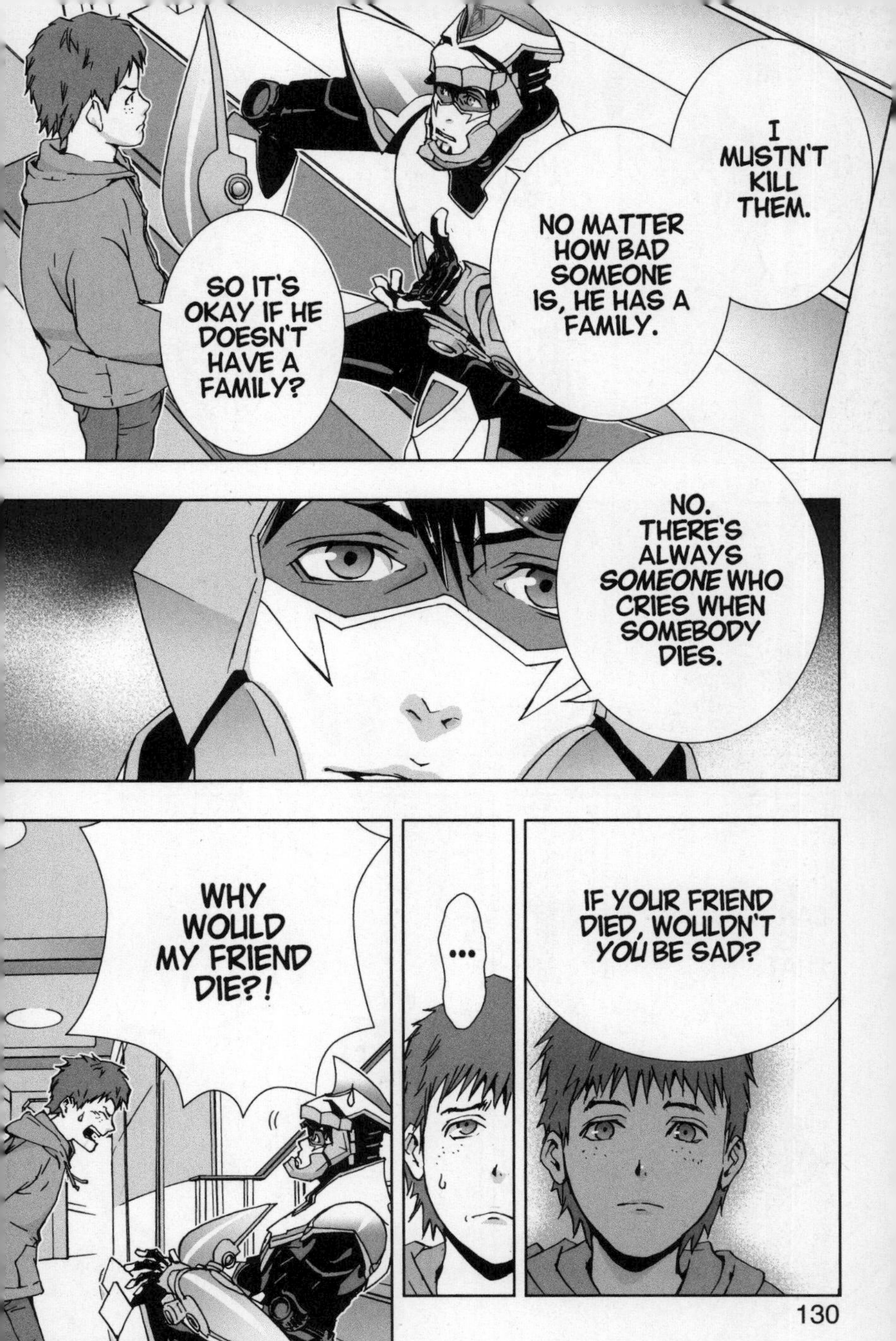
I MUSTN'T KILL THEM.
NO MATTER HOW BAD SOMEONE IS, HE HAS A FAMILY.
SO IT'S OKAY IF HE DOESN'T HAVE A FAMILY?
NO. THERE'S ALWAYS *SOMEONE* WHO CRIES WHEN SOMEBODY DIES.
IF YOUR FRIEND DIED, WOULDN'T *YOU* BE SAD?
...
WHY WOULD MY FRIEND DIE?!

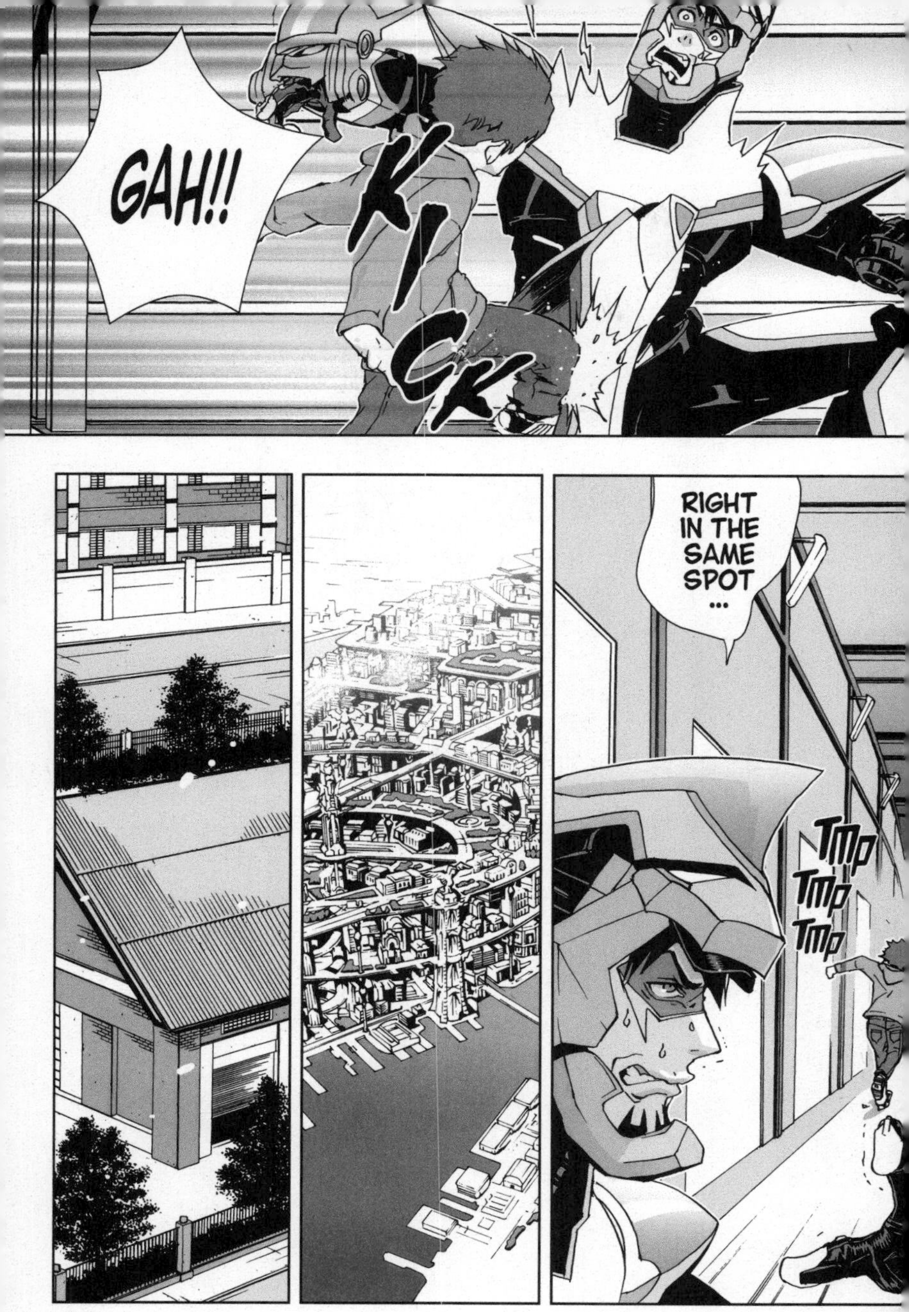
KICK
GAH!!
RIGHT IN THE SAME SPOT ...
Tmp Tmp Tmp

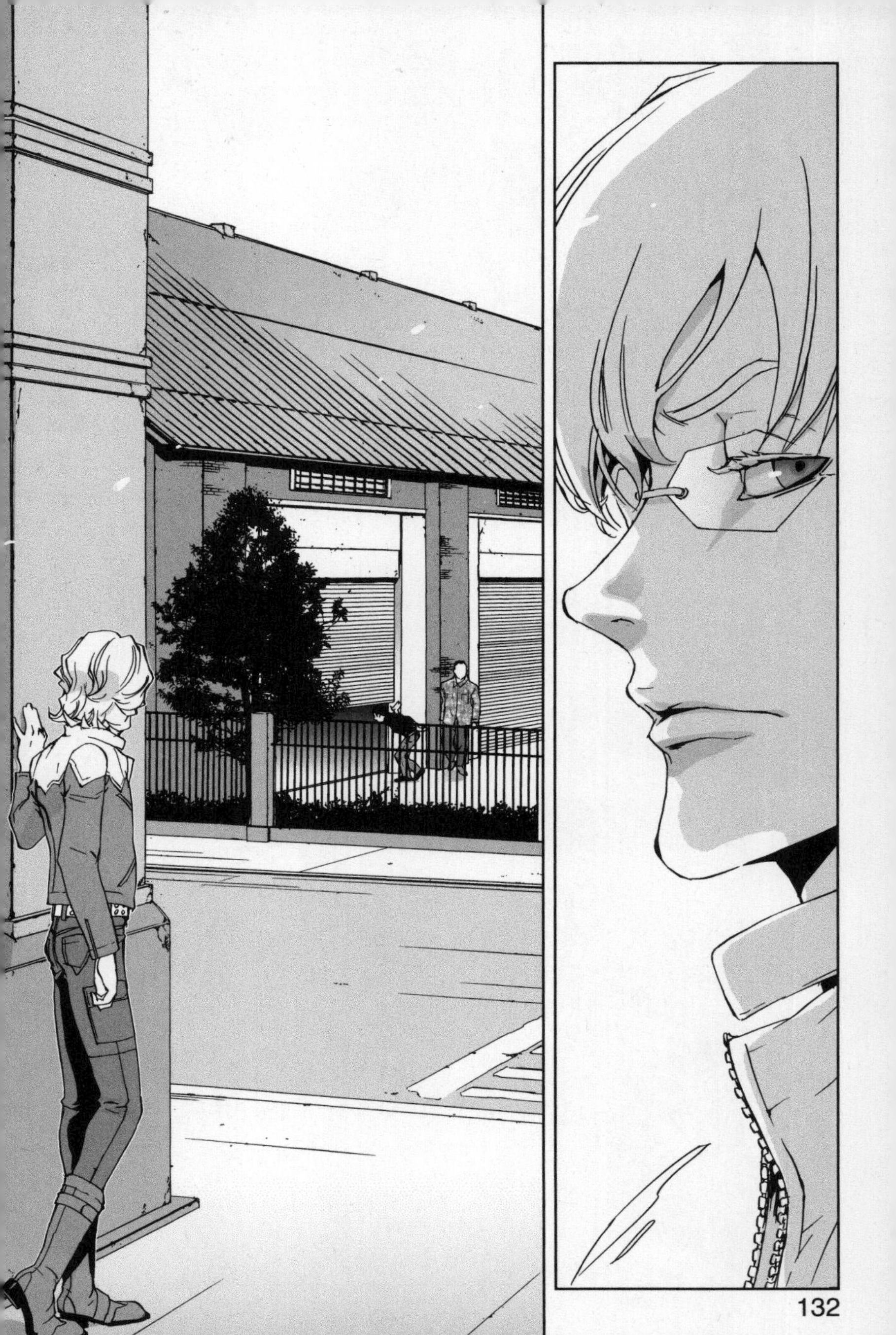

#13 The Wolf Knows What the Ill Beast Thinks

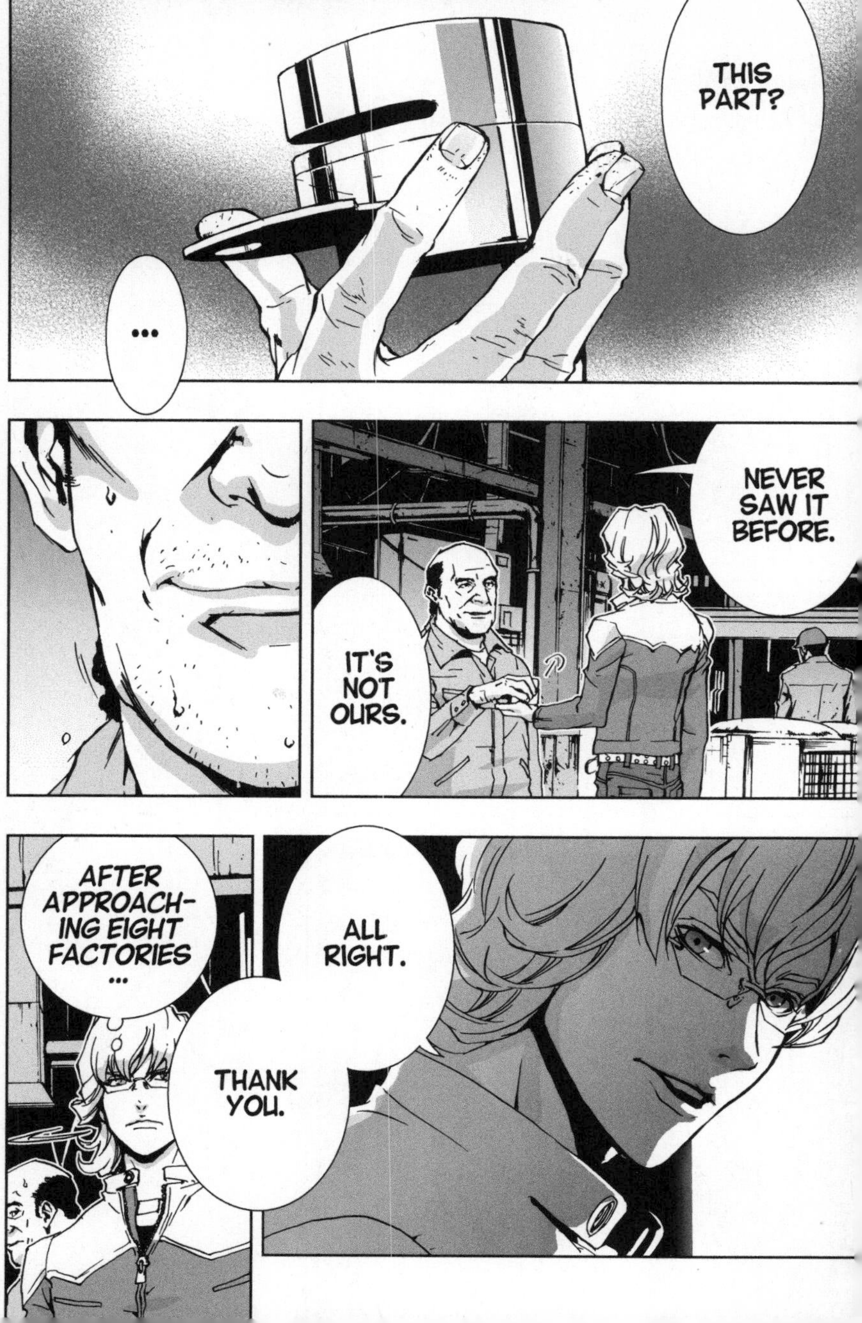
THIS PART?
...
NEVER SAW IT BEFORE.
IT'S NOT OURS.
ALL RIGHT.
THANK YOU.
AFTER APPROACH-ING EIGHT FACTORIES ...

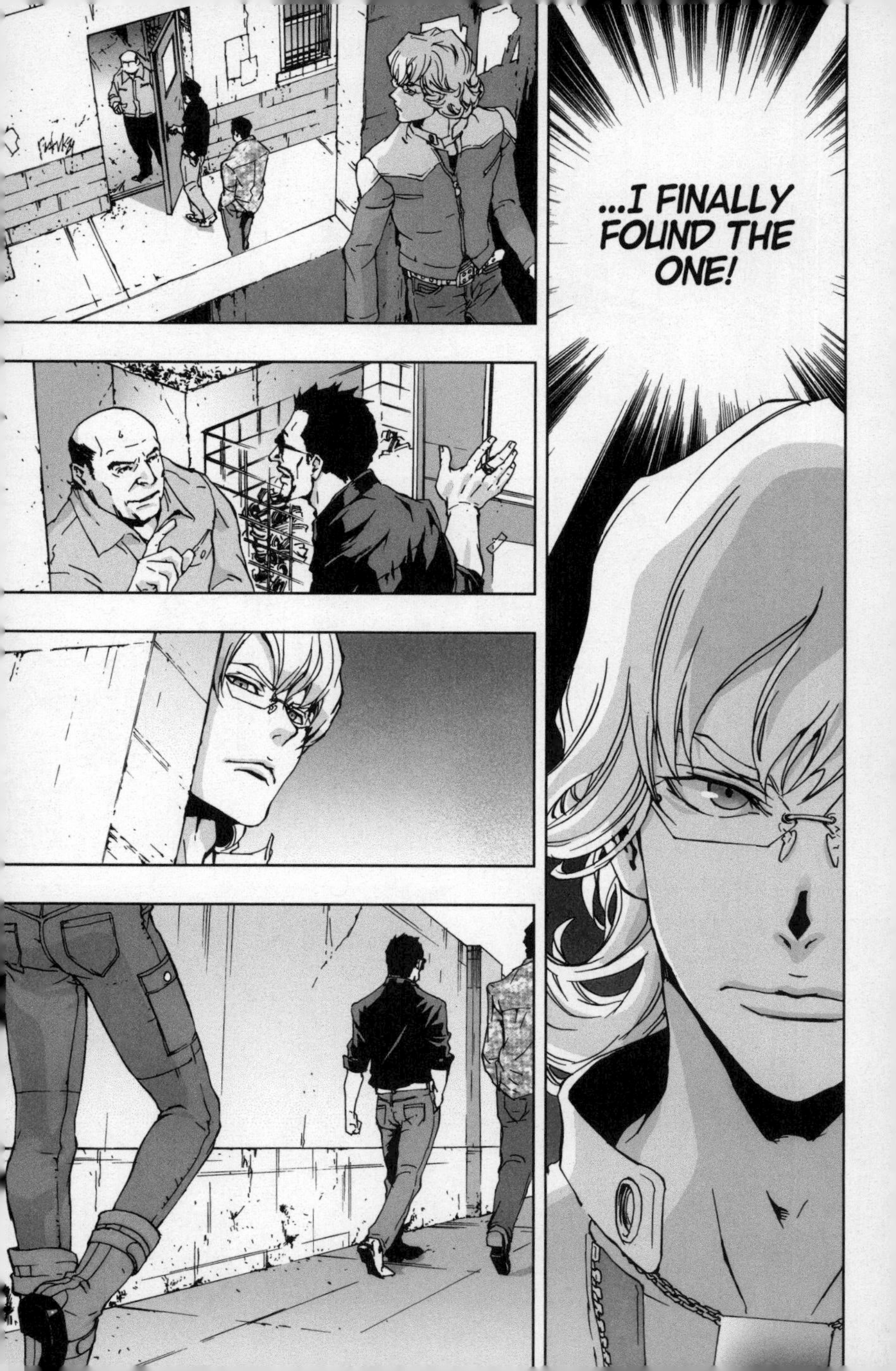
...I FINALLY FOUND THE ONE!

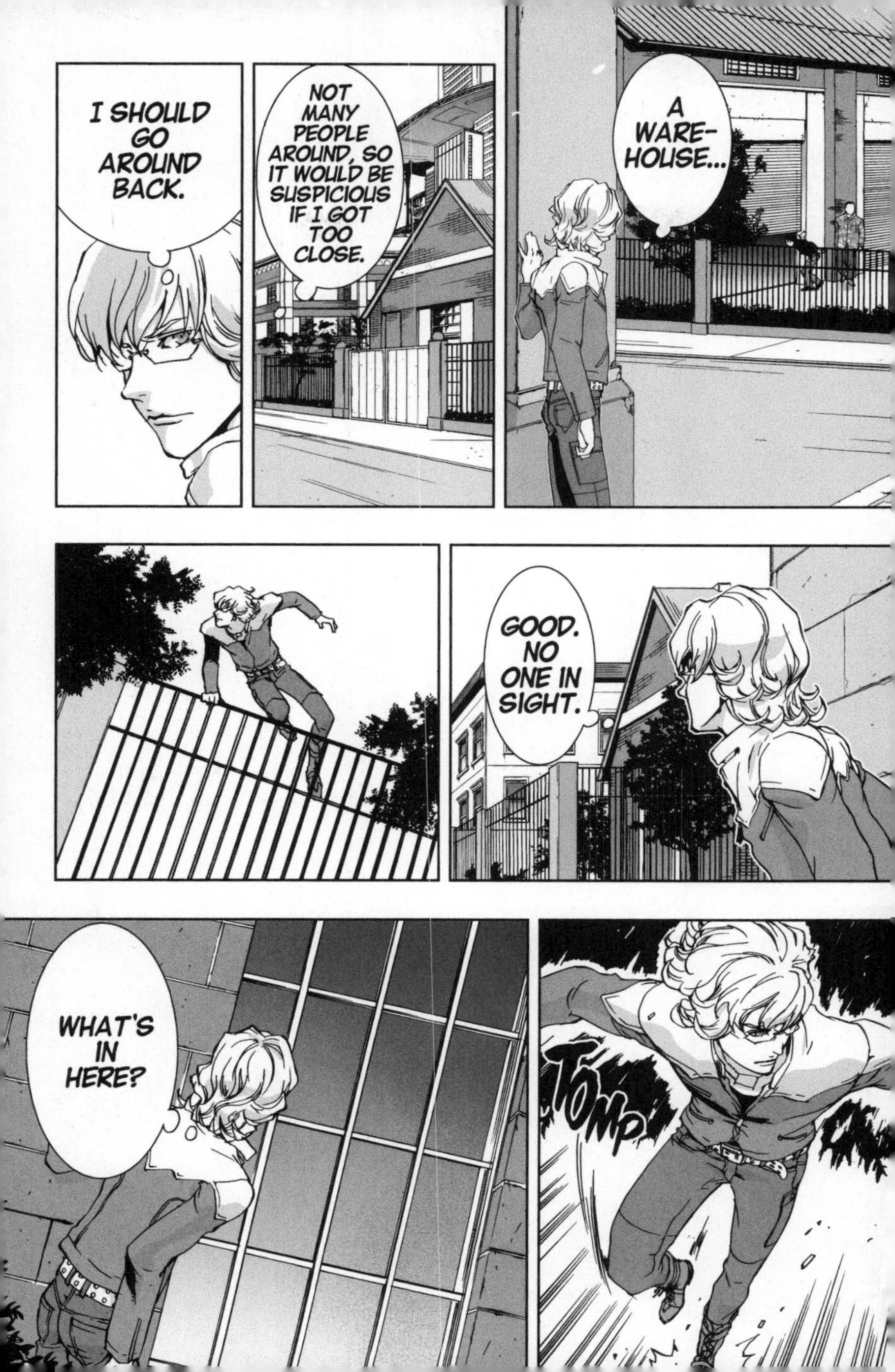
A WAREHOUSE...
NOT MANY PEOPLE AROUND, SO IT WOULD BE SUSPICIOUS IF I GOT TOO CLOSE.
I SHOULD GO AROUND BACK.
GOOD. NO ONE IN SIGHT.
TOMP
WHAT'S IN HERE?

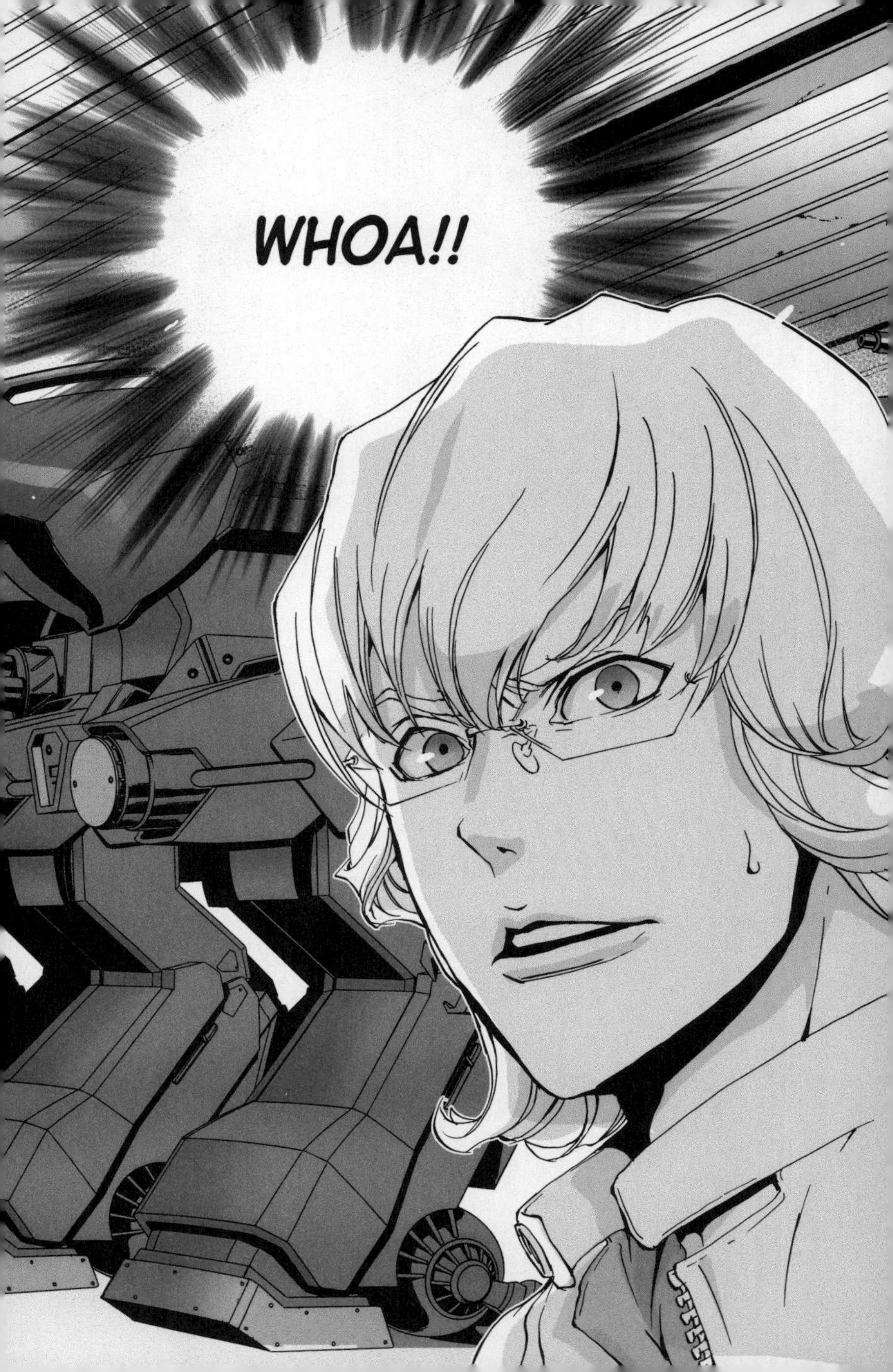
WHOA!!

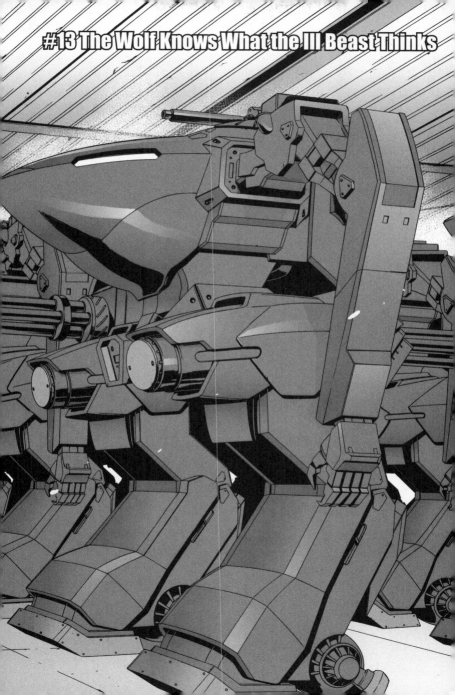

#13 The Wolf Knows What the Ill Beast Thinks

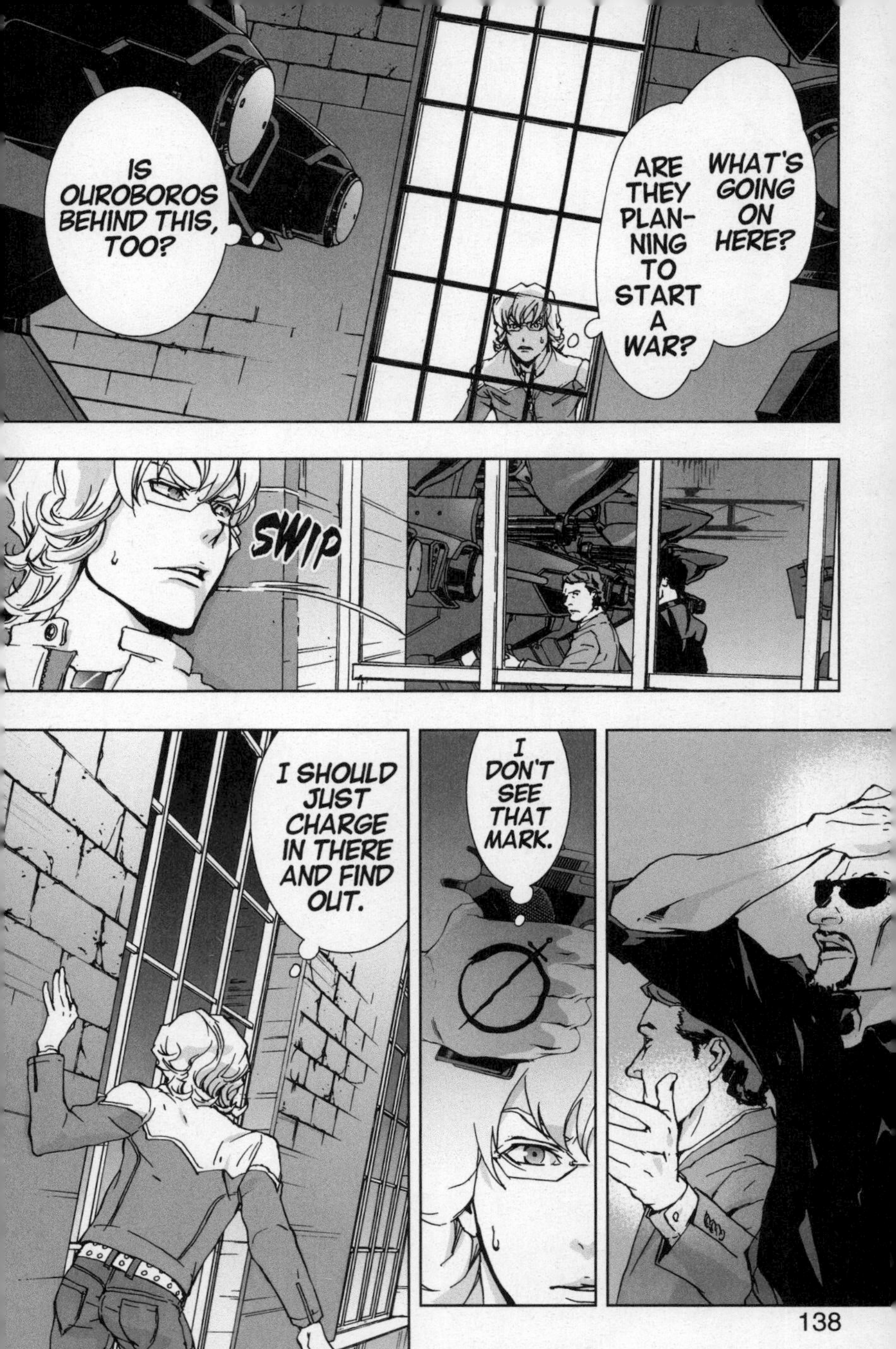
WHAT'S GOING ON HERE?
ARE THEY PLAN-NING TO START A WAR?
IS OUROBOROS BEHIND THIS, TOO?
SWIP
I DON'T SEE THAT MARK.
I SHOULD JUST CHARGE IN THERE AND FIND OUT.

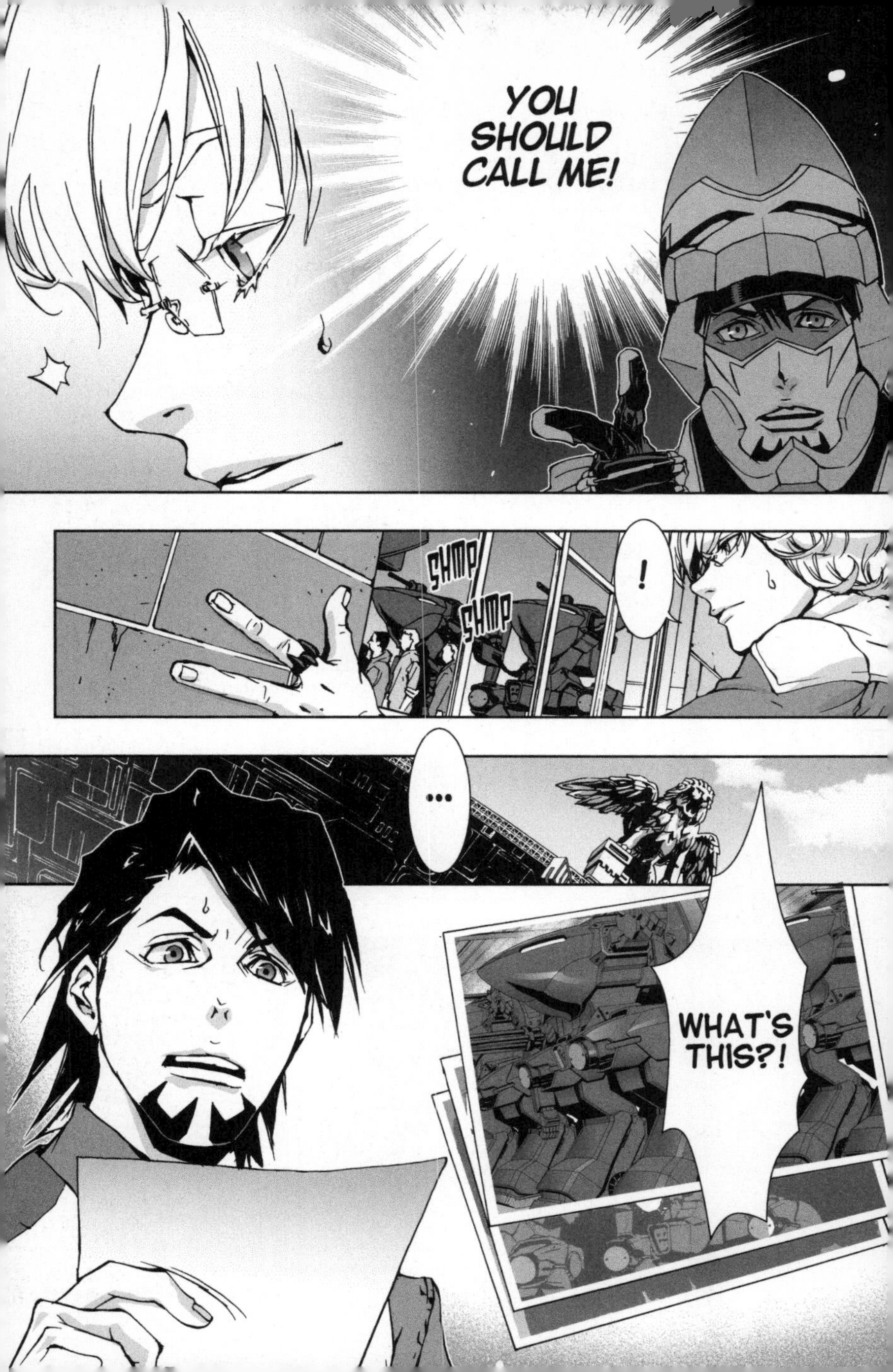
YOU SHOULD CALL ME!
!
SHMP
SHMP
...
WHAT'S THIS?!

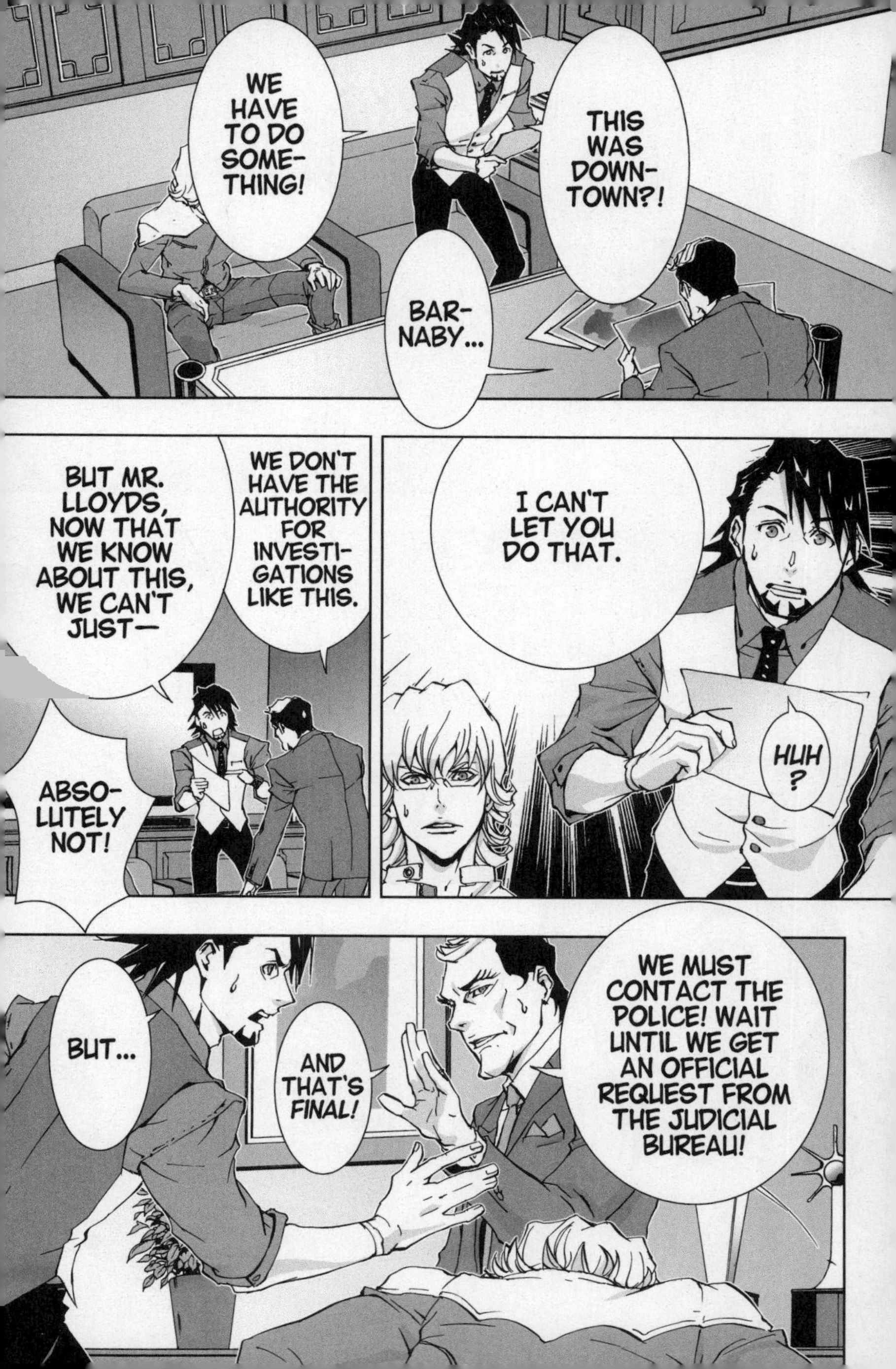
THIS WAS DOWNTOWN?!
WE HAVE TO DO SOMETHING!
BARNABY...
I CAN'T LET YOU DO THAT.
HUH?
WE DON'T HAVE THE AUTHORITY FOR INVESTIGATIONS LIKE THIS.
BUT MR. LLOYDS, NOW THAT WE KNOW ABOUT THIS, WE CAN'T JUST—
ABSOLUTELY NOT!
WE MUST CONTACT THE POLICE! WAIT UNTIL WE GET AN OFFICIAL REQUEST FROM THE JUDICIAL BUREAU!
AND THAT'S FINAL!
BUT...

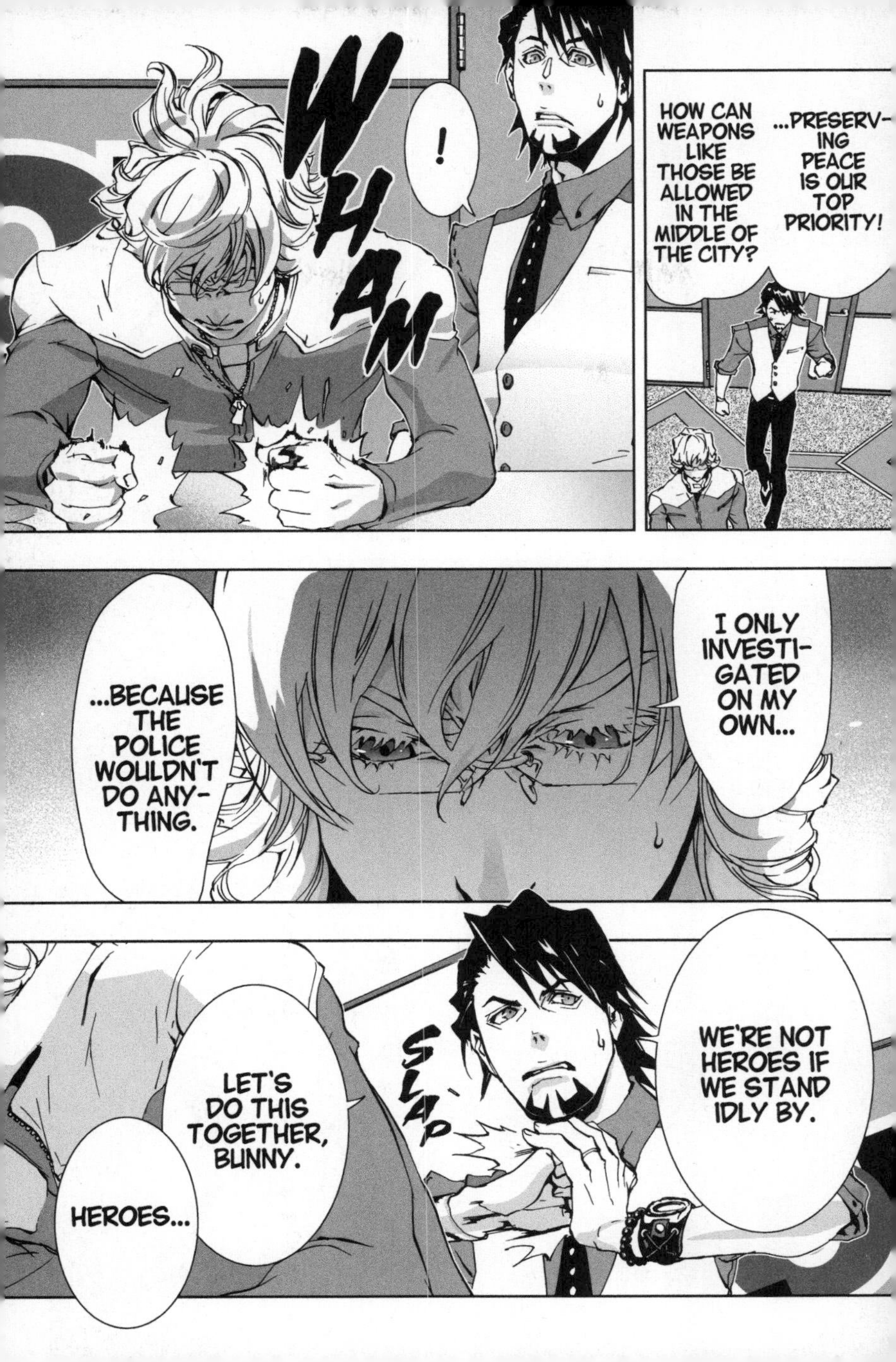
HOW CAN WEAPONS LIKE THOSE BE ALLOWED IN THE MIDDLE OF THE CITY?
...PRESERV-ING PEACE IS OUR TOP PRIORITY!
WHAM
!
I ONLY INVESTI-GATED ON MY OWN...
...BECAUSE THE POLICE WOULDN'T DO ANY-THING.
WE'RE NOT HEROES IF WE STAND IDLY BY.
SLAP
LET'S DO THIS TOGETHER, BUNNY.
HEROES...

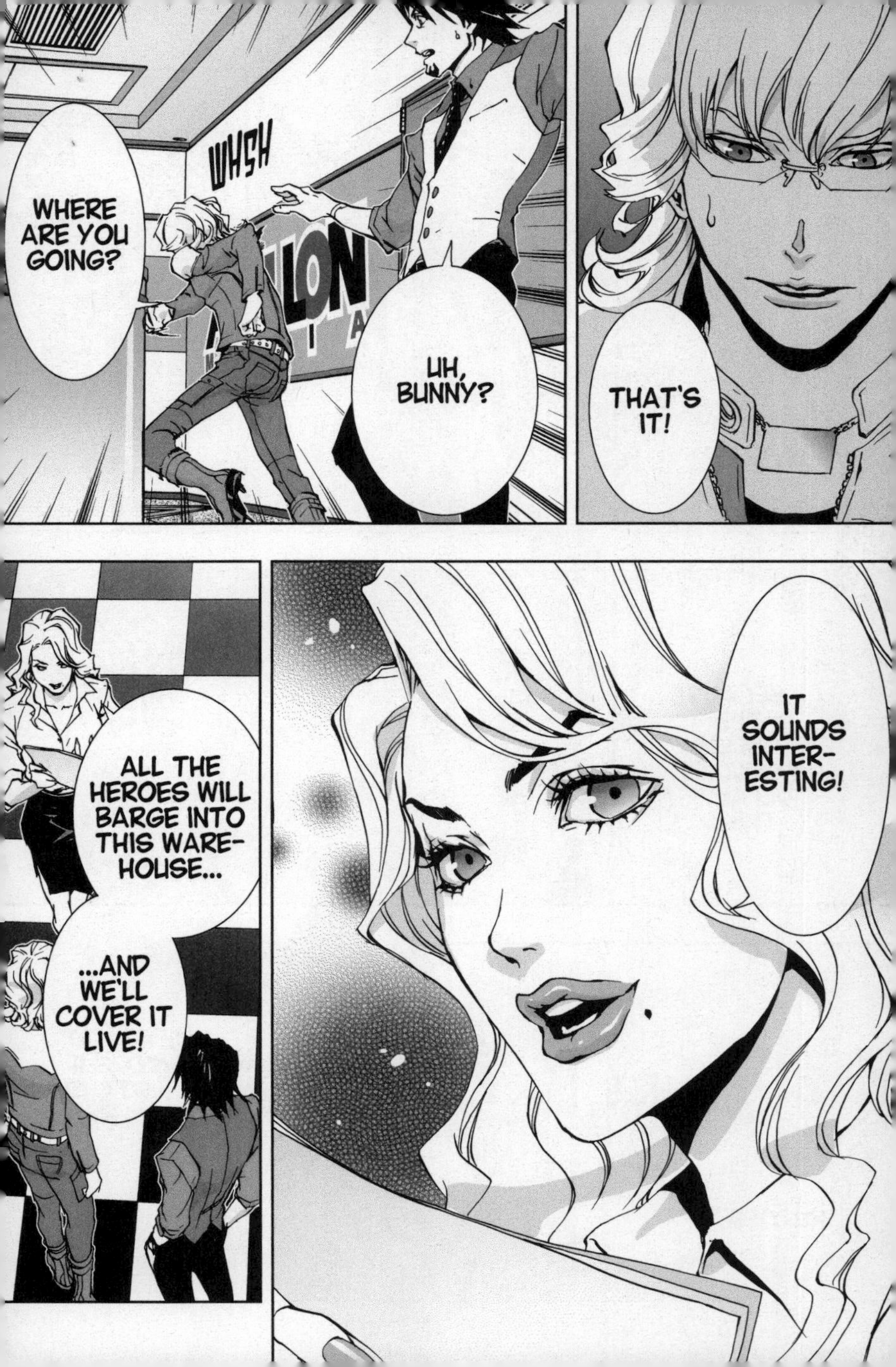
THAT'S IT!
WHSH
UH, BUNNY?
WHERE ARE YOU GOING?
IT SOUNDS INTER-ESTING!
ALL THE HEROES WILL BARGE INTO THIS WARE-HOUSE...
...AND WE'LL COVER IT LIVE!

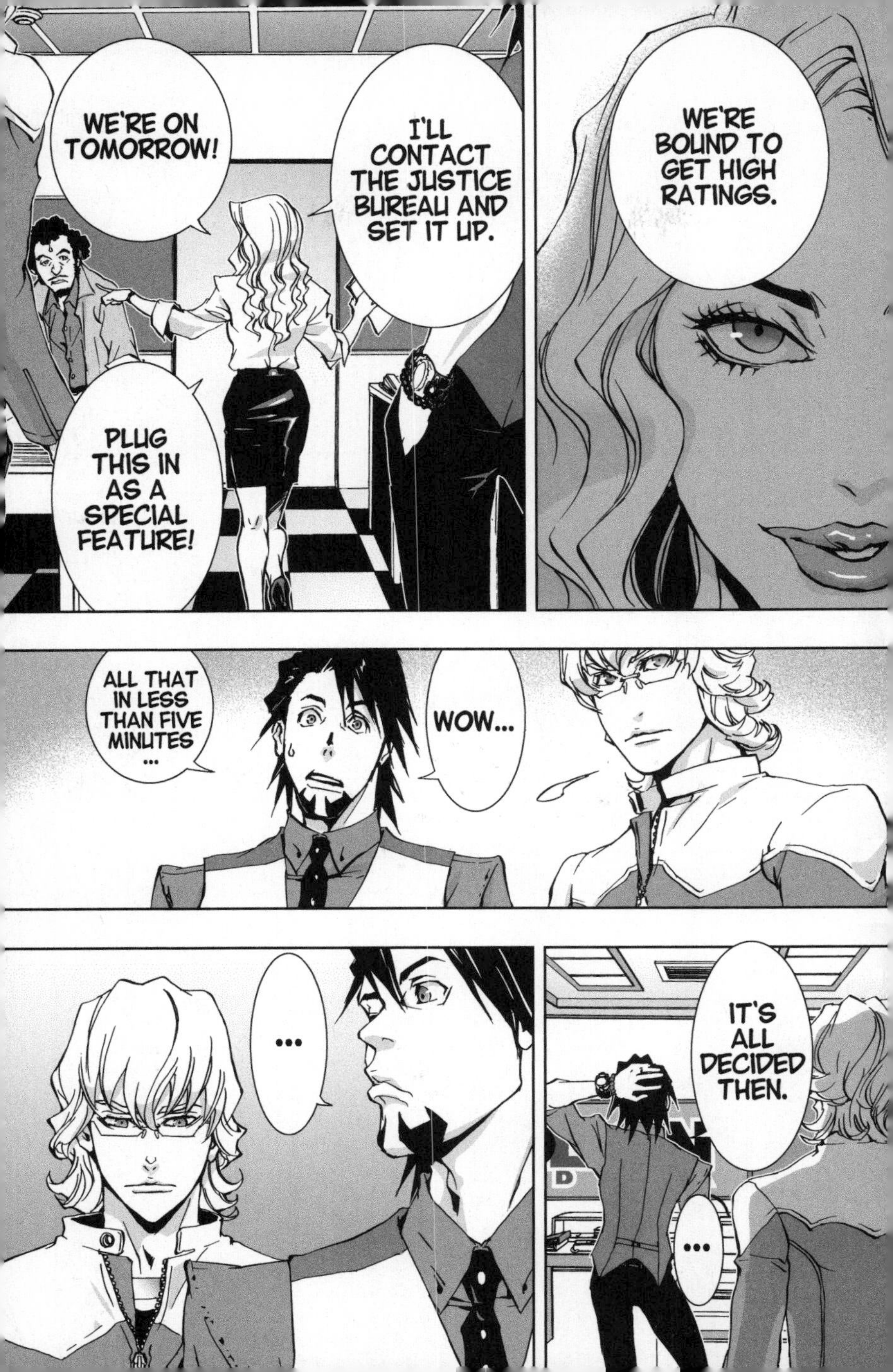
WE'RE BOUND TO GET HIGH RATINGS.
I'LL CONTACT THE JUSTICE BUREAU AND SET IT UP.
WE'RE ON TOMORROW!
PLUG THIS IN AS A SPECIAL FEATURE!
WOW...
ALL THAT IN LESS THAN FIVE MINUTES ...
IT'S ALL DECIDED THEN.
...
...

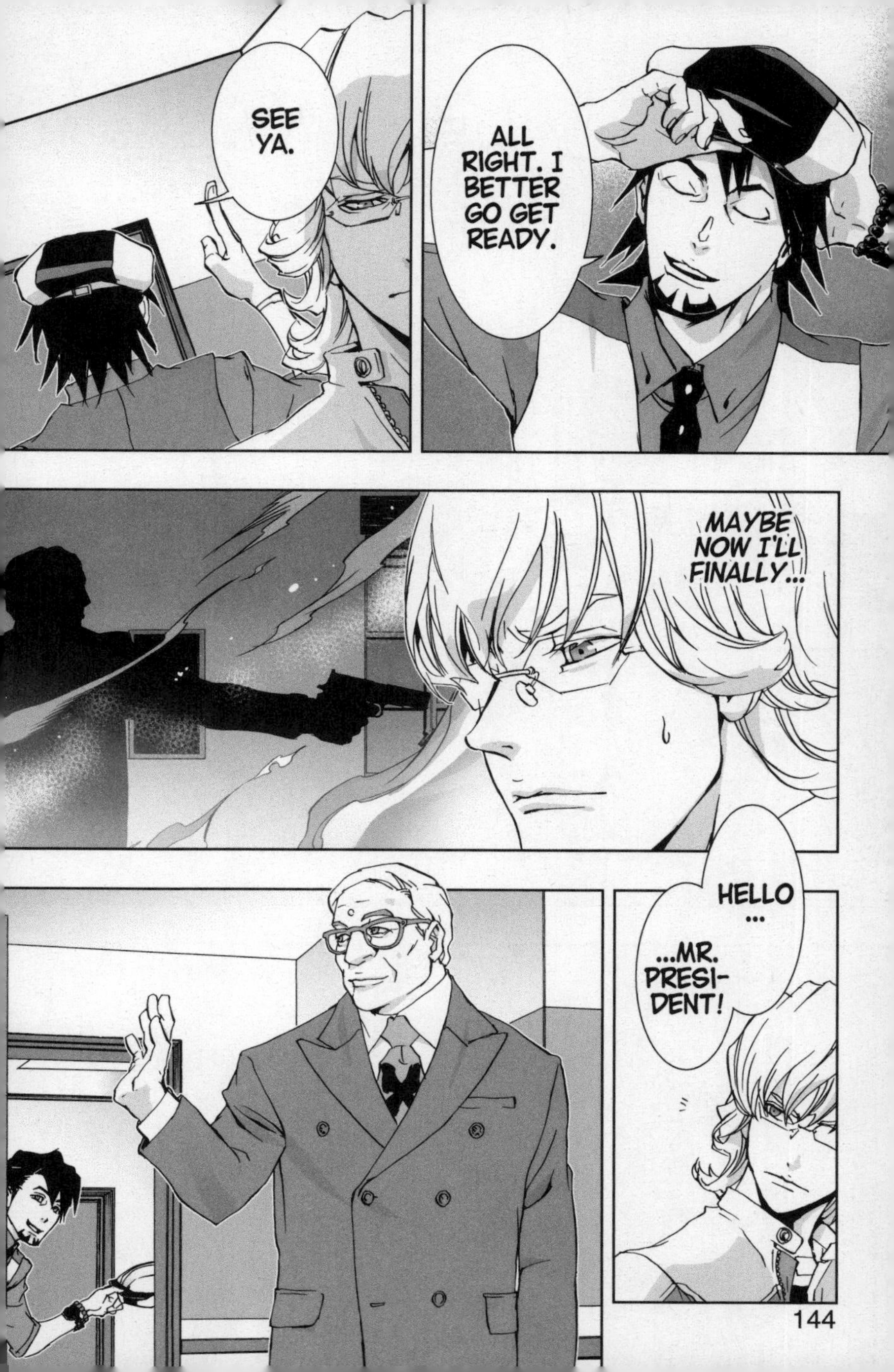
ALL RIGHT. I BETTER GO GET READY.
SEE YA.
MAYBE NOW I'LL FINALLY...
HELLO ...
...MR. PRESIDENT!

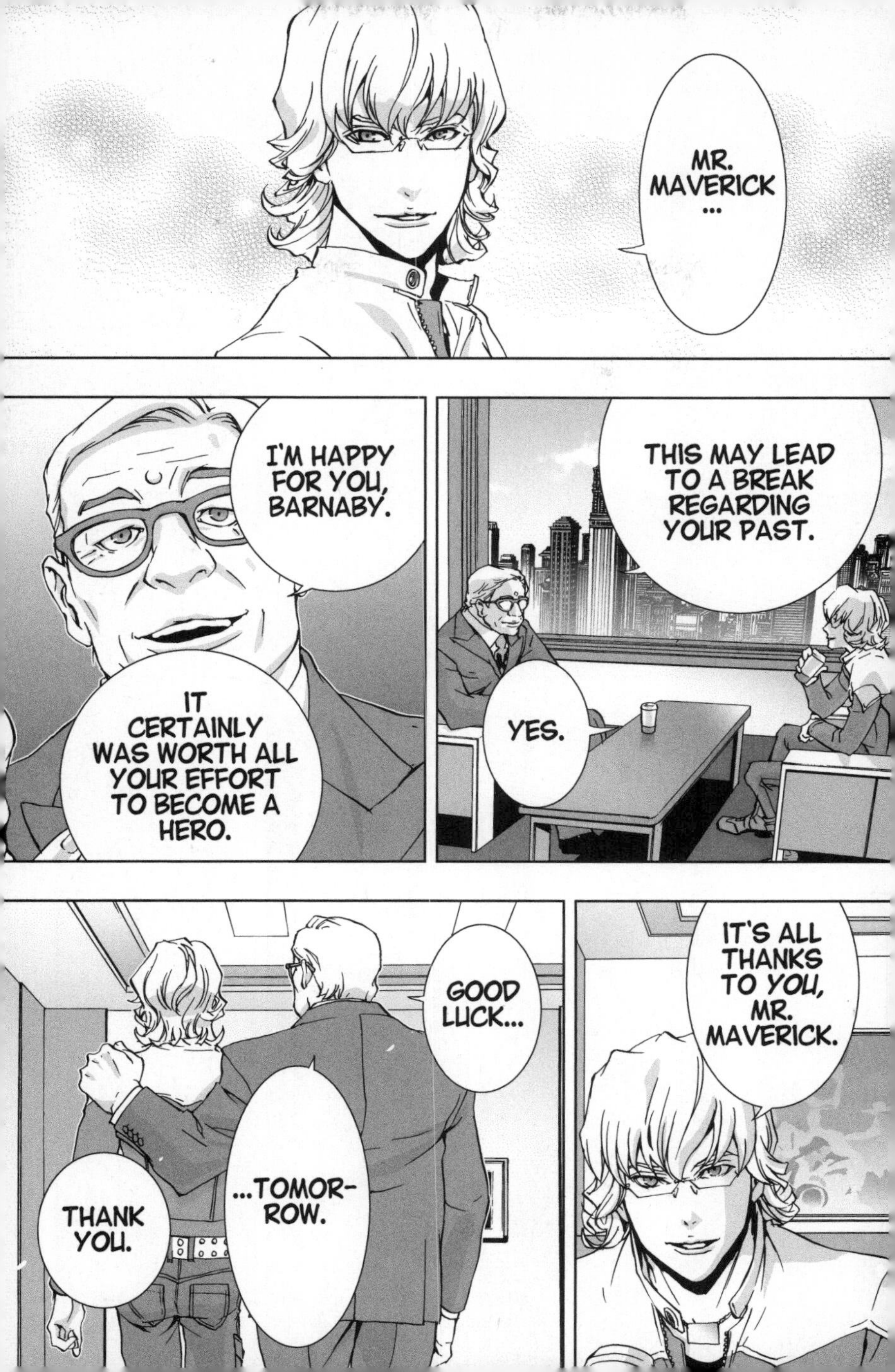
MR. MAVERICK ...
THIS MAY LEAD TO A BREAK REGARDING YOUR PAST.
YES.
I'M HAPPY FOR YOU, BARNABY.
IT CERTAINLY WAS WORTH ALL YOUR EFFORT TO BECOME A HERO.
IT'S ALL THANKS TO *YOU*, MR. MAVERICK.
GOOD LUCK...
...TOMOR-ROW.
THANK YOU.

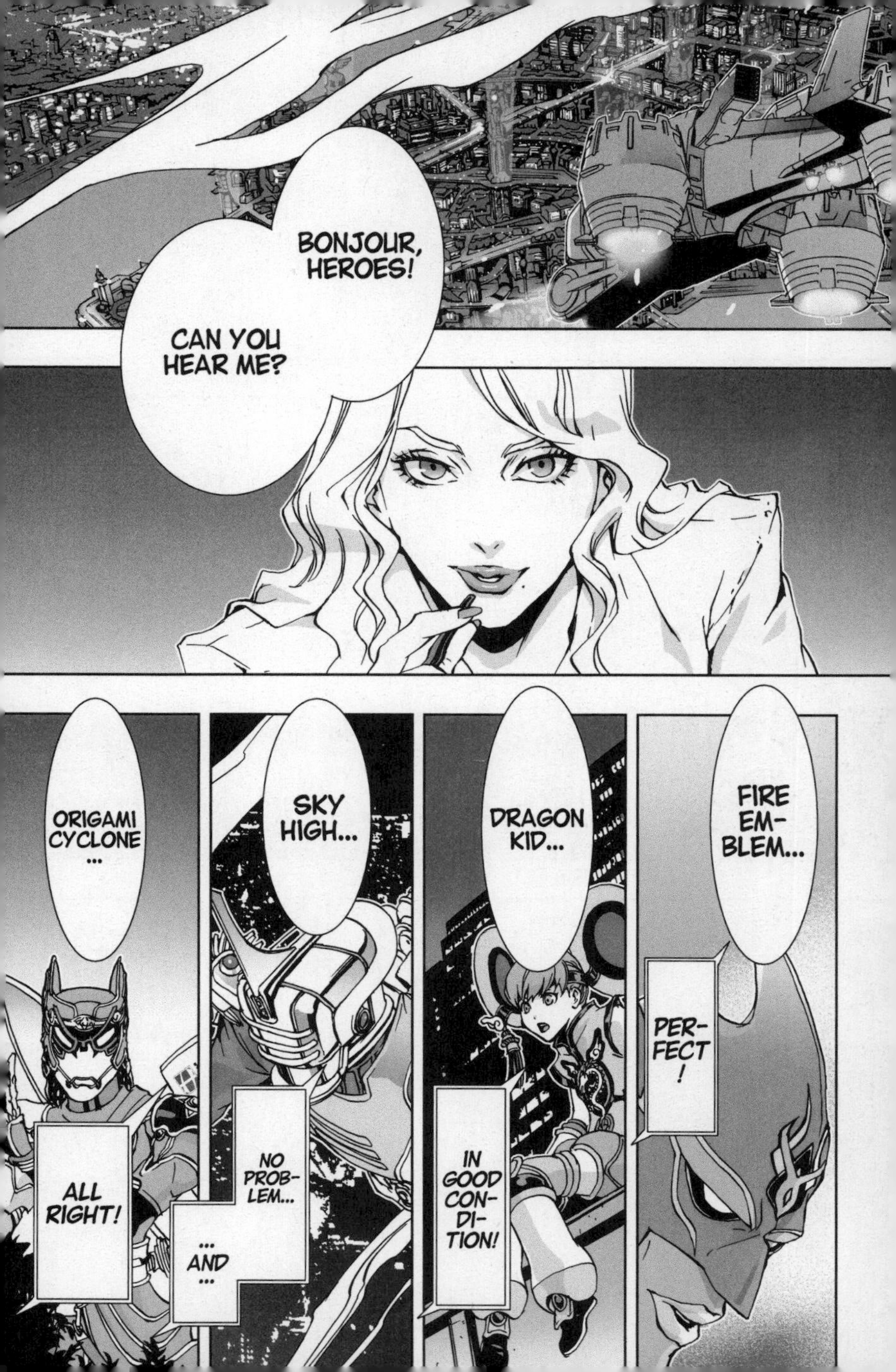
BONJOUR, HEROES!
CAN YOU HEAR ME?
FIRE EM- BLEM...
PER- FECT!
DRAGON KID...
IN GOOD CON- DI- TION!
SKY HIGH...
NO PROB- LEM...
... AND ...
ORIGAMI CYCLONE ...
ALL RIGHT!

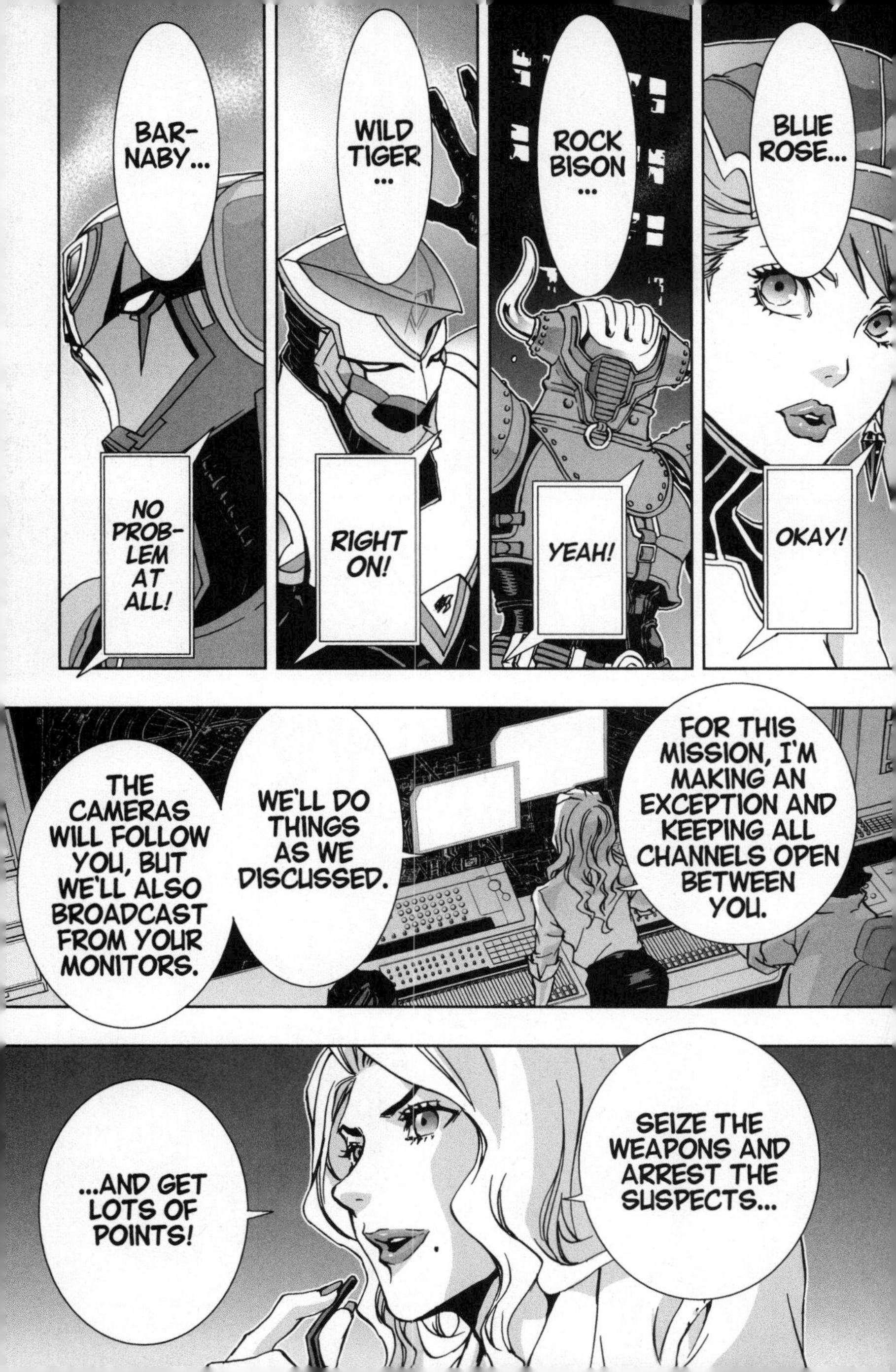
BLUE ROSE...
OKAY!
ROCK BISON ...
YEAH!
WILD TIGER ...
RIGHT ON!
BAR-NABY...
NO PROB-LEM AT ALL!
FOR THIS MISSION, I'M MAKING AN EXCEPTION AND KEEPING ALL CHANNELS OPEN BETWEEN YOU.
WE'LL DO THINGS AS WE DISCUSSED.
THE CAMERAS WILL FOLLOW YOU, BUT WE'LL ALSO BROADCAST FROM YOUR MONITORS.
SEIZE THE WEAPONS AND ARREST THE SUSPECTS...
...AND GET LOTS OF POINTS!

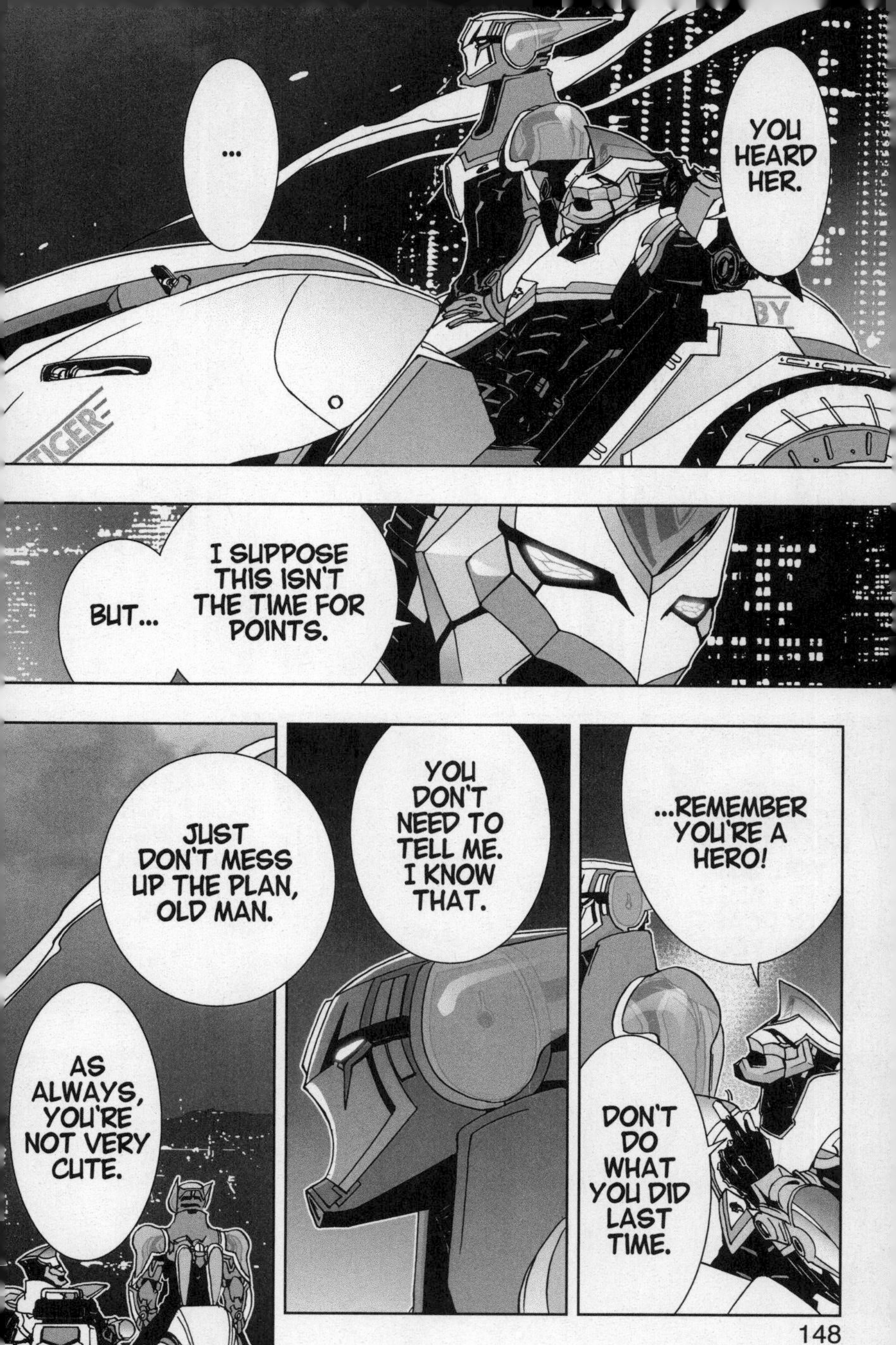
YOU HEARD HER.
...
TIGER
I SUPPOSE THIS ISN'T THE TIME FOR POINTS.
BUT...
...REMEMBER YOU'RE A HERO!
DON'T DO WHAT YOU DID LAST TIME.
YOU DON'T NEED TO TELL ME. I KNOW THAT.
JUST DON'T MESS UP THE PLAN, OLD MAN.
AS ALWAYS, YOU'RE NOT VERY CUTE.

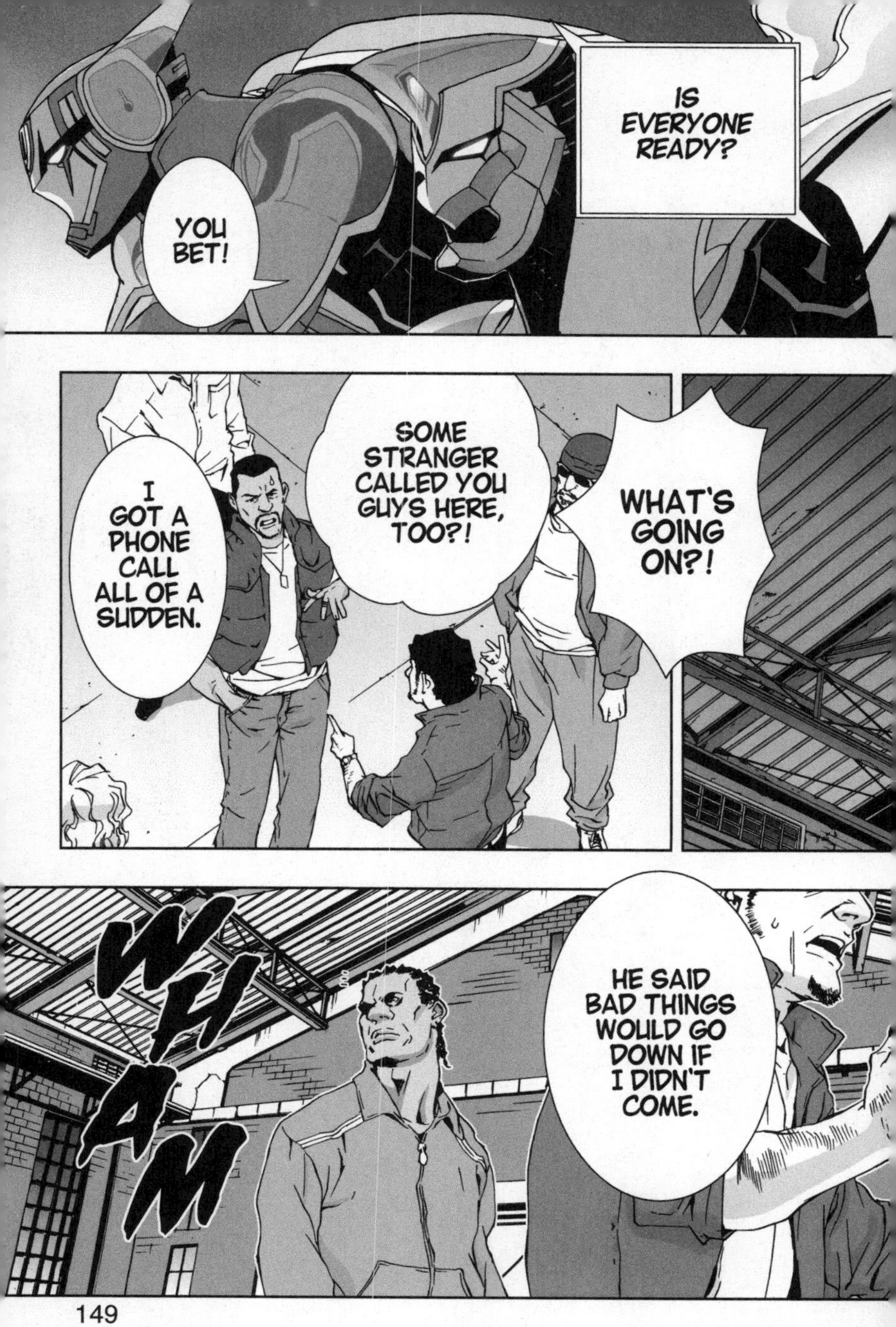
IS EVERYONE READY?
YOU BET!
WHAT'S GOING ON?!
SOME STRANGER CALLED YOU GUYS HERE, TOO?!
I GOT A PHONE CALL ALL OF A SUDDEN.
HE SAID BAD THINGS WOULD GO DOWN IF I DIDN'T COME.
WHAM

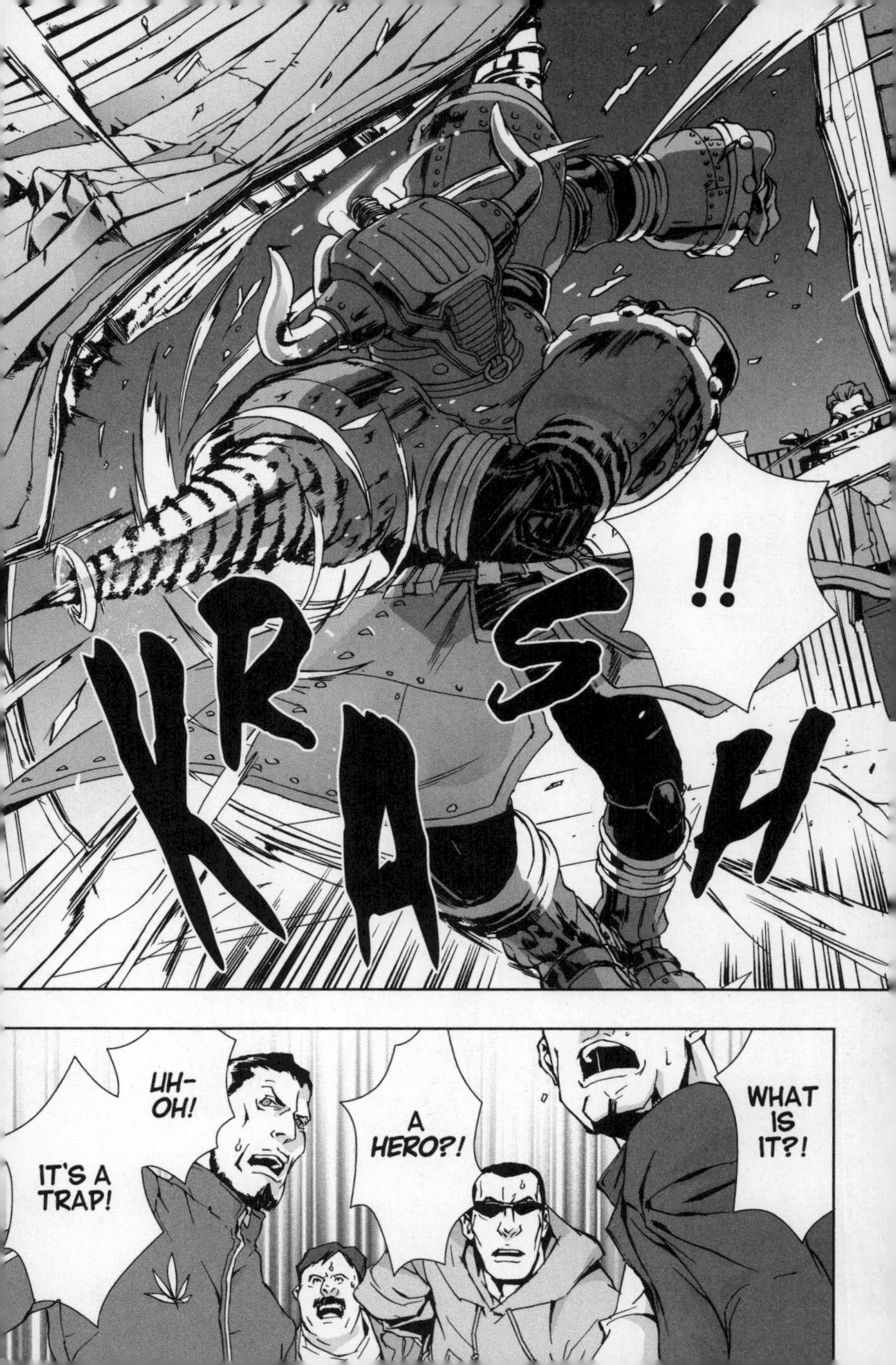
!!
KRASH
WHAT IS IT?!
A HERO?!
UH-OH!
IT'S A TRAP!

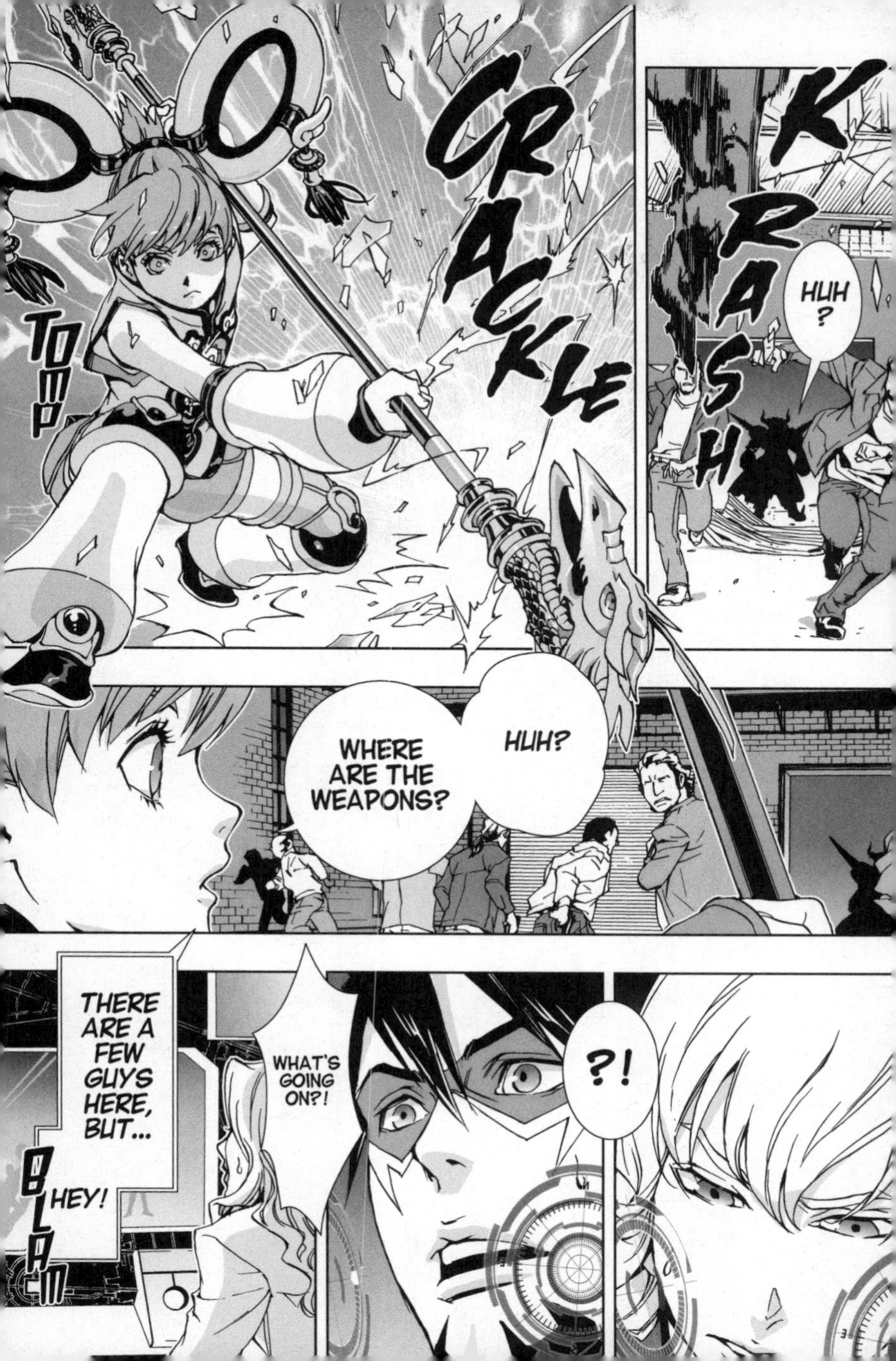
KRASH
HUH?
CRACKLE
TOMP
HUH?
WHERE ARE THE WEAPONS?
?!
WHAT'S GOING ON?!
THERE ARE A FEW GUYS HERE, BUT...
HEY!
BLAM

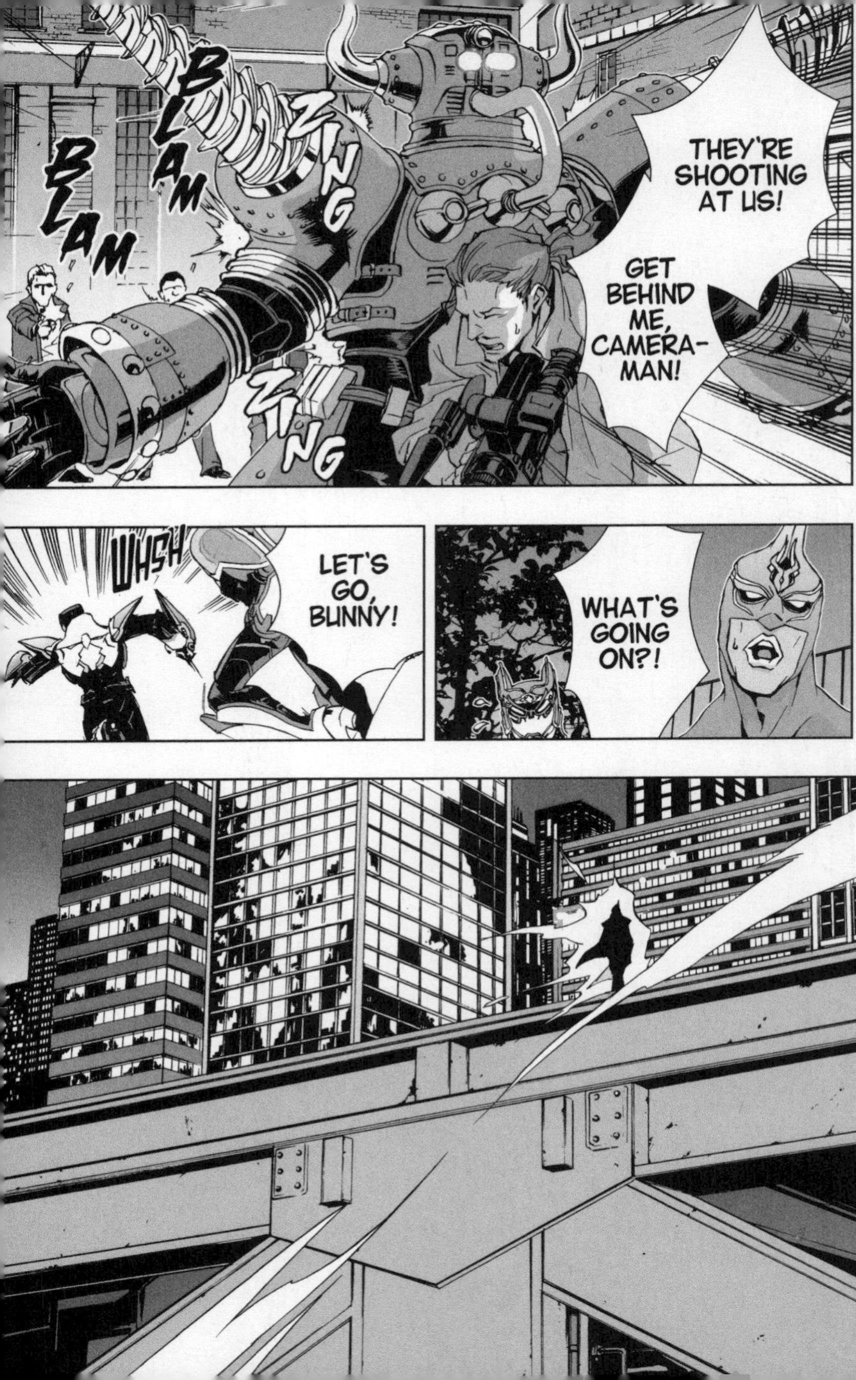
THEY'RE SHOOTING AT US!
GET BEHIND ME, CAMERA-MAN!
ZING
ZING
BLAM
BLAM
BLAM
BLAM
ZING
ZING
WHAT'S GOING ON?!
LET'S GO, BUNNY!
WHSH

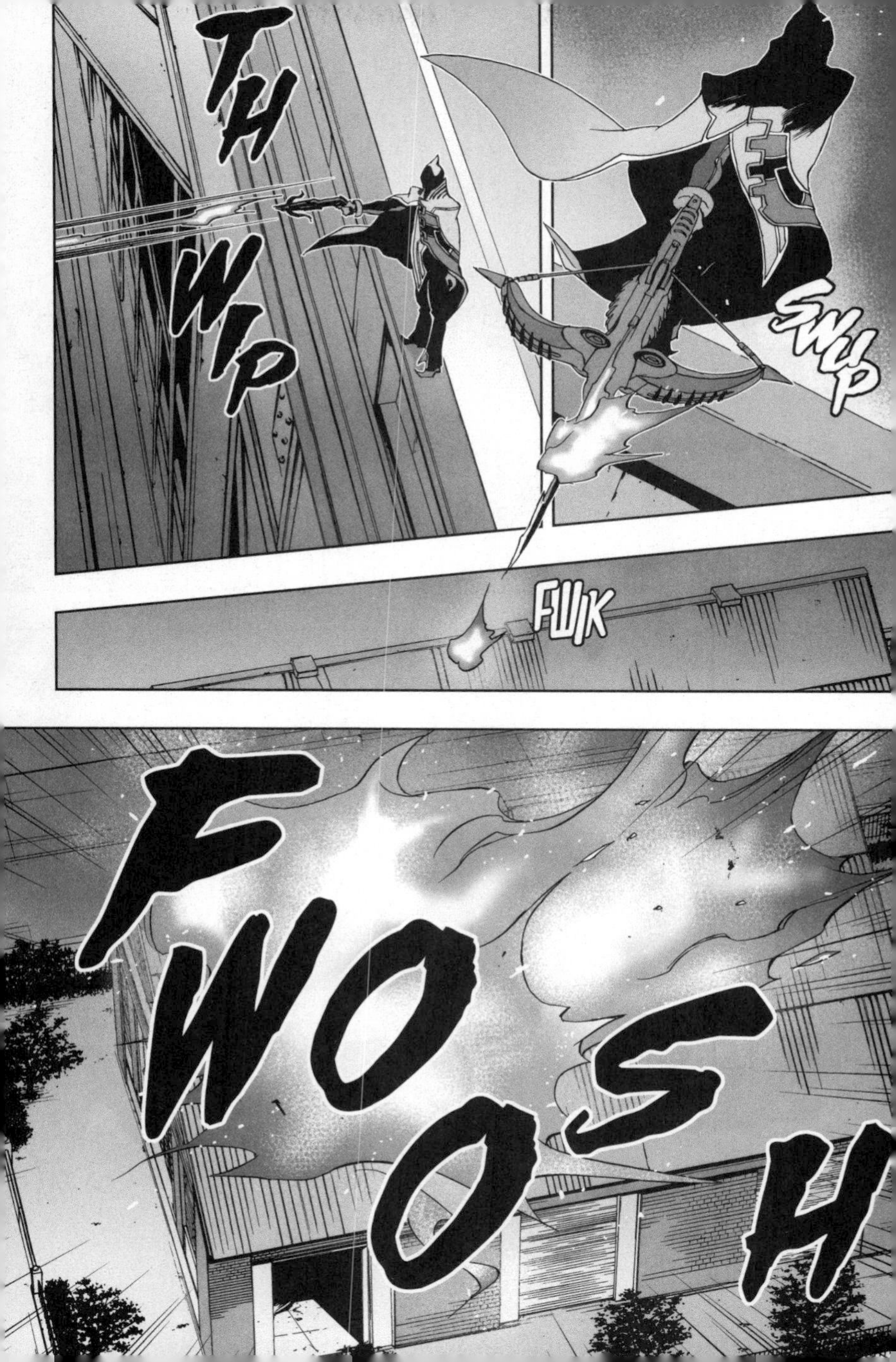
SWUP
THWIP
FWIK
FWOOSH

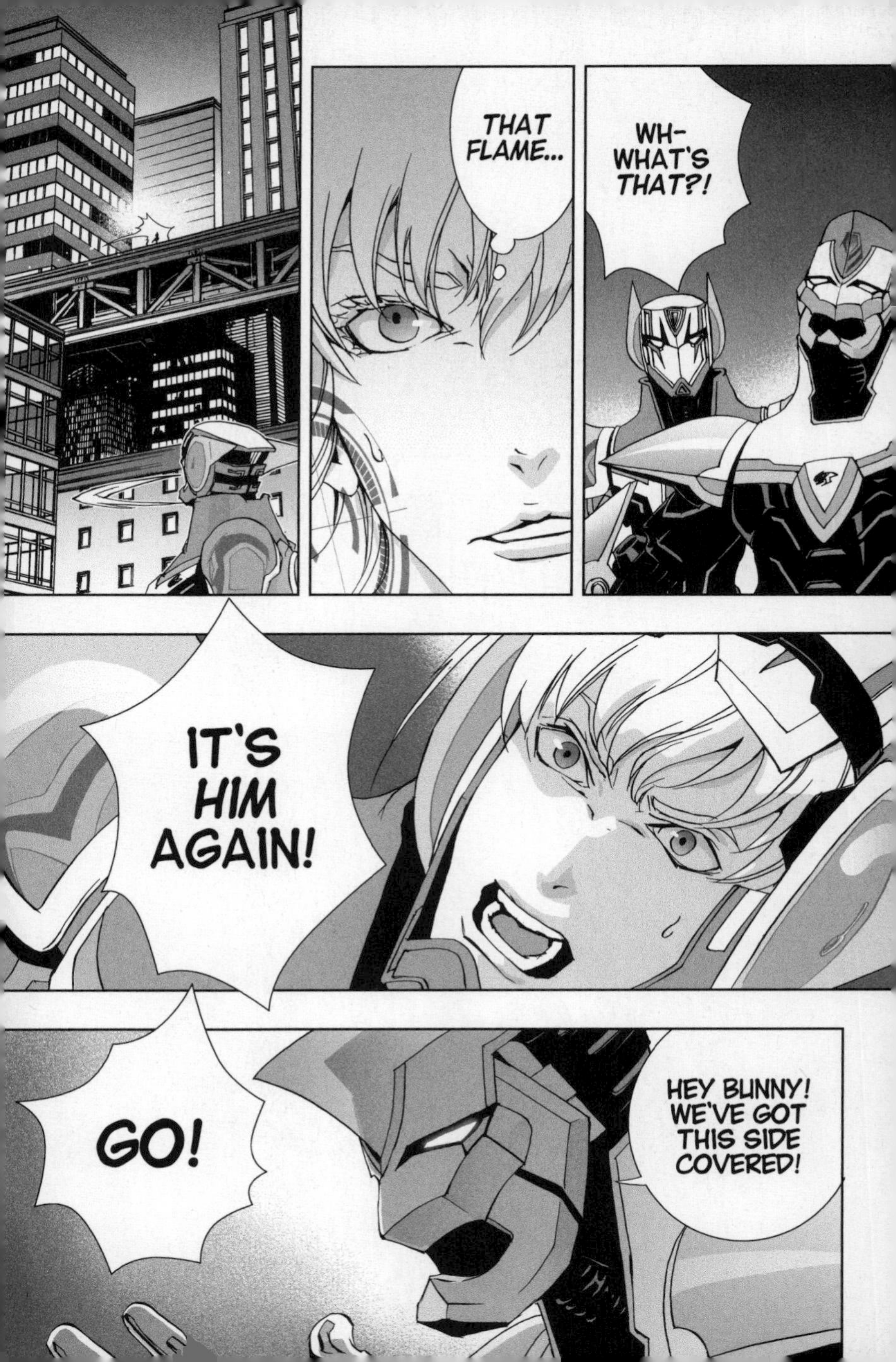
WH- WHAT'S THAT?!
THAT FLAME...
IT'S HIM AGAIN!
HEY BUNNY! WE'VE GOT THIS SIDE COVERED!
GO!

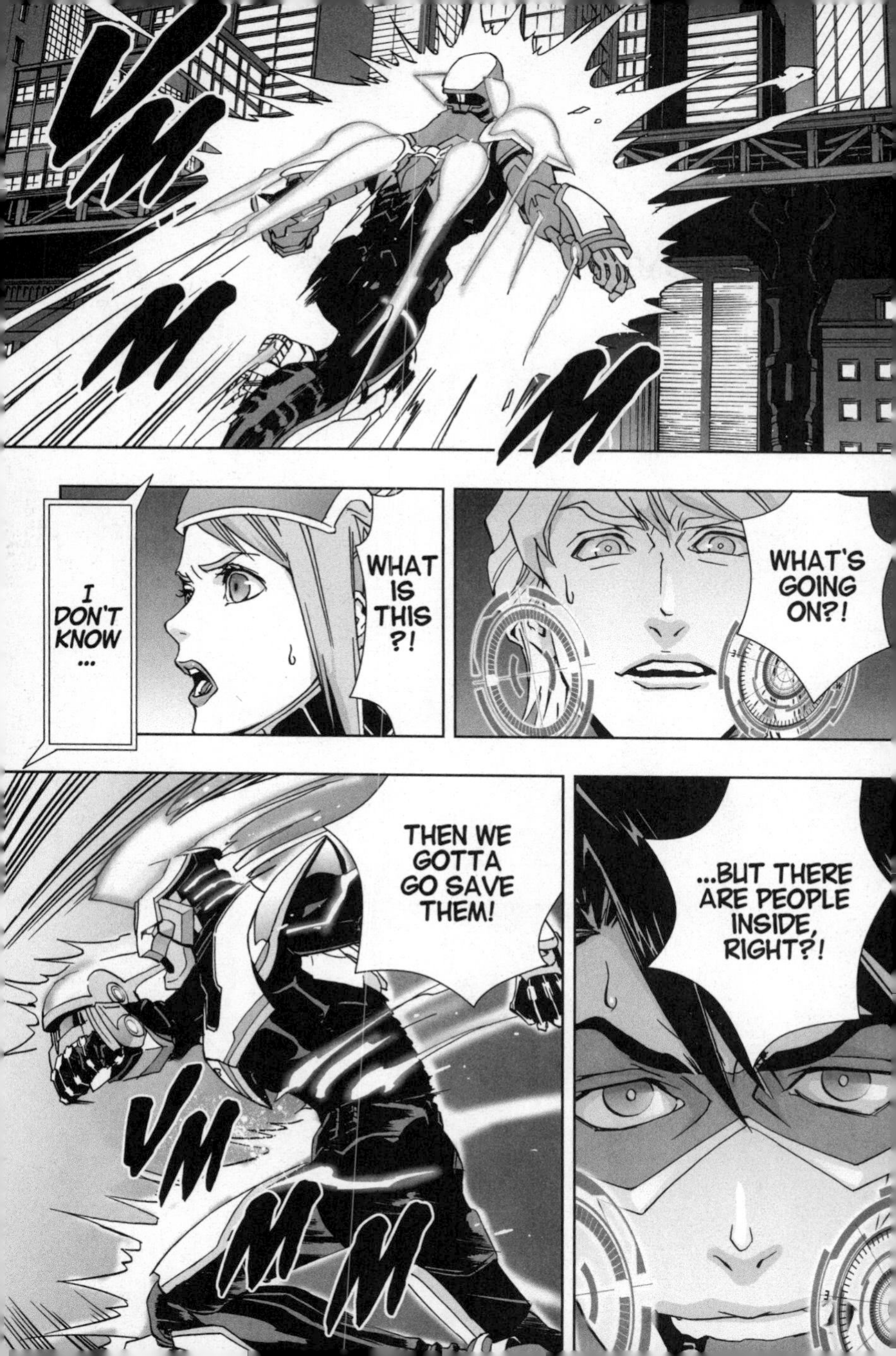
VM
M
M
WHAT'S GOING ON?!
WHAT IS THIS?!
I DON'T KNOW...
...BUT THERE ARE PEOPLE INSIDE, RIGHT?!
THEN WE GOTTA GO SAVE THEM!
VM
M
M
M

WHAM

KTH

UNK

AGH!

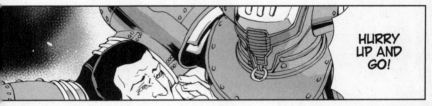

HURRY UP AND GO!

UGH!

WHAM

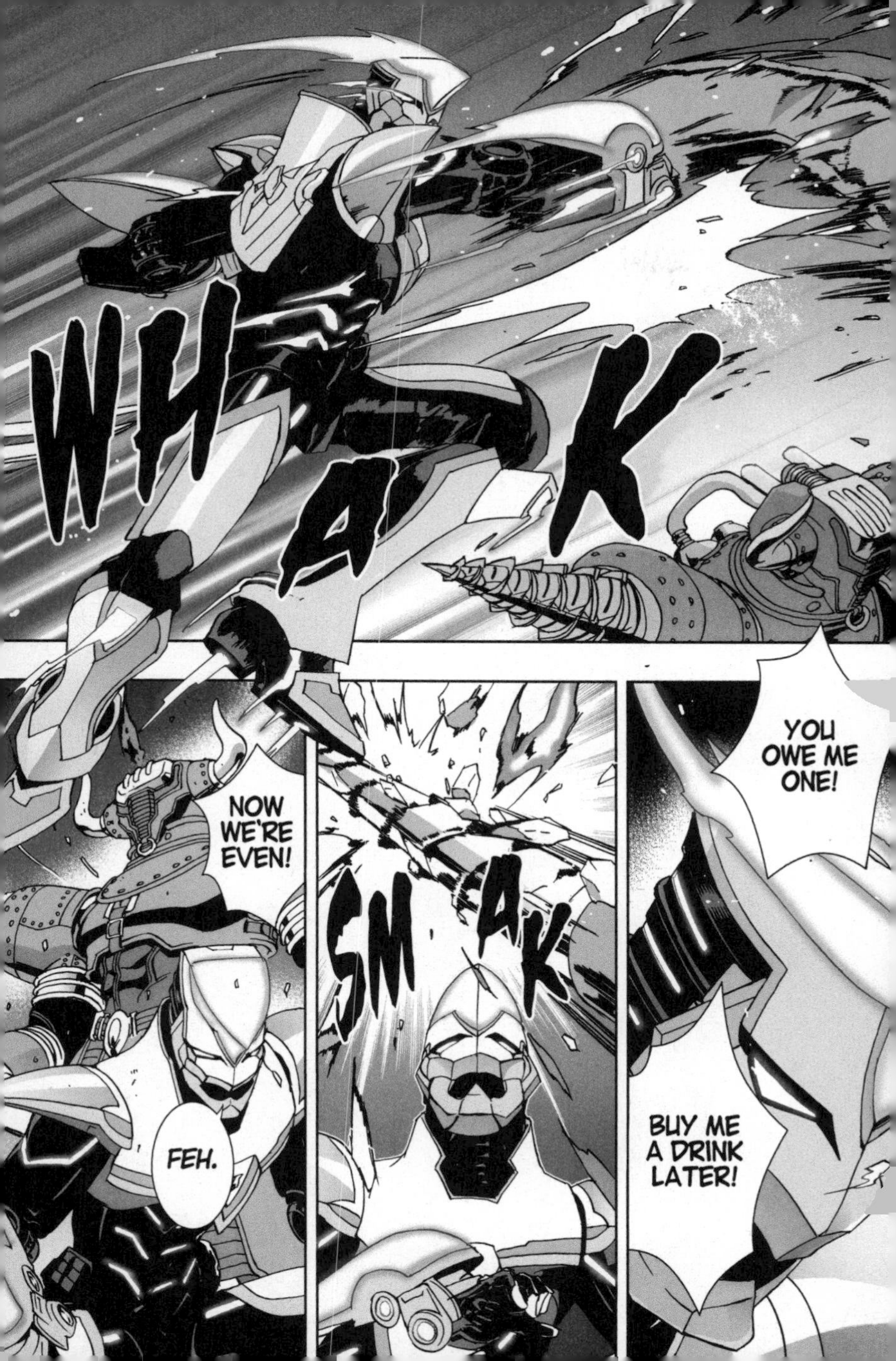
WHAK
YOU OWE ME ONE!
BUY ME A DRINK LATER!
SMAK
NOW WE'RE EVEN!
FEH.

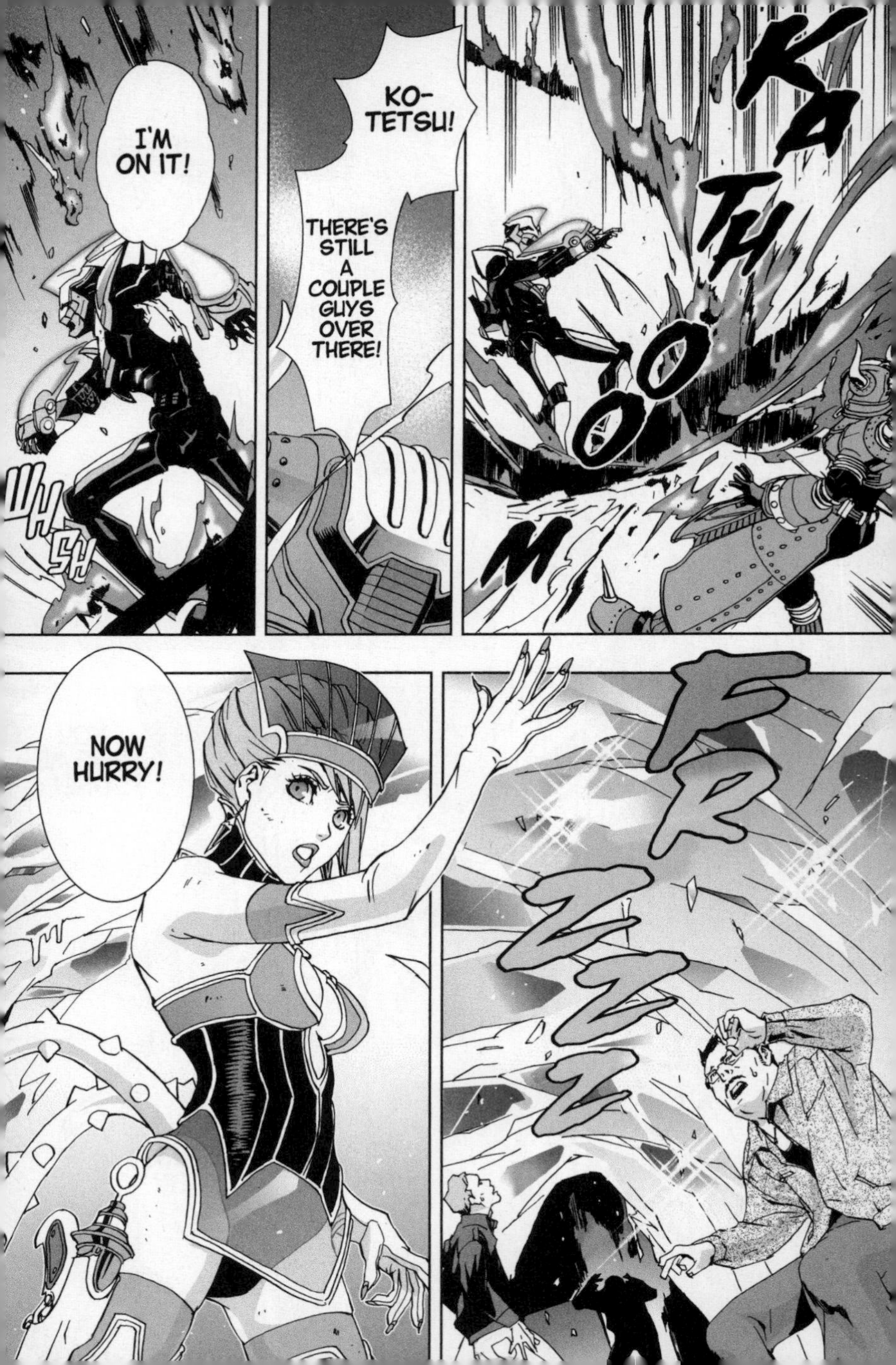
KATHOOOM
KO-TETSU!
THERE'S STILL A COUPLE GUYS OVER THERE!
I'M ON IT!
WHSH
FRZZZZ
NOW HURRY!

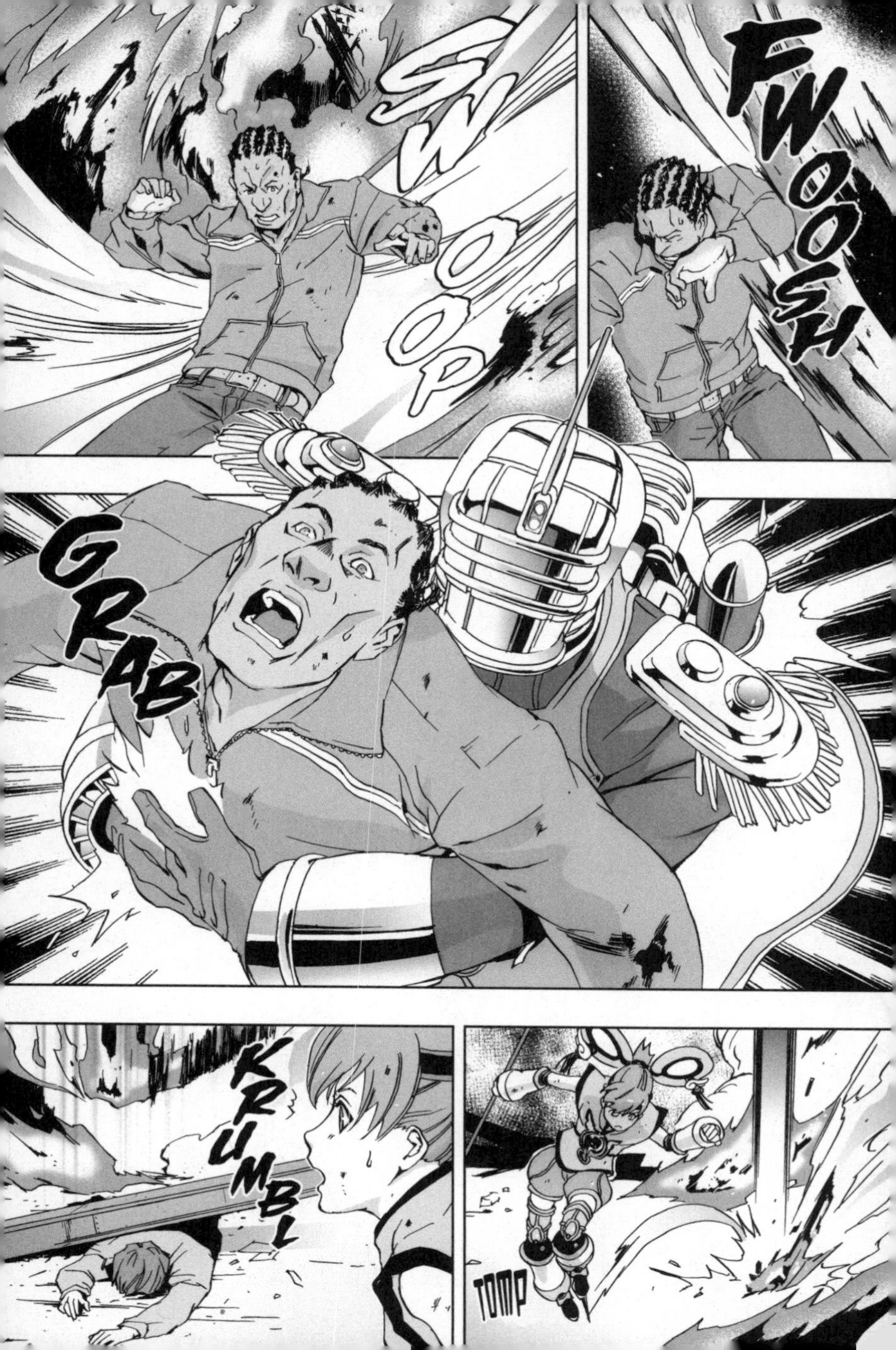
FWOOOSH
SWOOOP
GRAB
TOMP
KRUMBL

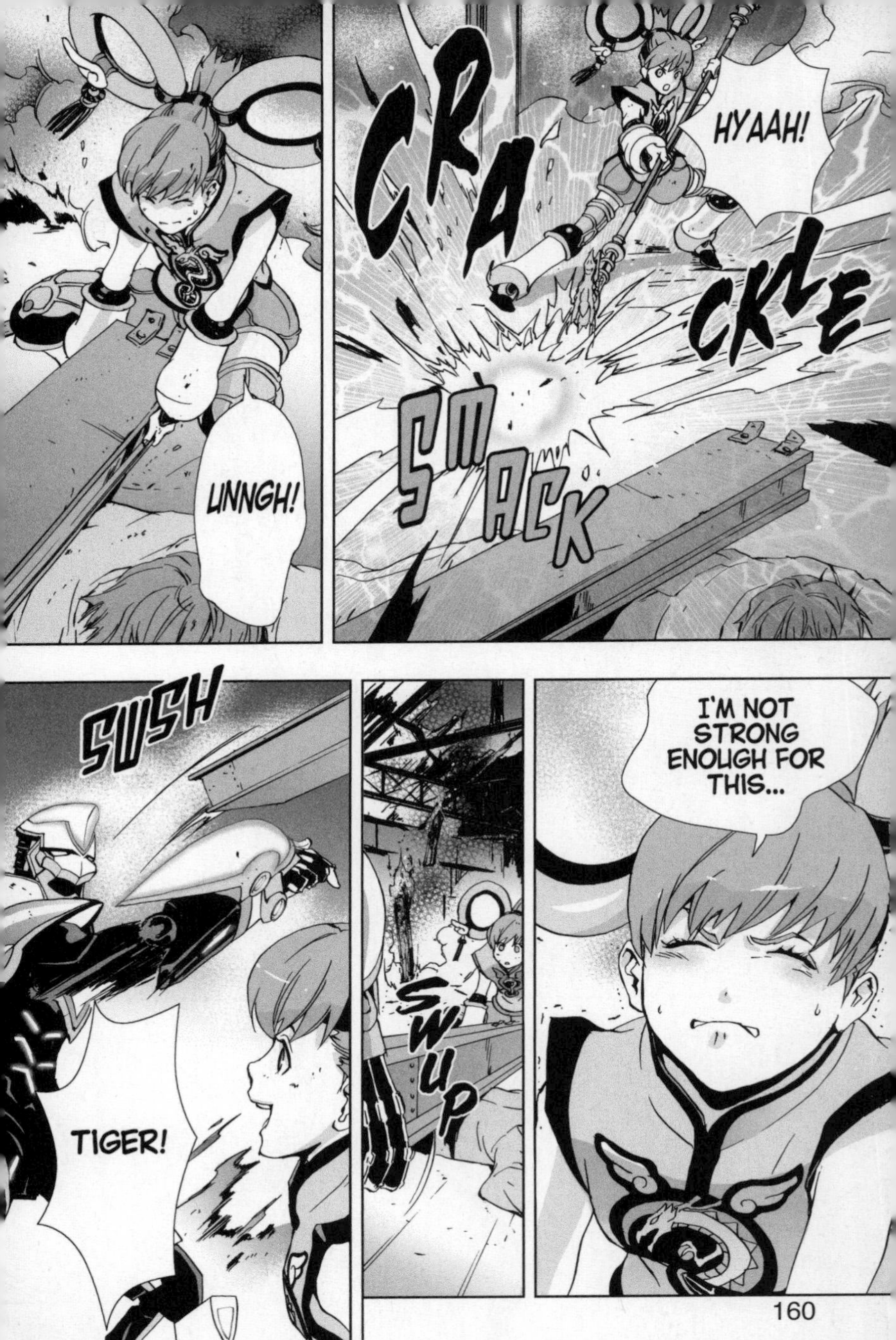

HYAAH!
CRACKLE
SMACK
UNNGH!
I'M NOT STRONG ENOUGH FOR THIS...
SWUP
SUSH
TIGER!

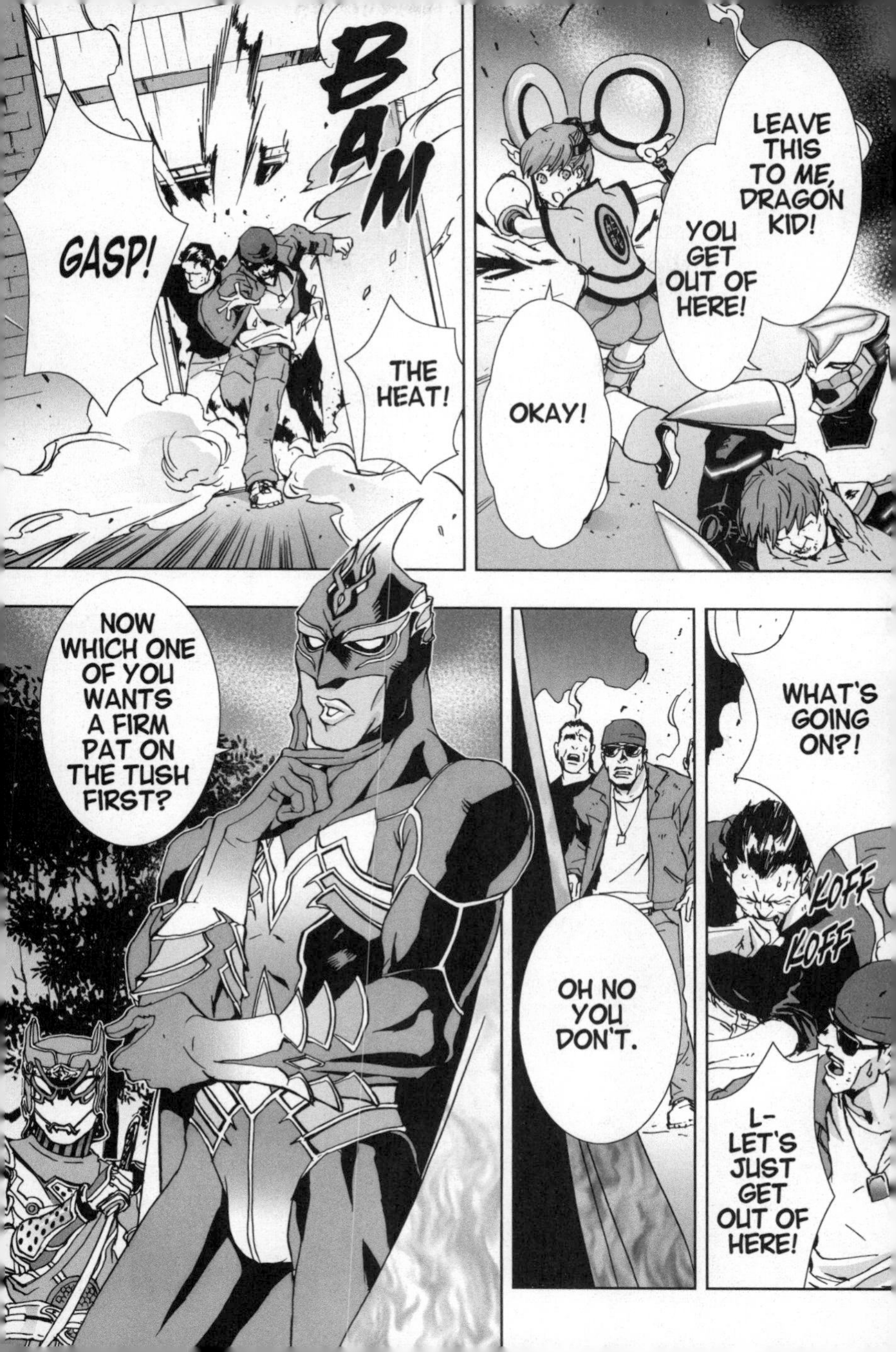
LEAVE THIS TO ME, DRAGON KID!
YOU GET OUT OF HERE!
OKAY!
BAM
GASP!
THE HEAT!
WHAT'S GOING ON?!
KOFF KOFF
L- LET'S JUST GET OUT OF HERE!
OH NO YOU DON'T.
NOW WHICH ONE OF YOU WANTS A FIRM PAT ON THE TUSH FIRST?

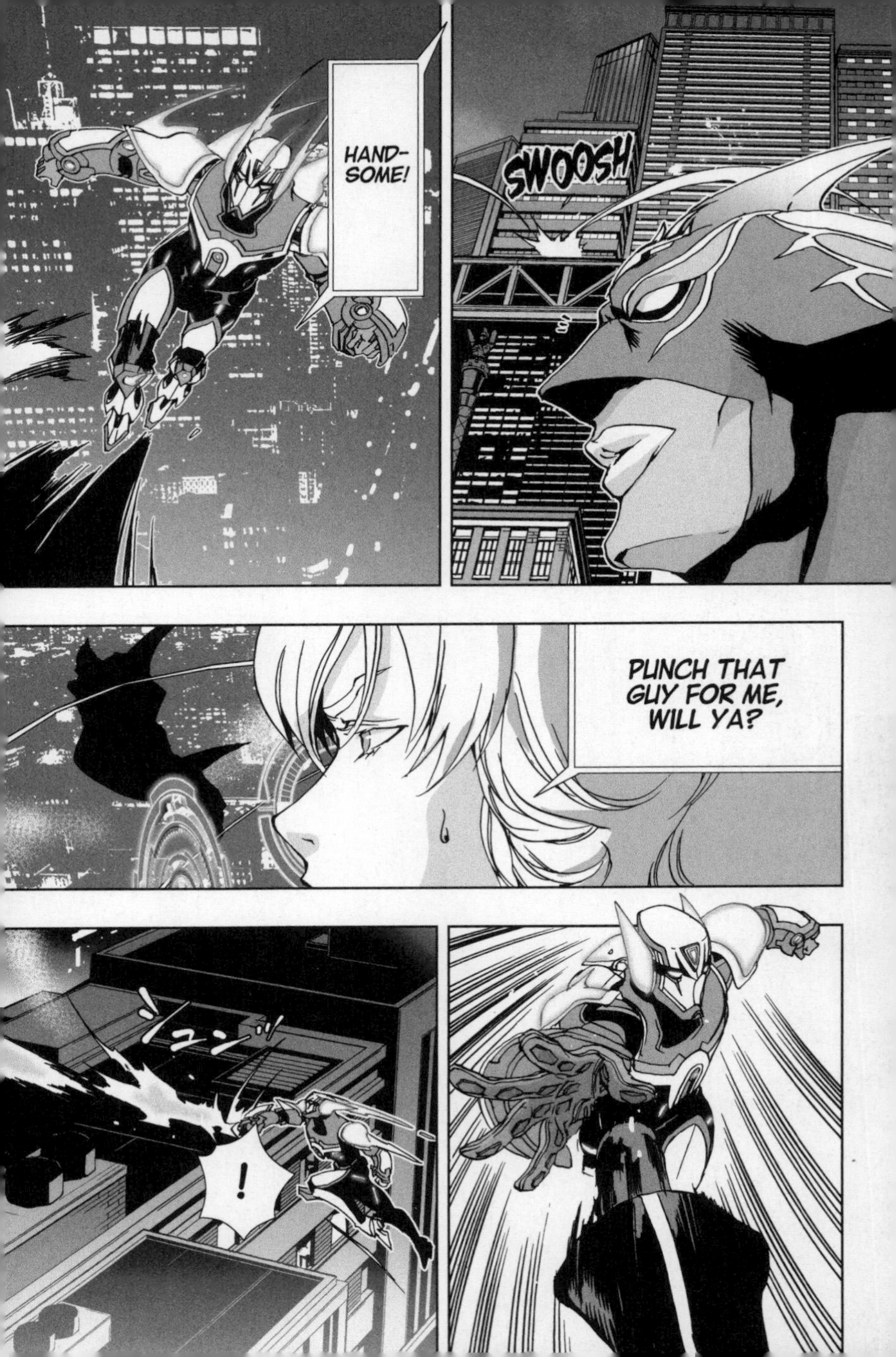
SWOOSH
HAND-
SOME!
PUNCH THAT
GUY FOR ME,
WILL YA?
!

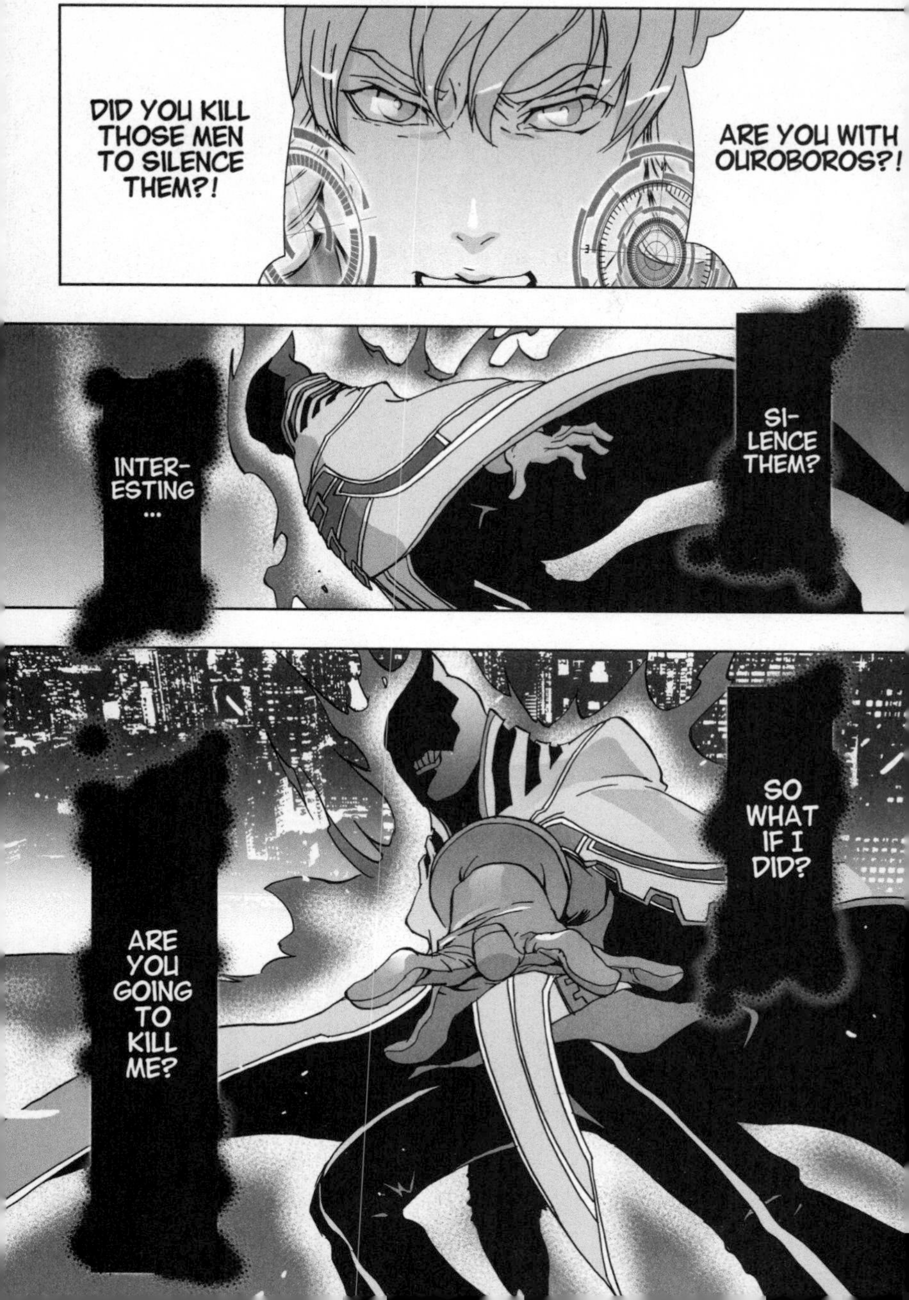
ARE YOU WITH OUROBOROS?!
DID YOU KILL THOSE MEN TO SILENCE THEM?!
SI- LENCE THEM?
INTER- ESTING ...
SO WHAT IF I DID?
ARE YOU GOING TO KILL ME?

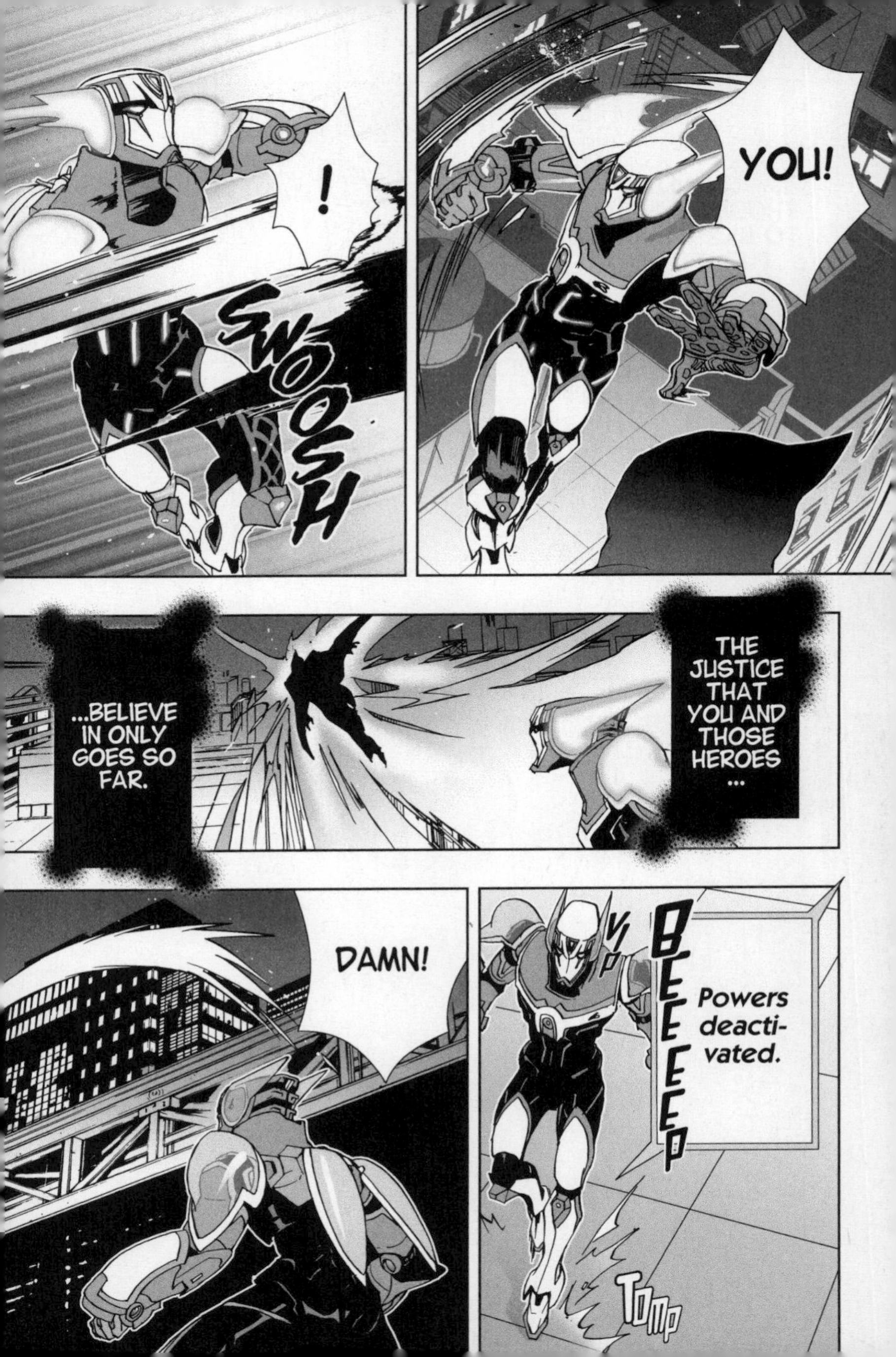
YOU!
!
SWOOSH
THE JUSTICE THAT YOU AND THOSE HEROES ...
...BELIEVE IN ONLY GOES SO FAR.
BEEEEP
VIP
Powers deacti-vated.
TOMP
DAMN!

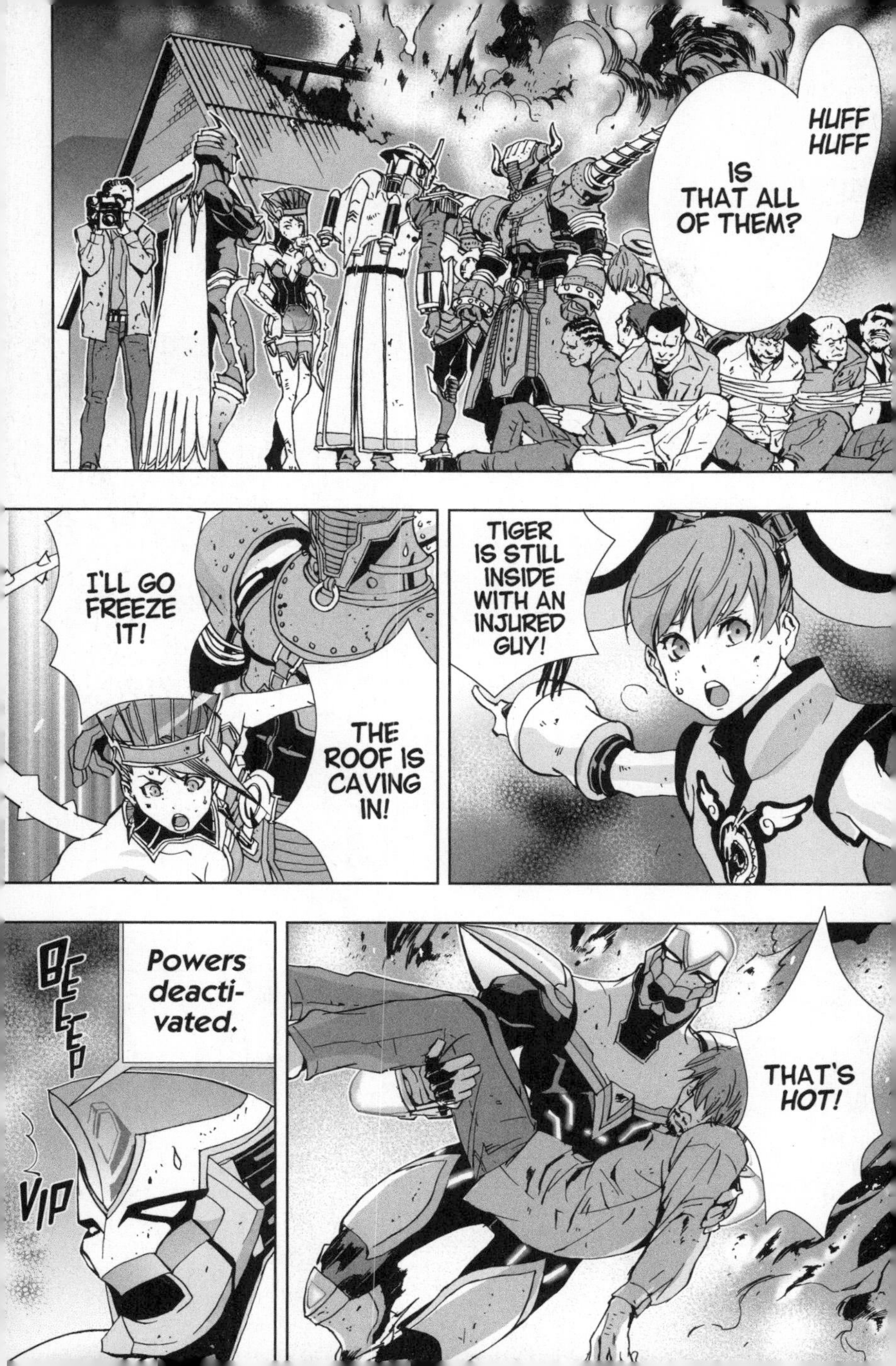
HUFF HUFF
IS THAT ALL OF THEM?
TIGER IS STILL INSIDE WITH AN INJURED GUY!
THE ROOF IS CAVING IN!
I'LL GO FREEZE IT!
THAT'S HOT!
Powers deacti-vated.
BEEEP
VIP

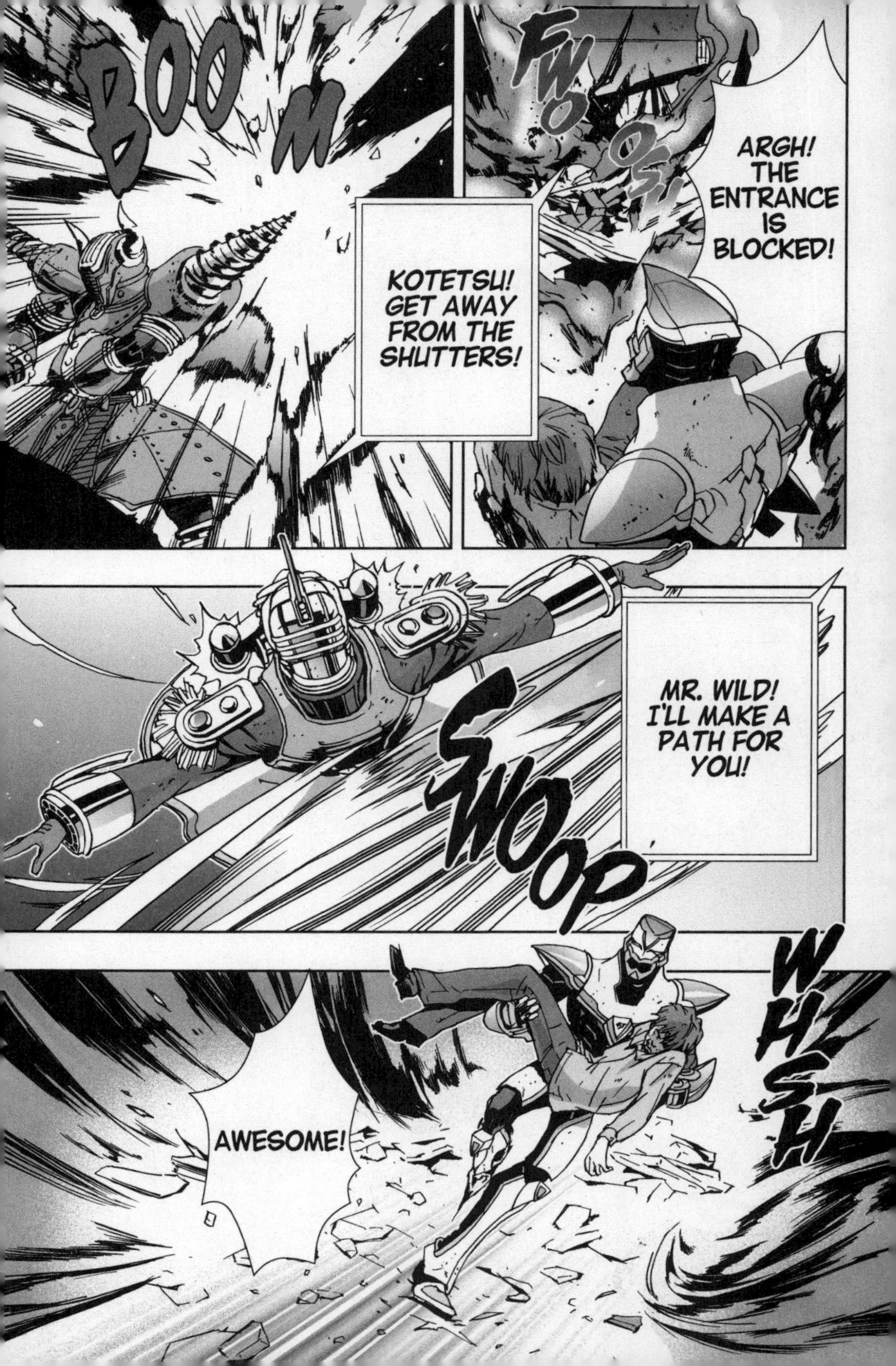
FWOOSH
ARGH! THE ENTRANCE IS BLOCKED!
KOTETSU! GET AWAY FROM THE SHUTTERS!
BOOM
MR. WILD! I'LL MAKE A PATH FOR YOU!
SWOOP
WHSH
AWESOME!

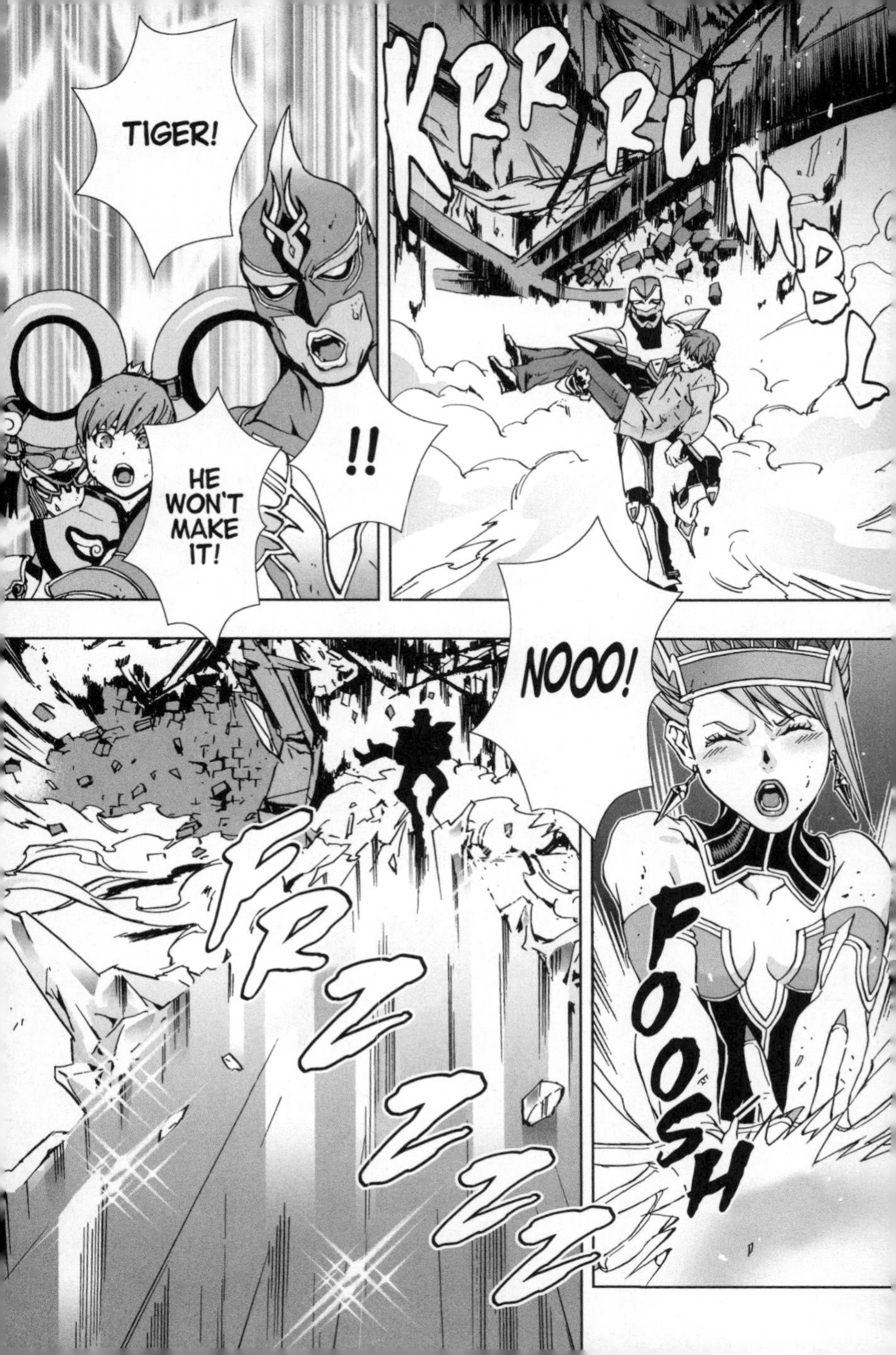
KRR RUMBL
TIGER!
!!
HE WON'T MAKE IT!
NOOO!
FOOSH
FRZZZZZ

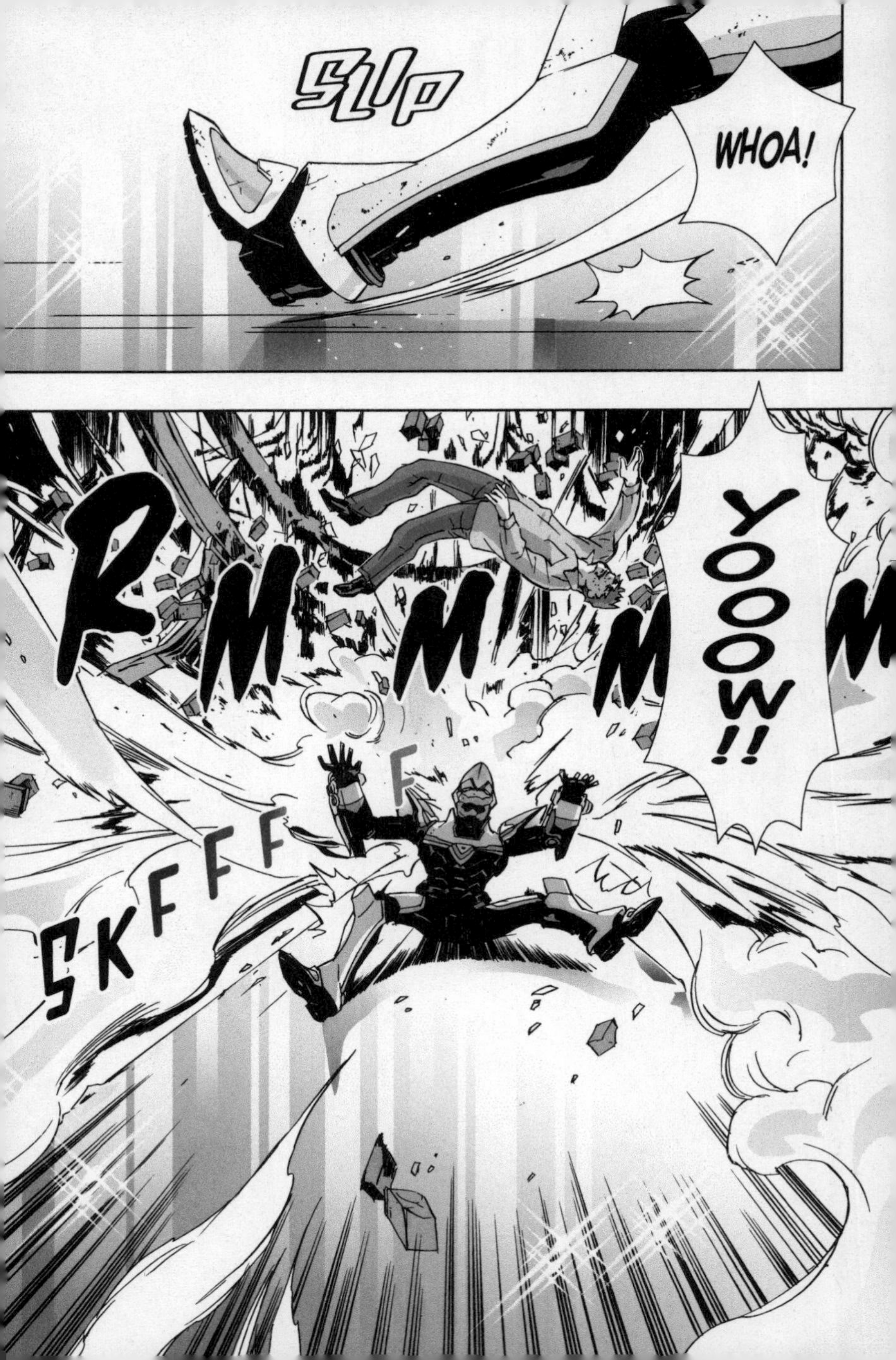
WHOA!
SLIP
YOOOOW!!
RMMMM
SKFFFF

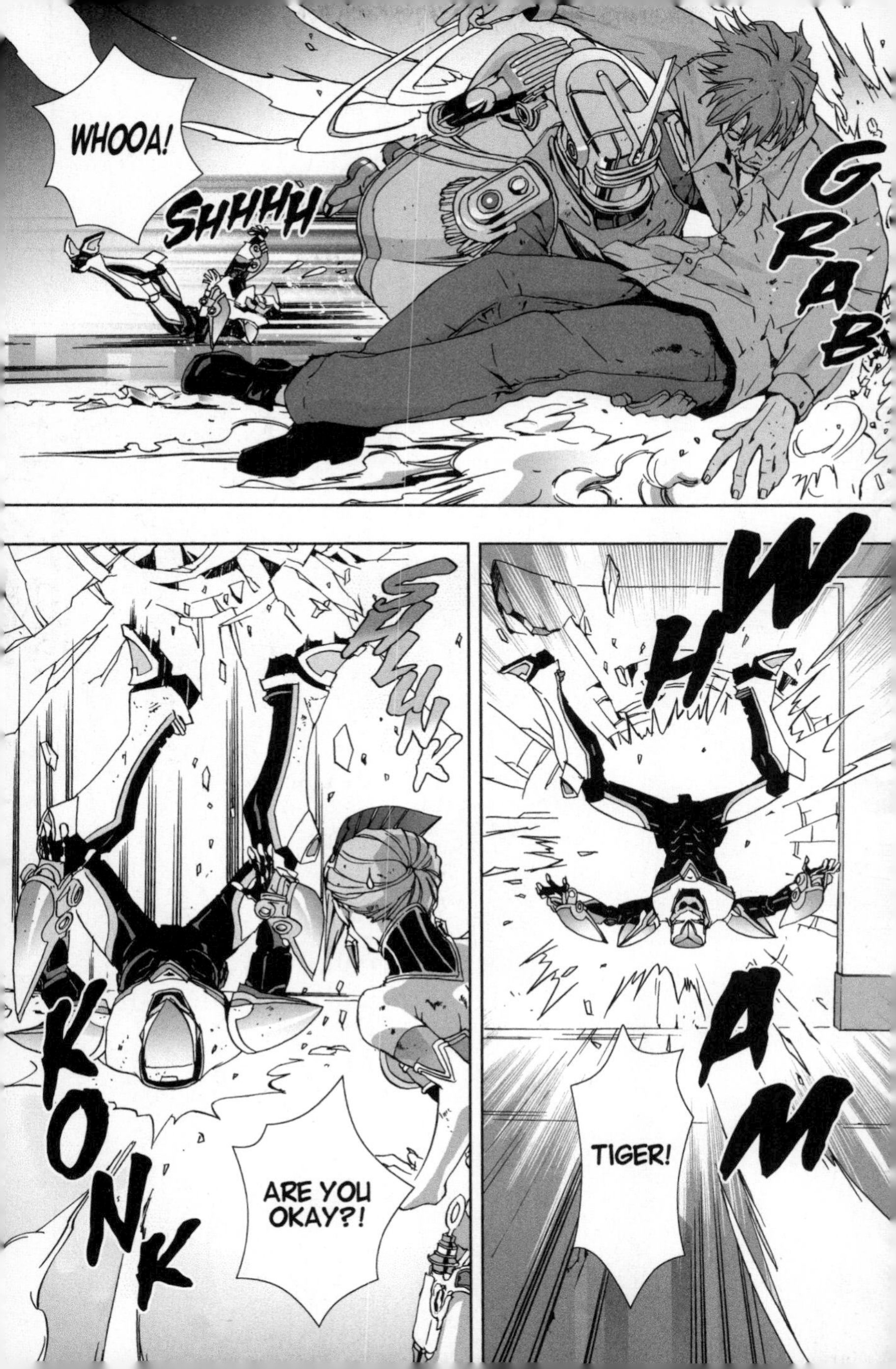
GRAB
WHOOA!
SHHHH
WHAM
TIGER!
SHUNK
KONK
ARE YOU OKAY?!

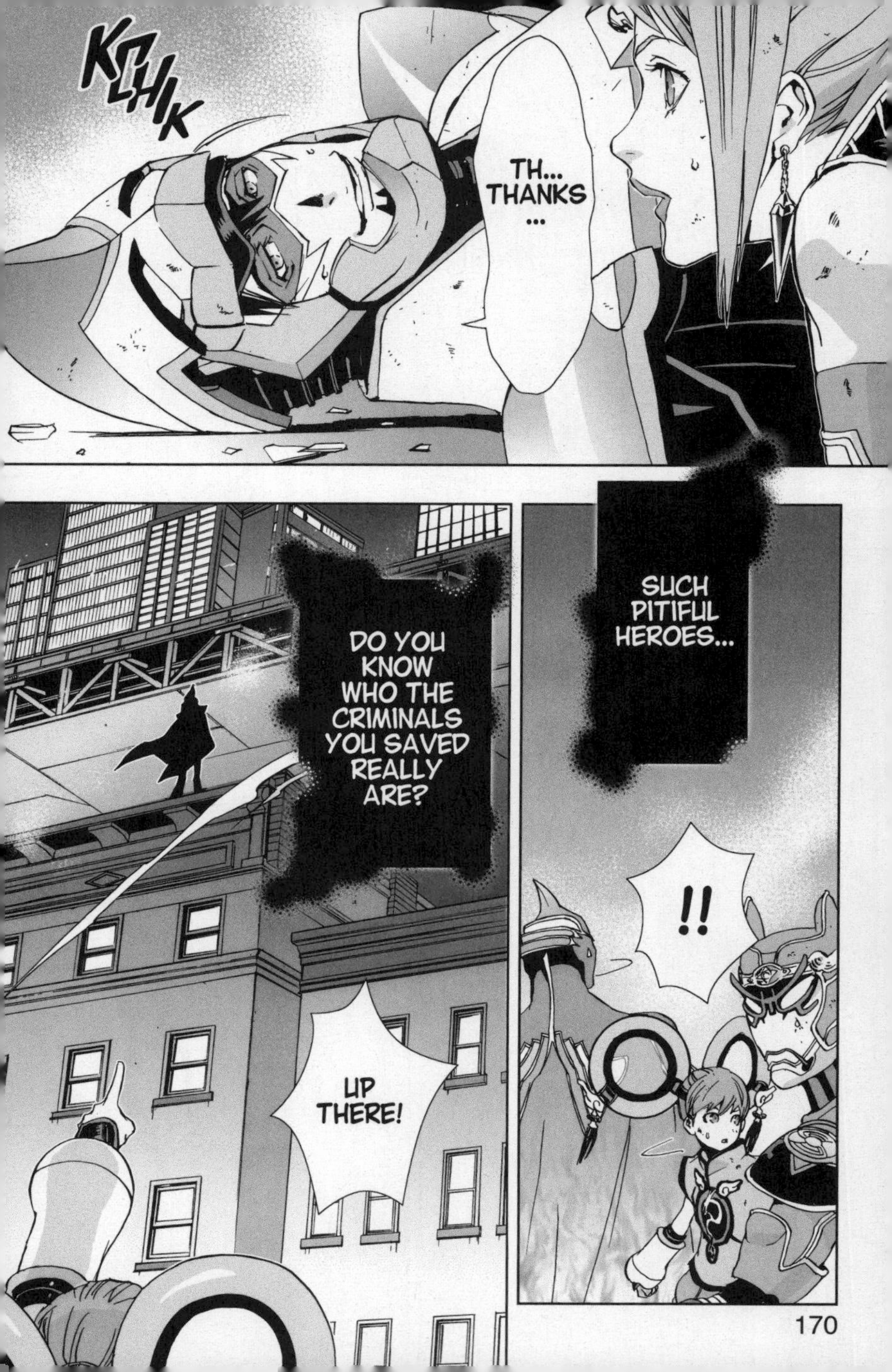
TH... THANKS ...
KCHIK
SUCH PITIFUL HEROES...
!!
DO YOU KNOW WHO THE CRIMINALS YOU SAVED REALLY ARE?
UP THERE!

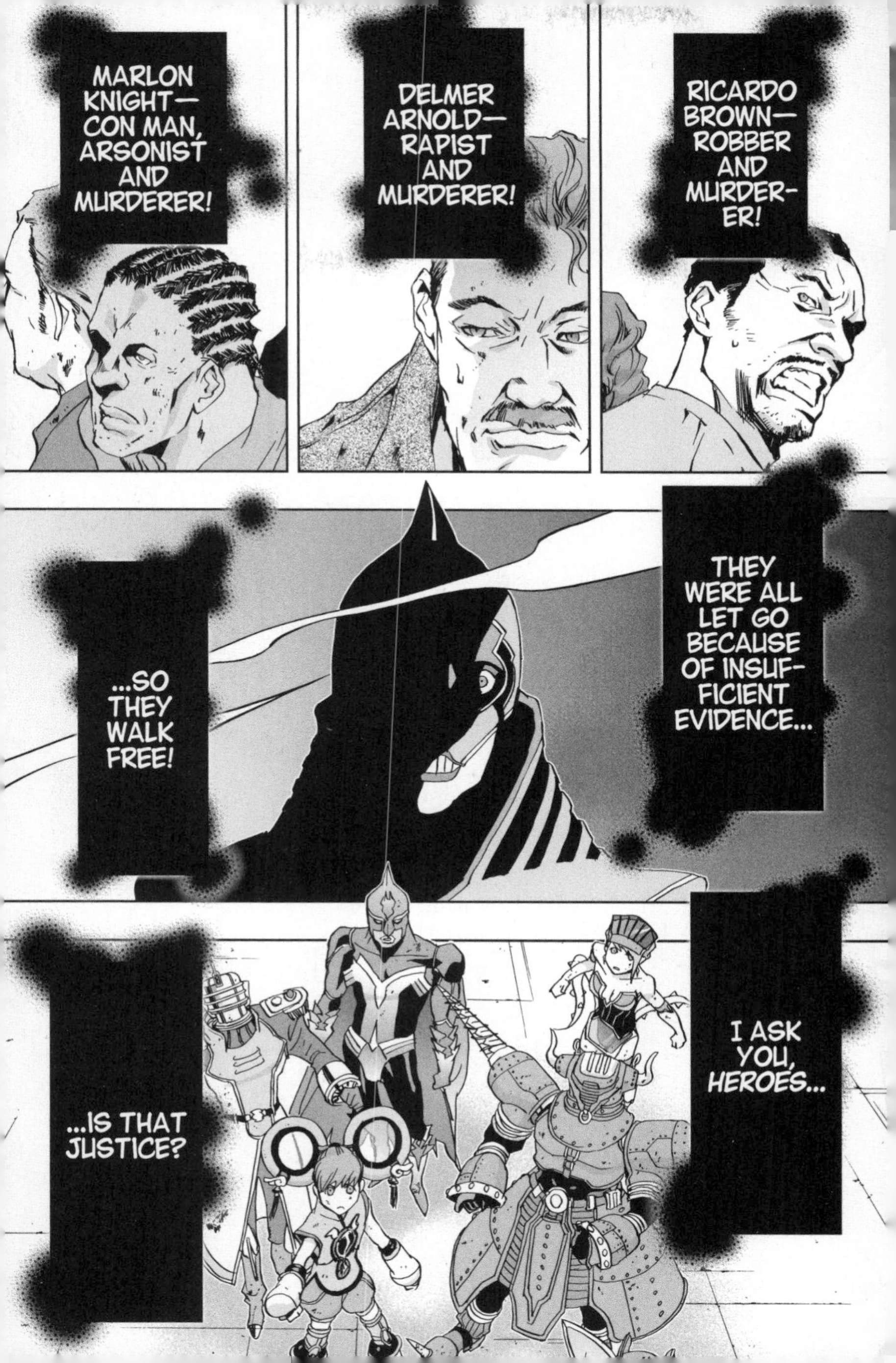
RICARDO BROWN—ROBBER AND MURDERER!
DELMER ARNOLD—RAPIST AND MURDERER!
MARLON KNIGHT—CON MAN, ARSONIST AND MURDERER!
THEY WERE ALL LET GO BECAUSE OF INSUFFICIENT EVIDENCE...
...SO THEY WALK FREE!
I ASK YOU, HEROES...
...IS THAT JUSTICE?

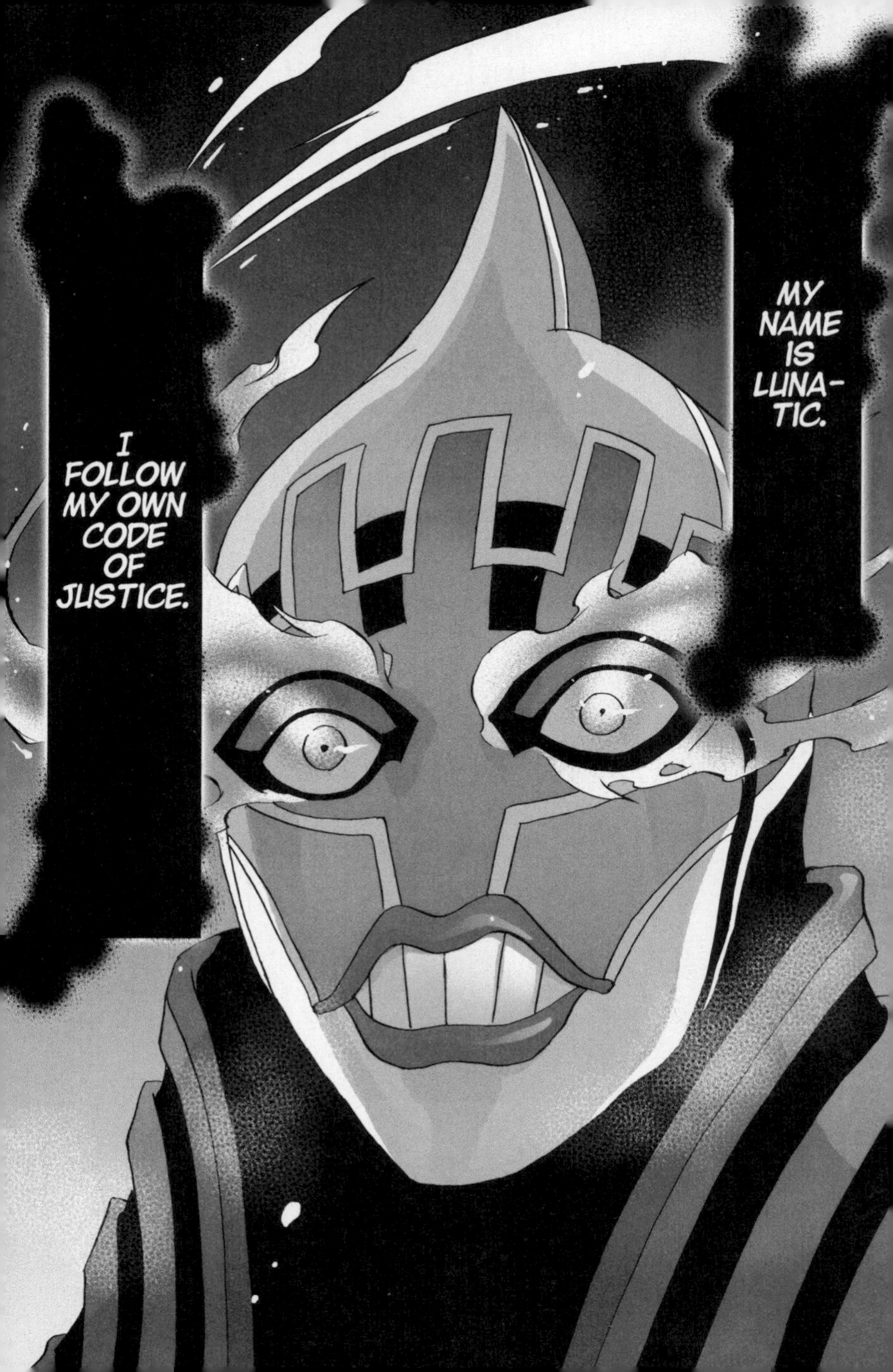
MY NAME IS LUNATIC.
I FOLLOW MY OWN CODE OF JUSTICE.

TIGER&BUNNY
To Be Continued

Mizuki Sakakibara

Assistants
Naoto Tsushima
Eri Saito
Sachiko Ito
Kiritachi
beth
Fuku

MIZUKI SAKAKIBARA

Mizuki Sakakibara's American comics debut was Marvel's *Exile* in 2002. Currently, *TIGER & BUNNY* is serialized in *Newtype Ace* magazine by Kadokawa Shoten.

MASAFUMI NISHIDA

Story director. *TIGER & BUNNY* was his first work as a TV animation scriptwriter. He is well known for the movie *Gachi☆Boy* and the Japanese TV dramas *Maoh*, *Kaibutsu-kun*, and *Youkai Ningen Bem*.

MASAKAZU KATSURA

Original character designer. Masakazu Katsura is well known for the manga series *WING MAN*, *Denei Shojo* (*Video Girl Ai*), *I"s*, and *ZETMAN*. Katsura's works have been translated into several languages, including Chinese and French, as well as English.

COMING NEXT VOLUME

4

The heroes face down the deranged NEXT killer, Lunatic. Lunatic's vigilantism has the city on edge, and the heroes find themselves having to convince everyone that NEXT are working for the good of Stern Bild City. Lunatic is in the wrong, but there is much more to the madman than anyone knows...

TIGER&BUNNY 3

VIZ Media Edition

Art **MIZUKI SAKAKIBARA**
Planning / Story **SUNRISE**
Original Script **MASAFUMI NISHIDA**
Original Character and Hero Design **MASAKAZU KATSURA**

TIGER & BUNNY Volume 3

First published in Japan in 2012 by KADOKAWA SHOTEN Co., Ltd., Tokyo.
English translation rights arranged with KADOKAWA SHOTEN Co., Ltd., Tokyo.

Translation & English Adaptation **LABAAMEN & JOHN WERRY, HC LANGUAGE SOLUTIONS**
Touch-up Art & Lettering **STEPHEN DUTRO**
Design **FAWN LAU**
Editor **MIKE MONTESA**

SKY HIGH

Printed in the U.S.A

Published by VIZ Media, LLC
P.O. Box 77010
San Francisco, CA 94107

10 9 8 7 6 5 4 3 2 1
First printing, October 2013

PARENTAL ADVISORY
TIGER & BUNNY is rated T for Teen and is recommended for ages 13 and up.
ratings.viz.com

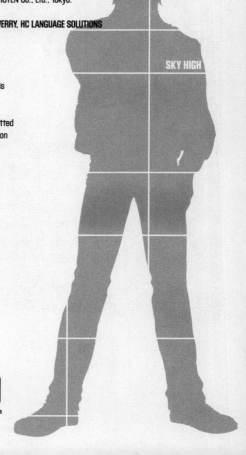

www.viz.com

VIZMANGA

Read manga anytime, anywhere!

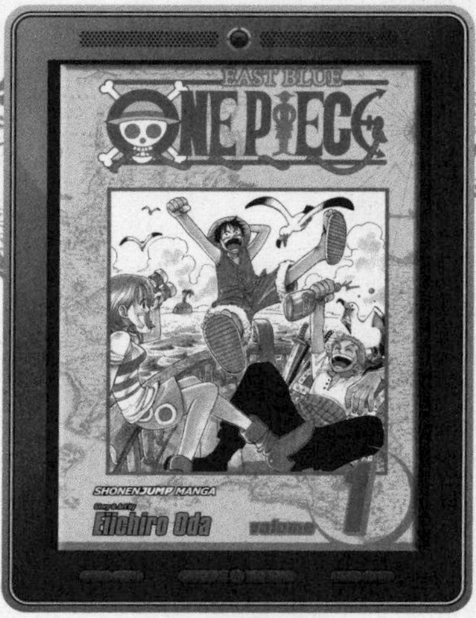
EAST BLUE
ONE PIECE
SHONEN JUMP MANGA
Eiichiro Oda
volume 1

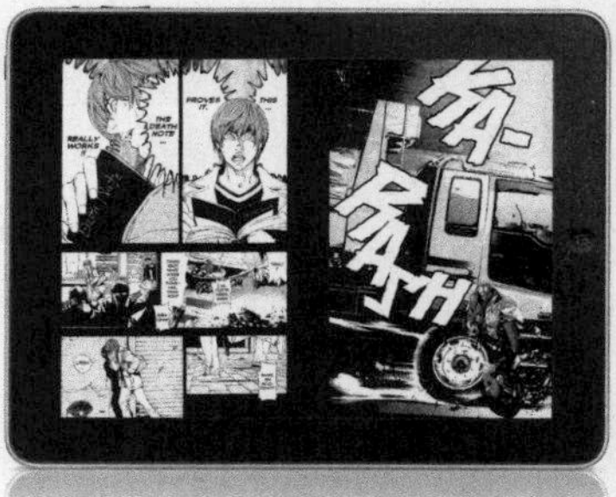

rom our newest hit series to the classics you know
nd love, the best manga in the world is now available
gitally. Buy a volume* of digital manga for your:

iOS device (**iPad®**, **iPhone®**, **iPod® touch**) through the **VIZ Manga app**

Android-powered device (**phone or tablet**) with a browser by visiting **VIZManga.com**

Mac or PC computer by visiting **VIZManga.com**

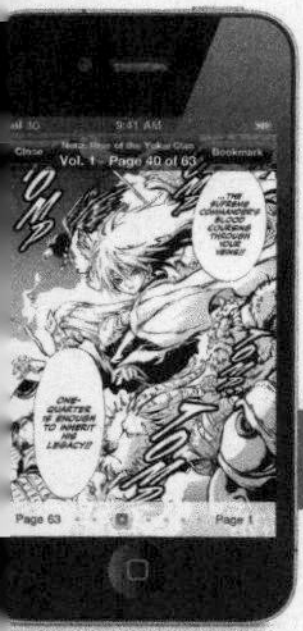

VIZ Digital has loads to offer:

- 500+ ready-to-read volumes
- New volumes each week
- FREE previews
- Access on multiple devices! Create a log-in through the app so you buy a book once, and read it on your device of choice!*

To learn more, visit www.viz.com/apps

* **Some series may not be available for multiple devices.**
Check the app on your device to find out what's available.

RATED T+ FOR OLDER TEEN ratings.viz.com

viz media

viz.com/apps

YOU'RE READING THE
WRONG WAY!

Tiger & Bunny reads from right to left, starting in the upper-right corner. Japanese is read from right to left, meaning that action, sound effects, and word-balloon order are completely reversed from English order.

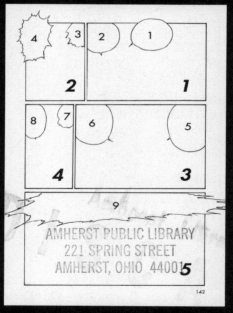

142